W9-BJB-644

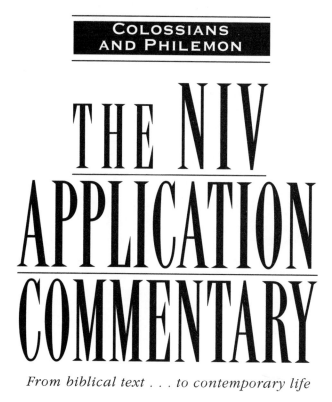

COLOSSIANS
AND PHILEMON

THE NIV
APPLICATION
COMMENTARY

From biblical text . . . to contemporary life

THE NIV APPLICATION COMMENTARY SERIES

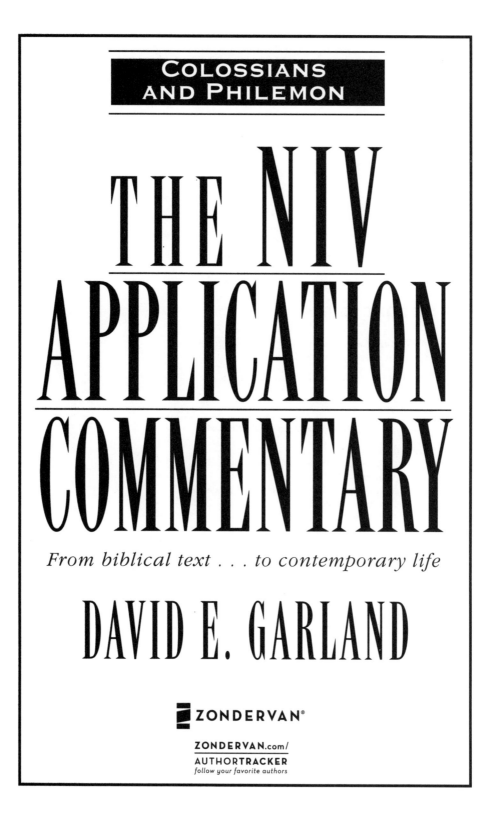

COLOSSIANS
AND PHILEMON

THE NIV APPLICATION COMMENTARY

From biblical text . . . to contemporary life

DAVID E. GARLAND

ZONDERVAN®

ZONDERVAN.com/
AUTHORTRACKER
follow your favorite authors

 **ZONDERVAN®**

The NIV Application Commentary: Colossians and Philemon
Copyright © 1998 by David E. Garland

Requests for information should be addressed to:

Zondervan, *Grand Rapids, Michigan 49530*

Library of Congress Cataloging-in-Publication Data

Garland, David E.
    Colossians and Philemon / David E. Garland.
        p. cm.—(NIV application commentary)
    Includes bibliographical references and indexes.
    ISBN-10: 0-310-48480-4
    ISBN-13: 978-0-310-48480-6
    1. Bible. N.T. Colossians—Commentaries. 2. Bible. N.T. Philemon—Commentaries. I.
Title. II. Series.
    BS 2715.3.G37 1997
    227'.7077—dc21   97-37306

This edition printed on acid-free paper.

Printed in the United States of America

07 08 09 10 11 12 13 14 • 20 19 18 17 16 15 14 13 12

Contents

NIV Application Commentary
Series Introduction

THE NIV APPLICATION COMMENTARY SERIES is unique. Most commentaries help us make the journey from the twentieth century back to the first century. They enable us to cross the barriers of time, culture, language, and geography that separate us from the biblical world. Yet they only offer a one-way ticket to the past and assume that we can somehow make the return journey on our own. Once they have explained the *original meaning* of a book or passage, these commentaries give us little or no help in exploring its *contemporary significance*. The information they offer is valuable, but the job is only half done.

Recently, a few commentaries have included some contemporary application as *one* of their goals. Yet that application is often sketchy or moralistic, and some volumes sound more like printed sermons than commentaries.

The primary goal of The NIV Application Commentary Series is to help you with the difficult but vital task of bringing an ancient message into a modern context. The series not only focuses on application as a finished product but also helps you think through the *process* of moving from the original meaning of a passage to its contemporary significance. These are commentaries, not popular expositions. They are works of reference, not devotional literature.

The format of the series is designed to achieve the goals of the series. Each passage is treated in three sections: *Original Meaning, Bridging Contexts,* and *Contemporary Significance.*

THIS SECTION HELPS you understand the meaning of the biblical text in its first-century context. All of the elements of traditional exegesis—in concise form—are discussed here. These include the historical, literary, and cultural context of the passage. The authors discuss matters related to grammar and syntax, and the meaning of biblical words. They also seek to explore the main ideas of the passage and how the biblical author develops those ideas.[1]

---

1. Please note that when the authors discuss words in the original biblical languages, the series uses the general rather than the scholarly method of transliteration.

After reading this section, you will understand the problems, questions, and concerns of the *original audience* and how the biblical author addressed those issues. This understanding is foundational to any legitimate application of the text today.

THIS SECTION BUILDS a bridge between the world of the Bible and the world of today, between the original context and the contemporary context, by focusing on both the timely and timeless aspects of the text.

God's Word is *timely*. The authors of Scripture spoke to specific situations, problems, and questions. Paul warned the Galatians about the consequences of circumcision and the dangers of trying to be justified by law (Gal. 5:2–5). The author of Hebrews tried to convince his readers that Christ is superior to Moses, the Aaronic priests, and the Old Testament sacrifices. John urged his readers to "test the spirits" of those who taught a form of incipient Gnosticism (1 John 4:1–6). In each of these cases, the timely nature of Scripture enables us to hear God's Word in situations that were *concrete* rather than abstract.

Yet the timely nature of Scripture also creates problems. Our situations, difficulties, and questions are not always directly related to those faced by the people in the Bible. Therefore, God's word to them does not always seem relevant to us. For example, when was the last time someone urged you to be circumcised, claiming that it was a necessary part of justification? How many people today care whether Christ is superior to the Aaronic priests? And how can a "test" designed to expose incipient Gnosticism be of any value in a modern culture?

Fortunately, Scripture is not only timely but *timeless*. Just as God spoke to the original audience, so he still speaks to us through the pages of Scripture. Because we share a common humanity with the people of the Bible, we discover a *universal dimension* in the problems they faced and the solutions God gave them. The timeless nature of Scripture enables it to speak with power in every time and in every culture.

Those who fail to recognize that Scripture is both timely and timeless run into a host of problems. For example, those who are intimidated by timely books such as Hebrews or Galatians might avoid reading them because they seem meaningless today. At the other extreme, those who are convinced of the timeless nature of Scripture, but who fail to discern its timely element, may "wax eloquent" about the Melchizedekian priesthood to a sleeping congregation.

The purpose of this section, therefore, is to help you discern what is timeless in the timely pages of the New Testament—and what is not. For example, if Paul's primary concern is not circumcision (as he tells us in Gal. 5:6), what *is* he concerned about? If discussions about the Aaronic priesthood or Melchizedek seem irrelevant today, what is of abiding value in these passages? If people try to "test the spirits" today with a test designed for a specific first-century heresy, what other biblical test might be more appropriate?

Yet this section does not merely uncover that which is timeless in a passage but also helps you to see *how* it is uncovered. The author of the commentary seeks to take what is implicit in the text and make it explicit, to take a process that normally is intuitive and explain it in a logical, orderly fashion. How do we know that circumcision is not Paul's primary concern? What clues in the text or its context help us realize that Paul's real concern is at a deeper level?

Of course, those passages in which the historical distance between us and the original readers is greatest require a longer treatment. Conversely, those passages in which the historical distance is smaller or seemingly nonexistent require less attention.

One final clarification. Because this section prepares the way for discussing the contemporary significance of the passage, there is not always a sharp distinction or a clear break between this section and the one that follows. Yet when both sections are read together, you should have a strong sense of moving from the world of the Bible to the world of today.

THIS SECTION ALLOWS the biblical message to speak with as much power today as it did when it was first written. How can you apply what you learned about Jerusalem, Ephesus, or Corinth to our present-day needs in Chicago, Los Angeles, or London? How can you take a message originally spoken in Greek and Aramaic and communicate it clearly in our own language? How can you take the eternal truths originally spoken in a different time and culture and apply them to the similar-yet-different needs of our culture?

In order to achieve these goals, this section gives you help in several key areas.

First, it helps you identify contemporary situations, problems, or questions that are truly comparable to those faced by the original audience. Because contemporary situations are seldom identical to those faced in the first century, you must seek situations that are analogous if your applications are to be relevant.

Second, this section explores a variety of contexts in which the passage might be applied today. You will look at personal applications, but you will also be encouraged to think beyond private concerns to the society and culture at large.

Third, this section will alert you to any problems or difficulties you might encounter in seeking to apply the passage. And if there are several legitimate ways to apply a passage (areas in which Christians disagree), the author will bring these to your attention and help you think through the issues involved.

In seeking to achieve these goals, the contributors to this series attempt to avoid two extremes. They avoid making such specific applications that the commentary might quickly become dated. They also avoid discussing the significance of the passage in such a general way that it fails to engage contemporary life and culture.

Above all, contributors to this series have made a diligent effort not to sound moralistic or preachy. The NIV Application Commentary Series does not seek to provide ready-made sermon materials but rather tools, ideas, and insights that will help you communicate God's Word with power. If we help you to achieve that goal, then we have fulfilled the purpose for this series.

The Editors

General Editor's Preface

THE TEMPTATION TO TRUST in the wrong things is strong. "In God We Trust" may be inscribed on the coins in our pockets, but too rarely is that phrase etched on the walls of our hearts. We trust in everything but God—the wrong things.

The wrong things include material prosperity, friends' opinions, corporate cultures, human philosophies, even gourmet food, diet programs, and exercise regimens. We trust in these things because we are insecure and are looking for the security that everyone claims their ideas and products have.

The book of Colossians is about trusting in the right things. Or to be more exact, about trusting in the right person, Jesus Christ. David Garland brings us back time after time to this central truth: The Colossians were trusting in the wrong things, and the way to be Christian was to trust in Jesus Christ.

This isn't an easy lesson for us to hear, any more than it was for the Colossians. They were blocked by the fact that Christianity was a minority religion, new and unestablished in their culture. When times got tough, it was hard to hang on to the hope offered in Jesus Christ. It was easier to hedge bets and go back to some of the tried and true stuff, whether long-established mystery religions, Greek philosophies, or even the rites and rituals of traditional Judaism.

We too are blocked from an elemental trust in Christ Jesus, but for different reasons. For us Christianity is not new and strange, it is old and familiar. We live in a culture that has plenty to offer, a culture so rich in material goods that it is tempting to buy the advertising pitch with which these bounties are sold—secure your health with our medicine, secure your finances with our insurance, secure your future with our financial plan. Even religious marketers get into the act—secure your eternal destiny by following our religion's rules.

By themselves none of these "securities" is bad. Medicine, insurance, financial planning, and religion are all good things. But they become bad when they are elevated from penultimate status to ultimate status. Ultimately they are not adequate. Medicines can't cure all disease, insurance doesn't cover all disasters, financial plans don't help heartaches brought by disaster, and religion without submission to Jesus Christ turns into self-help psychology.

The suffering Paul refers to in Colossians is different from his other sections. It is the low-grade, chronic suffering of insecurity, a slight lack of confidence, a lessening of hope that sends us chasing after every semblance of certainty the world has to offer. But this suffering is no less real, and it is all the more painful because of its chronic, ongoing nature. It is particularly painful in a world where the ideal is an all-too-attainable happiness brewed of one part wealth, one part love, one part fame, and one part security. Preaching the gospel should produce those four parts, but it doesn't—unless we reinterpret wealth, love, fame, and security through the only valid hermeneutical principle we have, Jesus Christ.

The way our culture is constructed, these penultimate "securities" that masquerade as the final answer are the real elemental powers of the universe (*ta stoicheia tou kosmou*). We have made simple creaturely comforts into gods that control our lives. We try to appease the insecurities brought on by our excessive individualism, and we appeal to these self-created elemental powers for security. They don't deliver, of course. Only Jesus Christ can do that. That is the message of Colossians.

When we are faced with a specific problem, such as Paul was with the situation Philemon brought him, Paul teaches us what to do: Orient all social problems within the context of our basic humility before Jesus, and fulfill our social responsibilities in light of the eternal security offered in Jesus. Suddenly what seemed like an insolvable problem becomes clear in light of God's reconciling work in the world—with Jesus Christ as center.

Terry C. Muck

Author's Preface

ONE INTERPRETER OF SCRIPTURE has written, "It is perhaps only to those who write them that commentaries are exciting."[1] Writing on Colossians and Philemon has been an exciting task, and one can only pray that this commentary helps make the reading of these letters more exciting and meaningful. In one of David Lodge's novels a character named Morris Zapp is a professor of English at a large state school. Zapp has set for himself an ambitious scholarly project. He intends to examine the novels of Jane Austen from "every conceivable angle, historical, biographical, rhetorical, mythical, Freudian, Jungian, existentialist, Marxist, structuralist, Christian-allegorical, ethical, exponential, linguistic, phenomenological, archetypal, you name it; so that when one had finished each commentary, there would be nothing further to say about the novel in question." The thought, "After Zapp, there would be silence," motivated and deeply satisfied him.[2]

Unlike Professor Zapp, this commentator has no pretension of trying to offer an exhaustive word. Rather, I simply intend to help readers to mine the wealth of spiritual riches in Colossians and Philemon and to understand ways in which they apply today. The spiritual power of these letters does not allow either a final word or silence. My goal is to assist readers in developing their own insights into Colossians and Philemon, so that the world might ring anew with their messages about the all-sufficiency of Christ and the brotherhood that comes from being in Christ and that crosses all barriers.

This work would not have been possible without the help of many friends. I would like to express my deepest affection and appreciation for Steve Dwinnells, who was especially helpful in the preparation of the manuscript, and for David Drinnon, who helped in chasing down references. I also want to express my heartfelt fondness to the following students who, along with Dwinnells and Drinnon, brought joy and insight in studying the text together: Brian Anderson, Stephen Awoniyi, Troy Bryant, Gary Cost, Brian Curry, Jeff Douglas, Jeff Elieff, Gerald Feulmer, Cal Hampton, David Hewitt, Teruaki Hirao, Gregg Hodge, Jeff Jordan, Matt Lockett, Alan Lusk, Lamar McAbee, Keith McKinley, Yoon Jung Na, Cory Pitts, Jonathan Propes, Rob Schettler, Michael Sharp, Scott Tilton, Bert Walker, and Mark Webb. I would

---

1. Ernest Best, "The Reading and Writing of Commentaries," *ExpTim* 107 (1996): 358.
2. David Lodge, *Changing Places* (London: Penguin, 1975), 44.

like to extend special thanks to Paul Debusman, reference librarian, for his many years of gracious and invaluable help in many research projects and especially this one.

I am particularly indebted to the close reading of the manuscript by Klyne Snodgrass, who offered much sage advice. I also appreciate greatly the input and encouragement of Jack Kuhatschek and Terry Muck and the careful and wise editing of Verlyn Verbrugge. I am also grateful for F. Matthew Schobert Jr. for his assistance in compiling the index. These persons naturally bear no responsibility for the weaknesses of this commentary, but their reading and those of the students listed above have provided tremendous help and stimulus, as did all who have written on this text before me.

I would like also to thank my wife, Diana, for her continued love and support, and my children, Sarah and John, who have brought such joy and delight to my life. This book is dedicated to the memory of Ruth Garland, a faithful missionary of Christ and loving mother.

David E. Garland
Professor of Christian Scriptures
George W. Truett Theological Seminary,
Baylor University

Abbreviations

AB	Anchor Bible
ABD	*Anchor Bible Dictionary*
ABW	*Archaeology in the Biblical World*
ACNT	Augsburg Commentary on the New Testament
ANRW	*Aufstieg und Niedergang der römischen Welt*
ATR	*Anglican Theological Review*
BBR	*Bulletin for Biblical Research*
BCBC	Believers Church Bible Commentary
Bib	*Biblica*
BibLeb	*Bibel und Leben*
BibRes	*Biblical Research*
BJRL	*Bulletin of the John Rylands University Library*
BSac	*Bibliotheca Sacra*
BTB	*Biblical Theology Bulletin*
CBQ	*Catholic Biblical Quarterly*
CGTC	The Cambridge Greek Testament Commentary
CNT	Commentaire du Nouveau Testament
DPL	*Dictionary of Paul and His Letters*
EKKNT	Evangelisch-Katholischer Kommentar zum Neuen Testament
EvQ	*Evangelical Quarterly*
ExpTim	*Expository Times*
FRLANT	Forschungen zur Religion und Literatur des Alten und Neuen Testaments
GTJ	*Grace Theological Journal*
HNT	Handbuch zum Neuen Testament
HTR	*Harvard Theological Review*
ICC	International Critical Commentary
IDBS	*Interpreter's Dictionary of the Bible Supplementary Volume*
Int	*Interpretation*
JB	Jerusalem Bible
JBL	*Journal of Biblical Literature*
JES	*Journal of Ecumenical Studies*
JETS	*Journal of the Evangelical Theological Society*
JR	*Journal of Religion*
JSJ	*Journal for the Study of Judaism*
JSNT	*Journal for the Study of New Testament*
JSNTSup	Journal for the Study of New Testament Supplement Series

Abbreviations

JTS	Journal of Theological Studies
KJV	King James Version
LCL	Loeb Classical Library
LXX	Septuagint
NASB	New American Standard Bible
NCBC	New Century Bible Commentary
NEASB	Near East Archaeological Society Bulletin
NEB	New English Bible
NICGT	New International Commentary on the Greek Testament
NICNT	New International Commentary on the New Testament
NIDNTT	New International Dictionary of New Testament Theology
NIV	New International Version
NIVAC	NIV Application Commentary
NJB	New Jerusalem Bible
NovTSup	Novum Testament, Supplements
NRSV	New Revised Standard Version
NTS	New Testament Studies
RB	Revue biblique
REB	Revised English Bible
RevExp	Review and Expositor
RSR	Researches de science religieuse
SBLASP	Society of Biblical Literature Abstract and Seminar Papers
SBLMS	Society of Biblical Literature Monograph Series
SJLA	Studies in Judaism in Late Antiquity
SJT	Scottish Journal of Theology
SNT	Studien zum Neuen Testament
SNTSMS	Society for New Testament Studies Monograph Series
SNTU	Studien zum Neuen Testament und seiner Umwelt
SUNT	Studien zur Umwelt des Neuen Testaments
TDNT	Theological Dictionary of the New Testament
TEV	Today's English Version
TNTC	Tyndale New Testament Commentary
TrinJ	Trinity Journal
TToday	Theology Today
TynB	Tyndale Bulletin
USQR	Union Seminary Quarterly Review
WBC	Word Biblical Commentary
WPC	Westminster Pelican Commentaries
WUNT	Wissenschaftliche Untersuchungen zum Neuen Testament
WTJ	Westminster Theological Journal
ZNW	Zeitschrift für die neutestamentliche Wissenschaft
ZTK	Zeitschrift für Theologie und Kirche

Introduction to Colossians

WE KNOW LITTLE ABOUT the agricultural town of Colosse in the time of Paul except where it was located—on the southern bank of the Lycus River in the territory of Phrygia (modern Turkey), about 110 miles east of Ephesus. At one time it was a notable city; but during Paul's day its neighboring cities, Laodicea, eleven miles to the northwest, and Hierapolis, twelve miles to the northwest on the opposite side of the river, had outstripped it in importance. Colosse was situated in a region prone to earthquakes, and one rocked the area in A.D. 61–62, causing severe damage and possibly destroying the city. Laodicea was also devastated but recovered quickly. Colosse may not have been rebuilt, since, according to Reicke, no references to the city appear in Christian or pagan sources after A.D. 61.[1] Consequently, Paul must have written this letter before this date when the earthquake destroyed the city.

Primary evidence about the city is sparse. In 1835, W. J. Hamilton identified the site that had lain in ruins since being destroyed by the Turks in the twelfth century. The mound has been surveyed but not excavated, and only a few literary references and a handful of inscriptions survive.[2] The unexcavated mound probably contains valuable information that might help in interpreting the letter.

Authorship

IN THE LAST two centuries, many scholars have questioned whether Paul wrote Colossians. The cumulative evidence of differences in vocabulary, style, and theology from the undisputed letters by Paul have led many to this conclusion.[3] Lohse, for example, claims that the differences point to someone else

---

1. Bo Reicke, "The Historical Setting of Colossians," *RevExp* 70 (1973): 430.
2. See W. H. Mare, "Archaeological Prospects at Colossae," *NEASB* 7 (1976): 39–59.
3. Walter Bujard, *Stilanalytische Untersuchungen zum Kolosserbrief als Beitrag zur Methodik von Sprachvergleichen*, SUNT 11 (Göttingen: Vandenhoeck & Ruprecht, 1973), challenges as inadequate the earlier stylistic analysis of Ernst Percy, *Die Probleme der Kolosser- und Epheserbriefe* (Lund: C. W. K. Gleerup, 1946), who defended Pauline authorship. Bujard investigates the language print in Colossians, found in such things as the connectives, sentence structure, and progression of thought, and concludes that it is not Paul's. Mark Kiley, *Colossians as Pseudepigraphy*, The Biblical Seminar (Sheffield: JSOT, 1986) adds a new criterion. All seven undisputed letters from Paul discuss financial transactions on behalf of his mission. Such discussion, he claims, does not appear in the letters that are disputed.

as its author—"not a secretary but an independently acting and judging theologian of Pauline stamp."[4]

The letter to Philemon reveals that Paul had some relationship to Colosse, and the city's destruction in the earthquake may have offered an excellent opportunity for someone to contrive a fictional correspondence to a church that no longer existed. Some contend that the references to Timothy and Paul's other colleagues were gleaned from the letter to Philemon to enhance the letter's authenticity. The command to send the letter to Laodicea (4:16) was concocted as a clever device to explain how it appeared in that city.

But why would such a ruse have been undertaken? The letter commands no specific actions and rebukes no specific persons. Some argue that it was drafted to introduce Paul to Asia Minor since Tychicus and Onesimus are to make known "the news about [Paul]" and "everything that is happening here" (4:7, 9). Such a letter would serve the purpose of advancing the apostolic position of Paul and of lending authority to his supporters.[5] This conclusion about the dual purpose of such a pseudepigraph is not convincing. If the letter to Philemon is any indication, Paul was not an unknown in these parts, and there would be no need to introduce him. If this were the aim of later Pauline supporters, why did they not choose to distribute one or more of his genuine letters instead?[6] The letter does not look like an introduction to Paul's thought, and "the news about [Paul]" in 4:7 (cf. v. 9) refers only to Paul's situation in prison, not his life and ministry. Tychicus and Onesimus come to tell the congregation how Paul is faring, not to introduce his theological perspective.

If the purpose of this letter, as some claim, were also to certify a "succession of teachers" commended by the apostle (4:7–15), why would the list of names in Philemon and Colossians be almost identical? Pokorný claims that Tychicus and Onesimus "represented the apostolic heritage in the Lycus

---

4. Eduard Lohse, "Pauline Theology in the Letter to the Colossians," *NTS* 15 (1969): 217–18.

5. Lohse, ibid., 218, concludes that the unknown author "composed the letter with the intention of making the apostle's word heard in the situation which had arisen with the appearance of the so-called philosophy in the Asia Minor churches. Just as Paul had ties with the churches through letters, so also for his students the letter was the appropriate form for making known to the churches the binding positions and statements." The list of coworkers in 4:7–17 certifies them as the legitimate bearers of the Pauline tradition.

6. Barth and Blanke, *Colossians*, 144, also ask, "If the author with the means to falsify the manuscript attempted to deceive the readers about its true authorship, then it is incomprehensible that he would have neglected the 'best' possibilities, for example imitating the typical Pauline style, especially in the preface."

Valley."[7] The description of Onesimus, however, does not give him any ministerial role; it simply identifies him as a Christian. The emphasis in 4:8 is not on the confirmation of these two brothers but on the Colossians' comfort. Moreover, we must also ask why the forger would list Demas (see 2 Tim. 4:10) and mention Nympha in Laodicea? The whole issue of "succession" seems anachronistically imposed on the text.

What can we say in defense of Paul as the author of this letter? (1) Much of the supposedly "unpauline" vocabulary occurs in the section dealing with the "philosophy." We should not expect Paul to express himself in the same way with the same ideas in every circumstance. This argument against Pauline authorship assumes that he was incapable of theological innovation in a fresh situation.[8] How do we limit the parameters of what Paul could or could not have said? How do we make judgments about what ideas Paul could or could not have entertained, particularly since he claimed that he could become all things to all men that he might save some (1 Cor. 9:22)? Distinctive vocabulary is an unreliable criterion to rule out Paul's authorship.

(2) Nothing in Colossians is completely inconsistent with Paul's theology known from his undisputed letters.[9] Some so-called theological differences have been pressed too far. For example, Lincoln argues that too much has been read into the statement that believers have already been raised with Christ (2:12).[10] While this assertion contrasts with Paul's affirmation in Romans 6:5, 8 that the resurrection with Christ lies in the future, Lincoln persuasively argues that the two passages represent opposite poles in Paul's thinking on the resurrection life—the "already" and the "not yet." Believers enter this resurrection life when they are joined to Christ, but "its consummation still lies in the future."[11]

---

7. Pokorný, *Colossians*, 191. He does not answer why it is that only Epaphras receives a full commendation. Epaphras, not Tychicus or Onesimus, is identified as a servant of Christ who labors on Paul's behalf (1:7) and as a servant of Christ Jesus (4:12).

8. The small sample of Pauline vocabulary from his letters is not exhaustive. Arnold, *The Colossian Syncretism*, 7, comments, "When one takes into consideration the Apostle Paul's ability for varied manners of expression, the arguments against the authenticity of the letter based on stylistic matters and *hapax legomena* are somewhat blunted." Cannon, *The Use of Traditional Materials in Colossians*, argues for Pauline authorship since Colossians contains a high percentage of pre-Pauline material.

9. See also the conclusions of Stanley E. Porter and Kent D. Clarke, "Canonical-Critical Perspectives and the Relationship of Colossians and Ephesians," *Bib* 78 (1997): 57–86.

10. Andrew Lincoln, *Paradise Now and Not Yet: Studies in the Role of the Heavenly Dimension in Paul's Thought with Special Reference to His Theology*, SNTSMS 43 (Cambridge: Cambridge Univ. Press, 1981). Erich Grässer, "Kol. 3,1–4 als Beispiel einer Interpretation secundum homines recipientes," *ZTK* 64 (1967): 139–46, makes this kind of argument.

11. Lincoln, *Paradise Now and Not Yet*, 122–23.

Colossians stresses the realized aspect of eschatology for two reasons. (a) It counters any doubt whether the Colossian Christians have already attained a heavenly dimension through Christ. (b) It makes unnecessary the visions and mortification of the flesh offered by the rival philosophy to reach a higher spiritual plane (2:18). In addition, the "not yet" aspect is present in Colossians in the assertion that our life in Christ is hidden and will not be revealed until he appears in glory (3:3–4). Paul's sense of eschatological urgency also emerges in 4:5. It fits Paul's "sense of the period of his mission as a time pregnant with eschatological importance, to be used to the full in proclaiming the gospel."[12] The presumed theological differences do not tip the scale against Paul's authorship of the letter.

(3) The differences in style are problematic but may be explained in a variety of ways.[13] Paul may have relied on a secretary who fleshed out the general line of thought, and Paul then signed the final copy. Some recent scholars attribute the differences in style and vocabulary to Timothy. He is identified as the coauthor of the letter but may have composed the entire letter. Dunn concludes that Paul did not write the letter, but his authority lay behind it:

If modern scholarship is persuaded by differences of style and emphasis that the letter cannot have been composed/dictated by Paul himself, that still leaves the possibility that Paul (incapacitated in prison) approved a letter written in his name and willingly appended his signature to a document whose central thrust and main outlines he

12. Dunn, *The Epistles to the Colossians and to Philemon*, 266. Colossians' affinities with the undisputed letters are significant: Paul's view of his calling (1:1, 25) as servant and apostle to the Gentiles (1:27; cf. Gal. 1:15–16; 2:7); his view of his suffering on behalf of the church (Col. 1:24; cf. 2 Cor. 1:1–7); his preaching on the basis of the revelation of a mystery (Col. 1:26; cf. 1 Cor. 2:1); his goal to bring his churches to maturity (Col. 1:28; cf. 1 Cor. 1:26; 14:20; Phil. 3:15); his understanding of the cross and redemption (Col. 1:14, 20, 22; 2:14); his understanding of Christ's exaltation (2:10, 15; cf. Phil. 2:10–11); his understanding of Christ's role in creation (Col. 1:15–16; cf. 1 Cor. 8:6); his understanding of baptism (Col. 3:12; cf. Rom. 6:1–14); his comparison of the church with a body and Christ's identity with it (Col. 1:18; 3:15; cf. 1 Cor. 12). Parallels in vocabulary and ideas with Philippians, another prison letter, are also striking.

13. The letter follows the Pauline pattern. Terence Y. Mullins, "The Thanksgivings of Philemon and Colossians," *NTS* 30 (1984): 288–93, shows that the Colossian thanksgiving section was not patterned on Philemon and expanded, as some have assumed. By charting the themes in the thanksgiving sections, he shows that Colossians has ten themes and includes only five of the nine themes in Philemon, whereas Philippians contains six of the nine themes found in Philemon. He also shows that the Colossian thanksgiving manifests the characteristic features of the Pauline thanksgiving by announcing basic themes to be dealt with in the letter. He concludes: "Structurally Colossians is a unit with thematic relationships appearing in a manner typical of Paul."

approved of, even if the details were not stated quite as he would himself.[14]

This view allows Timothy to be a theological and stylistic "wild card." His input can explain any differences from other Pauline letters.

The stylistic differences may be explained in another way. Paul's writing to a congregation that he did not found and did not know personally may be a key factor in the differences. When we look at Colossians, Ephesians, and Philemon, we can see how this works out.[15] Philemon is accepted as genuinely from Paul while the other two letters are disputed. But the differing purposes and audiences of the three letters, which I believe were written around the same time, explains the variations in the style and tone of the three letters. Philemon is a highly personal letter of request addressed to three individuals. It deals with a delicate private matter with explosive social consequences. Colossians is addressed to a whole church community that Paul has not founded and may never have visited.[16] He feels compelled to write to them about a particular problem to bolster their faith. Ephesians is a circular letter intended for several churches in different settings.

The theological issues in the three letters also differ. Philemon does not address a matter of theological controversy but a social issue. Colossians and Ephesians deal with similar theological issues from a different tack. Johnson cogently argues,

> The themes and images of Colossians are placed within the framework of a theological exposition concerning God's reconciling work in the world. The relation of Ephesians to Colossians is almost precisely that

---

14. Dunn, *The Epistles to the Colossians and to Philemon*, 44. On Paul's use of a secretary, see E. R. Richards, *The Secretary in the Letters of Paul*, WUNT 2/42 (Tübingen: J. C. B. Mohr [Paul Siebeck], 1991).

15. On the complex question of the relationship between Colossians and Ephesians, see John B. Polhill, "The Relationship Between Ephesians and Colossians," *RevExp* 70 (1973): 439–50; and for a more recent and different view, see Ernest Best, "Who Used Whom? The Relationship of Ephesians and Colossians," *NTS* 43 (1997): 72–96.

16. Paul has not had a direct, personal connection to the church (2:1), and the parallels with Romans, a church that Paul also did not know personally, are significant. In both letters, he opens with a Christological confession (Rom. 1:3–4; Col. 1:15–20). He refers to his apostolic commission to proclaim the gospel among Gentiles (Rom. 1:8–15; Col. 1:5–8, 24–29). He emphasizes that the Christian is joined to Christ's death in baptism (Rom. 6:1–11; Col. 2:11–13). The ethical exhortation follows a similar pattern (Rom. 12:1–15:6; Col. 3:1–4:6). Paul concludes both letters with a list of greetings from friends to reinforce his ties to the congregation (Rom. 16; Col. 4:7–18). See Lohse, "Pauline Theology," 219.

of Romans to Galatians; the issues forged in controversy are elevated to the level of a magisterial statement.[17]

Some contend that the agreements between Paul and his later followers who wrote in his name so outweigh the differences that the question of Paul's authorship of the letter is not important.[18] We should point out, however, that if Paul had nothing to do with the writing of Colossians, it must then be regarded as a deliberate forgery. The counterfeiter deliberately lifted names from Philemon to give verisimilitude to Colossians and to defraud readers into thinking that it was a genuine letter from Paul.[19] In contrast to Philemon, which has simply a list of names, the Colossian author supplies further remarks for each name, summarizing their circumstances and work in the churches. The hoax is intentional; "a clever trickster is at work."[20] Apparently the forger did not believe that the command not to lie to one another (3:9) applied in such a case. This problem is eliminated if Paul is the author of the letter. The close connection between Philemon and Colossians makes this the most reasonable conclusion.

Provenance

PAUL COULD HAVE written this letter from Ephesus, Caesarea, or Rome, and cases have been made for each place. Until recent times, it was taken for granted that the letter was written from Rome. The close connection between Colossians and Philemon means that what we decide about Philemon will determine where Colossians was written. In the introduction to Philemon we present more fully the arguments for a Roman origin for the letters.

---

17. Luke Timothy Johnson, *The Writings of the New Testament* (Philadelphia: Fortress, 1986), 352.

18. See, for example, Johannes Lähnemann, *Der Kolosserbrief, Komposition, Situation, and Argumentation*, SNT 3 (Gütersloh: Mohn, 1971), 174–77.

19. This conclusion presupposes that the letter to the Colossians is intended for churches other than those of Colosse and Laodicea. One would expect that the more general letter to the Ephesians would do the same, but except for the mention of Tychicus, the bearer of the letter, no other coworker is mentioned. Johnson, *Writings*, 352, asks a probing question, "Why should imitation of random biographical details from an obscure private note, which was not likely to have had wide circulation, have been expected to mark the letter as Pauline?"

20. Barth and Blanke, *Colossians*, 144. Johnson, *Writings*, 357, points out that pseudonymity most often was "a transparent fiction, employing the name of a person long dead and known to be so (Enoch, for example, in Apocalypses, or Socrates in the Cynic letters). Here, in contrast, we have a school producing a letter shortly after Paul's death, deliberately using signals—his autograph, the network of names—that make the enterprise more like a deliberate forgery."

Situation

PAUL'S LETTERS CARRY on conversations with his churches and serve as substitutes for his personal presence (2:5). The recipients did not need Paul to explain to them the things going on in their church that prompted his letter, but we might wish he had provided more information so that we would have a clearer understanding. We can only read between the lines to guess what was happening, and the letter to the Colossians is particularly puzzling. Anyone who has ever overheard a conversation on the telephone and tried to guess who was calling and what was being said on the other end of the line knows firsthand how easy it is to draw false conclusions.

A "philosophy" was apparently threatening the Colossian congregation, causing some concern for Paul and Epaphras, the missionary who founded the church. We do not know how Paul heard about the circumstances in Colosse. Unless he received a flash bulletin from someone in the church, Epaphras may have informed him of the brewing problems.[21] Epaphras's own imprisonment with Paul (Philem. 23) may have prevented him from coming in person to intervene.

In the past, it was common to refer to the problem as the "Colossian heresy." That term is misleading because it anachronistically assumes that there were widely accepted criteria for judging orthodoxy in the time of Paul. It also assumes that the opponents are Christians who are corrupting the Colossians' faith. Arnold uses the word "syncretism" to avoid prejudging the teaching as "bad, heretical, or unorthodox."[22] Paul, however, calls it a "philosophy" (2:8). Putting this term in quotation marks prevents us from understanding it as a logical system of truths and principles and allows it to apply to a religious way of life. What this "philosophy" was and how it threatened the congregation has occupied scholars' attention for some time and no consensus has been reached.[23]

---

21. The same verb "told us" (*deloo*) in 1:8 appears in 1 Cor. 1:11, where Paul says that Chloe's people gave him oral reports about the problems in Corinth. Conceivably, Tychicus or Onesimus relayed news about the church to Paul.

22. Arnold, *The Colossian Syncretism*, xiii, n. 1.

23. Most have assumed that Paul writes a rejoinder to false teaching that has invaded or challenged the church. Morna Hooker, "Were There False Teachers in Colossae?" in *Christ and Spirit in the New Testament*, ed. Barnabas Lindars and Stephen S. Smalley (Cambridge: Cambridge Univ. Press, 1973), 315–31, however, argues strongly against this scenario. She claims that since there is no clear reference to the supposed error and no sign of distress on Paul's part (no angry outbursts, no hint of rejection), there is no false teaching pervading the community. She claims: 'The teaching in Col. 1 is entirely positive, and it is only the assumption of some kind of situation such as has been outlined that leads commentators to assume that what Paul affirms, others have been denying" (316). Paul's description of the preeminence

To identify the "philosophy" we have only meager snippets in a short but clearly polemical section (2:8, 16–23). The problem is compounded because this section is the most unclear passage in the letter. Many interpreters look outside the text for some evidence in Paul's environment that will help stitch all the allusions in the letter together into a coherent pattern. It is like looking for a needle in a haystack, however. What is worse, the diverging conjectures reveal that scholars are looking in quite different haystacks for this magic needle. When one examines all the conflicting proposals by scholars who muster impressive primary evidence to buttress their arguments, the conflicting accounts resemble the story of blind men trying to describe an elephant when they are touching different parts of the animal.[24] This does not mean that if we piece together all the different proposals, we will have our answer. The evidence is confusing and enigmatic.

The nature of the error has a vital bearing on how one interprets the whole tenor of the letter and some of its individual phrases, but we cannot reconstruct it from a "shopping list of terms" that have parallels in other religious or philosophical movements of the time.[25] We must be aware that Paul may be using irony, caricature, and exaggeration. His purpose, after all, was not to describe its tenets for the Colossians but to dissuade them from being beguiled by it.[26]

We must also exercise caution and resist finding allusions to the "philosophy" everywhere in the letter. It is possible that Paul takes up favorite terms of the false teachers, which he then deftly turns to his own advantage. But

---

of Christ in creation and redemption in 1:15–20, for example, does not require that Paul is opposing some false teaching that believes otherwise.

24. J. J. Gunther, *St. Paul's Opponents and Their Background*, NovTSup 35 (Leiden: Brill, 1973), 3–4, lists 44 different suggestions, and more have been proposed since. Four recent major monographs in English on this topic arrive at four quite different conclusions. Sappington, *Revelation and Redemption at Colossae* (1991), contends the error is "an ascetical mystical piety from Jewish apocalypticism." DeMaris, *The Colossian Controversy* (1994), argues that it is "a distinctive blend of Middle Platonic, Jewish, and Christian elements that cohere around a pursuit for wisdom." Arnold, *The Colossian Syncretism* (1995), makes a strong case for a "syncretistic folk religion." Martin, *By Philosophy and Empty Deceit* (1996), contends that wandering Cynics are behind the error. The problem is compounded by the fact that the city of Colosse has never been excavated. The possibilities are abundant; our specific knowledge is limited.

25. Fred O. Francis, "The Christological Argument of Colossians," in *God's Christ and His People: Studies in Honor of Nils Alstrup Dahl*, ed. Jacob Jervell and Wayne Meeks (Oslo/Bergen/Tromsö: Unversitetsforlaget, 1977), 193.

26. J. Gewiess, "Die apologetische Methode des Apostels Paulus im Kampf gegen die Irrlehre in Kolossä," *BibLeb* 3 (1962): 264, argues that Paul often presents caricatures of his opponents and draws out the consequences from their teaching that they did not imagine in order to present them in the worst light possible.

almost every word in the letter has been identified by one commentator or
another as an echo of the opponents' teaching. Such arguments tend to be
circular.[27] We can expect Paul to refer to the false teaching in the strongly
worded polemical section (2:8, 16–23), but we should not expect to find
allusions to it throughout the letter.[28] In defining the nature of the "philosophy," we should therefore limit ourselves to direct statements from the polemical section of the letter and Paul's critical evaluation of it. We should also
consider Paul's direct injunctions to the Colossians.

(1) Direct statements in the polemical section reveal the following about
the "philosophy."

(a) It passes judgment on the Colossians for not submitting to the observances of certain holy days and food and purity restrictions (2:16). Doing so
will disqualify them in some way or rob them of the prize (2:18). Because the
opponents disparage the Colossians in these matters, the Colossian believers apparently have not yet submitted to them.[29]

(b) Its practices are linked to regulations regarding food and drink and
observing festivals, Sabbaths, and New Moons (2:16; 2:23). It issues prohibitions: "Do not handle! Do not taste! Do not touch!" (2:21).[30]

(c) It has an interest in self-abasement, angels, and visions (2:18).

(2) Paul's negative appraisal of the error reveals the following.

(a) The "philosophy" is vain deceit, based on human tradition and the elemental spirits (or principles) of the universe, and is not according to Christ
(2:8). It clearly deviates from Christian teaching.

(b) It has the "appearance of wisdom" (2:23). The opponents present persuasive, fine-sounding arguments (2:4) that can take the unwary captive

---

27. Hooker, "Were There False Teachers in Colossae?" 319, reminds us of the inevitable
danger of circularity in this process: "It is all too easy to use what hints there are in a letter
to build a false picture of events, and then read this back into what is said."

28. Colin J. A. Hickling, "Is the Second Epistle to the Corinthians a Source for Early
Church History?" *ZNW* 66 (1975): 284–87, offers a helpful caution. "We should not assume
that Paul's choice of subjects and of phraseology [is] dictated by the arguments of his competitors" (285). Paul more frequently gives an exposition of the truth than a refutation of error.
See also Jerry Sumney, "Those Who Pass Judgment: The Identity of the Opponents in
Colossians," *Bib* 74 (1993): 377–78. The letter's emphasis on the sufficiency of Christ, for
example, does not offer much guidance in identifying the opponents. We can only infer
that someone in or out of the church neglected this truth, misunderstood it, or rejected it.

29. The future tense in 2:8 translated literally ("Beware lest there will be someone who will
take you captive") indicates that this is a danger, not something that has already happened.

30. We must decide if Paul quotes their demands or lampoons their position. Clearly
the opponents' position is related to some kind of abstinence. Some measure of asceticism
is confirmed in 2:23, where "humility" and "harsh treatment of the body" are connected to
checking "sensual indulgence."

(2:8). The opponents may identify their teaching as "wisdom," or Paul may deride its deceptive appearance of possessing wisdom.

(c) The opponents have "lost connection with the Head," from which divine growth comes (2:19). We must decide whether the opponents would have disagreed with this statement if they were Christians or agreed with it if they were not.

(d) The regulations about food, drink, and the observance of holy days are only a shadow of things to come, which is found in Christ (2:17).

(e) The dogmas are based on the "basic principles [or elemental spirits] of this world," from which those in Christ have been set free (2:8).

(f) The rules are dismissed as the "human commands and teachings" (2:22; cf. v. 8), which cannot compare to divine revelation.

(g) The references to their "false humility" (NRSV, "self-abasement"), "worship of angels" (or "worship with angels"), the things a person "has seen," and "puffs ... up" in 2:18 are the most disputed phrases in the letter; but they are all associated with a "fleshly [NIV, unspiritual] mind."

(3) Paul gives the following direct commands to the Colossians, which shed further light on the "philosophy" and the Colossians' involvement with it.

(a) Paul applies the poetic material in 1:15–20 to the Colossians in 1:22–23 and tells them that they need to remain firm in the teaching they heard previously. He does not tell them that they need to renounce some error.

(b) Paul affirms in 2:9–10 that they are already complete, having attained fullness in Christ. We can infer from this statement that someone is claiming that they have not attained this fullness, that they need something more.

(c) Paul assures the Colossians of their status before God in Christ, who is "the head over every power and authority" (2:10) and who has secured for them the forgiveness of their sins.[31] We can infer from this that the Colossians are less confident of this status either because they have begun to doubt it themselves or because someone from the outside has cast doubt on it.

(d) Paul insists that Christ alone is sufficient for their salvation.

(4) Conclusion. Rather than rehearse all of the options that scholars have proposed as candidates for the "philosophy," I will argue the case for only one.[32] The evidence does not suggest that visitors from outside have somehow wormed their way into the church or that wrongheaded members of the church have become charmed by the lures of outside cults and practices.

31. These powers are referred to as the evil "dominion of darkness" (1:13), "the invisible ... thrones or powers or rulers or authorities"(1:16; cf. 2:10, 15), and *ta stoicheia tou kosmou* (2:8, 20), and perhaps "angels" in 2:18.

32. The following general categories have been proposed for the opponents: An incipient gnostic Judaism; a gnostic mystery religion; an ascetic, mystical Judaism; a form of Hellenistic philosophy; a syncretistic amalgam from the Hellenistic culture and religion.

The opponents are outsiders. Most have argued that the error has some Jewish dimension. Using Occam's razor, we can cut away the needless multiplication of assumptions about some pagan concoction with Jewish trimmings. The most streamlined view that adequately explains all the data is that newly formed Gentile Christians in Colosse are being badgered about their faith by contentious Jews who took affront over their claims.[33] Jews could argue persuasively from the same Scriptures used by Christians.[34] Consequently, they would be far more intimidating and devastating to a young, developing church than a pagan syncretistic philosophy, a mystery religion, or a folk religion with a potpourri of superstitions and practices.[35]

When the Colossians became Christians, they believed that they had become heirs to the promises of Israel. Paul affirms that they are "God's chosen people, holy and dearly loved" (3:12), the language of Jewish self-identity in the Scripture. It makes more sense that Jews would take umbrage at the presumption of Gentile Christians and respond by impugning their hope as false.[36] If we are to trust the evidence in Acts, indignant Jews are the most

---

33. When we say Judaism, we must recognize that first-century Jews expressed their faith in a variety of ways, particularly in the Diaspora. The Dura-Europa synagogue provides ample evidence of how variegated Judaism was.

34. See Titus 1:13–14: "This testimony is true. Therefore, rebuke them sharply, so that they will be sound in the faith and will pay no attention to Jewish myths or to the commands of those who reject the truth."

35. N. T. Wright, "Poetry and Theology in Colossians 1.15–20," in *The Climax of the Covenant: Christ and the Law in Pauline Theology* (Minneapolis: Fortress, 1992), 118, concludes that "the writer is not opposing an actual heresy in the church, but is writing to warn a young church against the blandishments of the synagogue which had proved so devastating to the young church in Galatia." Daniel J. Harrington, "Christians and Jews in Colossians," in *Diaspora Jews and Judaism. Essays in Honor of, and in Dialogue with A. Thomas Kraabel*, South Florida Studies in the History of Judaism, ed. J. Andrew Overman and Robert S. MacLennan (Atlanta: Scholars, 1992), 154, writes: "There is no indication that these Gentile Christians knew much about Judaism before becoming Christians. There is no debate about the interpretation of biblical texts. . . . It appears that they had come to know about Judaism after their conversion to Christianity and are attracted to it." Paul identifies the Colossians as having been "dead in your sins and in the uncircumcision of your flesh [NIV, sinful nature]" in 2:13. This judgment derives from the customary Jewish estimation of Gentiles without the law and outside God's covenant (see Eph. 2:12). Such a charge would have unsettled new, uncertain Gentile Christians.

36. Dunn, "Colossian Philosophy," 156, also envisages "a Jewish synagogue community or representative, conscious of the Jewish community's age and respectability, thus speaking dismissively of a (quasi-) Jewish sect so recently arrived on the scene." He concludes (179):

> If indeed there were Jews in Colossae confident in their religion (2:18) through faithfulness to what were traditional (Jewish) observances (2:16, 21–23), we should not be surprised if they professed such claims in dialogue and debate with other Colossians. And if there then grew up in their midst a new version of their own

likely opponents since most of the conflict incidents are struggles with Jewish contenders.[37] The opponents from a local synagogue are not prodding the Colossian Christians to follow their lead but informing them that they are disqualified from being part of the people of God as defined in the law.

There is no reason to believe, however, that they have already swept the Colossians from their theological moorings in Christ. Paul's concern is that they might undermine the new Christians' confidence in their hope. He is therefore writing to curb the insidious influence of a false "philosophy" and to confirm the Colossians' faith (2:4–5). They are to take care that no one preys on them and lures them into deceit (2:8). The warning against questions of food and drink, festivals, and worship of angels and visions assumes that they are not doing these things (2:16, 18), since it prompts the opponents' condemnation. Paul's response is therefore a warning shot across the bow; but, more importantly, it is a booster shot designed to inject greater assurance.

In 4:12, Paul mentions Epaphras's concerns for his friends in Colosse: "He is always wrestling in prayer for you, that you may stand firm in all the will of God, mature and fully assured." The key word is "fully assured." The letter's theme statement appears in 2:6–7, "So then, just as you received Christ Jesus as Lord, continue to live in him, rooted and built up in him, strengthened in the faith as you were taught, and overflowing with thankfulness." It shows that Paul worries about the congregation's crisis of confidence.[38] Under a torrent of hostile criticism, the Colossians may begin to perceive Christianity as only an abridged form of Judaism and may be fooled into thinking that only Judaism offered the fullness that they yearned for and the protection from malign forces. Paul responds that Christians will find completeness only in Christ (2:10) and that they have already been delivered from the powers and authorities.

The following evidence lends support to the view that the opponents are rival Jews.

---

teaching, proclaiming a Jewish Messiah and the fulfilment of ancient Jewish hopes (1:12 and 3:12), but intended for Gentiles, despite "the uncircumcision of the flesh" and their ignorance of Jewish law and tradition, then, again, it would hardly be a surprise if some of the more outspoken and religiously confident members of the synagogues spoke dismissively of the beliefs, devotion and praxis of the new movement as compared with their own.

37. See Acts 9:22–23; 13:45, 50 (Antioch of Pisidia); 14:2 (Iconium); 14:19 (Lystra and Derbe); 17:5, 13 (Thessalonica); 18:4, 12 (Corinth); 18:19; 19:33 (Ephesus); 20:3 (Greece); 20:19. See also Rev. 2:9 and 3:9 for a reference to the synagogue of Satan in Smyrna and Philadelphia.

38. This explains the noticeable lack of urgency in the letter. The opponents did not seek to make the Christians into Jewish proselytes but simply dismissed and denigrated the Christians claims.

---

(1) In the late third century B.C., Antiochus III (223–187 B.C.) transported a substantial Jewish population from Mesopotamia and Babylonia to Lydia and Phrygia (Josephus, *Antiquities* 12.3.4 §§ 147–53). Cicero reports that in 62 B.C. Flaccus, the governor of Asia, confiscated twenty pounds of gold that had been collected from this area for the temple tax (*Flaccus* 28.68); such a sum averages out to a Jewish adult male population of 10,000. The Jews in the Diaspora did not retreat into ghettoes but were well integrated into society and had open dealings with their Gentile neighbors. The church, therefore, would have informal contacts with Jews in the city, and that contact was likely to create friction. Devout Jews who refused to accept Jesus as the Messiah and who scorned the gospel that accepted Gentiles as coheirs would not sit idly by while Gentiles, in their opinion, pirated their Scriptures and stole their hopes.[39]

(2) Paul identifies the error as a "philosophy" in 2:8. Those defending Judaism to the Greco-Roman world commend their ancient tradition as a venerable philosophy.[40] They emphasized that Judaism was rational and that its laws were in accordance with nature, not against it. Judaism also gained a reputation for wisdom, for high ethical standards, and for esoteric knowledge (cf. 2:23).

(3) The mention of circumcision, Sabbaths, New Moons, food laws, and purity regulations are not random elements selected by a syncretistic pagan cult or philosophy enamored with Judaism. They are distinctive Jewish identity markers that set Jews apart in the ancient world and confirmed their special status as God's chosen people. In Justin Martyr's *Dialogue with Trypho*

---

39. To appreciate their reaction, we might compare the indignity of modern Christians with new sects or cults that adopt Christian features but reject orthodox Christian faith.

40. DeMaris, *Colossian Controversy*, 48, cites Philo's stress on the correspondence between Jewish piety and Greek philosophy and argues that the Sabbath allows for pursuit of philosophy (*The Life of Moses* 2.39 §§211–16). See further Philo, *On the Change of Names* 39, 223; *On the Contemplative Life* 26; *Embassy to Gaius* 23, 33, 156, 245; *On Dreams* 2.18, 127. See also *The Epistle of Aristeas* 256. Josephus used the word to classify the major "philosophies" of Judaism (*Jewish War* 2.8.2 § 119; *Antiquities* 18.2.2 §§1, 11, 23). The dismissal of Judaism by the tyrant Antiochus in 4 Macc. 5:11 sounds like Paul's: "Will you not awaken from your foolish philosophy, dispel your futile reasonings, adopt a mind appropriate to your years, philosophize according to the truth of what is beneficial?" To which Eleazar replies:

"You scoff at our philosophy as though living by it were irrational, but it teaches us self-control, so that we master all pleasures and desires, and it also trains us in courage, so that we endure any suffering willingly; it instructs us in justice, so that in all our dealings we act impartially, and it teaches us piety, so that with proper reverence we worship the only living God" (4 Macc. 5:22–24, NRSV).

---

the Jew, the rabbi Trypho urges Justin to be circumcised and to "keep the Sabbath, the festivals and the new moons of God"[41]

By referring to these practices—eating and drinking, religious festivals, New Moon celebrations, and Sabbath days—as "a shadow of the things that were to come," namely, Christ (2:17), Paul can hardly be referring to pagan rituals or regulations. He must be referring to the Old Testament.[42] On the other hand, if he is talking about Jewish ordinances, Paul could not renounce them as entirely useless. They were inadequate to accomplish salvation or perfection, but they did point to the forgiveness, reconciliation, and new life fulfilled in Christ.

(a) Paul brings up the circumcision issue in 2:11 to reaffirm that Gentile Christians were not handicapped or disqualified for remaining uncircumcised, as some Jews might claim. They received a spiritual circumcision in Christ, which made them a part of the elect of God.

(b) The dietary prohibitions in 2:16 best fit Jewish food laws, which were also important identity markers.[43] The parenthetical comment in 2:22 that the prohibitions listed in 2:21 are based on "human commands and teachings" alludes to Isaiah 29:13. Jesus appealed to this passage in his assault on Pharisaic interpretations of food laws and ritual purity (Matt. 15:9; Mark 7:7).

(c) Sabbaths, New Moons, and feasts appear in Jewish literature as a standard way of referring to the primary celebrations of Judaism.[44] These feasts, according to Ezekiel 20:18–20; 22:8, 26, "preserve the identity of this nation in a special way as the people of God; and they show that Yahweh is God

---

41. *Dialogue with Trypho the Jew* 8.4. Rabbi Trypho expresses amazement at the Christians' way of life in the world: "But this is what we are most at a loss about: that you professing to be pious, and supposing yourselves better than others, are not in any particular separated from them, and do not alter your mode of living from the nations, in that you observe no festivals or sabbaths, and do not have the rite of circumcision" (*Dialogue with Trypho the Jew* 10).

42. Barth and Blanke, *Colossians*, 340. See Gal. 3:19–26.

43. See Dan. 1:3–16; 1 Macc. 1:62–63; 10:3; Tobit 1:10–12; Judith 12:2, 19; Add. Esth. 14:17; *Joseph and Asenath* 7:1; 8:5; Josephus, *Against Apion* 2.31 §282. Some argue that the reference to food *and* drink does not make reference to Jewish food laws since the Old Testament does not contain any prohibitions regarding drink. But Rom. 14:17, 21 refer to drink along with food (see also *Letter of Aristeas* 142, quoted below).

44. 1 Chron. 23:31; 2 Chron. 2:4; 31:3; Isa. 1:13–14; Ezek. 45:17; 46:4–6; Hos. 2:11 (in reverse order, as in Col. 2:16); 1 Macc. 10:23; 1 Ezra 5:52; Judith 8:6; 1 Enoch 82:7–10; Jubilees 1:10, 14; 2:9–10; 6:34–38; 23:19. Numbers 28–29 lists sacrifices to be performed at the new moon, the first of every month. See also CD 3:14–15; 1QM 2:4–6; and 1QS 9:26–10:8, which refers to special revelation concerning "the holy sabbaths and glorious feasts." T. C. G. Thornton, "Jewish New Moon Festivals: Galatians 4:3–11 and Colossians 2:16," *JTS* 40 (1989): 97–100, suggests that the Christians at Colosse may be criticized for failing to keep the Jewish calendar.

of this nation."[45] The mention of the Sabbath is a smoking gun since it was distinctive to Jews.

(d) The reference to not touching (2:21) reflects a fear of impurity from physical contact (Lev. 5:2–3; 7:19, 21; 11:8, 24–28; Isa. 52:11). Dunn cites a parallel in *The Letter of Aristeas* 142: "So, to prevent our being perverted by contact with others or by mixing with bad influences, he hedged us in on all sides with purifications connected with meat and drink and touch and hearing and sight in terms of the law."[46]

(e) The phrase "worship of angels" in 2:18 is exceedingly difficult. It does not refer to some cult of angels but in my opinion fits in with widespread Jewish speculation about angels. Jews believed the law was delivered by angels (Acts 7:53; Gal. 3:19; Heb. 2:2), and insisting on strict obedience to the law could be likened to venerating angels.[47] Various strands of Judaism also reflect a great interest in angels.[48] One can easily get the impression from reading the "Songs of the Sabbath Sacrifice" (4Q400–405) from the Dead Sea Scrolls or the *Testament of Solomon* in the Pseudepigrapha, for example, that angels were objects of veneration.[49]

(f) The opponents are not Christians. Paul's assertion in 2:20, "Since you died with Christ to the basic principles of this world, why, as though you still belonged to it, do you submit to its rules," seems to imply that the opponents have not died with Christ as the Colossian Christians have. In Paul's estimation, the opponents have "lost connection with the Head" (2:19). Presumably, they hold to something else, such as human traditions (compare Mark 7:8).

(g) Paul's reaffirmation of the Colossians' relationship to Christ makes sense as a response to a Jewish challenge. God has revealed the mystery to them, hidden for ages and generations, and it is the good news that the Messiah is among the Gentiles (1:26–27). Gentile believers are "qualified" for the inheritance of the saints, Israel's inheritance (1:12). Paul declares in the strongest terms that "there is no Greek or Jew, circumcised or uncircumcised"

---

45. Barth and Blanke, *Colossians*, 339.

46. Dunn, "Colossians Philosophy," 166.

47. Caird, *Paul's Letters from Prison*, 199.

48. In addition to the Dead Sea Scrolls, see Pseudo-Philo, *Biblical Antiquities* 13:6; 1 Enoch 48:5; 62:6, 9; *Apocalypse of Zephaniah* 6:16; *Apocalypse of Abraham* 17:2; *Ascension of Isaiah* 7:21; *Adam and Eve* 13–15; Philo, *On Flight and Finding* 212; *On Dreams* 1.232, 238. Warnings against too great a veneration of angels in rabbinic literature may provide evidence that it was done (*t. Hul.* 2:18). Later Christians accused Jews of worshiping angels; see the evidence in Dunn, *The Epistles to the Colossians and to Philemon*, 179.

49. The term *ta stoicheia tou kosmou* ("basic principles [or elemental spirits] of the world") in 2:8, 23, is linked to Judaism in Gal. 4:3, 9.

for those renewed "in knowledge in the image of its Creator" (3:10–11). Consequently, Gentiles have become "God's chosen people, holy and dearly loved" (3:12). The Colossians therefore need to remember that their baptism in Christ's death is a far more effective circumcision than any trivial excision of flesh. They have nothing to gain from anything the opponents might offer and should not allow any criticism directed their way to fluster them.

What Colossians Means For Us Today

COLOSSIANS WAS WRITTEN to a negligible Phrygian Christian community almost two thousand years ago, and yet it still speaks relevantly today. It gives witness "to the finality, adequacy and all-sufficiency of the cosmic Christ—by whom and for whom all things were made, in whom they cohere, and with whom in God the life of the Christian and of the Church is hidden."[50] That truth will never go out of date.

But the situation facing the Colossians is also similar to ours today. They faced opponents who challenged and belittled the sufficiency of Christ and their hope. Christians today live in a secular society, which regularly scoffs at Christian faith. Many Christians in the West have become increasingly uncertain of their faith and consequently hold it uncertainly. The acids of criticism can eat away at the foundations of a weak and vacillating faith. There are also fewer cultural forces to keep people in the church. When confronted with the laughter and scorn of the modern-day scoffers, nominal church members may be tempted to capitulate. They will abandon their faith or trade it in for the latest craze. In Paul's language, they return to the darkness where the rulers of this age hold sway.

When Christians do not understand their faith, they are likely to water down the gospel and accommodate it to cultural expectations. They will cut out any offending articles of faith or append specious ones more in accord with the fashion of the age.[51] Paul wrote to the Colossians to help them grasp ever more firmly who Christ is and the rich glories of all that God has done in him.

When Christians have little confidence in their faith, they will be overly tentative in their claims and easily shaken by challenges. Paul hoped to fortify the Colossians in their assurance of the hope they had in Christ. The let-

---

50. James S. Stewart, "A First-Century Heresy and Its Modern Counterpart," *SJT* 23 (1970): 420.

51. Ibid., 423, mentions the danger of substituting "immanence for incarnation, evolution for redemption, psychological subjectivity for the Holy Spirit, progress for the Kingdom of God."

ter affirms that God's creation has a divine purpose, which is brought to fulfillment in and through Christ. It affirms the supremacy and sufficiency of Christ as the fullness of God and as our Creator and Redeemer.

When Christians do not live with a deep sense of gratitude for what God has done for them in Christ, they will become engulfed in anxieties and will be tempted to look for security in something other than Christ. Paul repeatedly urged the Colossians to be thankful for the victory already won for them by Christ's cross and resurrection. Salvation can be found only in Christ, and Christians do not need something else or something more. The cross brings redemption, the forgiveness of sin, and triumph over all the powers that would oppress human life. Every believer is made complete when placed under the complete claim of Christ, and all the spiritual ills of our world find their only cure in him.

When Christians live no differently from those around them who do not know God or who defy God's commands, they bring discredit to their faith and cause others to think that their claims are false. The letter to the Colossians argues that Christians must not only be solidly grounded in their faith. They must also be ethically above reproach. Discerning, confident, grateful, and ethical Christians lead lives worthy of the Lord, are pleasing to God, and will bear spiritual fruit in a spiritually blighted world. Paul intends in this letter to help form this kind of believer.

Outline of Colossians

I. Salutation and Thanksgiving (1:1–23)
  A. Salutation (1:1–2)
  B. Thanksgiving (1:3–23)
    1. Thanksgiving for the Reception of the Gospel in Colosse and the Whole World (1:3–8)
    2. Paul's Intercession for the Colossians (1:9–23)
      a. Living a Life Worthy of the Lord (1:9–14)
      b. Poetic Exaltation of Christ (1:15–20)
        (1) The Image of the Invisible God, the Firstborn over all Creation (1:15–17)
        (2) The Head of the Church, the Firstborn from Among the Dead (1:18–20)
      c. Remaining Firm and Established in the Faith (1:21–23)
II. Letter Body (1:24–2:23)
  A. Paul's Commission, Message, and Struggle (1:24–2:5)
  B. The Colossian Error (2:6–23)
    1. Theme Statement: Loyalty to Christ As Lord (2:6–7)
    2. First Warning (2:8)
    3. The All-Sufficiency of Christ (2:9–15)
    4. Rebuttal of the Errorist's Position (2:16–23)
      a. Second Warning (2:16–17)
        (1) The Issues Used to Condemn Others: Food, Drink, Feasts, New Moons, Sabbaths (2:16)
        (2) Paul's Evaluation: They Are Only Shadows of a Reality Already Here (2:17)
      b. Third Warning (2:18–19)
        (1) The Issues Used to Disqualify Others: Self-abasement, Worship of Angels, and Visions (2:18a–b)
        (2) Paul's Evaluation: They Lead to Arrogance and Separation from the Head (2:18c–19)
      c. Rhetorical Question and Answer (2:20–23)
III. Ethical Admonitions (3:1–4:6)
  A. Setting Your Hearts on the Things Above (3:1–4)
  B. The Old and the New Morality (3:5–17)
    1. The Vices of the Old Morality That Need to Be Renounced (3:5–9)

Selected Bibliography
on Colossians

Commentaries

Baggott, L. J. *A New Approach to Colossians*. London: A. R. Mowbray, 1961.

Barth, Markus, and Helmut Blanke. *Colossians*. AB. New York: Doubleday, 1994.

Beare, Francis. "The Epistle to the Colossians: Introduction and Exegesis," in *The Interpreter's Bible*. Nashville: Abingdon, 1955, 11:132–241.

Bruce, F. F. *The Epistles to the Colossians, to Philemon, and to the Ephesians*. NICNT. Grand Rapids: Eerdmans, 1984.

Caird, G. B. *Paul's Letters from Prison*. New Clarendon Bible. Oxford: Clarendon, 1976.

Calvin, John. *Commentaries on the Epistles of Paul the Apostle to the Philippians, Colossians and Thessalonians*. Ed. John Pringel. Grand Rapids: Eerdmans, 1948.

Dodd, C. H. "Philemon," in *The Abingdon Bible Commentary*. Ed. F. C. Eiselen, E. Lewis, and D. G. Downey. New York/Nashville: Abingdon, 1929, 1250–62.

Dunn, James D. G. *The Epistles to the Colossians and to Philemon: A Commentary on the Greek Text*. NIGTC. Grand Rapids: Eerdmans, 1996.

Harris, Murray J. *Colossians and Philemon*. Grand Rapids: Eerdmans, 1991.

Houlden, J. L. *Paul's Letters from Prison: Philippians, Colossians, Philemon and Ephesians*. WPC. Philadelphia: Westminster, 1970, 1977.

Hultgren, Arland J. "Colossians," in *The Deutero-Pauline Letters*. Proclamation Commentaries. Ed. Gerhard Krodel. Rev. ed. Minneapolis: Fortress, 1993, 24–38.

Lightfoot, J. B. *Saint Paul's Epistles to the Colossians and to Philemon*. Grand Rapids: Zondervan, 1959 (from the revised 1879 edition).

Lohse, Eduard. *Colossians and Philemon*. Trans. William R. Poehlmann and Robert J. Karris. Hermeneia. Philadelphia: Fortress, 1971.

Lucas, R. C. *The Message of Colossians and Philemon*. Downers Grove, Ill.: InterVarsity, 1980.

MacLeod, G. Preston. "The Epistle to the Colossians: Exposition," in *The Interpreter's Bible*. Nashville: Abingdon, 1955, 10:132–241.

Martin, Ernest D. *Colossians and Philemon*. BCBC. Scottsdale, Penn./Waterloo, Ont.: Herald, 1993.

Martin, Ralph P. *Colossians and Philemon*. NCB. London: Oliphants, 1974.

_____. *Ephesians, Colossians and Philemon*. Interpretation. Atlanta: John Knox, 1991.

Moule, C. F. D. *The Epistles to the Colossians and to Philemon*. CGTC. Cambridge: Cambridge Univ. Press, 1968.

O'Brien, Peter T. *Colossians, Philemon*. WBC. Waco, Tex.: Word, 1982.

Patzia, Arthur G. *Ephesians, Colossians, Philemon*. New International Commentary. Peabody, Mass.: Hendrickson, 1984, 1990.

Pokorný, Petr. *Colossians: A Commentary*. Trans. Siegfried Schatzmann. Peabody, Mass.: Hendrickson, 1991.

Radford, L. B. *The Epistle to the Colossians and the Epistle to Philemon*. Westminster Commentaries. London: Methuen, 1931.

Reumann, John H. P. *Colossians*. ACNT. Minneapolis: Augsburg, 1985.

Robertson, A. T. *Paul and the Intellectuals: The Epistle to the Colossians*. Ed. W. C. Strickland. Nashville: Broadman, 1959.

Schweizer, Eduard. *The Letter to the Colossians*. Trans. Andrew Chester. Minneapolis: Augsburg, 1982.

Scott, E. F. *The Epistles of Paul to the Colossians, to Philemon and to the Ephesians*. London: Hodder and Stoughton, 1930.

Stockhausen, Carol L. *Letters in the Pauline Tradition: Ephesians, Colossians, I Timothy, II Timothy and Titus*. Message of Biblical Spirituality. Wilmington, Del.: Michael Glazier, 1989.

Thurston, Bonnie. *Reading Colossians, Ephesians & 2 Thessalonians: A Literary and Theological Commentary*. New York: Crossroad, 1995.

Wall, Robert W. *Colossians and Philemon*. The IVP New Testament Commentary. Downers Grove, Ill.: InterVarsity, 1993.

Wright, N. T. *Colossians and Philemon*. TNTC. Grand Rapids: Eerdmans, 1986.

Yates, Roy. *The Epistle to the Colossians*. Epworth Commentaries. London: Epworth, 1993.

Monographs

Arnold, Clinton E. *The Colossian Syncretism*. WUNT 2/77. Tübingen: J. C. B. Mohr (Paul Siebeck), 1995.

Barclay, William. *The All-Sufficient Christ: Studies in Paul's Letter to the Colossians*. Philadelphia: Westminster, 1963.

Best, Ernest. *One Body in Christ: A Study in the Relationship of the Church to Christ in the Epistles of the Apostle Paul*. London: SPCK, 1955.

Cannon, George E. *The Use of Traditional Materials in Colossians*. Macon, Ga.: Mercer Univ. Press, 1983.

Crouch, J. E. *The Origin and Intention of the Colossian Haustafel*. FRLANT 109. Göttingen: Vandenhoeck & Ruprecht, 1972.

Selected Bibliography on Colossians

DeMaris, Richard E. *The Colossian Controversy: Wisdom in Dispute at Colossae.* JSNTSup 96. Sheffield: JSOT, 1994.

Francis, F. O., and Wayne Meeks, eds. *Conflict at Colossae.* Sources for Biblical Study 4. Missoula: Society of Biblical Literature, 1973.

Jones, Maurice. *The Epistle of St. Paul to the Colossians.* London: SPCK, 1923.

Martin, Troy W. *By Philosophy and Empty Deceit: Colossians As Response to a Cynic Critique.* JSNTSup 118. Sheffield: JSOT, 1996.

Sappington, Thomas J. *Revelation and Redemption at Colossae.* JSNTSup 53. Sheffield: JSOT, 1991.

Colossians 1:1–8

PAUL, AN APOSTLE of Christ Jesus by the will of God, and Timothy our brother,
²To the holy and faithful brothers in Christ at Colosse:
Grace and peace to you from God our Father.
³We always thank God, the Father of our Lord Jesus Christ, when we pray for you, ⁴because we have heard of your faith in Christ Jesus and of the love you have for all the saints—⁵the faith and love that spring from the hope that is stored up for you in heaven and that you have already heard about in the word of truth, the gospel ⁶that has come to you. All over the world this gospel is bearing fruit and growing, just as it has been doing among you since the day you heard it and understood God's grace in all its truth. ⁷You learned it from Epaphras, our dear fellow servant, who is a faithful minister of Christ on our behalf, ⁸and who also told us of your love in the Spirit.

THE FIRST TWO sections of Paul's letter to the Colossians consist of his customary salutation (1:1–2) and the prayer of thanksgiving that he offers to God on behalf of the believers in the churches (1:3–23). These sections help set the agenda for the rest of the letter.

The Salutation (1:1–2)

PAUL BEGINS HIS salutation identifying himself as "an apostle of Christ Jesus by the will of God." He does not write as a private interested party but as Christ's apostle who speaks with authority. By identifying himself in this way Paul is not trying to establish his badge of rank or to put his readers under his thumb. His authority is not increased by the use of the title *apostle*, just as it is not reduced when he omits it (1 Thess. 1:1; 2 Thess. 1:1) or substitutes "servant" (Phil. 1:1) or "prisoner" (Philem. 1). Being an apostle is simply what he is.

We therefore should not assume, as some do, that when Paul refers to himself as an apostle, he is defending his calling against bitter opposition.[1] Not everyone to whom Paul wrote was suspicious of his eligibility or adequacy as an apostle, and he was not always on the defensive. He praises the Colossians as a loving, supportive community, not a bickering, backbiting, spiteful group (1:8; Philem. 5). Though many in the Colossian church have not met Paul personally, the letter gives the impression that they esteemed both him and his coworker Epaphras, their evangelist.[2] Paul writes to them because they already accept his authority, which derives from the gospel he has been called to preach, a gospel they have learned from Epaphras.

When Paul says that his calling as an apostle came "by the will of God," it reflects his basic conviction that Christ called and empowered him to carry on a divine task that was entrusted to only a few. In the Old Testament, God appeared to prophets and sent them forth to proclaim the word. In Paul's case, Christ appeared to him and sent him out to proclaim a particular gospel (Gal. 1:12, 16; 1 Cor. 15:8–10). He did not decide to go into the apostolic ministry but understood himself to have been set apart by God from his mother's womb to carry the gospel to the nations (Gal. 1:15–16).[3] His authority was unique since it derived directly from Christ, but Paul did not see himself as set apart for high office from which he could rule the roost and issue divine directives (see 1 Cor. 4:9). God assigned him a task, not a status.

As Christ's apostle Paul is not tied to any one congregation but is obligated to all, particularly the Gentiles (Rom. 11:13; Gal. 2:7; Eph. 3:1–2). The world is his mission field. All he does as Christ's apostle involves Christ's church. Therefore, his charge to preach the gospel and build up the body of Christ by helping believers with their struggles in obedience leads him to intervene in the Colossian controversy.

Paul includes Timothy, "our brother," as a cosender of the letter.[4] Timothy appears as the cosender in five other letters: 2 Corinthians, Philippians, and

---

1. See Schweizer, *Colossians*, 28. Wall, *Colossians and Philemon*, 34, makes the statement without a shred of evidence: "While he has not yet met with his Colossian readers, no doubt there is opposition to his ministry and teaching among them." Paul is not trying to defend his apostleship to the Colossians because in 1:23 he simply designates himself as a "servant" (*diakonos*) of the gospel (like Epaphras, 1:7). He identifies himself as a "fellow servant" with others (1:7; 4:7). A later copyist apparently did not think Paul's status as a mere servant grand enough; the text of ℵ* reads "preacher and apostle" (*kerux kai apostolos*) and reflects a later preoccupation with titles and authority.

2. O'Brien, *Colossians, Philemon*, 16.

3. That imagery echoes the calling of prophets in the Old Testament (see Isa. 49:1; Jer. 1:5).

4. Other persons Paul designates as "brothers" are Quartus (Rom. 16:23), Sosthenes (1 Cor. 1:1), and Apollos (1 Cor. 16:12). See also 2 Cor. 8:18; 9:3, 5; 12:18.

Philemon, and with Silvanus in 1 and 2 Thessalonians. According to Acts 16:1–2, Paul met this young man during his ministry in Derbe or Lystra. Because Timothy's mother was Jewish, Paul made his status as a Jew official by circumcising him (Acts 16:3). Timothy joined Paul on his missionary travels, and Paul extolled him as a devoted son (1 Cor. 4:17; Phil. 2:22) and trusted him as a faithful emissary, sending him to various churches to help assuage anxious converts or to put out fires of conflict (1 Cor. 4:17; Phil. 2:19; 1 Thess. 3:2, 6). Although Timothy was not an apostle, Paul affirms him as one who carries on the same work (1 Cor. 16:10) and the same preaching task (2 Cor. 1:19).

We have no record of Timothy's direct connection to the Colossians. Possibly his name appears in the salutation because he composed the letter from Paul's dictation or at his direction. His inclusion also makes clear that what follows is not Paul's peculiar opinion. Paul is no maverick and does not stand alone on these issues. He works with a team of ministers, and this letter reflects the consensus of those who are with him (see 4:10–14).

Paul greets the church as "holy and faithful brothers in Christ."[5] Holiness has to do with being set apart from the world unto God and does not imply that these believers belong to some exalted echelon of saints. As God has made Paul his own as Christ's apostle, so God has made the Colossians as his covenant people in Colosse. The word "holy" (or "saints") was applied to Israel in the Old Testament, and Paul intentionally includes Gentile Christians under this category.[6] It means that they also belong to the eschatological people for whom all the promises apply.

Paul customarily identifies the recipients of his letters as "saints," but he does not usually address them as "faithful."[7] This expression most likely refers to their steadfastness under pressure. Some commentators take it to mean exactly the opposite of what it says. They suggest that Paul subtly hauls over the coals those in the church who have been unfaithful by forsaking the true gospel for the so-called "philosophy."[8] This reading assumes that Paul is

---

5. The NIV takes the word "holy" as an adjective. It could also be rendered as a substantive, "saints" (NRSV). Paul uses the word as a substantive in addressing the churches in his letters to the Romans, 1 and 2 Corinthians, Philippians, and Ephesians, and it has this meaning in 1:4. Since one definite article governs both "holy" and "faithful," it is likely that he intends an adjectival meaning; but it could be a careless usage that simply omits the article.

6. Dunn, *The Epistles to the Colossians and to Philemon*, 48.

7. The exception is Eph. 1:1.

8. Lightfoot, *Saint Paul's Epistles to the Colossians and to Philemon*, 130, suggests that Paul called them faithful in hopes of warding off any more unfaithfulness. He contends that by calling them faithful, Paul "obliquely hints at the defection" that has already occurred among some whose allegiance has been shaken (132). Wall, *Colossians and Philemon*, 38, concurs with this view: "In stressing *faithful brothers*, Paul may very well have the audience's religious confusion in mind."

being disingenuous. His praise becomes a backhanded compliment with a warning: "I am not fully convinced that you are faithful, so you better watch out." Commentators have unduly read the threat from the "philosophy" into every phrase of Colossians. But Paul's statements do not all contain some hidden nuance. If the Colossians were not faithful or were verging on abandoning their faith, Paul is perfectly capable of warning them forthrightly. He does not use "faithful" in Ephesians 1:1 in a reproving way, nor does it have any hidden meaning when he uses it to describe his coworkers Epaphras, Tychicus, and Onesimus (Col. 1:7; 4:7, 9; see also Eph. 6:21).

We should therefore accept the plain meaning of the text: The Colossians are genuinely "faithful," which is the reason for his thanksgiving. Their faith is not teetering on the brink of extinction, trapped in error, or at the mercy of those hawking false teachings. They are holding fast to the head (2:19), and Paul only warns them about others who do not. Their faith is not perfected, however, and Paul wants to buttress it further and revitalize their growth. In this greeting, he establishes their common commitments so that he can move on to instruct and warn them. His goal is to ensure that they remain securely established in their faith (1:23) and growing in their knowledge (1:10).

The NIV chooses not to retain the parallelism in the Greek text by translating 1:2, "To the holy and faithful brothers in Christ at Colosse." Literally, the Greek reads: "in Colosse ... in Christ." The parallelism implies that the recipients may reside in Colosse, but more importantly they live in the sphere of Christ. "In Christ" and related phrases appear frequently in Paul's writings, and the concept is central to his understanding of our salvation.

(1) To be in Christ means to be incorporated in him so that he encompasses the entire life of the believer. The recipients may be Colossians, but the only identity that matters to God is that they are Christians. That means that Christ determines everything in their lives. Paul will later make clear in the letter that his death becomes their death, his burial their burial, his resurrection their resurrection, his victory their victory (2:6–23).

(2) To be in Christ means that the Colossians are exclusively joined to him and to no other. One cannot be "in Isis," "in Artemis," or in any other god or goddess and also be in Christ.

(3) To be in Christ means that he determines the behavior of believers. One cannot be "in the world" or "into magic or drugs," for example, and be "in Christ." Elsewhere Paul uses this basic idea to denounce immorality: "Do you not know that your bodies are members of Christ himself? Shall I then take the members of Christ and unite them with a prostitute? Never!" (1 Cor. 6:15).

(4) To be in Christ means that believers are inseparably joined to him. Paul expresses this powerfully in Romans 8:38–39: "Neither death nor life, nei-

ther angels nor demons, neither the present nor the future, nor any powers, neither height nor depth, nor anything else in all creation, will be able to separate us from the love of God that is in Christ Jesus our Lord."

(5) To be in Christ means that believers are also joined to a new family where the dividing lines that separate and categorize persons have been erased (see Rom. 12:5). Their mutual faith in Christ has created a spiritual kinship that supersedes blood ties.

Being in Christ gives Christians their true identity beyond their race, nationality, or clan. Paul therefore calls the Colossians "brothers." Jews addressed fellow Jews as brothers (Acts 2:29, 37; 3:17; 7:2, 26; 13:15; Rom. 9:3), but for a devout Jew to call Gentiles brothers, many of whom he has never met, reveals the radical consequences of a gospel that swept away all racial prejudices isolating people from one another (see Col. 3:11; cf. Gal. 3:28; Philem. 16).

As many have noted, the customary greeting of letters, *chairein* ("greetings," Acts 15:23; 23:26; James 1:1), is transformed into a promise of "grace" (*charis*). The letter itself is intended to be a means of grace, and the word reappears in the concluding wish in Colossians 4:18. "Peace" was the traditional greeting in Hebrew (*šalom*).[9] The peace Paul has in view is peace that only God's salvation brings—harmony, wholeness, and serenity. These are things that human force or a balance of terror cannot establish. Paul shows an ardent concern that the effects of this peace from God be obvious in the life of Christian communities.[10] "Peace" becomes a key component of his moral exhortation and appears in his appeal to the Colossians in 3:15.[11]

Paul confesses that both grace and peace come "from God our Father." The thanksgiving that follows is based on all that God has done and will continue to do (1:7, 12–13). The image of father conveyed power, authority, and loving care. The nearness and love of God as Father was something particularly esteemed by Christians, and Paul usually identifies God as the Father of Jesus Christ, as he does in 1:3.[12] For Christians, God is our Father because he is the

---

9. Peace appears in all the greetings of letters attributed to Paul (Rom. 1:7; 1 Cor. 1:3; 2 Cor. 1:2; Gal. 1:3; Eph. 1:2; Phil. 1:2; 1 Thess. 1:1; 2 Thess. 1:2; 1 Tim. 1:2; 2 Tim. 1:2; Titus 1:4; Philem. 4) and in many of his closing benedictions (Rom. 16:20; 2 Cor. 13:11; Gal. 6:16; Eph. 6:23; Col. 1:2; 2 Thess. 3:16; see Phil. 4:9).

10. Buttrick, "Philemon," 563, comments: "The grace is God's free unmerited favor to sinful men through the forgiving Cross and the enabling resurrection of his Son, and the peace is the consequent reconciliation of men with God."

11. See Rom. 12:18; 14:17, 19; 1 Cor. 7:15; 14:33; 2 Cor. 13:11; Eph. 4:3; 1 Thess. 5:13; 2 Tim. 2:22; see also Rom. 3:17; 8:6; Eph. 2:14–17; Col. 1:20.

12. See Rom. 1:7; 1 Cor. 1:3; 2 Cor. 1:2; 11:31; Gal. 1:3; Eph. 1:2; 6:23; Phil. 1:2; 2 Thess. 1:2; Philem. 3. It may well be that Paul omits mention of Jesus Christ here because he wants to affirm his monotheism prior to the Christological hymn.

Father of Jesus Christ, to whom we belong.[13] The Father is not an impenetrable and invisible God but one who makes himself known through his Son (see Matt. 11:27). Both Father and Son can be known even by those disdained as "babes" by the so-called "wise and learned" (Matt. 11:25).

The Structure of the Thanksgiving (1:3–23)

PAUL ADOPTED THE custom in ancient letter writing of offering a prayer of thanks to the gods and transformed this convention by expanding it and filling it with Christian meaning. His thanksgiving is not some perfunctory nod to various divinities for blessings received and misfortunes averted. It is a prayer to be read aloud in Christian worship and thereby becomes a witness of Christian faith and a means of Christian instruction. Paul never trots out some stock, all-purpose prayer but carefully tailors it to the situation of the church he is addressing. He sensitively weaves together the church's progress in the faith, their needs, and his hopes for them into a beautiful tapestry of praise and thanks to God.[14] One should not ignore the thanksgiving proems in Paul's letters as unimportant devotional meditations unrelated to the key themes of the letter. They lay the groundwork for what follows in the letter, previewing its major themes and setting the tone of the letter.

The thanksgiving section in Colossians extends from 1:3 through 1:23 and includes the Christological prose hymn in 1:15–20. The key ideas of "faith," "hope," and "hearing" in the opening (1:4–6) are repeated in 1:23 to form an inclusio—a rhetorical device in which the beginning of a unit is repeated in its ending. The thanksgiving divides into two parts, 1:3–8 and 1:9–23. The first part focuses on the effects of the gospel in Colosse and the whole world, the second on Paul's intercession for the Colossians and his celebration of the salvation accomplished by Christ.

In 1:3–5, Paul tells the Colossians that he always thanks God for them because of their faith in Jesus Christ and their love for all the saints. The focus on the community suddenly shifts in 1:6 to the whole world as he exults over the universal effects of the gospel. In 1:7–8 he returns to how the gospel took root in Colosse through Epaphras's ministry. This first section of the thanksgiving forms a chiasm, a literary pattern in which two or more terms, phrases, or ideas are stated and then repeated in reverse order (ab ba):

---

13. Barth and Blanke, *Colossians,* 168.

14. Caird, *Paul's Letters from Prison,* 165, insightfully observes that when Paul begins with a thanksgiving, he can inform the readers how he is pleased with them "yet protect them from smugness by a reminder that their Christian faith and life are the product of God's unmerited grace."

A v. 4: We have heard of your *faith* in Christ Jesus and of *the love* you have
for all the saints

   B v. 5: the faith and love that spring from the hope stored up for you
in heaven and that you have already *heard* about in the word of *truth,*
the gospel

      C v. 6a: that has come to you. All over the world this gospel is
bearing fruit and growing,

   B' v. 6b: just as it has been doing among you since the day you *heard*
it and understood God's grace in all its *truth.*

A' vv. 7–8: You learned it from Epaphras, our dear fellow servant, who is
a *faithful minister of Christ* on our behalf, and who also told us of *your love*
in the Spirit.

From this structure we see that the heart of the first part of the prayer is
verse 6a, in which Paul gives thanks for how the gospel has spread throughout the world.

The second section of the thanksgiving consists of Paul's intercession for
the Colossians (1:9–14). Paul restates that he does not cease praying for
them (1:9; cf. 1:3), and in 1:9–11 he reiterates in reverse order the key
phrases in 1:3–6. He repeats the phrase "since the day we heard about you"
(1:9; 1:6, "since the day you heard it") and then lists how he intercedes for
them. He prays that they will increase in "bearing fruit" and "growing" (1:10;
cf. 1:6) and in "the knowledge of [God's] will" (1:9; cf. 1:10, "of God"; see
1:6, of "God's grace"). In 1:11–12 he also prays that they may be "strengthened with all power according to his glorious might" and that they may
give thanks joyfully.

He lists three reasons for giving thanks in 1:12–14.[15] Some question
whether 1:12–14 are part of the prayer and treat it as an introit leading in
to the anthem to Christ in 1:15–20. Paul is not working from a precise outline, however, and we should regard 1:12–14 as part of his intercession. It
gives the reasons for joyfully giving thanks to God and flows naturally
into glorifying Christ. These verses therefore place 1:15–20 in the context
of the celebration of redemption rather than abstruse, metaphysical rumi-
nations.[16]

---

15. The traditional verse division puts "joyfully" (literally "with joy") in 1:11 and connects it with what precedes, "so that you may have great endurance and patience with joy."
The NIV correctly renders the prepositional phrase with the participle that follows. It
matches a syntactic pattern in 1:10–11: (lit.) "in every good work bearing fruit," "growing
in the knowledge of God," "with all power being strengthened," and "joyfully giving thanks."

16. Lohse, *Colossians and Philemon,* 33; and Yates, *The Epistle to the Colossians,* 10.

The prose hymn to Christ in 1:15–20, which affirms Christ's absolute and universal supremacy, bursts forth like a supernova, whose resplendence eclipses everything around it. The verses surrounding this poetic celebration, however, also offer up praise for what God has done for us through Christ. God has made the Colossians fit for a share in an inheritance for which they did not previously qualify as Gentiles (1:12). God has rescued them from the dominion of darkness (the plight of pagans) and brought them in a new Exodus to the kingdom of God's beloved Son (1:13). God has redeemed them and forgiven their sins (1:14) and has reconciled them through Christ to present them holy, without blemish, and free from accusation (1:22).

In the final verses of the thanksgiving (1:21–23), Paul recounts how the Colossians accepted this reconciliation (1:21–22). He mentions again (1:23) the hope held out in the gospel (see 1:5), their hearing of it (1:5), and how it has been proclaimed to every creature under heaven (1:6) so that it can bear fruit and grow. He concludes the thanksgiving with mention of his own role as a servant of this gospel (1:23), a topic he will take up in the next section (1:24–2:5). This long, rhapsodic thanksgiving lays the foundation for the exhortation beginning in 2:6.[17]

In sum, 1:3–23 is like a mighty river meandering through stunningly beautiful terrain. To appreciate fully the theological landscape, we will need to break up the unity of this segment by discussing it in separate sections in the commentary.

Thanksgiving for the Colossians' Reception of the Gospel (1:3–8)

PAUL INFORMS THE Colossians that he regularly prays for the church and gives thanks for them in every prayer.[18] Thanking God for their faith and love implies that he gives God the credit for it, not them. The theme of

---

17. Wright, *Colossians and Philemon*, 48.

18. The "we" in 1:9 may be a literary plural, a royal "we," which would mean that Paul has only himself in mind. Since he switches from the plural to the singular in 1:24, it is more likely that the "we" refers also to his coworkers (see Barth and Blanke, *Colossians*, 166–68). The "always" may go with "we give thanks" to God (NIV) or "praying for you" (so KJV). The NIV translation implies that every time Paul prayed for the Colossians he gave thanks for them (see 1 Cor. 1:4; Eph. 1:16; 1 Thess. 1:2). Wright, *Colossians and Philemon*, 50, argues, however, that "always" should go with "praying." Paul wants to convey that he "does not pray haphazardly only when the mood strikes him, but keeps regular hours of prayer (probably morning, noon, and evening), and the church in Colosse is always mentioned." Dunn, *The Epistles of Colossians and to Philemon*, 56, imagines that Paul prayed during his travel or long hours of stitching. Paul may also have continued in his Jewish tradition of praying at the three hours of prayer (see Dan. 6:11; Acts 3:1; 10:3).

thanksgiving is an important facet of this letter and reappears in 1:12; 2:7; 3:15, 16, 17; 4:2. Here Paul gives thanks for three developments in their spiritual life.

(1) He is thankful for their faithful acceptance of the gospel, which has spilled over into their love for others.[19] If Paul is writing from Rome, news of their faithfulness has even reached the capitol of the empire. Their active love is a sign of a genuine faith based on a solid hope. We meet the familiar triad of faith, love, and hope (see 1 Cor. 13:13; 1 Thess. 1:3; 5:8), but they are not coordinate here. The Colossians have faith and love because of "the hope that is stored up . . . in heaven." In this letter, hope becomes "the greatest of these" (see 1 Cor. 13:13) because it is the very thing that the Jewish critics have disparaged: What hope do Gentiles have? (see Eph. 2:12). Paul is not concerned about a so-called "false doctrine" that "tended to cheat them of their hope."[20] Instead, he wants to counter those who have belittled and maligned the Colossians' hope, prompting some of them to develop nagging doubts. This backdrop best explains why the opening thanksgiving emphasizes their hope of glory (1:5, 23; see 1:27). Paul wants to revive their faith in the certainty of what the gospel promises (1:23).

The faith that Paul commends in 1:5 is not faith in general but *faith in Christ Jesus*.[21] It refers specifically to the belief that God raised Jesus from the dead and that he offers all believers, Jew and Gentile, the same promise of life. In 2:12, Paul reminds his readers that they were raised with Christ through faith in the power of God, who raised him from the dead. This faith is not something that can be possessed like a piece of property or enshrined in a creed. It is a vibrant force that expresses itself in how we live. Consequently, Paul commends them for faith proven by tangible demonstrations of love for the saints (see 2 Cor. 8:1–15; 9:6–16). He rejoices in its firmness (Col. 2:5), but he would also like to see it more securely established (1:23; 2:7).

"Love" refers to the mutual love that Christians have for one another, a basic Christian virtue. Faith directed toward Jesus Christ is embodied in love for others. It is a "supernatural, God-given love," because he refers to it a

---

19. Paul gives thanks for the same thing in Philem. 5.

20. See Lightfoot, *Saint Paul's Epistles to the Colossians and to Philemon*, 134.

21. Dunn, *The Epistles to the Colossians and to Philemon*, 57, points out that Paul does not normally use the noun "faith" followed by the preposition *en* plus the dative, "faith in Jesus Christ," but instead uses the phrase "faith of Jesus Christ" (Rom. 3:22, 26; Gal. 2:16, 20; 3:22; Phil. 3:9). Paul uses the verb "to believe" followed by the phrase "in Jesus Christ" (Rom. 10:14; Gal. 2:16; Phil. 1:29). The phrase "faith in Jesus Christ" appears in letters that many scholars claim are post-Pauline (Eph. 1:15; 1 Tim. 3:13; 2 Tim. 1:13; 3:15). W. H. P. Hatch, *The Pauline Idea of Faith* (Cambridge, Mass.: Harvard Univ. Press, 1917) 46, argues that "faith of Christ," "faith in [*en*] Christ," and "faith in [*eis*] Christ" all mean essentially the same thing (noted by Harris, *Colossians and Philemon*, 16).

second time as "your love in the Spirit" in 1:8.[22] Christians are not united solely by their mutual interest in personal salvation but are knit together in love. This love is a force within that seeks release by giving itself to others, not a vacuum that selfishly craves to be filled by what others can give to us. True disciples of Christ, inspired by love, intend every action to bring benefits to others.[23]

A sure hope is the source of faith and love.[24] What is interesting in this formulation is that hope is not grounded in faith, but the reverse—faith is grounded in hope. "Hope," therefore, does not refer to the "subjective attitude of expectation." Rather, it refers to the thing hoped for.[25] Paul does not clarify what that hope precisely is except that it is stored up in heaven (see Rom. 8:24; Titus 2:13; Heb. 6:18).[26] We can assume that he has in mind the glorious future that Christ has established for believers (see Col. 3:4, 24; cf. Rom. 8:18). The "hope of glory" in Colossians 1:27 is based on Christ's being in us. Christ is the image of God, in whom all things were created, and the firstborn from among the dead. The implication in Colossians is that Christians are also being transformed into the image of God and will know the resurrection from the dead. This hope encapsulates "the word of truth, the gospel" (1:5).

(2) The second feature for which Paul gives thanks is the universal impact of the gospel as it sprouts up everywhere on earth, including Colosse.[27] The gospel's effects testify to its truth. Paul applies two criteria here to judge the genuine power of the gospel: its "universality and effectiveness."[28] (a) Paul

---

22. Caird, *Paul's Letters from Prison*, 169. Love heads the list of the fruit of the Spirit (Gal. 5:22; see Rom. 5:5). This reference to the Spirit in 1:8 is the only one in the letter. Schweizer, *Colossians*, 38–39, offers an engaging explanation:

> The Spirit is extremely difficult to control by the use of objective criteria. Appeal is made to the Spirit in every kind of sectarian movement for which Christ has become incidental or nothing more that a cipher for something altogether different. In Christology, by contrast, the criteria for distinguishing between true and false teaching are more readily available.

23. Paul shows his own love for others by risking imprisonment as he seeks to spread the gospel and perfect others' faith so that they might stand faultless before the Lord. We find a clear illustration of what Paul means by love from his letter to Philemon. He expects Philemon to ignore social conventions and economic self-interest and respond to his appeal for Onesimus on the basis of love (Philem. 8–9).

24. The NIV paraphrases well the Greek phrase "because of the hope" by translating it "the faith and love that spring from the hope."

25. See 2 Cor. 3:12; Gal. 5:5; Eph. 1:18; 4:4; 2 Thess. 2:16; see also Titus 1:2; 3:7.

26. "Stored up in heaven" may connote both a spatial idea and a temporal idea: It is laid up for future use.

27. Paul's vision is all-embracing; the word "all" appears in the Greek text in 1:4, 6, 9, 10, 11.

28. Caird, *Paul's Letters from Prison*, 168.

---

notes how the gospel has swept across geographical and racial barriers. Against all odds, it has found a ready reception throughout the world; and this power to surmount provincial resistance testifies to its truth.[29] The message of God's love for all humankind and Jesus' sacrificial death to redeem us by grace speaks in any language or culture. It speaks to the universal condition of every human being—male or female, slave or free, Jew or Gentile (and whatever other divisions humans may create). The "individual churches" composed of converted Gentiles "were for Paul a sign of the universal scope of God's saving purposes and hence of still greater things to come."[30]

(b) The truth of the gospel is also effective, "bearing fruit and growing" (1:6). Schweizer comments that "just as a tree without fruit and growth would no longer be a tree, so a gospel that bore no fruit would cease to be a gospel."[31] The gospel, however, continues to produce harvest after harvest.[32] "Bearing fruit" has been interpreted since Chrysostom as referring to "a crop of good deeds," but Paul has in mind converts (see Rom. 1:13; Phil. 1:22).

Most, however, would not have called the advance of the gospel in the Greco-Roman world a triumphant success. The church was not taking the world by storm. The Jewish historian Josephus, penning his history of the Jewish war and of the Jews at the end of the first century, hardly gave men-

---

29. Wright, *Colossians and Philemon*, 51, comments that Paul presents the gospel "almost as a personified force"; it comes, and it bears fruit as a plant.

30. Ibid., 53. Lightfoot, *Saint Paul's Epistles to the Colossians and to Philemon*, 134—35, contends that by contrast, "the false gospels are the outgrowths of local circumstances, of special idiosyncrasies; the true Gospel is the same everywhere. The false gospels address themselves to limited circles; the true Gospel proclaims itself boldly throughout the world. Heresies are at best ethnic: the truth is essentially catholic."

31. Schweizer, *The Letter to the Colossians*, 37.

32. The order of bearing and increasing is found in the parable of the sower (see Mark 4:8). Wright, *Colossians and Philemon*, 53—54, connects the imagery of a growing plant to Gen. 1:22, 28, where the animal kingdom and the man and woman are to be fruitful and increase. He writes:

> This theme from the creation account is picked up at several key points in the story of the creation of Israel, the family of Abraham, highlighting the Jewish belief that in the call of Israel God was fulfilling his purposes for the whole world, undoing the sin of Adam by creating for himself a holy people. It is completely in line with Paul's rethinking of Jewish belief in the light of the gospel that he should transfer to that gospel ideas belonging to creation, and the divinely intended recreation, of the world. Paul gives us an advance glimpse of the theological position soon to be stated in full (1:15—20). God is doing through the gospel what he always intended to do. He is sowing good seed in the world and preparing to reap a harvest of human lives recreated to reflect his glory.

The image of a growing tree could also match that of Wisdom taking root and flourishing in Sir. 24:13—17.

tion to Christians. The Roman historian Tacitus mentioned Christians only as Nero's scapegoats for the fire of Rome. By contrast, Paul could see what they could not. A seed as small as the mustard had been sown, and it would produce magnificently because of God who gives the growth (1 Cor. 3:7). The gospel was bursting forth in small groups of Christians not only in such vital centers of the empire as Rome, Corinth, and Ephesus, but also in declining towns such as Colosse, in the hearts of slaveowners such as Philemon, and in runaway slaves such as Onesimus. The gospel is growing the way kudzu takes over in some parts of the American South. Originally imported as a groundcover, kudzu overruns everything. The difference is that the gospel is not some alien import or a noxious infestation but something deeply rooted in human need and in God's purposes for the whole creation.

(3) The third cause for Paul's giving thanks is how Epaphras has laid a solid foundation for the Colossians in the true gospel (1:7–8). The gospel can only bear fruit successfully when people faithfully proclaim it and when others respond with understanding and obedience. This is the only thanksgiving section in which Paul mentions the name of a particular person. He identifies Epaphras as a "dear fellow servant," the one who first taught them the gospel, and as "a faithful minister of Christ on our behalf."[33]

Paul did not believe that as an apostle he was the only one qualified to preach the gospel. He was commissioned by God to preach to the Gentiles, but he could not be everywhere. He rapidly equipped his converts to spread the gospel in places where he could not go himself. Apparently, Epaphras represented Paul in his home territory and may have founded all three churches in the Lycus valley: Colosse, Laodicea, and Hierapolis (Col. 4:13).[34] Paul firmly believed in the unity of the missionary effort (1 Cor. 3:5–9), and he identifies himself here with Epaphras as a "fellow servant" of Christ. He regards what this servant has done in Colosse as an extension of his own ministry, without wanting to take credit for it, for both work together in the same field. He does not view Epaphras as one of his underlings but treats him as his collaborator and clarifies that both serve Christ. Epaphras does not have two masters, Christ and Paul. He has only one—Christ.

---

33. Our word "deacon" derives from the Greek noun *diakonos*, used here to describe Epaphras, but it does not describe a formal office here. A textual variant has faithful servant of Christ "in behalf of you." The two words "your" and "our" would have been pronounced identically, which explains the many variants confusing the two. The NIV reflects the reading in the best textual witnesses (p⁴⁶, ℵ, A B, Dᵍʳ, G itᵍ, Ambrosiaster).

34. Paul may have commissioned Epaphras to evangelize the outlying areas while he concentrated on the major cities.

Some claim that Paul mentions Epaphras because the latter needed an extra boost from an external authority figure.[35] It does not follow, however, that because Paul commends someone, others must have been condemning him. While Paul may have in the back of his mind that Epaphras stands over against the teachers of philosophy with their sham wisdom (2:8), he mentions him primarily because he is his entrée to a congregation that he has not personally founded. Paul's close association with Epaphras and Epaphras's close association with the Colossians is the mutual bond that allows the apostle to write this friendly letter to them filled with instructions. How could Paul have mentioned Epaphras's founding work in Colosse without also commending him?

IN HELPING TO bridge the context of this opening paragraph with the twentieth century, we will look at two issues. In earlier centuries Paul was revered as a saint; in ours his authority has been increasingly questioned. We look at this issue as well as the problem of claiming to have exclusive truth in an age of relativism.

Paul's authority. Our generation does not readily accept historic traditions or traditional authority. Paul has fallen victim to these misgivings. I have found that many Christians nurse negative opinions about Paul. Some have the false impression that Paul was too pushy, too prickly, and too authoritarian. Few today would wax as eloquently about Paul as Chrysostom did at the end of his homilies on Romans, that he loved the city of Rome best not for its gold or columns or other display but because that is where Paul was buried.

> Would that it were now given me to throw myself round the body of Paul, and be riveted to the tomb, and to see the dust of that body that "filled up that which was lacking" after "Christ" (Col. 1:24), that bore "the marks" (Gal. 6:17) that sowed the Gospel everywhere yea, the dust of that body through which he ran to and fro everywhere! the dust of that body through which Christ spoke, and the Light shone forth more brilliant than any lightning, . . . Fain would I see the dust of hands that were in a chain, through the imposition of which the Spirit was furnished, through which the divine writings were written. . . .

---

35. See, for example, Wall, *Colossians and Philemon,* 42–43. C. Masson, *L'Épître de Saint Paul aux Colossiens* (CNT 10; Neuchâtel: Delachaux, 1950), 156, went even further by saying that Epaphras had a reputation for incompetence and laziness, which allowed the false teachers to succeed. There is no evidence to support such speculation.

Fain would I see the dust of those eyes which were blinded gloriously, which recovered their sight again for the salvation of the world; which even in the body were counted worthy to see Christ, which saw earthly things, yet saw them not, which saw the things which are not seen, which saw not sleep, which were watchful at midnight, which were not effected as eyes are. I would also see the dust of those feet, which ran through the world and were not weary; which were bound in the stocks when the prison shook, which went through parts habitable or uninhabited, which walked on so many journeys.[36]

Others, this side of the Enlightenment, hold deeply hostile views of Paul. Nietzsche called him an apostle "so greatly troubled in mind and so worthy of pity, but who was also very disagreeable to himself and to others."[37] George Bernard Shaw wrote, "There has really never been a more monstrous imposition perpetrated than the imposition of the limitation of Paul's soul upon the soul of Jesus."[38] William James dismissed Paul's vision on the Damascus road as "a discharging lesion of the occipital cortex, he being an epileptic."

Suspicion is now a widespread phenomenon in our culture, and biblical texts and figures have not escaped it. Some might think that Paul would fit into the developmental pattern of the guru (from the Sanskrit, meaning "one who brings light out of darkness"), as proposed by Anthony Storr, a British psychiatrist.[39] He suggests that gurus share the following characteristics: an isolated childhood, extreme narcissism, a sense of personal destiny, illness, mental and sometimes physical depression, "conversion," and the unshakable conviction that one has a profound insight into the nature of reality and a mission to lead others.

We know nothing of Paul's childhood, but we do know that he experienced a profound conversion, that he possessed a clear sense of personal destiny, that he suffered from illness (a thorn in the flesh, which some scholars have connected to depression among many other guesses), that he had an unshakable conviction that he had profound insight into the nature of reality, and that he had a compelling sense of mission to lead others to the truth. After his call/conversion, Paul reenvisioned who God was, what God's purposes were, and how God worked. As God caused the light to blaze in the

36. John Chrysostom, "Epistle to the Romans," in *A Select Library of the Nicene and Post-Nicene Fathers of the Christian Church*, ed. Philip Schaff (Grand Rapids: Eerdmans, 1980), 11:562.

37. Friedrich Nietzsche, "The First Christian," in *The Writings of St. Paul*, ed. Wayne A Meeks (New York/London: W. W. Norton, 1972), 289.

38. George Bernard Shaw, "The Monstrous Imposition Upon Jesus, " in *The Writings of St. Paul*, 300.

39. Anthony Storr, *Feet of Clay: Saints, Sinners and Madmen: A Study of Gurus* (New York: Free Press, 1996).

darkness of his own heart, he believed God called him to flood a darkened world with that same light. But what makes him different from so many others who have crowded the stage of history?

He was not narcissistic or self-absorbed. He says in 1:23 that he has become a servant (minister) of the gospel; the lack of a definite article shows that he does not regard himself as *the* minister. He was not some maverick but saw himself bound up with others in the community. In his letter to the Colossians, the mention of so many coworkers shows that he did not offer his idiosyncratic opinion on these issues but spoke the consensus of all who were with him. Mentioning Timothy as a joint writer adds a second witness to his regulating and exhorting the community (cf. Deut. 17:6; 19:15; Matt. 18:16).[40] He hardly mentions the conditions of his imprisonment and only asks for their prayers so that he might be free to expand his mission opportunities (4:2). His whole life is consumed by this mission goal.

Paul did not use the gospel in a manipulative way, that is, as a tool to exercise selfish power. He was not dictatorial—the complementary letter to Philemon should make that obvious. Paul did write to his churches as an apostle with an authority entrusted to him by Christ and not simply as a private, interested party. His counsel, however, was authoritative, not authoritarian. He had no intention of lording over his churches (2 Cor. 1:23). He makes it clear to the Colossians that he has the right to speak to them because:

- he is a servant of the gospel, which they have heard and was preached in all the world (1:23);
- he has been praying daily for them;
- he has struggled for their sake (1:24; 2:1) in fulfilling God's commission to present the word of God to everyone, including them (1:25, 28).

Paul writes to the Colossians because they need reminders of their faith and their hope to deepen and strengthen their maturity in Christ (1:28), not to strengthen their commitment to him personally. He is concerned (see 2 Cor. 11: 28) and wants to help them brush off the opponents' detractions of their hope and to fend off the "philosophy's" fatal attractions.

Truth in an age of relativism. In the opening verses of Colossians, Paul refers to understanding "God's grace in all its truth" (1:6). Christians used to believe that truth did not shift like a kaleidoscope, but pragmatic relativism

---

40. Pokorný, *Colossians*, 33. Caird, *Paul's Letters from Prison*, 169, notes that Paul mentions fourteen fellow workers in his letters, four fellow prisoners of war, two fellow soldiers, two fellow slaves, and one yokefellow. Wright, *Colossians and Philemon*, 54, reminds us, "In an individualistic age we do well to remind ourselves how often Paul's you is plural—and that not merely referring to a collection of individuals, but indicating a corporate unity, the Body of Christ."

increasingly rules in our culture today and has even infected many believers' perceptions of things. This relativism assumes that an idea cannot be inherently true, but it is good if it works for now. Fewer Christians today take for granted that Christianity provides the standard of truth and morality by which all life and all other religions can be assessed. Many assume that we all worship the same God and that whatever a person chooses to believe about that God is valid or just as good as another's belief. To question one's belief system is to be unpardonably judgmental and intolerant.

Most generally now adhere to the principle that whatever works for me or works for you must be true. Robert Wuthnow has documented this disturbing trend in modern spirituality:

> Spirituality is no longer true or good because it meets absolute standards of truth or goodness, but because it helps me get along. I am the judge of its worth. If it helps me find a vacant parking place, I know I am on the right track. If it leads me into the wilderness calling me to face dangers I would rather not deal with at all, then it is a form of spirituality I am unlikely to choose.[41]

Wade Clark Roof confirms these findings. He notes that people do not approach truth objectively but want to know what it can do for them and how it can do it more efficiently.[42] A consumerist mentality allows each person to choose his or her particular brand of truth just as he or she might choose a ccrtain make of automobile or toothpaste, according to preferences and perceived needs. Each person then acts in accord with the chosen standards. In a Malcolm Bradbury novel, Professor Treece muses: "It's a funny age, isn't it? There are so many literatures, so many religions, so many cultures, so many philosophies, one doesn't know where to turn."[43]

Many today assume that one religion is as good as another. The American comedian Bob Hope expresses the general mindset with this crack: "I do benefits for all religions—I'd hate to blow the hereafter on a technicality." Even Christian theologians compare the different faiths to a rainbow. John Hick maintains that there are many faiths but only one ultimate object of faith, so that the refractions of light producing the rainbow come from one

---

41. Robert Wuthnow, "Small Groups Forge New Notions of Community and the Sacred," *The Christian Century* 110 (Dec. 8, 1993): 1239–40. Wuthnow's book, *Sharing the Journey: Support Groups and America's New Quest for Community* (New York: The Free Press, 1994), shows that people in Bible study groups tended to use the Bible as a self-help book. The Bible is considered true because it has helped one get whatever it was that one wanted.

42. Wade Clark Roof, *A Generation of Seekers* (San Francisco: HarperCollins, 1993), 195.

43. Malcolm Bradbury, *Eating People Is Wrong* (New York: Alfred A. Knopf, 1960), 133.

light source. Who is to say, he asks, that one band of the rainbow is better than another?[44]

Pannenberg notes that "a public climate of secularism undermines the confidence of Christians in the truth of what they believe."[45] He cites Peter Berger's *A Rumor of Angels* (1969), which argues that believers' standard of knowledge deviates from what is publicly taken for granted and goes against the grain of what those around them believe. But Christians who live in a dominantly secular culture face powerful psychological pressure to conform to the views and beliefs of those around them. In this secular milieu, we do not necessarily deal with the outright rejection of Christian teachings: "Large numbers of people have not the vaguest knowledge of what those teachings are." This unawareness results in less tolerance for Christianity. "The more widespread the ignorance of Christianity, the greater the prejudice against Christianity."[46]

An example of ignorance combined with prejudice against Paul is captured in a skit by two British comedians about the Ephesians as they receive a letter from Paul:

> Dear George and Deidre and Family, Stop having a good time, resign yourselves to not having a picnic, cover yourself with ashes and start flaying yourselves, until further notice, Signed Paul.[47]

Paul never said any such thing, but people may have the impression that he did. Pannenberg claims that when such persons turn away from the secular culture's spiritual void and superficiality, they do not turn to Christianity but show interest in "alternative religions." The whole problem, he argues, is exacerbated by "the cultural relativizing of the very idea of truth." Today, many, including Christians, assume that "Christian doctrines are merely opinions that may or may not be affirmed according to individual preference, or depending on whether they speak to personal felt needs."[48] Pannenberg writes:

> The dissolution of the idea of truth—of truth that does not need my approval in order to be proved true—severely undercuts the Christ-

44. John Hick, *The Rainbow of Faiths* (London: SCM, 1995), ix–x.

45. Wolfhart Pannenberg, "How to Think About Secularism," *First Things* 64 (June/July 1996): 27.

46. Ibid.

47. Peter Cook and Dudley Moore, "Religions," in *Dud and Pete: The Dagenheim Dialogues* (London: Methuen, 1971), 139, cited by Brian J. Dodd, *The Problem with Paul* (Downers Grove, Ill.: InterVarsity, 1996), 10.

48. Pannenberg, "How to Think About Secularism," 27.

ian understanding of evangelization or mission. Missionary proclamation was once understood as bringing the truth to others, and was therefore both legitimate and extremely important. For many today, the missionary enterprise is a matter of imposing our personal preferences and culturally conditioned prejudices upon others, and is therefore not only illegitimate but morally offensive.[49]

Many have concluded that Christianity is simply one among many options leading up the same mountain, and it may not even be the best option. In their study of religion in Middletown, USA, researchers discovered a dramatic change in 1978 from a survey done in 1924. They write that "about half of the Middletown adolescents who belong to and attend a church and who believe in Jesus, the Bible, and the hereafter do not claim any universal validity for the Christian beliefs they hold and have no zeal for the conversion of non-Christians."[50]

The pervasiveness of this view was confirmed for me when I overheard a teenager who had recently moved discuss a visit to a new Sunday school class. The teenager expressed outrage that they said in the class that Islam was wrong. "How do they know?" was the indignant response. Many raised in Christian homes and churches have failed to grasp that there is anything special about Christianity. They have accepted the prevailing idea that "My truth is just as good as your truth if it works for me." This hesitancy about the universal truth of the Christian faith is compounded by the well-publicized moral failings of professed Christians. They evoke a common response: Those who are not Christian act more Christian than the Christians. That statement is revealing, however. Christianity does provide the ideal by which to measure people's behavior.

In bridging the contexts, we must remember that Paul's context was no less pluralistic and relativistic than ours. The problems we face in our culture are similar to the problems faced by the Colossians. The popular cultural values ran counter to their faith commitments; and, in addition, outsiders subjected their faith to demeaning criticism.

The Greeks, and later the Romans, were normally tolerant in their attitude toward various religions and cultures. Every nation had its own ancestral traditions, its own temples and gods. The conquering Romans did not insist that everyone worship Greek or Roman gods alone. From a practical standpoint, such a policy would have needlessly alienated the worshipers of

---

49. Ibid., 27–28.
50. Theodore Caplow, Howard M. Bahr, Bruce A. Chadwick (et al.), *All Faithful People: Change and Continuity in Middletown's Religion* (Minneapolis: Univ. of Minnesota Press, 1983), 98.

the regional deities within the empire. From a theoretical standpoint, the intellectual elite assumed that the gods were symbolic representatives of some ultimate ground of being. Therefore, they said, you may continue to worship your gods and goddesses; we will also worship them, and you can worship ours. That way no one's god will get slighted. This openness to other gods is reflected in the altar to an unknown god (Acts 17:24)—which I paraphrase, "To whatever god we may have forgotten to honor, we are sorry. Don't hold it against us."

There was a relative disinterest in doctrine and a greater emphasis on the utility of the gods for making human life better. Consequently, most in the ancient world could accommodate a medley of gods and goddesses into their religious beliefs, and the selection was indeed large in the great religious melting pot of the Roman empire. Many believed that there was "safety in numbers." The more cults into which one was initiated the better. The more gods one honored the better. The temple of Demeter in Pergamum, for example, had altars to the gods Hermes, Helios, Zeus, Asclepius, and Heracles.[51]

Many in the western part of the empire were fascinated with and attracted to the more mysterious and awe-inspiring gods of the East. These Eastern gods were not like the vamps of the Olympian pantheon and spoke with more fearsome voices. Strange new cults also offered fresh ways of experimenting with religion and worship. But many others also looked down their noses at these Eastern religions as superstitions, in the same way modern Americans might view Shi'ites or Hare Krishnas. The only time that Roman officials became upset with foreign religions was when they were perceived as threatening peace and security, engaging in gross immorality, or drawing people away from their normal civic duties.

In the context of this pluralism, Jews and Christians stood out. They differed from everybody else because of their unswerving allegiance to one God. This religious "intolerance" led others to label Christians as "atheists" because they did not believe in the gods, only their one God. Apuleius describes a certain baker's wife in his novel as "an enemy of faith and chastity" because she was a "despiser of all the gods whom others did honor" (*Metamorphoses* ["*The Golden Ass*"] 9.14). Christians were labeled "misanthropes, haters of humankind," because they refused to participate in the worship and

---

51. In one papyrus fragment, the writer says: "I pray to all gods" (P. Oxy. 1766 [18]); an inscription reads: "We magnify every god" (SIG 1153). S. Angus, *The Mystery-Religions and Christianity* (New York: Charles Scribner's Son, 1925), 192, cites the private chapel of the Emperor Alexander Severus, which contained shrines of Orpheus, Abraham, Apollonius of Tyana, and Jesus.

sacrificial meals to local, traditional gods in pagan temples and in the great festivals of towns and cities.

Christians were not simply rejected as religious party poopers; their denial of the gods was deemed to have serious consequences for the community. Since the gods were also revered as the ones who preserved the state and order, rejecting them opened the community to divine disfavor and catastrophe. They were also considered strange because they had no temples or national temple; they met in private homes at night and greeted each other with a holy kiss, and they partook of the body and blood of one who was executed by Roman authorities in a provincial backwater. But they claimed boldly that they knew the truth about the one true God and that this God could only be known fully through Jesus Christ, whom God has raised from the dead.

In other words, Paul lived in an age no less pluralistic than ours, and it was no less scandalous for Christians to reject the pervasive idolatry and to claim exclusive truth in a culture that prized tolerance. Paul does not blush to say that God's full self-revelation is summed up in Christ and that this revelation is more true and more moral than any other. Pokorný notes that Paul does not introduce God speculatively in the opening verses of Colossians.[52] He does not introduce God as merely the creator and ruler of nature or the God of Abraham, Isaac, and Jacob (Ex. 3:6). The God Paul worships is also not some generic god, some divine force field, but the one who acts in history and who has acted specifically in the life, death, and resurrection of Jesus of Nazareth, his beloved Son.[53] Stewart cites Alexander Pope's "Universal Prayer":

> Father of all! in ev'ry age,
> > In ev'ry clime adored
> By saint, by savage, and by sage,
> > Jehovah, Jove, or Lord!

He comments: "Not much there of the ancient word—'I the Lord God am a jealous God'!—a divine logion which the Christian revelation has illuminated but certainly not displaced."[54]

---

52. Pokorný, *Colossians*, 37.

53. Wright, *Colossians and Philemon*, 50, comments: "Though Judaism knew God as Father, the precise nature of his paternal love could not be conceived until it had been revealed in the cross of the Messiah. Nor could that cross be understood, conversely, until it became clear that it was the climax of the saving plan of the God of Israel, and that therefore this God had now exalted the crucified one and given him the title 'Lord'. . . ."

54. James S. Stewart, "A First-Century Heresy and Its Modern Counterpart," *SJT* 23 (1970): 424.

PAUL CALLS THE gospel "the word of truth" (1:5).
We will first address how we must proclaim this
word of truth in our contemporary setting, and
then look at the continuing relevance of the triad
of faith, love, and hope.

Proclaiming the word of truth. Pannenberg argues, "The idea of truth is
absolutely vital for the Christian faith."[55] We do not search for truth but start
from it. Therefore, Christians cannot shrink from the challenge to refute the
misconception that all truth is relative, a view that legitimates secular culture,
and to present the distinctive biblical truth in plausible and persuasive ways.
Paul did not simply reject the "philosophy" as error or heresy; he gave reasoned arguments why the Christian faith is better. The opening paragraph
in Colossians speaks to our contemporary need to understand, uphold, and
proclaim the Christian vision of the truth.[56]

(1) Those who are able to detect counterfeit bills learn everything they can
about a genuine bill; this same principle applies to distinguishing truth from
falsehood. We must know what is truth before we can recognize what is false.
Our pragmatic relativism has blurred the distinction between the two. If we are
to go as God would have us go, however, we need to know God's unchanging
truth. Paul places an emphasis here on understanding and "growing in the
knowledge of God" (see 1:6, 10; 2:2). Only through such knowledge can we
debunk what is false. We must be thoroughly rooted in our historic faith if it
is to produce fruit. We must also guard against ignorance and the superficiality of a culture that replaces one era's delusions with new ones. We will not win
others through quick fix adjustments to cultural fads. Christians in the early centuries attracted others by their monotheism, their powerful and loving God,
their offer of hope, their appraisal of the human condition of alienation, and the
solution to that plight offered by the forgiveness through Christ's death.

(2) We must offer social support to one another in order to sustain and
bolster our faith (1:4). Many in our culture feel a sense of isolation and loneliness. Thus, many Christians may think they are all alone in their faith. But
we are not alone, and we need to link up with and encourage one another
in the faith. In Christ individuals are joined to others in a loving community
with worldwide associations.

---

55. Pannenberg, "How to Think About Secularism," 28.

56. J. Richard Middleton and Brian J. Walsh, *Truth Is Stranger Than It Used to Be* (Downers Grove, Ill.: InterVarsity, 1995), deal with the problem of claiming truth in a postmod-
ern setting. Alister McGrath, *A Passion for Truth* (Downers Grove, Ill.: InterVarsity, 1996)
sets forth the ground on which evangelicalism can constructively engage the world with its
vision of the truth.

(3) The best argument for the Christian faith is for believers to live out its principles: to "live a life worthy of the Lord" (1:10). Reasoned and persuasive arguments are effective, but they will be even more effective if others can see evidence for what we claim in how we live. This is why Colossians contains a lengthy section of ethical exhortation. Until Christians act like Christians, following their Lord and imbued with his Spirit, they will have little or no impact on their world.

(4) We must live life with thanksgiving and joy. One wonders if people will not be more attracted to the Christian faith by our joyful thanksgiving than by our dogmas and arguments.

(5) We must exercise Christian grace in proclaiming our truth and be wary lest we become prey to arrogance (see 1 Peter 3:15). When a seminary student was asked how he would minister to persons who might be different from him, he responded, "I wouldn't. They must change to my point of view, because I am right." We do a grave injustice to our faith when we become imperialistic, paternalistic, narrow, and bigoted toward others. Wright recognizes, "To assert today that the one Creator God has revealed himself fully and finally in Jesus Christ is to risk criticism on the grounds of arrogance or intolerance."[57] We have the truth, but we must remember Paul's words that we have not arrived or attained it all (Phil. 3:12–16).

Faith, love, hope. *Faith.* Mark Twain said that "faith is believing what you know ain't so." If that is the case with our faith, then it will not survive the first challenge. In the New Testament, faith knows that God spoke once and for all in Jesus. R. Buckminster Fuller has said, "Faith is much better than belief. Belief is when someone *else* does the thinking." Faith requires more than intellectual assent that the fullness of deity dwells in Christ, for example. Wright comments on 2:12 that faith is not identified as faith in Jesus Christ but as "faith in the power of God." "To believe that God raised Jesus from the dead *is* to believe in the God who raises the dead. Such faith not merely assents to a fact about Jesus, it recognizes a truth about God."[58]

Faith is not just something to think about and discuss but something that is lived. Faith acts on what it believes. Vincent J. Donovan tells of a conversation with a Masai elder about how the word for "faith" was to be translated into his language. The elder contended that the word chosen was unsatisfactory because it meant "to agree to." He said that it was

---

57. Wright, *Colossians and Philemon*, 79. He adds that Christianity "does not commit Christians to the proposition that there is no truth to be found in others religions." They may reflect some truth, but they are at best "doorways" into the one truth, which is Christ.

58. Ibid., 108. Schweizer, *Colossians*, 35, reminds us that truth in this context does not pertain to something that can be shown from "empirical proof or logical deduction"; it refers to "reliability." The truth believers place their faith in does not disappoint or fail.

similar to a white hunter shooting an animal with his gun from a great
distance. Only his eyes and his fingers took part in the act. We should
find another word. He said for a man really to believe is like a lion
going after its prey. His nose and eyes and ears pick up the prey. His
legs give him the speed to catch it. All the power of his body is
involved in the terrible death leap and single blow to the neck with
the front paw, the blow that actually kills. And as the animal goes
down the lion envelops it in his arms (Africans refer to the front legs
of an animal as its arms), pulls it to himself, and makes it part of himself. This is the way the lion kills. This is the way a man believes. This
is what faith is.[59]

Love. The theme of love dominates popular music: "Love is all you need";
"Love is all around"; "Love is the answer." Love in our culture has come to
mean an emotion, a feeling. In the New Testament, however, love is commanded. Feelings cannot be commanded. New Testament love does not
have to do with emotions but has to do with actions that aim at improving
the welfare of others. It follows the pattern of a loving God who gave his Son
for a lost world.

William Blake's poem "The Clod and the Pebble" captures this meaning
and contrasts it with a worldly love that is like a vacuum that craves to be
filled and desires others only for itself.

Love seeketh not itself to please
Nor for itself hath any care
But for another gives its ease
And builds a Heaven in Hell' despair.
So sang a little Clod of Clay
Trodden with the cattle's feet,
But a Pebble of the brook
Warbled out these metres meet:
Love seeketh only self to please
To bind another to its delight
Joys in another's loss of ease
And builds a Hell in Heaven's despite.[60]

The power of the new love we have in Christ is that it transforms the old
kind of love and expels the hankering for the things of this fallen world. A
soldier watching a nurse clean and dress the gangrenous wounds of those

59. Vincent J. Donovan, *Christianity Rediscovered* (2d ed.; Maryknoll, N.Y.: Orbis, 1982), 63.
60. William Blake, "Songs of Experience," in *The Complete Writings of William Blake* (New York: Random House, 1957), 211.

fallen in battle said to her, "I wouldn't do that for a million dollars." "Neither would I," came the nurse's response.

Hope. In our culture, hope has become associated with wistfulness, a blind optimism without any foundation: "I hope the Cubs will win the pennant." Or, as Lloyd George, addressing the House of Commons on Armistice day in 1918, said, "I hope we may say that on this fateful morning came an end to all wars." Hope in these examples means "I hope so." In response to this kind of yearning, Alexander Pope wrote, "Blessed is he who expects nothing for he shall never be disappointed."

In the New Testament, hope refers to the confident expectation that God will fulfill his promises, not our personal dreams. Christians expect everything, and this hope will not disappoint. Paul does not refer to a subjective experience of hope but to a reality that God has yet to make fully manifest. The hope Paul has in mind has to do with the glorious future Christ has established for Christians. It pertains to something that exists objectively beyond our existence in this life.[61] It resides "in heaven" and recognizes what Schweizer calls "the beyondness of salvation." This affirmation may be difficult to convey to a contemporary generation that places so much value on personal experience. But, as Schweizer recognizes, it checks "the subjectivity of a faith based only on itself, resting on the experience of one's own soul's stirrings; and, along with this, it does understand hope as an effective act which actually generates faith and love." He comments further:

> Human beings, dwelling on an earth that has become heavenless, are told that they derive their life from the fact that the whole meaning of life lies neither in one's self, nor in humanity, nor in nature, but in the one who is encountered in (though he is also beyond) them both.[62]

Some might misconstrue the claim that salvation, our hope, lies outside this world. It may lead to a world-denying gnosticism or to tolerance of evil assuaged only by promises of "pie in the sky bye and bye." But the belief that salvation is only to be found in the potentialities of this world is no less dangerous. A fallen humanity in a fallen world offers no hope. Many people today place their confidence in science, but all our great advances have produced as many problems as have been solved. In many ways, science has shattered hope. It has become more difficult for some to believe in a God that would care about or even notice our existence. Consequently, many people live without any hope of salvation in this life, let alone a life beyond.

---

61. Pokorný, *Colossians*, 100, observes that one of the problems is that willful, sinful humanity does not want to accept that it must rely completely "upon a gift from the outside."
62. Schweizer, *Colossians*, 34.

Paul affirms that Christ is behind creation and that his death on our behalf reveals God's love and secures our hope. Hope, as Moule points out, is not wishful thinking but confidence.[63] In Romans 4:18–21, Paul identifies Abraham as the prototype of hope and trust. Hayes observes that "Abraham wrestled with his doubts, discounted his own experience, rejected skepticisim, and clung to the promise of God," and thus he became the mode for the community of faith.[64] The hope is secure because God guarantees it, and it is ours through his grace.

---

63. Moule, *Colossians and Philemon*, 84.

64. Richard B. Hayes, "Salvation By Trust? Reading the Bible Faithfully," *Christian Century* 114/7 (Feb. 26, 1997): 219.

Colossians 1:9–14

FOR THIS REASON, since the day we heard about you, we have not stopped praying for you and asking God to fill you with the knowledge of his will through all spiritual wisdom and understanding. ¹⁰And we pray this in order that you may live a life worthy of the Lord and may please him in every way: bearing fruit in every good work, growing in the knowledge of God, ¹¹being strengthened with all power according to his glorious might so that you may have great endurance and patience, and joyfully ¹²giving thanks to the Father, who has qualified you to share in the inheritance of the saints in the kingdom of light. ¹³For he has rescued us from the dominion of darkness and brought us into the kingdom of the Son he loves, ¹⁴in whom we have redemption, the forgiveness of sins.

Original Meaning

PAUL CONTINUES THE thanksgiving section (1:3–23) by informing the Colossians how he and Timothy specifically intercede for them in prayer. The initial success of the gospel in Colosse does not lull them into slackening their prayer efforts for the Colossians. Quite the reverse, it leads to even more intense prayer. They have continued to pray for them because of what God has already done for them and because of their faith and love ("for this reason," 1:9).[1] By sharing his petition on their behalf, Paul reacquaints them with their blessings, their obligations, and their potential in Christ.

Intercession for the Colossians (1:9–14)

PAUL PRAYS THAT God will fill the Colossians with the knowledge of God's will through spiritual wisdom and discernment of every sort.[2] The knowledge

---

1. Paul put into practice what he tells the Colossians to do, "Devote yourselves to prayer, being watchful and thankful" (4:2). Wright, *Colossians and Philemon*, 57, comments: "He will not offer teaching, advice, and encouragement except in the context of prayer."

2. The idea of a person being filled by God prepares for the concept of fullness in 1:19 and 2:9, and Paul is probably not introducing the language of the false teachers here. Caird, *Paul's Letters from Prison*, 170, notes that the three terms *knowledge*, *wisdom*, and *understanding* occur together in the Old Testament (Ex. 31:3; 35:31; Isa. 11:2; see also Sir. 1:19; 1QS 4:4; 10:9, 12; 1QSb 5:21; 1QH 2:18; 11:17–18; 12:11–12). Similar prayers occur in Eph. 1:17; Phil. 1:9; Philem. 6, where there is no hint of false teachers.

that Paul has in view has nothing to do with some secret lore reserved only for the elite or some hidden key that unlocks the mysteries of the universe or of the inner person. For Paul, understanding God's will involves recognizing how Christ is the fulfillment of God's redemptive purposes (1:27; 2:2), how God's salvation is open to all people, and how God intends for Christians to live in whatever situation they find themselves.

In Judaism, one finds knowledge of God's will exclusively through the law (see Rom. 2:17–20; Bar. 3:24–4:4; Sir. 24:23). For Paul, Christ is the end of the law (Rom. 10:4), and God's will is embodied in the person of Christ.[3] Full knowledge comes only through the Spirit and our complete commitment to Jesus Christ.[4] This knowledge is extremely important in the Colossians' situation. If they sufficiently grasp that all of God's creation and his plan for the redemption of the cosmos revolves entirely around Christ, they will not be confused by the challenges of opponents or duped by engaging notions that have the appearance of wisdom (2:8).

Paul does not want his readers to gain knowledge purely for its own sake. Knowledge of God's will always has ethical implications, because it requires us to bring our daily conduct and thinking into line with it.[5] This reality may explain why many people do not want to know that will or why they attempt to tranquilize themselves with a more agreeable and seemingly more sophisticated wisdom. But wisdom that excludes Christ or makes him subordinate is counterfeit. The goal of being filled with knowledge of God is to "live a life worthy of the Lord and [to] please him in every way" (lit., "unto all pleasing"). "Spiritual wisdom and understanding" help us know what is truly important in life from God's perspective. God gives us knowledge to lead us to deeper faith, greater virtue, and more devout service.

Paul lists four traits of the spiritual life that are pleasing to the Lord, each expressed by a participle linked to a prepositional phrase:

- "bearing fruit in every good work"
- "growing in the knowledge of God"[6]

---

3. In the Dead Sea Scrolls (1QS 11:18–19), God's plan of salvation lies hidden; for Paul, it has been fully revealed in Christ (Col. 1:15–20).

4. Caird, *Paul's Letters from Prison*, 170, comments: "In the spiritual realm there is no knowledge without commitment."

5. The word *epignosis* ("knowledge") may also refer to "moral and religious insight, recognition, acknowledgment." The adjective "spiritual" governs the two nouns "wisdom" and "understanding" and refers to something given by the Spirit, which contrasts with what emerges from an unspiritual mind (2:18).

6. The phrase translated in the NIV "growing in the knowledge of God" can also be rendered, "growing by the knowledge of God." The growth is not *in* knowledge but comes *as*

- "being strengthened[7] with all power according to his glorious might[8] so that you may have great endurance and patience"
- "joyfully giving thanks to the Father."

In 1:12–14, Paul specifies three reasons for "joyfully giving thanks" for what God the Father has done in Christ. Each is expressed by a verb in the aorist tense.[9] (1) Paul says that God "has qualified [them] to share in the inheritance."[10] The phrase "the share of the inheritance" (lit. trans.) was originally identified with the land apportioned to each tribe after the conquest.[11] After the Exile some Jews used this inheritance language to refer to a divine bequest beyond history and connected it to the resurrection life to come.[12] Nearly all Jews regarded the inheritance as exclusively Israel's; and, like most heirs, they did not want to share with strangers and enemies (1:21) what they believed rightfully belonged to them alone.[13] Gentiles have no natural right to the inheritance, but through Christ they have been made full legal heirs (see 3:24; Rom. 8:16–17; Gal. 3:29; 4:1–7). "In the kingdom of light" translates literally "in the light."[14] The word "kingdom" does not appear in the

---

the result of the knowledge of God. As Patzia, *Ephesians, Colossians, Philemon*, 23, explains, "Moral and spiritual growth comes from knowing and doing the will of God."

7. The passive voice indicates that the strength comes entirely from God. Pokorný, *Colossians*, 49, comments that Paul refers to the redeeming power by which God is able to bring about the transformation of the situation of sinful humanity, and it is expressed in words such as "deliver," "transfer into the kingdom of his Son" (1:13), "reconcile," and "present before him" (1:22).

8. The phrase "his glorious might" reads literally, "according to the power of his glory." See the power of God in Eph. 1:19; 3:7, 16, 20; 6:10.

9. Lohse, *Colossians and Philemon*, 34, points out that the word "thanks" does not appear often in the LXX and is often interchanged with the word for confession. He cites Origen's remarks, "To say 'I confess' is the same as saying 'I give thanks'" (*Orat.* 6).

10. Paul uses the verb *hikanoo* and its cognates to describe God "making him fit" (2 Cor. 2:16, "equal," NIV; 2 Cor. 3:5–6, "competent," NIV) for a ministry for which he felt "unfit" (1 Cor. 15:9, "do not even deserve," NIV).

11. See Num. 18:20; Deut. 10:9; 12:12; 14:27, 29; 18:1; Josh. 13:1–19:51.

12. James D. G. Dunn, "The Colossian Philosophy: A Confident Jewish Apologia," *Bib* 76 (1995): 158, citing Dan. 12:13; Wis. 5:5; 1 Enoch 48:7; 1 QS 11:7–8; 1QH 11:10–12.

13. Some claim that "the saints" (1:12) refers to angels, "holy ones in the light" (see Dan. 7:18, 22; Wis. 5:5; 1QH 11:7–8), and that Paul begins here to undermine the Colossians' mistaken veneration of angels by affirming that they are joint heirs with them. Elsewhere in Colossians, however, the word "saints" (*hagioi*) refers to believers (1:2, 4, 26; 3:12); and Paul always uses this word to refer to human saints (including 1 Thess. 3:13; 2 Thess. 1:10). In Eph. 1:18; 2:19, *hagioi* refers to the Jews who believe. The passage matches Paul's speech to the Ephesian elders in Acts 20:32 and to Agrippa in 26:15–18, which refers to humans sanctified in Christ.

14. The translation accords with the interpretation of Abbott, *Epistles to the Ephesians and Colossians*, 207.

Greek text, but this translation may help the reader see that Paul refers to the salvation from God that has been inaugurated by Christ.

(2) Paul affirms that God "has rescued" them from the harsh rule of the power of darkness.[15] Paul characterizes the life of Gentiles before becoming Christians as an ethical and theological darkness (Eph. 5:8; 1 Thess. 5:4–5; see also 1 Peter 2:9; 1 John 1:5–7).[16] Immorality, anger, strife, vengeance, violence, and oppression thrive in such murk. The Gentiles were in bondage to the prince of darkness (the pretender to light, 2 Cor. 11:14) and his evil dominion (see Eph. 6:12). C. S. Lewis's description of the fictional land of Narnia, where it was always winter and never Christmas, expresses the same idea with different imagery. All humans need deliverance from a wasted life of sin and from the cosmic powers that keep them captive in sin. When the mob comes with swords and clubs to arrest Jesus in Gethsemane, he declares that it is the hour of the power of darkness (Luke 22:53), when violence rules. In Christ, God tears believers away from this dark power and moves them into the light.

(3) Like victorious kings who uproot whole populations and resettle them in other lands, God has wrested believers from the tyrannical rule of darkness and "brought [them] into the kingdom of the Son he loves" (lit., "the Son of his love"). Changing lordships means changing kingdoms. The image pictures a reverse exile.[17] God's domain is filled with light, and its charter is love. Because God loves his Son, all those who belong to him also are objects of divine love. The following verses affirm that Christ reigns over all malevolent powers in the universe, and Paul affirms in Romans that no force in heaven or earth, physical or supernatural, can separate his followers from God's love (Rom. 8:34–39). Since these powers cannot obstruct our relationship with God, Christians need not fear them and must not pay them homage.

Paul caps off the mention of the beloved Son with the benefits he has bestowed on us, namely, "redemption, the forgiveness of sins."[18] Christ has removed the barrier of sin. Wright helps us see that the forgiveness of sins

---

15. The phrase "dominion of darkness" (*exousia tou skotous*) refers to a sphere in which the power is exercised (see Eph. 2:2).

16. Paul applies the image to himself (2 Cor. 4:6). He lived in a theological darkness before the veil was lifted so that he could see Christ clearly. In the Old Testament, darkness represents death (Job 10:22; Ps. 143:3), Sheol (Ps. 88:12), and God's judgment (Ps. 105:28; Jer. 23:12; Ezek. 32:8; Amos 5:18, 20; Zeph. 1:15).

17. Many have noted that Josephus uses the verb *methistemi* for relating how Tiglath-Pileser, the Assyrian king, took captive the conquered population, "transferring them to his own kingdom" (*Antiquities* 9.11.1 § 235).

18. Some may find it surprising that Paul rarely refers specifically to the forgiveness of sins (see Eph. 1:7).

"is not merely good news for troubled consciences." Jeremiah (31:31—34) and Ezekiel (36:16—36) speak of it as "one of the specific blessings of the new covenant."[19] The blessings of our final redemption have already broken into the present. Forgiveness of sins is not simply a liberation from the past; it sets us free for the present and future. It opens the possibility of living a life worthy of the Lord (Col. 1:10). Paul says that the Colossians used to give their lives to sin, which brings only God's wrath (3:5—7), but now they give their lives to Christ, which brings joy and light (2:6).

THIS PASSAGE BRIDGES easily into our culture, but we should pay special attention to three issues: the Exodus imagery, the emphasis on growing in the knowledge of God, and the idea of bearing fruit in every good work.

The imagery of liberation. Old Testament prophets envisioned the new age in terms of a new Exodus. Paul couches his belief that the promised new age has begun in Christ in the imagery of Israel's beginnings, when Israel was ransomed from slavery in Egypt and led to the promised land. The parallels are clear. God first rescued the Hebrew people from the enslavement and tyranny they endured in Egypt. Now God has rescued a renewed Israel from darker, more vicious powers, which overshadow the present world order. God has delivered them to a new inheritance, a spiritual promised land, which is immune to the invasions of despots and demonic onslaughts—the kingdom of Christ. Paul compares Israel's entering Canaan, when each tribe was given its allotment of land, to the new Israel, composed of Jews and Gentiles entering the kingdom of Christ, the realm of light. The difference is that this emancipation is not from physical slavery or political tyranny, but from sin.[20] This liberation also includes Gentiles.[21]

Most Americans today know the Exodus story from the movie "The Ten Commandments," often shown on TV during religious holidays. As a consequence, the Exodus imagery has become insipid and shallow to many people. It may be helpful to recapture the imagery by appealing to other, more vivid images of liberation for it to have its effect. One might compare the Christian Exodus, for example, to the liberation of concentration camps by

---

19. Wright, *Colossians and Philemon*, 63. See also 1QS 3:6—12; 11:2—5.

20. Caird, *Paul's Letters from Prison*, 172.

21. In my opinion, the Exodus imagery is particularly apt because Paul wishes to counter Jewish objections to the inclusion of Gentiles in salvation. From the Jewish perspective, Gentile Christians were usurping their hopes, which they interpreted as rights and privileges belonging solely to them.

Allied troops after World War II. The stark pictures of the piles of corpses and the emaciated, hollow-eyed survivors provide a good image for what happens to humans under the power of sin. The Holocaust survivors, however, were not welcomed with open arms by the world and continued to suffer travail and humiliation. Christians, though liberated from sin's power, continue to live in a world dominated by sin. They must still endure and have patience. The difference is that their hope lies secure in a kingdom of light untouched by the crossfire of international politics and the ravages of sin.

Growing in the knowledge of God. The catchy title of the book *All I Needed to Know I Learned in Kindergarten* unfortunately reflects the attitudes of some Christians toward growing in knowledge in their Christian faith. They think they learned all they needed to know in the early days of their church schooling and are complacently apathetic about progressing beyond their elementary knowledge. Many would just as soon leave faith and doctrine to others, who then dictate to them what they need to believe. The result is that they remain woefully ignorant about what they believe and why and have only a dim awareness of God. Calvin wrote: "Faith rests not on ignorance, but on knowledge. And this is, indeed, knowledge not only of God but of the divine will."[22]

A Christian's growth in the knowledge of God and his will is vital to Paul for two reasons. (1) Knowledge of God is essential for proper living. We do not lack for knowledge in our age, but the knowledge explosion has not translated into wiser living. We possess lots of know-how but little appreciation for knowing who made things as they are or knowing where everything is being directed. Those who are enemies of God in their minds (1:21) have consigned themselves to dark ignorance and produced a society where immorality and other evil behavior are at home. To be "holy ... without blemish and free from accusation" (1:22) in such a society requires spiritual insight that directs one in going against the tide.

Such knowledge about God does not have a saving function; we are saved by faith (1:12). Knowledge, however, is a means by which one grows in faith, which in turn leads to a life pleasing to God. Ambrose Bierce defined faith as "belief without evidence in what is told by one who speaks without knowledge, of things without parallel."[23] This definition may apply to some persons, but this kind of faith is little more than superstition. A strong faith requires that we can recognize the truth, think it through carefully, and allow

22. John Calvin, *Institutes of the Christian Religion*, ed. John T. McNeill, trans. Ford Lewis Battles (Philadelphia: Westminster, 1960), 1:545.

23. Ambrose Bierce, "The Devil's Dictionary," in *The Collected Writings of Ambrose Bierce* (New York: Citadel, 1946), 237.

it to permeate our lives. The opposite of understanding God's will is a life given over to foolishness (Eph. 5:18).

(2) A thorough knowledge of God's will enables us to shield ourselves from false teaching. The grave danger for those who are not solidly grounded in their faith is that they will unknowingly allow the values and practices of our culture to dilute it beyond recognition. We wind up with mushy sentimentality or worse, bizarre beliefs reinforced by herd mentality. Christians may not know more than others, but they should know better.

Bearing fruit in every good work. The phrase in 1:10, "bearing fruit in every good work," allows us to remind people that Christians need to work out their faith in the way they live. Some, it is true, mistakenly assume that they still must do something more to earn their salvation. They attend faithfully, give sacrificially, and accumulate a long history of good works so that they can make themselves feel worthy before God. Paul's condemnation of salvation based on works of law (Rom. 3:28) has led many to see such attempts as a vain endeavor. But others err in thinking that they need do nothing. They mistakenly assume that all that God requires of us is to give token allegiance to Christ by getting baptized, joining a church, attending occasionally, and giving nominally.

Paul's denunciation of "works" does not mean that Christians can safely ignore "work" (see Eph. 2:8–10). When Paul opposed faith to works, he used the plural "works" and generally described them as "works of law" (lit., Rom. 3:28, NIV, "observing the law"; cf. Gal. 3:2–10). These works included ritual acts of piety such as circumcision and observing food laws. Paul was reacting against those who believed that when they obeyed such laws, they placed God in their debt: "I have done what was required, and now God owes me something." The basic goal of human beings is to please God (Rom. 8:8; 12:1–2; 1 Cor. 7:32; 2 Cor. 5:9; Eph. 5:10; Phil. 4:18), but that cannot be accomplished through a calculating obedience to a manageable set of rules and regulations (see 2:21).

The problem as Paul expounded it is that some rely on their obedience to the law for salvation. This belief used to direct Paul's life, and Paul could reel off a long list of proud religious accomplishments (Phil. 3:5–6; cf. Gal. 2:13–14). If anyone had grounds for boasting religiously, it was the apostle Paul. But when Christ was revealed to him, he learned that his boast was empty, that he was still a sinner. He also learned that Christ "gave himself for me" (Gal. 2:20), and therefore salvation comes from God's gracious gift alone. Faith for Paul is a trusting openness to what God has done for us in Christ. But when Paul contrasted faith and works (in Romans, Galatians, and Philippians 3), he was addressing the issue of how one receives salvation, not how salvation works itself out in our daily life.

Paul was not opposed to moral obedience to the law or even ritual obedience for Jews as long as one did not think that salvation comes from one's own achievements or racial heritage. The apostle uses the singular "work" in a positive sense to describe how salvation works itself out in our daily lives. In 1 Thessalonians 1:3 he refers to "your work produced by faith." He also writes that faith works through love (Gal. 5:6) and contends that while we are not saved by works, we are created *for* them (Eph. 2:10; see "good work [deed]" in 2 Cor. 9:8; 2 Thess. 2:17).

Paul's speech in Acts 26:20 captures his basic belief. He urges others to repent, to turn to God, and to do deeds worthy of their repentance. Paul argues in Romans 2:13 that it is not the hearers of the law who are righteous before God, but the doers of the law who will be justified.[24] He also contends that God raised Christ from the dead so that we might bear fruit to God (Rom. 7:4), and so that on the day of Christ we might be "filled with the fruit of righteousness that comes through Jesus Christ—to the glory and praise of God" (Phil. 1:11).

Like the owner of the vineyard who plants a fig tree and expects a return of fruit (Luke 13:6–9), God expects fruit from every Christian. Jesus warned his disciples that trees that do not bear good fruit will be cut down and thrown into the fire (Matt. 7:19; see 3:10; 12:33–35). Wicked vineyard tenants, who do not produce the fruits in their seasons, will be destroyed (21:41, 43). In the Gospel context, bearing fruit refers to obedience to Jesus' commands, but our obedience to his commands can only come from a life that has been changed at its very core. How can persons claim to be saved if what makes them who and what they are and do remains completely unchanged? Only the truth that enters our existence and transforms it is saving. A good fruit tree produces fruit naturally and spontaneously because it is the nature of a good fruit tree to produce fruit. A useless tree, no matter how healthy, remains a useless tree. Only true Christian existence can produce fruit. If there is a continuity between the being of a person and his or her works, it is good fruit. If there is no such continuity, it is sham spirituality.

THE OPENING THANKSGIVING prayer allows us to see the importance of prayer in Paul's life and our calling to please God. In applying this text to our contemporary situation, we will look at how Paul develops these two issues.

---

24. On "good work" in Paul, see Rom. 2:7; 13:3; 1 Cor. 3:14; 2 Cor. 9:8; Gal. 6:10; Eph. 2:10; Phil. 1:6; 2:12; 1 Thess. 1:3; 2 Thess. 2:17; Titus 1:16.

The significance of prayer. The thanksgiving sections in Paul's letters reveal how important prayer was for Paul. We can learn from Paul's habit of praying constantly for others.

(1) *Praying regularly.* E. D. Martin points out that "Paul's asking has been regular, intense, focused, and intentional. Such deliberateness stands in sharp contrast to the bland suggestion of prayer in the comment, 'I'll be thinking of you.'"[25] One can imagine that Paul prayed regularly for a list of churches, perhaps as he stitched his tents. We are prone to pray only in emergencies— for those in need, in trouble, or in hard circumstances. Paul prayed contin- uously for his churches; he wrote them letters when trouble was brewing. Spiritual fortitude depends on regularity in prayer.

(2) *Praying with praise and thanksgiving.* Paul always praises and thanks God in his prayers. Sometimes we lack the joy and thanksgiving in offering up our prayers because we are too preoccupied with the evil that we fear is lurking around the corner. We sometimes resort to prayer only when we feel under siege and then focus only on our problems. Paul gave thanks in every situa- tion, because he could always see God's resplendent grace at work through- out the world.

(3) *Praying for others.* An important facet of our communal faith is that we pray for others, and they pray for us. Such mutual concern becomes crucial during those dark times when we may feel, for various reasons, unable to pray. We can rest assured that in our family of faith we are cared for, prayed for, and supported. But we tend to remember others in prayer only when we become aware of immediately pressing issues. We then beseech the Lord to intervene. E. D. Martin notes that Paul's intercessory prayers "do not have him asking God to 'fix' people." Instead, he exercises "preventive maintenance." Most would have to concede that Martin is right: "Too often intercession waits until there is a problem."[26] When things seem to be going well for us or others, we may neglect prayer. C. S. Lewis was aware of this danger and wrote to his friend, Sister Penelope Lawson:

> I specially need your prayers because I am (like the pilgrim in Bunyan) traveling across "a plain called Ease." Everything without and many things within are marvelously well at present.[27]

(4) *Praying for spiritual development.* Paul recognizes that what his churches need most is to grow in the knowledge that will govern their faith and deci- sions. He prays that they will be filled with spiritual wisdom and will know

---

25. E. D. Martin, *Colossians and Philemon*, 46.

26. Ibid., 56.

27. W. H. Lewis, ed., *Letters of C. S. Lewis* (New York: Harcourt, Brace and World, 1966), 232.

---

the hope to which God has called them and will live accordingly. We should note that Paul specifically prays for the Colossians' spiritual development in this passage. He prays that they will blossom in the soil of God's grace so that they will please God. He provides a model of intercessory prayer that we do not often emulate.

Pleasing God. Paul prays that the Colossians will please God in every way. He then lists four ways that are crucial for pleasing God.

(1) *Bearing fruit in every good work.* An abundant harvest of good fruit reveals that a fruit tree is healthy. An abundant harvest of good works reveals the spiritual health of a Christian. The good news of the forgiveness of sins and the promise of an inheritance from God should change our lives. "Things to be believed (*credenda*) do matter. But things to be done (*agenda*) matter also."[28]

Unfortunately, Christians do not always put the truth they believe into practice. Marva J. Dawn draws from Neil Postman's work *Amusing Ourselves to Death* and argues "that television has habituated its watchers to a low information-action ratio, that people are accustomed to 'learning' good ideas (even from sermons) and then doing nothing about them."[29] We learn enough to talk about it intelligently but never follow through on action. Sometimes preachers feel they have done their job by merely presenting the information or the need. Paul does not praise the Colossians simply because they have learned the truth from Epaphras (1:7) but because their faith has led to concrete results. The test of faith is whether it makes any difference in the way we live and treat others.

(2) *Growing in the knowledge of God.* The axiom that the rich get richer is particularly true in the spiritual sphere: Knowledge of God's will brings even more knowledge and spiritual growth. Sin becomes a vicious cycle as it plunges us deeper and deeper into degradation. Knowledge of God becomes a virtuous cycle as it leads us deeper and deeper into fulfilling God's sovereign purposes. As Wright puts it, "Understanding will fuel holiness; holiness will deepen understanding."[30]

Living as God desires leads to greater understanding. E. D. Martin outlines a progressive pattern:

To receive the gospel is to come to know God.
To know God is to do his will.
To do his will is to know more and more of God.[31]

---

28. Robertson, *Paul and the Intellectuals*, 33.
29. Marva J. Dawn, *Reaching Out Without Dumbing Down: A Theology of Worship for the Turn-of-the-Century Culture* (Grand Rapids: Eerdmans, 1995), 21.
30. Wright, *Colossians and Philemon*, 58.
31. E. D. Martin, *Colossians and Philemon*, 47.

The goal is to come ever closer to having the mind of Christ, which automatically affects all that we do (1 Cor. 2:16; Phil. 2:5). We can never be satisfied that we have fully mastered it (Phil. 3:12), and Paul's spiritual maturity shines through in his fervent desire to know Christ and his sufferings better (3:10).

Knowing God becomes even more crucial in an age that prizes knowing everything *but* God. A member of the Moscow patriarchate of the Russian Orthodox Church responded to a recent witch hunt in which a woman was killed and four of her five children were severely beaten.

> We have had in this country a very long period of total absence of spiritual education, and people completely forget what religion really means. ... People have lost their spiritual immunity to resist evil. They have become confused and they often have trouble knowing what is good and bad.[32]

Many technologically sophisticated people today are also shockingly gullible and ignorant when it comes to theological understanding. Those without solid doctrinal ballast are candidates for shipwreck as they jib back and forth on a never-ending sea of doubt.

(a) Every spiritual crisis derives from a failure to know God. When people shut God out of their knowledge, God gives "them over to a depraved mind, to do what ought not to be done" (Rom. 1:28). The catalog of social ills listed in Romans 1:29–32 inevitably results.

(b) All Christians need to move beyond rudimentary fundamentals (Heb. 5:12, 14) and cursory confessions if our faith is to have any effect on the way we think or live.[33]

(c) Our knowledge should result in more than just knowing good from evil but in doing good. Knowledge leads to a transformed relationship with God and others. If Christians understand God's will, they are expected to follow through and do it (see Luke 6:46, "Why do you call me, 'Lord, Lord,' and do not do what I say?").

(d) Knowledge of God results in understanding what is happening around us so that we are not taken by surprise or shaken. We know assuredly that God is working out the divine purposes for the world and often in unexpected ways. Insight into God's will enables us to see God's purpose in each new circumstance.

For Christians to grow in the knowledge of God, the church needs to be a rigorous biblical and moral training ground. The need for moral discern-

---

32. Michael Specter, "In Modern Russia, a Medieval Witch Hunt," in *The New York Times*, 146 (Apr. 5, 1997): 1, 4.

33. Wall, *Colossians and Philemon*, 51–52.

ment derived from biblical Christianity could not be greater. Surveys have revealed that the Bible has an incredible penetration level into American homes. Nine out of ten Americans own one, but most rarely read it and consequently know practically nothing about it. People have not allowed the biblical truth to penetrate their hearts and minds. They fail to read it for themselves; and when they do, they do not read it systematically or have a context for understanding it. They may flip through the pages in hopes to find something meaningful, as if the Bible were some kind of Ouija board. The result is a woeful degree of biblical ignorance that has grave consequences. Christians must be willing to study God's Word to achieve a greater understanding of their faith.

(3) *Being strengthened with all power according to his glorious might.* Knowledge alone does not enable obedience. Paul petitions God to give his readers not only spiritual discernment of his will but also the divine power to do it. That power has been revealed in the resurrection: "Christ was raised from the dead through the glory of the Father" (Rom. 6:4). That same power gives Paul strength to toil for the gospel (1:29) and empowers other Christians to live lives pleasing to God. Christianity is not a do-it-yourself religion; the believer can only be strong through God. E. D. Martin writes that "salvation is more than a matter of restoring standing with God; it is a transformation in which God is at work *in* believers as well as *for* them."[34]

Paul recognizes, however, that Christian life and growth "takes place in a world antagonistic both to his faith and to his good works."[35] Christians will meet with adversity and affliction, which will require "great endurance and patience." As Pokorný recognizes, these are not "merely passive virtues; rather, they are expressions of the power of the Risen One who makes possible the life of the church as life in togetherness within the Christian communities."[36]

(a) In this context, "endurance" is exercised toward circumstances. It is the power to cope and be content in all circumstances (Phil. 4:11–13), even when we are deluged by suffering. It is, therefore, the opposite of complaining, grumbling, or becoming despondent. When our faith in Christ fails to deliver ease or greater earthly rewards but instead brings persecution and suffering, those who endure do not abandon their faith for something that looks less demanding and more promising. Endurance refers to hanging on during tough times.

Robert Coles provides a beautiful example of endurance in his description of the experience of Tessie, one of four African-American girls who initiated

---

34. E. D. Martin, *Colossians and Philemon,* 299.
35. Caird, *Paul's Letters from Prison,* 171.
36. Pokorný, *Colossians,* 49.

school desegregation in New Orleans in 1961. They were six years old, and for months federal marshals had to escort them to their school. Each morning they endured adults spitting out a fusillade of obscenities at them as they were led through a crowd of protesters. More than once, someone in the mob yelled out a death threat. One day when Tessie was worn down by the strain and tried to beg off going back to school, her grandmother gave her an inspiring pep talk. She lamented that she could not go with her and "call those people to my side, and read to them from the Bible, and tell them, remind them, that He's up there, Jesus, watching over all of us—it don't matter who you are and what your skin color is." Coles reports that she stopped briefly to swat at a bee that was buzzing around the kitchen. She picked it up still alive; but instead of squashing it, she took it outside and let it free. She then connected her rescue of the bee to her granddaughter's situation.

> You see, my child, you have to help the good Lord with His world! He put us here—and He calls us to help Him out. That bee doesn't belong here; it belongs out there. You belong in that McDonogh School, and there will be a day when everyone knows that, even those poor folks— Lord, I pray for them!—those poor, poor folks who are out there shouting their heads off at you. You're one of the Lord's people; He's put His Hand on you. He's given a call to you, a call to service—in His name! There's all those people, scared out of their minds, and by the time you're ready to leave the McDonogh School they'll be calmed down, and they won't be paying you no mind at all, child, and I'll guarantee you, that's how it will be![37]

This wise grandmother offers keen insight on how we can endure difficulties. (i) We need a sense of calling, a belief that we have been deputized by God so that we can brave oppression. Tessie's grandmother said: "We're the lucky ones to be called, and we've got to prove we can do what the Lord wants, that we're up to it." Her words echo those of the first disciples when they had to endure suffering. After the Sanhedrin gave them the third degree, they left "rejoicing because they had been counted worthy of suffering disgrace for the Name" (Acts 5:41).

(ii) We need a sense of calling to service, not just to friends but to those who mistreat us. We need to see things as an opportunity to serve God rather than as trouble that we would like to avoid. We should view ourselves as more than simply the beneficiaries of God's grace; we are benefactors through whom God's grace reaches others.

---

37. Robert Coles, *The Call of Service: A Witness to Idealism* (Boston/New York: Houghton Mifflin, 1993), 3–4.

(iii) We need a sense that we are allied with what God is doing in the world. The grandmother's lesson sank in. Tessie herself said, "If I can help the good Lord and do a good job, then it'll all be okay, and I won't be wasting my time."[38]

(b) "Patience" differs from endurance in that it is exercised toward people (see 3:12). It refuses to succumb to bitter feelings or to strike back in vexation when wounded by malicious people. Augustine said that the one who shows patience "prefers to endure evil so as not to commit it rather than to commit evil so as not to endure it."[39] Patience is what Paul expects Philemon to show toward his errant slave Onesimus. But patience is close to endurance in that we can also be patient in our circumstances. Paul also expects Onesimus to show patience. Nouwen writes:

> The word *patience* means the willingness to stay where we are and live the situation out to the full in the belief that something hidden there will manifest itself to us. Impatient people are always expecting the real thing to happen somewhere else and therefore want to go elsewhere. The moment is empty. But patient people dare to stay where they are.[40]

(4) *Joyfully giving thanks.* It is said that Joseph Stalin considered gratitude a sickness suffered by dogs. That attitude may explain his vicious nature and the horrifying purges he visited upon his people. Joyful gratitude, however, is basic to Christians. M. Scott Peck says that he once commented to Theodore Gill that gratitude was one of the characteristics of any genuine Christian. Gill countered, "Gratitude is not one of the characteristics; it is the primary characteristic." Peck goes on to say, "Indeed, gratitude is so basic it is like salvation itself."[41] G. K. Chesterton has remarked, "When it comes to life, the critical thing is whether you take things for granted or take them with gratitude."[42]

Thanksgiving is more than a happy feeling that causes one to bubble with joy. Since Paul commands thanksgiving, it must be more than a feeling over which we have no control. It is something we can decide to do. Therefore it can become a discipline in which we can grow. Chronic complainers are never satisfied and always feel cheated in some way. They also become more susceptible to heresies in their desperate search to find something good in something else. True Christians experience God's grace intensely and

---

38. Ibid., 5.

39. Augustine, *On Patience* 2; cited by E. D. Martin, *Colossians and Philemon*, 287.

40. Henri J. M. Nouwen, "A Spirituality of Waiting: Being Alert to God's Presence in Our Lives," *Weavings* 1 (1986): 9.

41. M. Scott Peck, *What Return Can I Make?* (New York: Simon and Schuster, 1985), 162.

42. G. K. Chesterton, *Irish Impressions* (London: Collins, 1919), 24.

allow their gratitude for what God has done in Christ to shape their whole life. This gratitude makes life richer, happier, and more wondrous.

According to Nouwen,

> Gratitude in its deepest sense means to live life as a gift to be received gratefully. But gratitude as the gospel speaks about it embraces *all* of life: the good and the bad, the joyful and the painful, the holy and not so holy.[43]

For this reason, gratitude is a difficult discipline. The wear and tear of daily living can chip away at our trust in God and our appreciation for the bounty of life in Christ.

One of my students asked, "Why is it that I can effortlessly find things to complain about while remaining ungrateful for that with which I have been blessed? What is it in me that is so unsatisfied?" Perhaps our materialistic culture breeds our discontent. We are goaded by advertisers always to want more, and they promise that fulfillment, bliss, and well-being are just a phone call away. To get these magical things, many "max out" multiple credit cards and mortgage themselves to the hilt. The anxiety this high-debt lifestyle creates naturally chokes out any sense of gratitude. Those who can appreciate Jesus' response to the devil's temptation, "It is written: 'Man does not live on bread alone, but on every word that comes from the mouth of God'" (Matt. 4:4), know that abundant life does not come from an abundance of things (cf. Luke 12:15–21). Life in the here and now is not all there is.

Sometimes we forget or have not yet fully recognized or cherished what God has done for us in Christ. When we do remember and value it over all things, our gratitude abounds to God and spills over to others. A thankful spirit keeps us mindful that our lives depend entirely on God, not on ourselves. It crowds out selfish pride and checks anxiety and fear. It directs our feelings outward toward others instead of inward, where they can congeal into viscous lumps of self-pity.

Paul mentions two things for which Christians will be eternally grateful—an "inheritance ... in the kingdom of light" and our "redemption, the forgiveness of sins" (1:12, 14). Christ makes this present life bearable, and Christ promises a new life in his heavenly kingdom. Helen Keller, who became blind and deaf at a very early age, wrote in her autobiography: "For three things I thank God every day of my life: thanks that he vouchsafed me knowledge of His Works; deep thanks that He has set in my darkness the lamp of faith; deep deepest thanks that I have another life to look forward

---

43. Henri J. M. Nouwen, "All Is Grace," *Weavings* 7 (1992): 39.

to—a life joyous with light and flowers and heavenly song." She claimed that so much had been given to her that she had no time to think about what had been denied her. John's Gospel records that Lazarus had a foretaste of the power that will bring that new life (John 11:28–44). In O'Neill's play "Lazarus Laughed," a guest recalls the scene after Jesus raised Lazarus from the dead.

> And then Lazarus knelt and kissed Jesus' feet and both of them smiled and Jesus blessed him and called him "My Brother" and went away; and Lazarus, looking after Him, began to laugh softly like a man in love with God![44]

The forgiveness of sins we have through Christ should quicken the joy that was wordlessly poured out by the woman who bathed Jesus' feet with her tears (Luke 7:36–50). Sin cripples; God's grace in Christ frees. Diane Komp, a pediatric oncologist, tells the story of Arthur, who developed cancer when he was three years old. He had multiple relapses over a five-year period and was often close to death. His parents were wonderful, she says, patient with his treatment, never losing hope.

One day Arthur's mother called the doctor to ask something that had been weighing her down for years. She said that in the early years of her marriage, she had an affair and left her husband for another man. She became pregnant by him. When he learned of her pregnancy, he gave her something to swallow in hopes of inducing an abortion. It did not work, and he abandoned her. She returned to her husband, pregnant with Arthur. She asked for and received his forgiveness. He knew the truth but always loved and treated Arthur as his own son. Her question to the oncologist was this: "Do you think that the concoction I drank to abort the pregnancy caused the cancer?" Dr. Komp wisely responded that we will never know what caused the cancer. But doctors cannot heal guilt, and the mother suffered for many years with her terrible burden. Deep within her soul she must have felt that her sin caused all this suffering for her son.

Arthur's mother later wrote the doctor that she had grown up in a church that preached forgiveness through Christ's sacrifice. In spite of this religious tradition,

> she had never been able to forgive herself and had rejected the forgiveness that God had offered in Jesus. There was no one in her church with whom she could share her burden. When she finally forgave herself, she underlined every passage in her Bible that referred to God's forgiveness and was amazed that the burden was finally lifted. The

---

44. Eugene O'Neill, *The Plays of Eugene O'Neill* (New York: Random House, 1955), 1:277.

healing of memories and guilt can sometimes be more difficult than healing cancer.[45]

Arthur was one of the first in the country to receive a new experimental drug. It worked. His mother called the doctor to invite her to his wedding. One can imagine that it was going to be a big celebration. How else can one respond to God's gifts?

---

45. Diane M. Komp, "Hearts Untroubled," *TToday* 45 (1988): 278.

Colossians 1:15–23

H E IS THE image of the invisible God, the firstborn over all creation. ¹⁶For by him all things were created: things in heaven and on earth, visible and invisible, whether thrones or powers or rulers or authorities; all things were created by him and for him. ¹⁷He is before all things, and in him all things hold together. ¹⁸And he is the head of the body, the church; he is the beginning and the firstborn from among the dead, so that in everything he might have the supremacy. ¹⁹ For God was pleased to have all his fullness dwell in him, ²⁰and through him to reconcile to himself all things, whether things on earth or things in heaven, by making peace through his blood, shed on the cross.

²¹Once you were alienated from God and were enemies in your minds because of your evil behavior. ²²But now he has reconciled you by Christ's physical body through death to present you holy in his sight, without blemish and free from accusation—²³if you continue in your faith, established and firm, not moved from the hope held out in the gospel. This is the gospel that you heard and that has been proclaimed to every creature under heaven, and of which I, Paul, have become a servant.

Original Meaning

PAUL'S MENTION OF the kingdom of the beloved Son in 1:13 leads to the poetic praise of Christ in 1:15–20. This section divides into two parts, each with its own theme: Christ is mediator of creation, victor over the powers, and Lord over all of God's created order (1:15–17); and Christ is also Lord over God's new order, the church, where one finds reconciliation (1:18–20). Every part of the created cosmos, visible and invisible, was created in, by, and for him; and every part will be touched by Christ's reconciling work on the cross. Christ's cosmos-encompassing supremacy undergirds the status and power of those who have been brought into his kingdom. The universal supremacy of Christ matches the universality of the gospel (1:6) and assures believers of the sufficiency of Christ.[1]

---

1. Jones, *The Epistle of St. Paul to the Colossians,* 73.

Is Colossians 1:15–20 an Early Christian Hymn?

WHILE A SPECIAL commissioner in Pontus-Bithynia, the younger Pliny wrote to Emperor Trajan asking advice on what to do about the Christians. He reported that they met "on a certain fixed day before it was light, when they sang in alternate verses a hymn to Christ as to a God" (*Epistles* 10.96; see Eph. 5:19; Col. 3:16). Most scholars contend that Paul has preserved a fragment of early Christian hymnody in 1:15–20.[2] Interpreters, however, have reached no consensus about the supposed hymn's structure, original author, background, purpose, or possible glosses by the author of Colossians.

I join the minority opinion that does not think that Paul took up a liturgical tradition and inserted it (with annotations) into his letter.[3] Our passage is undeniably poetic, but I think it best to regard it as hymnic prose composed by Paul himself, perhaps drawing from traditional material. Although R. P. Martin argues that it is a liturgical hymn, he concedes that "religious speech tends to be in poetic form; and meditation upon the person and place of Jesus Christ in the Church's life and in the experience of the believer is not expressed in a cold, calculating way, but becomes rhapsodic and ornate."[4] The Greek verb "to hymn" (*hymno*) initially meant simply "to praise," and it was used for praise of something beyond humans.[5]

Paul was not writing this letter as a document to be studied in a seminar or interpreted in a commentary but as something he knew would be read aloud as part of the church's worship. He could express his faith with majes-

---

2. They base this conclusion on the use of the relative clause, which begins with "who is," as a common opening for Christological hymns, the rhythmically balanced units, the quantity of unusual vocabulary in such a short space ("visible," "thrones," "hold together," "beginning," "supremacy," "making peace," "his blood, shed on the cross" [lit., "the blood of the cross"]), and the self-contained content that can stand alone apart from its context in the letter.

3. See, for example, J. C. O'Neill, "The Source of the Christology in Colossians," *NTS* 26 (1979): 87–100; Seyoon Kim, *The Origin of Paul's Gospel* (Grand Rapids: Eerdmans, 1981), 144–47; John F. Balchin, "Colossians 1:15–20: An Early Christian Hymn? The Arguments from Style," *Vox Evangelica* 15 (1985): 65–93; Steven M. Baugh, "The Poetic Form of Col 1:15–20," *WJT* 47 (1985): 227–44; and N. T. Wright, "Poetry and Theology in Colossians 1.15–20," in *The Climax of the Covenant: Christ and the Law in Pauline Theology* (Minneapolis: Fortress, 1992), 99–119. Just because the subject is Christological does not mean it derives from a previously formed liturgical tradition. Balchin, "Colossians 1:15–20," 76, comments that such a conclusion "would be tantamount to saying that the New Testament writers were incapable of making statements about Christ as occasion demanded without quoting liturgical material."

4. R. P. Martin, "Aspects of Worship in the New Testament," *Vox Evangelica* 2 (1963): 21.

5. Edgar Krentz, "Epideiktik and Hymnody: The New Testament and Its World," *Biblical Research* 40 (1995): 52, 83. Described as a work in progress, Krentz provides the most useful treatment in English of the hymn form and its use in the New Testament.

tic poetry.[6] His letters reveal that he can write as prophet and psalmist, and he is a master of "the liturgical style, which soars high above the dusty street of everyday prose, which, almost in the language of the seer of another world, bears witness to the wonderful secret of that other world."[7] Since 1:12–14 also exhibits this elevated style, scholars disagree over the length of proposed liturgical material that the writer adopts. Some begin in verse 12; others, in verse 13. A more reasonable conclusion regards 1:12–23 as all springing from Paul hymning praise to his Redeemer.[8] Enclosed by references to the redemption offered in Christ (1:14, 21–22), the poem fits the context well.

We should not read our modern assumptions about what constitutes a hymn into this passage. The many proposals for the hymn's structure indicate, for example, that its metrical structure is not immediately obvious.[9] Many have excised any words or phrases that do not fit their reconstruction of a hypothetical, more metrical pre-Pauline form.[10] Such speculation, in my

---

6. See Rom. 8:31–39; 11:33–36; 16:25–27; 1 Cor. 1:18–31; 13:1–13; 2 Cor. 4:7–10; 6:3–10; 11:33–36; Gal. 5:16–26; Phil. 2:5–11; 1 Thess. 5:14–22. On Phil. 2:5–11, see Gordon D. Fee, "Philippians 2:5–11: Hymn or Exalted Pauline Prose?" *BBR* 2 (1992): 29–46. Dunn, *The Epistles to the Colossians and to Philemon*, 83–84, admits that "it can never be finally proved that preformed material has been taken up here. It is always possible that Paul himself became lyrical at the thought of all that Christians owed Christ (1:13–14) or simply struck a purple passage." Werner Georg Kümmel, *Introduction to the New Testament*, rev. ed., trans. Howard Clark Kee (Nashville: Abingdon: 1975), 343, concludes that it is far more likely "that the author of Col himself formed the hymn utilizing traditional material." Basic expressions from the passage can be found elsewhere in Paul's letters; see Rom. 5:1; 8:29; 11:36; 1 Cor. 2:8; 8:6; 2 Cor. 4:4.

7. Adolf Deissmann, *The New Testament in Modern Research* (Garden City, N.Y.: Doubleday, Doran, 1929), 98.

8. Balchin, "Colossians 1:15–20," 69, points out that if a traditional hymn has been inserted into the context, the introductory line "who is" omits the antecedent; and it therefore must begin with the hymn's second line. In the context, however, the relative pronoun does not mark a syntactical break but follows naturally what precedes.

9. Balchin (ibid., 78) lists twenty-five differing proposals. Pierre Benoit, "L'hymne christologique de Col 1, 15–20," in *Christianity, Judaism and Other Greco-Roman Cults*, ed. Jacob Neusner, SJLA 12 (Leiden: Brill, 1975), 1:226–63, graphs twenty reconstructions. Wright, "Poetry," 106, n. 25, comments that few scholars ever raise the question about "what sort of rhythm one might have a right to expect." Balchin ("Colossians 1:15–20," 68) argues that the careful parallel structure is best explained as coming from one who was "steeped in the poetic background of the Old Testament, where not only hymns but also prophetic productions were cast in parallel form. . . . It should not be surprising that he expressed himself in those forms which he had been reared to associate with the divine message."

10. Schweizer, *Colossians*, 57, for example, deletes four phrases—"thrones or dominions or principalities or authorities," "the church," "that in everything he may be pre-eminent," "making peace by the blood of his cross"—to get back to the original hymn. See most

opinion, gets us nowhere. Not only is it unprovable, it also creates a strange scenario. If the hymn were familiar to the Colossians, Paul's tinkering with it would be more likely to mystify rather than enlighten them.[11] Wright critiques Schweizer's notion that the community would recognize the opening words and join in reciting it, coupled with his theory that the author interpolated bits. "Nothing would be more calculated to puzzle a congregation than tampering with a hymn they are in the act of singing."[12]

Since many consider this passage to contain primitive traditional material, they have also tried to trace its origins in the many-faceted philosophical world of Hellenism or the various streams of Judaism. None of this helps us interpret its meaning in Colossians. Learning the source of the paints on Vincent van Gogh's palette when he painted "Sunflowers," for example, does not help us appreciate more its representation of nature bursting with life.

Nevertheless, I am convinced that the Old Testament and pre-Christian Jewish reflection on Wisdom provided the seedbed that nourished the ideas in this passage.[13] The best explanation for how such an august poem could come to birth is Burney's theory that it derives from an intricate exposition

---

recently, Jerome Murphy-O'Connor, "Tradition and Redaction in Col 1:15–20," *RB* 102 (1995): 231–41. That Paul would take over a pre-Christian, heretical hymn to make his theological case with a few alterations seems highly unlikely (see Barth and Blanke, *Colossians*, 244). Why cite a tradition whose theology one feels compelled to correct?

11. Larry R. Helyer, "Recent Research on Col 1:15–20," *GTJ* 12 (1992): 67, puts it more forcefully: "Enormous time and energy have been expended in the vain attempt to recover, rearrange and explain the original hymn and its background." O'Neill, "The Source of the Christology in Colossians," 89, exposes the fallacy behind proposing hypotheses upon hypotheses and "pretending that the additional theories actually render the first hypothesis more likely rather than less likely."

12. Wright "Poetry," 100. An attempt to change the familiar phrase "that saved a wretch like me" in the first stanza of the beloved hymn "Amazing Grace" to a more updated, higher self-esteem version, "who saved and strengthened me," raised a hue and cry of protest in some churches.

13. Helyer, "Recent Research," 66, concludes that "Paul's cosmic Christology is rooted in the OT teaching of a creator-redeemer God and Paul's personal encounter with Jesus the Lord on the Damascus Road." Wright ("Poetry," 108) contends that the poem should be read in light of the entire Jewish worldview: "There is one God; he made the world, and is neither identified with it (as in pantheism and its various pagan cousins) nor detached from it (as in dualism); he is in covenant with Israel; and he will, in fulfilling that covenant, reclaim and redeem his whole creation from that which at present corrupts or threatens it." It makes far more sense that Old Testament traditions lie behind this poem than superficial parallels in Gnosticism, Stoicism, or other Hellenistic literature. Paul was more at home with Palestinian Jewish exegetical techniques and traditions than many commentators acknowledge. Wright goes on to argue that while the poem may contain "verbal echoes of ideas current in other world views, its overall emphasis belongs within the broad and rich tradition of Jewish psalmody."

of the opening words of the biblical creation account in Genesis 1:1, "In the beginning God created the heavens and the earth," and from the poetic exaltation of Wisdom and her involvement in creation in Proverbs 8:22, "The Lord begat me as the beginning of his way, the antecedent of his works, of old" (Burney's translation).[14]

The opening word of Genesis, "in the beginning" (*bršyt*), is amplified by playing on three meanings of the Hebrew preposition *b*, "in," "by," and "for." We are told that all things were created "in" (*en*) Christ, "by" (*dia*) Christ, and "for" (*eis*) Christ (1:16). The meanings of the Hebrew word *ršyt* ("beginning," "sum-total," "head," and "firstfruits") are developed in the poem. Christ "is before all things" (beginning); "in him all things hold together" (sum total); "he is the head of the body"; and he is "the firstborn [firstfruits] from among the dead." Christ therefore fulfills every possible meaning of the word *bršyt*, the first word in the Bible.

In Proverbs 8:22–31, Wisdom is praised as the preexistent agent in God's ordering and directing creation (see Sir. 1:4; Wis. 9:9). The poem asserts that Christ realizes and supersedes all the notions associated with Wisdom.[15] Christ is God's agent in creation, revelation, and redemption; and all of God's purposes for the universe are accomplished through him.

Structure of the Passage

ANOTHER DISPUTED ISSUE concerns the structure of the poem. I divide it into two strophes.

15 **Who is** the image of God,

                    the invisible one

      firstborn over *all* creation

16   **because in him**   *all* things were created

                          in the heavens and upon the earth

                          the visible and invisible things

                          whether thrones or dominions

---

14. C. F. Burney, "Christ as the APXH of Creation: Pr 8, 22, Col 1,15.18, Rev 3, 14," *JTS* 27 (1925–26): 160–77. See also W. D. Davies, *Paul and Rabbinic Judaism* (London: SPCK, 1948), 150–52; Frederic Manns, "Col 1, 15–20: Midrash Chrétien de Gen. 1, 1," *RSR* 53 (1979): 100–10; T. E. Pollard, "Colossians 1,12–20: A Reconsideration," *NTS* 27 (1981): 572–75; and Wright, "Poetry," 107–13.

15. Wisdom is connected to creation in Prov. 8:22–30; Sir. 1:4; 24:9; Wis. 9:9; but nowhere is it claimed that "all things were created in her," as is affirmed about Christ (1:16, "for in him [NIV, by him] all things were created"). Nowhere do we find it said of Wisdom that "all things hold together in her," as is affirmed about Christ in 1:17. According to Wis. 1:7, the Spirit of the Lord has filled the world and holds all things together, not Wisdom. See Sappington, *Revelation and Redemption at Colossae*, 174.

whether rulers or authorities

all things have been created by [*dia*] him and
for [*eis*] him

17 **and he is** before *all* things and *all* things in him hold
together

18a **and he is** the head of the body, the church

18b **Who is** the beginning,

firstborn from the dead

so that he might come to have first place in *all* things

19 **because in him** it pleased *all* the fullness to dwell

20 and **by** [*dia*] **him** *all* things will be reconciled
for [*eis*] him

making peace through the blood of his cross
(through him)

whether things upon the earth or things in the
heavens.[16]

The first strophe begins with the affirmation "who is" (1:15), followed by
an explanation, "because" (1:16), and ending with another affirmation "and he
is" (1:17). The second continues with another "and he is" affirmation (1:18a),
followed by a "who is" affirmation (1:18b), and ending with an explanation
"because" (1:19–20). The two strophes draw a parallel between the creation of
all things and the new creation. Together they affirm that the Creator of all
things in heaven and on earth is the one the Colossians know as their Redeemer.
The key ideas come together in the middle (1:17–18a): Christ is preeminent
over natural creation. He is not simply one among a number of spiritual powers; he is supreme. Christ is also preeminent over his new moral creation, the
church. In Christ, his community experiences reconciliation to God as an
accomplished fact and awaits the cosmic reconciliation of all things.[17]

The Image of the Invisible God, the Firstborn Over All Creation (1:15–17)

THE FIRST STROPHE proclaims that Christ is the firstborn over all creation
and the agent of creation; it concludes with the majestic affirmation that all
things hold together in him.

(1) **The image of the invisible God.** The poem begins by affirming that
Christ is "the image of the invisible God" (see 2 Cor. 4:4; Phil. 2:6; Heb.

---

16. The parallelism has been adapted from Wright, "Poetry," 104.

17. Ephesians emphasizes the reconciliation between Jew and Gentile; Colossians, the
reconciliation of the cosmos.

1:3). This may sound strange to us. How can something invisible have an image? In Greek philosophy, however, the image has a share in the reality that it reveals and may be said to be the reality. An image was not considered something distinct from the object it represented, like a facsimile or reproduction.[18] As the image of God, Christ is an exact, as well as a visible, representation of God (Col. 1:19; 2:9), illuminating God's essence.[19]

In Romans, Paul insists that "since the creation of the world God's invisible qualities—his eternal power and divine nature—have been clearly seen, being understood from what has been made, so that men are without excuse" (Rom. 1:20). As God's representation and representative, Christ brings clarity to our hazy notions of the immortal, invisible God, who lives in unapproachable light (1 Tim. 1:17; 6:16).[20] In Christ we see who God is—Creator and Redeemer; what God is like—a God of mercy and love; and what God does—one who sends his Son to rescue people from the dominion of darkness and brings about the reconciliation of all creation through his death on a cross. Calvin comments that in Christ God shows us "his righteousness, goodness, wisdom, power, in short, his entire self."[21]

Human beings are also made in God's image (Gen. 1:26–27), but the Son is the only satisfactory likeness of God. As the perfect image of God, Christ teaches us what God intended humans to be: "renewed in knowledge in the image of [our] Creator" (Col. 3:10; see 1 Cor. 15:45; 2 Cor. 3:18).

(2) **The firstborn over all creation.** Christ is also acclaimed as "the firstborn over all creation."[22] We usually associate the term *firstborn* with birth, and it connotes to us the first child. This meaning occurs in Luke 2:7; Jesus is the "firstborn" son of Mary. But Paul's usage has a quite different sense. While it implies priority in time, it does not mean that Christ was the first being created or born. In the Old Testament this title expresses status. It appears in Psalm 89:27 as a title of sovereignty: "I will also appoint him my firstborn, the most exalted of the kings of the earth." God bestowed this title on Israel because of her divine election (Ex. 4:22; Isa. 64:8; Jer. 31:9; Psalms of Solomon

---

18. Hermann Kleinknecht, "εἰκών," *TDNT*, 2:389.

19. Harris, *Colossians and Philemon*, 43.

20. We find this core belief expressed in different ways elsewhere in the New Testament (John 1:14, 18; 6:46; 8:19; 12:45; 14:9; Heb. 1:1–3). Divine Wisdom was also regarded as the image of God: "For she is a reflection of eternal light, a spotless mirror of the working of God, and an image of his goodness" (Wis. 7:26). Philo regarded the Logos as the image of God and the firstborn of creation (*Allegorical Interpretation* 1.43; *On the Confusion of Tongues* 97). In Paul's thinking, Christ has taken over all the functions of divine Wisdom.

21. Calvin, *Commentaries on the Epistles of Paul the Apostle to the Philippians, Colossians and Thessalonians*, 150.

22. In the letter to the Laodiceans in Rev. 3:14, Christ is called the "ruler of God's creation" (*arche*, "the origin of God's creation," NRSV)

18:4; 4 Ezra 6:58). The metaphor, therefore, distinguishes Christ from all created things as before them in time and as supreme.[23] He outranks all things in creation. The NIV correctly renders the Greek (lit., "of all creation") as a genitive of subordination, "firstborn *over* all creation."[24] Paul asserts Christ's "primacy over creation, and not just within creation."[25]

(3) **All things created in him.** The next statement explains why Christ is preeminent over all creation (1:16–17). Verse 16 contains a series of prepositional phrases: All things were created "in [*en*] him," "through [*dia*] him," and "for [or with respect to, *eis*] him."[26] The NIV translates the first preposition as a dative of agency (instrumental), "by him." It is better, however, to read it as a dative of sphere (locative), "in him." Paul frequently uses "in Christ" or "in him" in this sense. Since the last part of this verse states that all things have been created through him (*dia*), it is unlikely that the apostle intends to repeat the idea of Christ's agency in creation. The first prepositional phrase maintains Christ was "the location from whom all came into being and in whom all creation is contained."[27]

The imposing list of powers visible and invisible created by Christ accents his all-encompassing role in creation—all things in heaven and earth. In the ancient world heaven was not perceived as some distant outpost that had no impact on human life on earth. Rather, invisible powers exerted their influences for good or ill (see Eph. 6:12). The pattern is chiastic:

> heaven
> > earth
> > visible
> invisible

---

23. See Philo's discussion of Logos in *On the Confusion of Tongues* 62–63; *On Husbandry* 51; *Who Is the Heir?* 205–6; *Allegorical Interpretation* 3.175; *Questions and Answers on Exodus* 2.117.

24. Grammar is important. Arius, who denied Christ's divinity, misinterpreted the phrase as a partitive genitive, "firstborn *out of* creation," reducing Christ to the status of a created being. Paul does not think of Christ as "the first" of the Lord's works in creation, as was said of Wisdom in Prov. 8:22. See Larry R. Helyer, "Arius Revisited: The Firstborn Over All Creation (Col 1:15)," *JETS* 31 (1988): 59–67.

25. Dunn, *The Epistles to the Colossians and to Philemon*, 90.

26. One can compare this to the Stoic hymn of praise to all nature in Marcus Aurelius, *Meditations* 4.23.2: "O nature, from you all things, in you all things, unto you all things." See Philo *On the Cherubim* 125–26. Though similar words appear, they express quite different ideas.

27. H. Wayne House, "The Doctrine of Christ in Colossians," *BSac* 149 (1992): 182. See also Harris, *Colossians and Philemon*, 44–45. Wall, *Colossians and Philemon*, 68, contends that "in Christ/in him" is a "metaphor for restored relationships or, even more specifically, the spiritual home of those who belong to Christ, where he (rather than the evil one) rules over them (v. 13)." In 1:17, it "presumes that the destiny of the whole created order—both its spiritual and physical realms—is linked to the Christ's destiny."

We can see the tangible powers on earth, but we cannot see the invisible forces of heaven. The invisible things are identified as the "thrones . . . powers . . . rulers . . . authorities" and perhaps refer to heavenly host.[28] They may be good or evil, that is, mediators of divine knowledge or malevolent foes in league with the power of darkness (1:13), or simply human patterns of authority (see 1 Cor. 8:6). The point Paul celebrates is that Christ has majesty and power over all of them, whatever shape they take (see Col. 2:10, 15). They, like all things, were created by him and for him.

(4) **The controlling principle of all creation.** This first strophe concludes with a reassertion of Christ's universal preeminence: "He is before all things, and in him all things hold together." Christ has precedence over all things in terms of time and status and is a kind of divine glue or spiritual gravity that holds creation together.[29] God did not simply start things off and then withdrew from his creation; Christ continues to sustain the whole universe. As H. C. G. Moule memorably put it, "He keeps the cosmos from becoming a chaos."[30]

---

28. Jewish texts use the same terms for angelic powers. See the references in Arnold, *The Colossian Syncretism*, 253. We find in Jubilees 2:2 the belief that on the first day God not only created the heavens and the earth and the waters but also "all of the spirits which minister before him":

> the angels of the presence, the angels of sanctification, and the angels of the spirit of fire, and the angels of the spirit of the clouds and darkness and snow and hail and frost, and the angels of resounding and thunder and lightning, and the angels of the spirits of cold and heat and winter and springtime and harvest and summer, and all the spirits of his creatures which are in heaven and on earth.

The "thrones" refer to the angelic potentates sitting on heavenly thrones. The "powers . . . rulers . . . authorities" are those supernatural viceroys who exercise lordship, rule, and control in heavenly realms. The same roster of powers appears in 2 Enoch 20:1 (plus "cherubim" and "seraphim"), and the differing order suggests that Paul does not list them in any hierarchical order.

29. This idea has a parallel in Stoic philosophy and makes its appearance also in Jewish writers. Sirach concludes a long poem of praise for the natural order (Sir. 42:22–43:26) with a reference to the Logos: "By his word all things hold together" (43:26; see Wis. 1:7). Fred B. Craddock, "'All Things in Him': A Critical Note on Col. I. 15–20," *NTS* 12 (1965): 79, points out, however, that the similarity is deceiving because Christ is pictured as preexisting:

> He is not in all things but all things are in him. The Logos of the Stoics gave unity, order, and meaning to all things because it permeated all things as *dia-existent* principle; the Colossian hymn praises him in whom all things begin, continue, and conclude because they are in, through, and unto him as a *pre-existent* being.

30. H. C. G. Moule, *Colossians Studies* (London: Doran, 1898), 78. Schweizer, *Colossians*, 129–30, points to evidence that some Jews believed that the whole cosmos would fly apart were it not for the Jewish New Year Festival, which reconciled the elements to one another each year and maintained the harmony of the upper and lower world. The high priest's holy vestments had embroidered symbols of the cosmos, which served to remember the universe to God whenever he entered the temple. Christ makes the high priest and the temple passé.

But this may be saying too little. The verb "hold together" (*synistemi*) can imply that they have their existence in him. Christ is more than the force that preserves the orderly arrangement of the cosmos; he is its rationale, its rhyme and reason. Wink interprets it to mean that Christ is "the System of the systems."[31] He is the basic operating principle controlling existence.[32] The universe is not self-sufficient (as in the deistic model), nor are individuals, no matter how much they may deceive themselves into thinking they are.[33] Even those who do not acknowledge Christ's reign and those who actively oppose him are entirely dependent on him.

The Head of the Church, the Firstborn from Among the Dead (1:18–20)

THE FIRST STROPHE lauds Christ as the sphere of creation, the mediator of creation, the preserver and controller of creation, and creation's aim. But Paul does not exult in some heavenly abstraction. The poem's second strophe brings the cosmic Christ down to earth, where blood flows from a body strung up on a cross. Christians know the supreme Creator and Sustainer of all things as the crucified and resurrected Lord. Paul anchors Christ's cosmic supremacy in salvation history and in his Lordship over the church. The image of the invisible God entered the plane of human experience in order to reconcile all things in heaven and on earth by means of his humiliating death. Christ establishes his Lordship in house churches, prison cells, and families, as well as in the furthest reaches of the heavens. His sacrificial death shows that "the fundamental rationale of the world is 'caught' more in the generous outpouring of sacrificial, redemptive love (1:14) than in the greed and grasping that is characteristic of 'the authority of darkness' (1:12)."[34] Christ also reveals more of the ultimate aims of this invisible God.

(1) **The head of the church.** The second strophe begins by proclaiming that Christ is "the head of the body, the church." It was not uncommon in

---

31. Walter Wink, *Naming the Powers* (Philadelphia: Fortress, 1984), 115.

32. We might compare it to the motherboard of a computer, the operating system that makes it work. No program can be run on the computer without interfacing with that operating system.

33. Harris, *Colossians and Philemon*, 45, argues that uses of the perfect tense "has been created" (*ektistai*, "were created, " NIV)

emphasizes the state resulting from the past event of creation, pointing not to continuous acts of creation (true though such an idea may be in a limited sense) but to the permanent "createdness" of creation. All things have been created, and remain in their created existence, through Christ and for him. Thus the universe (τὰ πάντα) has an ongoing relationship to Christ.

34. Dunn, *The Epistles to the Colossians and to Philemon*, 94.

Paul's time for philosophers to compare the cosmos to a body, but Paul applies it to the church, a historical entity.[35] If Christ is the head of the church, it means that the destinies of creation and the church are bound together and that God's purposes for all creation gestate in the church's congregational life.[36] The church does not exist to meet the needs of its members or to insure its institutional survival, but to fulfill the redemptive purposes of Christ, its head. It should therefore reflect the image of the divinely ordered cosmos. The creative principle flourishes in the church as it bears fruit all over the world (1:6) through its preaching the gospel and living worthily of Christ.

The focus is on Christ, however, not the church. When Paul uses the body metaphor elsewhere (see 3:15; Rom. 12:4–5; 1 Cor. 12:12–31), he stresses the interdependence of church members. In this passage, Paul emphasizes the body's organic and dependent relation to Christ as head (see also Eph. 4:15; 5:23).[37] "Head," "beginning," and "firstborn" all derive from the same root in Hebrew (*ršyt*). Each affirms Christ's sovereignty in the new creation and in the old. What is more important, "head" can also indicate source or origin.[38] Christ is the source of the church's life. The metaphor "head" designates him both as supreme over the church and as the source of the church's life. In the image of a living body, the head not only directs and governs the body, it gives it life and strength. Best comments:

> The life of the Church is a new Life, not the life of the old or first creation but the life of the New Creation, achieved through his cross and resurrection. So he is preeminent in all things.[39]

This second strophe includes three declarations that explain why Christ is head of the church.

(2) **The beginning and the firstborn from the dead.** The poem moves from creation to a new creation by identifying Christ as "the beginning and

---

35. See Lohse, *Colossians and Philemon*, 53–55; Best, *One Body in Christ*, 123.

36. Wall, *Colossians and Philemon*, 57. He comments that "the new creation has erupted in the midst of a fallen creation, and the promised blessings of the new age are now being realized within the history of the church" (70).

37. Wright, *Colossians and Philemon*, 74.

38. This meaning for the term *head* has prompted much debate. See Stephen Bedale, "The Meaning of *Kephale* in the Pauline Epistles," *JTS* 5 (1954): 211–15; Wayne A. Grudem, "Does *Kephale* Mean 'Source' or 'Authority over' in Greek? A Survey of 2,336 Examples," *TrinJ* 6 NS (1985): 38–59; Richard. S. Cervin, "Does *Kephale* Mean 'Source' or 'Authority' in Greek Literature? A Rebuttal," *TrinJ* 10 NS (1989): 85–112; Joseph A. Fitzmyer, "Another Look at *KEPHALE* in 1 Corinthians 11.3," *NTS* 35 (1989): 503–11; Clinton E. Arnold, "Jesus Christ: 'Head of the Church,'" in *Jesus of Nazareth: Lord and Christ*, eds. M. M. B. Turner and J. B. Green (Grand Rapids: Eerdmans, 1994), 346–66.

39. Best, *One Body*, 129–30.

the firstborn from among the dead."[40] Christ's resurrection is the source of the new life for others. He is the first in a sequence that opens new possibilities for others who follow: "Because I live, you also will live" (John 14:19).

Wright draws out the eschatological implications of such a perspective. Rather than view the resurrection as some "large-scale, single event at the end of time," as many Jews did, Paul "believed that God brought forward the inauguration of the 'age to come,' the age of resurrection, into the midst of the 'present age,' in order that the power of the new age might be unleashed upon the world while there was still time for the world to be saved."[41]

The goal of the resurrection is not merely to give individual believers the hope that they might also defeat death. God is not satisfied for Christ to be head only over a small band of devoted followers. The goal expressed in 1:18b is far grander: Christ is firstborn of the dead "so that in everything he might have the supremacy."

This poses a paradox. Does Christ not already have supremacy as the firstborn over all creation? Wright offers a helpful explanation: What Christ had by natural right he had not yet exercised. "The puzzle is caused by sin: though always Lord by right, he must become Lord in fact, by defeating sin and death."[42] The poem assumes that creation is somehow out of harmony, fallen, disordered, and fractured, without touching on how it got out of whack.[43] All creation awaits the consummation, when it will be drawn into complete harmony with the Father. Christ's death and resurrection were all part of the divine purpose to accomplish this end, and this mystery can now be seen by all. In the meantime, Christ exercises his worldwide rule in his church.

(3) **The fullness of God.** The next clause in 1:19 explains that Christ differs from other supposedly divine emanations in the world (such as angels). He is a full, not a partial, embodiment of God (see 2:9, "For in Christ all the fullness of the Deity lives in bodily form").[44] In the Old Testament, God

---

40. Christ is not born from the dead but raised from the dead, and the term *firstborn* means that he is the first one raised from the dead (Acts 26:23; 1 Cor. 15:20, 23; Rev. 1:5).

41. Wright, *Colossians and Philemon*, 74–75.

42. Ibid., 75. Christ's Sonship is demonstrated on the cross and in the resurrection (Rom. 1:3–4).

43. We need to turn to the early chapters of Genesis to read about the fallout from human sin—enmity between husband and wife, between humans and animals, between humans and the earth (Gen. 3:15–19), and between brothers (4:1–16).

44. The NIV translation, "For God was pleased to have all his fullness dwell in him," supplies "God" as the implied subject of the verb. The word "God" does not appear in the Greek text, and "all the fullness" is the subject in the Greek. Translating it literally, "all the fullness was pleased to dwell," makes God the unexpressed agent working his will on creation. It preserves the parallel of this *hoti* clause to the one in the first strophe (1:16), which

---

chose a place for his name to dwell and to express divine care.[45] The Lord particularly chose to dwell on Zion (Ps. 68:16; 132:13–14; Isa. 8:18).[46] God also fills heaven and earth (Isa. 6:3; Jer. 23:23). The "fullness" is a circumlocution for God: God pleases to dwell fully and permanently only in Christ. Christ supplants the temple, or any other house made with hands, and represents God in person.[47] As Bruce states it, "all the attributes and activities of God—his spirit, word, wisdom and glory—are disclosed in him."[48] We especially see God's redemptive power in Christ.[49]

(4) **The one who reconciles all creation through his death.** The sequence "in him . . . through him . . . to him" (lit. trans.) in 1:16 is repeated in 1:19–20.[50] In the beginning, God created all things through Christ; in the end, God will reconcile all things through Christ. Christ's majesty is rooted in God's love, shown in the earthly, historical reality of the cross. He is not the Lord of some spiritual netherworld, alien or hostile to this material realm, but one

---

expresses God's agency with a divine passive, "in him [*not* by him, NIV] all things were created." The verb "pleased" is in the aorist tense but is timeless, referring to God's purpose, and should not be pressed to refer to some particular moment in Jesus' life. The verb expresses God's will in the Old Testament (see Ps. 44:3; 147:11; 149:4). When God is said to be "well pleased" or expresses "good pleasure," it refers to an "inscrutable decree," in the sovereignty and mystery of God's choice (B. W. Bacon, "Notes on New Testament Passages," *JBL* 16 [1897]: 136–39; "Supplementary Note on the Aorist εὐδόκησα, Mark i. 11," *JBL* 20 [1901]: 28–30). See Luke 12:32; Eph. 1:4–9; 1 Cor. 1:21; Gal. 1:15; 2 Peter 1:17.

45. See Deut. 12:5, 11; 14:23; 16:2, 6, 11; 26:2; Jer. 7:7; 2 Macc. 14:35; 3 Macc. 2:16; Acts 7:48–50.

46. Sir. 24:3–12 refers to Zion, where Wisdom pleased to dwell.

47. Note the emphatic position of "in him" (*en auto*): God dwells in him. The *Epistle to Diognetus* from the late second century provides an apt commentary of what this affirmation would mean in the ancient world. God did not establish his truth on earth by sending

> an angel or ruler, or one of those who direct earthly things, or one of those who are entrusted with the dispensations in heaven, but the very artificer and Creator of the universe himself, by whom he made the heavens, by whom he enclosed the sea in its own bounds, whose mysteries all the elements [*ta stoicheia*] guard faithfully; from whom the sun received the measure of the courses of the day, to whose command the moon is obedient to give light by night, whom the stars obey, following the course of the moon, by whom all things were ordered, and ordained, and placed in subjection, the heavens and the things in the heavens, the earth and the things in the earth, the sea and the things in the sea, fire, air, abyss, the things in the heights, the things in the depths, the things between them—him he sent to them (7:2).

48. Bruce, *The Epistles to the Colossians, Philemon and to the Ephesians,* 207.

49. H. Wayne House, "The Doctrine of Christ in Colossians," 186, comments: "God the Father was pleased to have all redemptive power dwelling in Christ."

50. Note that the NIV has omitted the extra "through him" after "his cross." Even though it may sound awkward, "it reemphasizes the fact that reconciliation was achieved through Christ alone" (Wright, *Colossians and Philemon,* 76).

---

who took on the flesh of creation. Christianity has not been founded on a mythical salvation drama, as was true of the rival mystery religions of Paul's day. Agonizing suffering in history (see 2:14–15, "nailing it to the cross") achieved our redemption.

The death of an obscure Jew on a seemingly God-forsaken hillock in a backwater of the Roman empire attracted no notice from the historians of the era, but it was the event that reconciles heaven and earth. The world may be corrupted, disordered, and ravaged by sin, but God still loves it; and God intends for it to fulfill its destiny in Christ.[51] Sin has defaced Christ's work in creation, but he came to undo its consequences and to bring concord in a universe out of harmony with God.

The grim reference to Christ's "blood" and "cross" brings us down from the lofty heights of preeminence and fullness to the squalid depths of human pain and suffering. These two words are combined to express cost and violence. Blood refers to death by violence (see Matt. 23:30, 35; Rev. 6:10; 19:2); the cross refers to humility and shame (Phil. 2:8). The head of the church is the one who was shamefully crucified (see Col. 2:9, 14, 20; 3:3). These last lines affirm, however, that God's ultimate purpose is not to judge and to destroy, but to reconcile and to renew—to make peace (see Rom. 5:1–5; 2 Cor. 5:19).[52]

Paul also uses "blood" to refer to the work of Christ's atoning sacrifice.[53] The cross establishes a new relationship between God and humans, which overcomes the rupture created by sin—estrangement from God, estrangement from other humans, and estrangement from created things. That peace can only be found now in his body. It is not yet an accomplished fact in the cosmos, but God's "purpose, means, and manner" of making peace have already been established.[54]

The pacification of all things, human and nonhuman, does not mean that the enemies of God are won over in obedience to him. It is not a peace among equals, "but one forcefully brought about by a triumphant victor."[55] When Paul promises that every knee will bow at the name of Jesus and con-

---

51. God's patience and persistence is captured by the lament in Ezek. 33:11: "Say to them, 'As surely as I live, declares the Sovereign LORD, I take no pleasure in the death of the wicked, but rather that they turn from their ways and live. Turn! Turn from your evil ways! Why will you die, O house of Israel?'"

52. I am attracted by the interpretation in the *Epistle to Diognetus* 7:3–5, which says that God did not send the Creator of the universe "in sovereignty, fear and terror" but "in gentleness and meekness," "saving and persuading," not "compelling," "calling, not pursuing," "loving, not judging."

53. Rom. 3:25; 5:9; Eph. 1:7; 2:13; see also Heb. 9:14; 10:29; 13:12; 1 Peter 1:19; 1 John 1:7; Rev. 1:5.

54. Dunn, *The Epistles to the Colossians and to Philemon*, 103.

55. Lars Hartman, "Universal Reconciliation (Col 1, 20)," *SNTU* 10 (1985): 120.

fess that he is Lord (Phil. 2:10–11), he means that every being will finally acknowledge who is Lord of the universe. The unconditional surrender of the Axis troops in World War II brought a cessation to the hostilities, but war crimes tribunals still awaited those who perpetrated evil (see Rom. 8:19–21; 1 Cor. 15:24–28).

The Relation of the Prose Hymn to the Argument in Colossians

HOW THIS PROSE hymn to Christ fits in Colossians, not its hypothetical pre-history or redaction, is the only thing important for interpreting Colossians. Key affirmations in 1:15–20 buttress Paul's arguments against the opponents that appear later in the letter.

(1) If Christ is the image of God (1:15) and all the fullness of God dwells in him (1:19), then the Colossians will not find fullness in anything else (2:10).

(2) If all the "things in heaven and on earth, visible and invisible, whether thrones or powers or rulers or authorities" were created by him (1:16), he brings to naught all supposed threats posed by these powers.

(3) God's plan from before creation was to reconcile all things through Christ, and that design has not been revised. The Colossians do not need a supplemental salvation plan and cannot attain this peace and reconciliation through heavenly visions or rigorous asceticism (2:16–23). Instead, attention to these things may disqualify them.

(4) Christ is supreme over all, but that supremacy manifests itself most visibly in the church. Christ is the head of the body, the church (1:18), and those who lose connection with the head, "from whom the whole body, supported and held together by its ligaments and sinews, grows as God causes it to grow" (2:19), will wither and die. One can cut off any extremity of the body except the head and still live.

(5) The supremacy of Christ over the whole cosmos assures believers of the sufficiency of Christ. Therefore, they should not allow their hope in Christ, the firstborn of the dead, to be shaken when it is challenged or denigrated by others.

(6) If Christ sustains the entire universe, then Christ can sustain individual believers.

Remaining Firm and Established in the Faith (1:21–23)

COLOSSIANS 1:21–23 CONCLUDES the opening thanksgiving section. The key words "faith," "hope," and "heard" (1:23) are repeated from the opening verses (1:4–6). These verses also restate the theme in 1:12–14, that redemption comes in Christ. Thus, this theme encases the poem in 1:15–20.[56] These concluding words of the thanksgiving recall the believers' past ("once," 1:21), present ("now," 1:22), and future ("if," 1:23). They also declare the means of their redemption ("he has reconciled," 1:22), its effects ("holy," "without blemish," and "free from accusation," 1:22), and the extent of its impact ("to every creature under heaven," 1:23).[57]

This conclusion also contains a warning. If believers are to be holy, without blemish, and free from accusation in the future, they must remain steadfast in the faith in the present. They cannot take their new status for granted, be nonchalant about its responsibilities, or be fooled into thinking that other avenues to God exist. Christ alone offers the solution to human alienation in the world.

The word "alienated" (1:21) implies isolation, loneliness, and a deep sense of not belonging. The phrase "from God" is not in the Greek text but fits a Jewish perspective that all Gentiles by definition lived apart from the one true God. It clarifies the heart of the problem besetting all humans (see Eph. 4:18). Humans have worshiped false gods and have become enslaved to sin so that the ways of the true God seem alien. Being "enemies in your minds" (cf. Rom. 5:10; 8:17) does not limit the hostility only to the intellectual aspect of our lives. When we are out of relationship with God, it mars our entire life. Thoughts and behavior are intertwined. Chronic sinful behavior twists the mind so that it becomes even more at enmity with God, and the twisted mind hurtles us into ever greater depravity. The depraved mind then commends evil behavior as good or natural or as an alternative lifestyle. It produces and condones fear and suspicion of others and an urge to hurt and destroy them. Those who become enemies of God become Sin's lackeys, and Sin inflicts only ruin on them as their lives spiral out of control.

Reconciliation in Christ breaks the cycle of sin, heals the ruptured relationship with God, and brings us into accord with God's holy character and purpose (1:22). By referring to "Christ's physical body" (lit., "the body of his flesh"), Paul reemphasizes that the one who is fully identified with God (1:19; 2:9) is fully identified with sinful humanity. He shared our life, experienced our suffering, bore our sin, and endured the full brunt of the consequences of our sin, namely, death (Rom. 5:10a). Those who are members of

---

56. Verses 21–22a are another way of saying that believers have been delivered from the dominion of darkness (see 1:13) and have received forgiveness of sins (see 1:14). Verse 22b is another way of saying that God has qualified them to share in the inheritance of the saints in the kingdom of light (1:12–13).

57. Lohse, *Colossians and Philemon*, 66, comments, "The cosmic scope of the Christ-event, as it was developed in the hymn, is thereby applied to the gospel that is directed to the whole world."

Christ's body find their sin already canceled by his death (3:14–15) and the dominion of darkness with its menacing powers and authorities already defeated (3:15).

The imagery of being "without blemish" comes from the world of sacrifice. Animals offered in sacrifice to God had to be unblemished. Caird reminds us that "when a man offered an animal in sacrifice, he laid his hand on it in order to identify himself with his offering and to express his aspirations to be himself holy and unblemished."[58] Paul, however, believes that this aspiration has become a reality. Through the sacrifice of Christ, who knew no sin, we blameworthy sinners have become "the righteousness of God" (2 Cor. 5:21). This leads to the law court imagery. When we are presented before the judgment seat of God, no accusation will be raised against us. In Christ we will be irreproachable.

Paul emphasizes that Christ has accomplished this perfection for us; it does not come from our own striving. But God's goal of making us a holy and blameless people in Christ is still a work in progress, and it requires some response on our part. Christians need to recognize that they have been reconciled to God to live a life that God approves. Moule thoughtfully expresses the truth of the New Testament doctrine of reconciliation: "Christ does for us what we could not do for ourselves; but we must do, for our part, what he will not do for us. He 'offers' us to God, but it is none the less our own offering."[59]

The promise of blamelessness is, therefore, not unconditional. If the Colossians allow outsiders to dislodge them from their foundation in the gospel—what they had heard and received from Epaphras—they will find themselves removed from their hope. Therefore, they need to be planted ever more deeply in the faith that they first heard preached and which is preached throughout the world, lest they become like the seed in the shallow earth that bursts into bloom but then quickly withers and dies under persecution (Mark 4:16–17).[60]

In concluding his thanksgiving, Paul expresses his deepest conviction that God's plan for the world, kept secret from the dawn of history until

---

58. Caird, *Paul's Letters from Prison*, 182.

59. Moule, *Colossians and Philemon*, 73.

60. "Faith" could refer to the fixed tenets of faith as outlined, for example, in the prose hymn (see Gal. 1:23), that Christ makes the invisible God visible, is the agent, center, and crown of God's creation, and accomplishes God's objectives to reconcile the world through his cross. It also could refer to the Colossians' personal faith (see NIV). The latter is more likely. Paul is talking about something that should bear fruit and grow, not something fixed in a creed. The Colossians must accept by faith God's act of reconciliation in the death and resurrection of Christ, persevere in their convictions, and grow in their discernment of God's purposes.

now, has at last been disclosed in Christ.[61] "[It] has been proclaimed to every creature under heaven"—an expression that echoes Old Testament language (see Rom. 10:18 = Ps. 19:4) but which Paul does not intend it literally.[62] It means that the gospel is not obscure or some secret mystery. This verse also defines the scope of the church's mission field: The gospel is to go out to everyone everywhere.

THANKSGIVING FOR OUR Lord Jesus Christ bursts forth in the highest praise and the highest Christology in this section. We may not be able to penetrate fully its theological depth, but we can appreciate its profundity. We will examine the poetic affirmation of Christ's preexistence, incarnation, and universal rule as issues that need further attention for bridging the contexts.

The preexistent Christ. The poetic praise of Christ in 1:15–20 lauds him as the regent and reconciler of all creation. Caird asks a vital question, "How could claims of this magnitude be made about a man who died little more than thirty years ago, and who was remembered as a personal friend by men and women still living when the letter was written?"[63] That is, how could anyone believe that Jesus of Nazareth was the image of the invisible God and preexistent agent of creation? It is easier to accept that this Jesus offered himself as a sacrifice for the world's redemption on the cross than it is to believe that he was also active in creation.

The poem contains a paradox wrapped inside a mystery that has puzzled theologians for centuries. It affirms the complete humanity of Jesus, who shed his blood on a cross, and his full divinity, in whom the fullness of God dwells and by whom and for whom all things were created. Caird comments on how difficult it is "for creatures of space and time to say anything about eternity without misleadingly clothing it in temporal or spatial imagery. Appearing in the midst of time, Christ so fully represents and reveals the divine purpose and wisdom that only the language of eternity can do him justice."[64] Perhaps poetry is the only means that can express such truth. In try-

---

61. Paul understands himself to be a servant of this reconciling gospel, and no more so than when he tries to reconcile a runaway slave to his master in the letter to Philemon. In using such a generic term as *servant*, Paul emphasizes the hard service as opposed to the high status of his calling.

62. See Gen. 1:9; 6:17; 7:19; Ex. 17:4; Deut. 2:25; 4:19; 9:14; 25:19; see Luke 17:24; Acts 2:5; 4:12.

63. Caird, *Paul's Letters from Prison*, 175.

64. Ibid., 179.

ing to convey the idea of preexistence to our time and culture, however, we need to be mindful of some key issues.

(1) The qualities ascribed to Wisdom in Jewish tradition have influenced the poem's language in glorifying Christ. This tradition regarded Wisdom as something far more than simply a savvy philosophy of life. Jewish writers portrayed the figure of Wisdom as the personification of God's will, as the underlying principle of the universe, and as having the same essence as God, though separate from him.

Wisdom originates with God as the breath of his power, a pure emanation of his glory, a reflection of eternal light, a spotless mirror of his working, and an image of his goodness (Wis. 7:25–26; Sir. 1:1; 24:9). Wisdom pervades and penetrates all things (Wis. 7:24), renews all things (7:27), and orders all things well (8:1). Wisdom shares God's throne (9:4; 1 Enoch 84:3), was with him from the beginning (Job 28:25–27; Wis. 9:9; Sir. 1:4), was the agent of creation (Prov. 3:19–20; 8:22–31; Wis. 8:4–6), and is the agent of providence (Wis. 1:7; 8:1, 4) and of revelation (7:26–27; 11:1). God sends Wisdom into the world (Bar. 3:37; Wis. 9:10–17; Sir. 24:8) to save (Wis. 10:1–21), and Wisdom returns to heaven again (1 Enoch 42:1–2). Wisdom seeks out humans and makes personal claims and promises (Prov. 1:20–33; 8:1–21; 9:4–6), is associated with the Spirit (Ex. 31:3; Isa. 11:2; Wis. 1:6; 7:7, 22; 9:17; Sir. 39:6), and is an agent of judgment (Wis. 1:8).[65]

The poem in Colossians affirms that Christ is the realization of everything attributed to Wisdom in this Jewish tradition and more. The "more" has to do with his incarnation. Wisdom had an ambiguous status between a rational principle that encompassed all truth everywhere and an ethereal individual being. Personified Wisdom "oscillates between being an attribute of God (a picturesque way of saying 'God in his wisdom') and the divine plan for human life which is incidentally the ground plan for the universe, capable of being identified with the Torah (Sirach 24:7–12, 23)."[66] In this tradition, Wisdom was incarnate only in the Law. By contrast, Christ is a personal being who became fully human and shed his blood on a cross.

(2) The poem flows from creation to redemption, but we can understand creation only by moving back from redemption. Paul affirms that as redemption begins with Christ, so God's purpose in creation began with Christ. We can witness God's ultimate intention for creation in Christ's redemptive death, which is the source of the new creation. The same creative power that triumphed on the cross in Christ created and sustains our world. "The cross firmly fixes the central event of the purposes of God for the whole creation

---

65. See Balchin, "Paul, Wisdom and Christ," 208.
66. Caird, *Paul's Letters from Prison*, 177.

in the *terra firma* of history"—in an event "located and dated in history."[67] It reveals the essence of God and shows that the Creator of all things is also the Redeemer of all things. The poem declares that God's full presence and power that was in Christ's reconciling work and in his resurrection was the same presence and power working in creation.

(3) What "is pre-existent is not Christ in person, but the power of God that came to be active in him."[68] Wright comments that the poem does not say that Jesus "pre-existed in human form," but that it "was utterly appropriate for him, as the pre-existent one, to become man." He explains with an analogy. If one says that Queen Elizabeth II was born in 1926, that does not mean that she was queen when she was born. It affirms that the one we now know as the queen was born then. Paul is saying something similar. The person we know as Jesus, the Messiah, was "God's pre-existent agent" in creation.[69] Wright contends that any idea of *human* preexistence would have been completely foreign to this world of thought.[70] Instead, the passage asserts that Jesus is "the predestined human lord of the world"; he has appropriately "become what he always was." "The pre-existent lord of the world has become the human lord of the world, and in so doing has reflected fully, for the eyes of the world to see, the God whose human image he has now come to bear."[71] Christ embodied God's salvific purposes from before creation.

(4) Paul attributes to Jesus what the Old Testament attributes to God as Creator (see Ps. 96:5; 146:5–6; Isa. 40:12–31). Jesus does not displace the God of the Old Testament or become a second God; "he has made him known."[72] Wright argues that Paul "does not in this poem abandon the Jewish doctrines of monotheism and election. He redefines them." It fits what Wright calls "christological monotheism" (see 1 Cor. 8:6). Paul modifies "Jewish monotheism so as to place Jesus Christ within the description, almost the definition, of the one God."[73] The poem, according to Wright, contains "a form of Jewish monotheism not before envisaged, in which the Messiah himself is the dwelling-place of the divine wisdom, the immanent presence of the transcendent God, the visible image of the invisible God."[74] This

---

67. Fred B. Craddock, *The Pre-Existence of Christ in the New Testament* (Nashville/New York: Abingdon, 1968), 97–98, 166.

68. John Ziesler, *Pauline Christianity* (Oxford: Oxford Univ. Press, 1983), 124.

69. Wright, *Colossians and Philemon*, 68–69.

70. Bo Reicke, "πρό," *TDNT*, 6:687, argues that "preexistence" is not related to "an abstract idea of timelessness, but to God's dominion over the world and history." It affirms "that God foreordained 'before all times' or 'before the foundation of the world.'"

71. Wright, "Poetry," 116.

72. Wright, *Colossians and Philemon*, 66.

73. Ibid., 67.

74. Wright, "Poetry," 118.

means that any who claim to know God and do not recognize God in Jesus Christ do not know the true God. Any who claim to hear God and do not hear God speaking in Jesus Christ are deaf to God's message.

(5) Paul wanted to make clear that Christ, not Wisdom or the Law, is God's agent in the world. All things were created for him and by him and are subject to him. According to Wright, the poem undermines the claims of Judaism. All they "hoped to gain by belief in the one God, whose Wisdom was given to them in the form of the Torah, is now to be gained through Christ."[75] The poem also exposes the error of dualism and polytheism: There is only *one* Creator-Redeemer God, not a countless horde of gods with differing powers and assignments.

The Christ of flesh and blood. Since the poem maintains that Christ reconciles all things to himself, it implies that all things were previously unreconciled. It assumes that the world is fallen and that sin has ravaged the image of God in humankind and embroiled the world in discord. Sin created a gulf between God and creation. The poem declares that Christ has bridged the chasm between God and humankind, between heaven and earth, by making God's presence, power, love, and grace known to all creation. What is more, the life, death, and resurrection of Christ did not simply rectify the Fall but created in a human being the image that God had always intended to be in humankind.[76]

This reconciliation could not be achieved by intermediate beings, but only by the One whose love "moves the stars and leads the universe to its appointed goal" and whose love took on our flesh and died for us on the cross. Stewart explains why it could only be done in the Christ of flesh and blood: "Because he is himself highest and lowest, thoroughly historical, yet outside all the normal categories of men: which is precisely the truth for which at a later day and in a different form the Nicene theologians so vigorously contended."[77] The poem exalts Christ as the image of God and agent of creation but checks any extreme view that would magnify Jesus' divine nature to the exclusion of his human nature.

How this could be done remains a mystery of our faith. C. S. Lewis remarks:

> We cannot conceive how the Divine Spirit dwelled within the created and human spirit of Jesus: but neither can we conceive how His human spirit, or that of any man, dwells within his natural organism. What we can understand, if Christian doctrine is true, is that our own

---

75. Ibid.

76. Caird, *Paul's Letters from Prison*, 175.

77. James S. Stewart, "A First-Century Heresy and Its Modern Counterpart," *SJT* 23 (1970): 432–33.

composite experience is not the sheer anomaly it might seem to be, but a faint image of the Divine incarnation itself—the same theme in a very minor key.

He goes on to say that it reveals

the power of the Higher, just in so far as it is truly higher, to come down, the power of the greater to include less. Thus solid bodies exemplify many truths of plane geometry, but plane figures are not truths of solid geometry; many inorganic propositions are true of organisms but no organic propositions are true of minerals; Montaigne became kittenish with his kitten but she never talked philosophy to him. Everywhere the great enters the little—its power to do so is almost the test of its greatness.[78]

We may never fully comprehend the miracle of the Incarnation, but it has enormous relevance for us today. (1) It reveals God's true majesty. As Guthrie puts it:

He is not like a king who preserves his majesty and honor only by shutting himself up in the splendor of his palace, safely isolated from the misery of the poor peasants and the threat of his enemies outside the fortress. His majesty is the majesty of a love so great that he leaves the palace and his royal trappings to live among his subjects as one of them, sharing their condition even at the risk of vulnerability to the attack of his enemies. If we want to find this king, we will find him among the weak and lowly, his genuine majesty both revealed and hidden in his choosing to share their vulnerability, suffering, and guilt and powerlessness.[79]

(2) Revealing himself by hiding himself in human flesh and blood affirms the goodness of his creation. When people still consider the world of creation to be "a rotten ship in polluted waters (and good that it should sink)," this word needs to be heard.[80] We have UFO cults making headlines when they commit mass suicide, gladly shedding what they called their bodily containers. They yearn to escape this world and evolve to a higher form of life—in this particular case, by hitching a ride on a space ship they believed was trailing the comet Hale-Bopp. Such beliefs may seem bizarre, but they

---

78. C. S. Lewis, *Miracles: A Preliminary Study* (New York: Macmillan, 1947), 134.

79. Shirley C. Guthrie, Jr., "The Nearness and Distance of God," *International Documentation* 71 (1976): 41–42.

80. Artemio M. Zabala, "Advent Reflections on Colossians 1:15–20 in the Philippine Setting," *Asian Journal of Theology* 3 (1989): 316.

reflect an age-old gnostic disdain for this material world and the human body. We find the same sentiments expressed in a passage from the Hermetic literature, which speaks of how to behold God fully:

> But first you must tear off this garment which you wear,—this cloak of darkness, this web of ignorance, this [prop] of evil, this bond of corruption,—this living death, this conscious corpse, this tomb you carry about with you,—this robber in the house, this enemy who hates the things you seek after, and grudges you the things which you desire.[81]

In bridging the contexts, we must make clear that Christianity is a world-affirming religion, rightly understood. God's creation is good, and salvation is not found by trying to escape the body. Paul's poem in Colossians 1 declares that the Creator and Sustainer of the universe took on our flesh and blood and will reconcile this world to himself.

The universal Christ. Markus Barth asks, "Does it make sense to speak of a cosmic rule of Jesus Christ and of the reconciliation of all things, the whole universe, through him? Or are his person and work related only to the salvation of humankind?"[82] Many scholars have argued that we must avoid cosmological statements about Jesus and should focus only on what his death means for the salvation of individuals, the church, and society. This view assumes that nature does not benefit from Christ's work and that humanity has a monopoly on Christ's divine mercy. Nature was simply the stage on which the drama of salvation was played out and does not take part in redemption. Barth contends that such a view is the legacy of two intellectual developments: Bultmann's demythologization of the New Testament and his existential interpretation, and Kant's view of the mechanical concept of nature, which assumes that nature is governed by general laws and that only the realm of spirit is governed by freedom.

Some years ago, J. B. Phillips made the case that we often considered our God to be too small. The same might be said about our Christ. Popular studies on the historical Jesus have made Christ even smaller, to the point of inconsequence. They have classified Jesus variously as a political revolutionary, a messianic schemer, a Galilean charismatic holy man, a wandering peasant, or a countercultural crusader. The Jesus of history usually comes out looking remarkably like the theological image of the historians. They leave little room for Christ's divinity, let alone his universal rule.

---

81. *The Corpus Hermeticum* 7.2b, in Walter Scott, ed., *Hermetica* (Oxford: Clarendon: 1924), 1:173.

82. Markus Barth, "Christ and All Things," *Paul and Paulinism: Essays in Honor of C. K. Barrett*, ed. M. D. Hooker and S. G. Wilson (London: SPCK, 1982), 160.

Such views deviate significantly from Paul's. For him, Christ was far more than a Jewish reformer. He is Lord over all creation (see Rom. 8:37–39; 1 Cor. 8:5–6; Phil. 2:10), who bore the fissure between God and creation in himself and united the whole universe. We cannot reduce him to simply a Mediterranean peasant who went about doing good and spouting pithy maxims without gutting the historic Christian confession that has sustained the church for centuries. Paul's poem checks the extreme view that would understand Christ's significance only in human terms while neglecting his divine nature and universal significance.

This hymn affirms that there is no sphere in creation over which Christ is not sovereign. Conjectures about intelligent life on other planets in this vast universe have escalated. The possible evidence of microbial traces in a "spud-sized meteorite" that smacked into the Antarctic and is purported to be from Mars feeds the speculation. If intelligent life exists elsewhere, they will not know Christ as Jesus of Nazareth; but Christian theology insists that they will know him as Lord. In raising this question, C. S. Lewis cited Alice Meynell's poem, "Christ and the Universe":

> . . . in the eternities
> Doubtless we shall compare together, hear
> a million alien Gospels, in what guise
> He trod the Pleiades, the Lyre, the Bear.[83]

Lewis questioned the word "doubtless," but the point is well taken. Nothing falls outside the orbit of Christ's rule. Such a Christology has ethical implications. If Christ reigns over all things and reconciles all things, then every aspect of our lives should come under his rule.

HUMANS STILL ASK if there is a God and if this world has any purpose. Paul assumes in Romans 1:19–20 that humans may learn of God from the work of creation, but the key for understanding who God is and all that God has done, is doing, and will do is found in Christ.

Christology, cosmology, and praiseology. Perhaps the best way to try to capture the mystery of creation, incarnation, and redemption is in the poetry of our hymns. This poem shimmers in the exultant celebration of Christ's creative and redemptive work. It praises who he is, what he has done, and what he will do. It forms the basis of Paul's intercession and instruction in the letter, which is filled with exhortations to be thankful.

---

83. C. S. Lewis, "Religion and Rocketry," in *The World's Last Night* (New York: Harcourt, Brace, 1960), 86.

Unfortunately, we have become less skillful singers of praise to God and Christ and may have even forgotten how to speak the language of adoration. Those who have lost an immediate sense of God's presence and glory tend to turn God into an object of study and the subject of theories instead of praise and adoration. Schweizer argues that "God is not an object that we could take in our hands in order to analyze it and describe it exactly. God is always God in action, and the life and death and resurrection of Jesus specifies this as action of love."[84] This love in action for us and all the world should evoke our amazement, our awe, and our praise.

Miller writes that "doxology celebrates human impossibilities that became God's possibilities."

> In a world that assumes the *status* is *quo*, that things have to be the way they are and that we must not assume too much about improving them, the doxologies of God's people are fundamental indicators that wonders have not ceased, that possibilities not yet dreamt of will happen, and that hope is an authentic stance.[85]

Being able to voice such praise to Christ is a sign of a secure and deeply rooted faith. We exult because we know that we do not live in a God-indifferent world. We also exult because we know that we have nothing to fear. God is with us through Christ, and God will deliver us in Christ. We need to cultivate more the spirit of praise we see in the psalmists (Ps. 8; 19; 33; 104) and in the New Testament's poetic praise that glorifies Christ.

The supremacy of Christ. Although human nature has not changed, the modern world differs vastly from Paul's world. Some today may wonder whether the Jesus who walked the dusty roads of Palestine years ago has any relevance for a modern world filled with the technological wonders of computers, instantaneous communication, nuclear power, and space stations. One boy asked in Sunday school, "If Jesus came back today, would he be able to understand computers?" This lad recognized that the world he knew was totally different from the world Jesus knew, but his question expressed a hidden fear that Jesus might be overwhelmed and lost in this modern age. He wanted assurance that Jesus could make a difference in such a world as today—that he is Lord over all this too.

Stewart's comments are apropos:

> This age tends to be more aware of the achievements of man than of the Word of God by which all achievements are judged; and more

---

84. Eduard Schweizer, "Christ in the Letter to the Colossians," *RevExp* 70 (1973): 457.
85. Patrick D. Miller, Jr., "In Praise and Thanksgiving," *TToday* 45 (1988): 186.

intimidated by the pressure of inexorable forces than emboldened by the exhilaration of the gospel.[86]

When we are so impressed with our own achievements and scientific genius, which can bring the tremendous forces of nature to heel and unleash them as well, Christ may indeed seem irrelevant. He can be easily dismissed as a fading relic of past religious piety, who has nothing to offer for the unprecedented issues facing us today. What does Christ have to say to a world in which humans have the power to clone animals and alter the genetic makeup of plants and animals? Stewart recognizes that Colossians answers these questions theologically and ethically. The letter affirms that only in Christ can we ever unveil the mystery of God's purpose in our world. It also affirms that Christ is "the cohesive force of penetrating and supporting all creation."[87]

The letter also has an ethical thrust. Paul insists that "life will ultimately work only one way—God's way made manifest in the humanity of Jesus once and for all."[88] If we ignore that way or spurn it, we will face the same fate as the builders of the tower of Babel, who exalted themselves over their Creator. The only way we can ever make sense of life and find our own way in it is to recognize that Christ is the converging point of the transcendent God's activity in the arena of human history. He is the interpretive key for understanding the meaning of creation, the purpose of life, and its goal (John 14:6).

Scientists continue their search for the "holy grail" of science, the "theory of everything," the simple set of laws that explains every complex detail of our universe. This poem professes that, in a way, Christ is the theological "theory of everything." He is the key who unlocks the meaning and purpose of the universe. But he is not a set of physics laws; he is a person, who has shown his love for us by giving his life. Wink writes that this passage gives the principle uniting the universe "a heart," a "purpose," and a "face."[89] Knowledge of him is also not confined to an elite circle of scientific geniuses. God did not wait for the advent of the scientific method to make known to humans his purposes and love. They have been made known through the cross of Christ and through his church, in which he reigns as head.

The hymn affirms that all things "hold together" in Christ, and this fact justifies our own attempts to bring order to the lives of individuals and to society as a whole. The hymn affirms that God will reconcile all things through Christ, and this fact blesses all our efforts to bring reconciliation to others.

---

86. Stewart, "A First-Century Heresy and Its Modern Counterpart," 421.

87. Ibid.

88. Ibid.

89. Walter Wink, "The Hymn of the Cosmic Christ," in *The Conversation Continues: Studies in Paul and John*, ed. R. T. Fortna and B. R. Gaventa (Nashville: Abingdon, 1990), 242.

We identify ourselves with what God is doing in the world through Christ when we seek to become peacemakers. The hymn affirms that good will triumph over evil. When we give our lives to Christ, no matter what the cost, we know that we will triumph with him.

Does this world have any purpose? Like toddlers entering preschool and learning to cope with the rude awakening that they are not the center of the universe, we humans are learning that our home, earth, is not the center of created reality. We now know that our earth is a tiny planet in a minor solar system on the outskirts of a modest galaxy among billions of galaxies. Some have wrongly inferred from the earth's physical insignificance that it must also be spiritually insignificant. How could a God care about what happens on such a minor planet in such a vast universe? Many have despaired that the more we have learned and theorized from scientific discoveries about our universe, the more meaningless it seems to be.

Scientists today describe the beginning of our universe as a "Big Bang," in which the cosmos exploded in a blind scatter of inanimate lumps. Many accept on faith that life arose from an unsupervised, impersonal, unpredictable, and natural process of ordinary chemistry and physics on our planet, which coincidentally happened to possess the appropriate conditions. Some scientists, who claim to have cracked part of the cosmic code, attribute the advent of humans to the complex outcome of chance mutations. But even those who forcefully argue for such a view must continually remind themselves not to be fooled by any evidence to the contrary. Francis Crick, for example, admits, "Biologists must constantly keep in mind that what they see is not designed, but rather evolved."[90]

Apart from any religious heritage that might influence people today, the internal evidence that this universe has any divine purpose is at best ambiguous. The more we learn, the less we see some divine pattern. Some have removed God completely from creation and live as if the only reality that matters is what they experience and what can be explained in scientific terms. Others have relegated God's role to taking care of whatever afterlife there might be. The laws of nature have taken God's place as the ruler of the world. Because science describes and analyzes these forces, people look more often to it for the answers to life. Science has become the sacral way of knowing and has replaced revelation as the final answer. Physicists and geneticists have become the new high priests of our knowledge. The answer they give is that we live in a mathematical universe captive to the meaningless dance of atoms and the chance alignment of DNA. Survival belongs to the fittest

---

90. Francis Crick, *What Mad Pursuit* (New York: Basic Books, 1988), 138. I am grateful to C. Ben Mitchell for this reference.

in a nonmoral, aspiritual struggle, which sanctions cruelty and ignores the weak.

Combined with this sense that life is only a fortuitous concourse of atoms is a fear that our world is a dangerous place. The mood of many today parallels the despair in Paul's time. Many felt forsaken by God, although they had forsaken God first. The local gods seemed totally impotent before the might of Rome and seemed lost in Rome's vast and growing empire. How could such people stem the tide of chaos that they believed was always threatening to engulf the world? The supreme gods who might have power to intercede were as far away as the emperor and just as indifferent to the fates of individuals. This sense of meaninglessness was frequently expressed in cosmic terms, but there remained a longing for salvation that would bring harmony to the world and deliverance from the collapse to come.

Today we may not fear the same things or express our fears in the same way, but most still believe that we live in a threatening world. Some forego any hope; others look for some kind of security to protect themselves. The ancient anxiety that the elements would disintegrate and tear everything into chaos parallels the modern fear of a nuclear holocaust or an asteroid striking the earth and blowing things to bits. Our anxiety is increased by the speed in which news of disasters around the corner and around the world appears instantaneously before our eyes—terrorist bombings, serial killings, drive-by shootings, church burnings, workplace massacres, gang wars, floods, tornadoes, hurricanes, earthquakes, and drought. This news reinforces the impression that the world is dark and dangerous. Random violence reinforces the belief that everything in the world is aimless. It becomes harder to believe that this creation, which seems to be going so sour, can be redeemed by its Creator and Sustainer, and easier to believe that no such Creator and Sustainer exists. To some it may seem that randomness rules, not Christ.

One wonders if we will ever put the "meta" back in physics. But the scientific search to know everything will reach a dead end. Jastrow, an agnostic astronomer, confesses as much in describing a scientist's scaling the mountains of ignorance and now climbing the highest peak—the beginning of time. "As he pulls himself over the final rock, he is greeted by a band of theologians who have been sitting there for centuries."[91] Ferguson explains the irony: It is not that the theologians had it all explained for a long time but that they have been saying for centuries that "we are dealing with a mystery human beings will *never* be able to explain, and now the scientists, by dint

---

91. Robert Jastrow, *God and the Astronomers* (London: W. W. Norton, 1978; repr. 1992), 107; cited by Ferguson, *The Fire in the Equations*, 97.

of hard labour trying to find that explanation, have to their chagrin arrived at the same conclusion."[92]

G. K. Chesterton admitted as much about his own search for the obvious:

> I am the man who with utmost daring discovered what had been discovered before. ... I freely confess all the idiotic ambitions of the end of the nineteenth century. I did, like all other solemn little boys, try to be in advance of the age. Like them I tried to be some ten minutes in advance of the truth. And I found that I was eighteen hundred years behind it.[93]

Knowledge can become error and blindness if it is not in Christ.

Christians are sustained in all this by their faith that God's gracious purposes for this world are being worked out and will be worked out. A gracious and loving God will determine our destiny, not capricious and fluky chance. Paul affirms for us that the world is not a purposeless accident in the chemistry lab of the universe. But he also makes clear that we cannot understand God, creation, or God's purpose for creation apart from Christ. If creation has been created by Christ and exists for Christ, then it is never meaningless. If we belong to Christ, then it means that we too have a place in the cosmic story. History is not just one thing after another; it has a purpose and is moving somewhere. Proof of this will never show up in a laboratory experiment, in pictures from the space telescopes, or in atomic microscopes.

We see through a glass darkly (cf. 1 Cor. 13:12), but science is an even darker glass for finding the meaning to life. It has unlocked many mysteries of life, but it can never unlock *the* mystery of life. Science can observe, describe, and analyze what is already there; but it cannot give answers to the question why. C. S. Lewis wrote, *"In the whole history of the universe the laws of Nature have never produced a single event.* They are the pattern to which every event must conform, provided only that it can be induced to happen." A billiard ball hitting another billiard ball follows the laws of physics, but those laws did not set the ball in motion; someone with a cue did. "The laws are the pattern to which events conform: the source of the events must be sought elsewhere."[94] In other words, the meaning of the universe can only be found outside of creation. Christians can have some understanding of its purposes only because of their knowledge in Christ, who is beyond creation yet within it.

Christians need to make clear for our turn-of-the-century world with its technological wizardry and terrors, its great economic prosperity and

---

92. Ferguson, *The Fire in the Equations*, 97.

93. Gilbert K. Chesterton, *Orthodoxy* (New York/London: John Lane, 1909), 18.

94. C. S. Lewis, "The Laws of Nature," in *Undeceptions: Essays on Theology and Ethics*, ed. Walter Hooper (London: Geoffrey Bles, 1971), 53–54.

economic despair, that our universe is not a godless and impersonal gaming house. Jesus Christ is its center, its origin, and its destiny.[95] The "resurrection victory of God in Christ" is grounded "in the very fabric of the cosmos."[96] In spite of all appearances to the contrary, God still has plans for this shadowy, hellish earth, suffocated by hatred and violence, and he will accomplish the glorious purposes intended from the beginning. We are meant to be here, and God has not left this world to the caprice of impersonal forces.

The wrong concept of creation leads to the wrong view of humanity, sin, and salvation. Many moderns may feel less acutely some kind of cosmic defect than they do some defect in their own lives. Things may be going extremely well for them in their careers and their families, but they still sense that something is missing. In the movie "Love and Death," two characters discuss their emptiness.

> Boris: I feel a void at the center of my being.
> Friend: What kind of void?
> Boris: An empty void. I felt a full void a month ago, but it was just something I ate.[97]

Many feel this kind of void because they have no real relationship with the One who created them. They try to fill that emptiness with anything that promises fulfillment and to drown out the hiss of the vacuum that sucks all meaning from their lives with the clatter of aimless pursuits.

I have heard Fred Craddock use the conch shell as an illustration of our need for God. When you hold the shell up to your ear, it will always make the sound of the ocean until it is returned to the ocean. We too will always have that empty ring of a raging torrent within us until we return to God. As the psalmist declares, "As the deer pants for streams of water, so my soul pants for you, O God" (Ps. 42:1). Paul rejoices that God is not some absentee landlord but as near as the confession on our lips (Rom. 10:6–13).

He has the whole world in his hands. Christians may sing the song "He Has the Whole World in His Hands" heartily, but they may not believe it in their hearts. That is because we are inclined to emphasize only Christ's work in redemption and think of salvation too individualistically—that it involves only me and my Lord. Another hymn sung heartily contains the line, "You ask me how I know he lives? He lives within in my heart." That may be true,

95. Stockhausen, *Letters in the Pauline Tradition*, 61.
96. Wink, "The Hymn of the Cosmic Christ," 242.
97. Cited by Gary Commins, "Woody Allen's Theological Imagination," *TToday* 44 (1987): 236.

but we cannot reduce Christ's reign to the confines of our own little existence as our personal spiritual director. Stewart writes, "You cannot have Christ in the heart and keep him out of the universe."[98] God's salvation is universal in scope. God began with all creation and will end with all creation. Christ reigns supreme over all; the whole universe is held in his loving hand.

If Christ is Lord over all creation, then Christ is also Lord over every aspect of human life.[99] This includes our social world, our Christian community, and our physical environment. Our forgiveness by God is part of God's purpose for the whole cosmos to reconcile all creation to himself. God does not restrict this reconciliation to one segment of creation—humans. The whole creation groans and longs for the revealing of the sons of God (Rom. 8:15–29), when the world will be brought back to its "divinely created and determined order."[100]

This redemption has ecological significance, and Christians are now becoming more aware of the need to become involved and in the forefront of such issues. The native American proverb that we do not inherit the land from our ancestors but borrow it from our children rings true. God's word over Nineveh reveals a love for creation beyond just humans: "But Nineveh has more than a hundred and twenty thousand people who cannot tell their right hand from their left, and many cattle as well. Should I not be concerned about that great city?" (Jonah 4:11).

In *The Brothers Karamazov*, Father Zosima says:

> Brothers . . . love all creation, the whole and every grain of sand in it. Love every leaf, every ray of God's light. Love the animals, love the plants, love everything. If you love everything you will perceive the divine mystery in things. Once you perceive it, you will begin to comprehend it better every day. And you will come at last to love the whole world with an all-embracing love. Love the animals: God has given them the rudiments of thought and joy untroubled. Do not trouble it, don't harass them, don't deprive them of their happiness, don't work against God's intent. Man, do not pride yourself on superiority to the animals; they are without sin, and you with your greatness, defile the earth by your appearance on it, and leave traces of your foulness after you—alas, it is true of every one of us.[101]

---

98. Stewart, "First-Century Heresy," 420.

99. Wall, *Colossians and Philemon*, 64–65.

100. O'Brien, *Colossians and Philemon*, 56.

101. Fyodor Dostoevsky, *The Brothers Karamazov* (London: William Heinemann, 1912), 332.

God does not intend for us to escape, to rape, or to subdue creation as if it were an enemy. All creation is destined also to be reconciled in Christ, and we must treat it so.

Victory in the cross. The first half of the poem asserts that Christ is sovereign over all creation as the one in whom and for whom all things were created. The second half of the poem explains how Christ exercises his sovereignty by reconciling the world through shedding his blood on a cross. Pailin contrasts how children might understand sovereignty from observing them playing "king of the castle" on a mound of sand on a beach.

> One child stands on top of the castle and taunts the others by proclaiming, "I'm king of the castle." . . . Others then attempt to dethrone the king by scrambling on to the castle and supplanting the incumbent. The result is a melée in which there is much shoving and pushing during which most find that their reign at the top is precarious and brief. In the end, the game has to stop because the castle has been destroyed by the assaults upon it.[102]

The game shows what children assume it means to reign supreme, and it also provides a parable for our world. The struggle for ascendancy among the powers and individuals results in ruin. It contrasts dramatically with what we see in Christ and his cross. Christ wins his victory and is proclaimed king when he is lifted up on a cross.

Bonhoeffer says that God lets himself be pushed out of the world onto the cross. He is weak and powerless in the world, and that is precisely the way, the only way, in which he is with us and helps us. It gives us a glimpse of a divine plan so vast in scale that we can barely fathom it. It reveals the means to accomplish it, which is scandalous and foolish to the human mind. Part of the great mystery is that the Agent of creation and its Sustainer can be met in the humble and tiny group of Colossian Christians who form his body. This mystery is proclaimed by one who takes the role of a humble table servant and who is chained in prison and is afflicted with suffering. Paul understands that victory is won through suffering and giving life, not taking it.

For the beauty of the earth. In her review of three books by parents trying to deal with the tragic circumstances and excruciating pain of losing a child, Travis notes a common thread in the authors' attempts to make sense of things. Trying to answer why such calamities occur, they assume that God either does not exist or is "an accomplice to murder." The authors do not find

---

102. David A. Pailin, "On the Significance of the Sovereignty of God," *TToday* 53 (1996): 35.

a community or a religious or philosophic framework to help them make sense of things and to make the deaths more endurable. Rather, the antidote to their despair comes from "the reassurances of nature." One writer is heartened by the "golden flower poking up through the ankle-deep snow." Another "looks out over the hills into the sky," thinking maybe his daughter is out there somewhere. A third sees that "the light behind the trees was spring light." Travis concludes her review, "Each book ends with its author lost and alone in thoughts of his daughter, each man comforted by nature—but not by another human being."[103]

Humans can detect something of God in nature (Acts 17:24–29), but they consistently have perverted what they learn by turning it into idolatry (Rom. 1:21–23). Without doubt, nature is filled with marvelous wonders, beautiful to behold. Everyone can probably think of some garden spot where the beauty of the earth radiates God's glory. For me, it is the Rocky Mountains. The snow-capped peaks glisten; the air is crisp and the sky clear; the wild flowers bloom gloriously in meadows where elk and deer graze. The wind whistles through the pines, sometimes drowning out the chatter of squirrels and chipmunks. Coyotes howl regularly; a mother bear and her cubs occasionally make midnight visits. Mountain lions and bobcats are there even though they never make their presence known.

But I have also seen that same sky filled with smoke from forest fires. Elk have been shot by hunters; deer have been chased and lacerated by predators. My own dog has caught and killed chipmunks only to wonder what to do with the carcass; her instinct told her to chase and kill, but for no purpose. Landslides have buried campers under tons of rock. Nature may be beautiful; but it is also cold and impervious, offering little comfort in times of mourning. God's evidence in nature is at best ambiguous; God can only be fully known through Christ.

Because creation is fallen, we can know God fully only through the process of redemption. We may be able to see God's glory in nature, but we can also see its fallenness. Nature is not God. C. S. Lewis wrote, "Nature never taught me that there exists a God of glory and of infinite majesty. I had to learn that in other ways. But nature gave the word *glory* a meaning for me."[104]

Nature may provide us with an image of glory, but it does not provide "a direct path" that leads to an increasing knowledge of God.

> The path peters out almost at once. Terrors and mysteries, the whole depth of God's counsels and the whole tangle of the history of the universe, choke it. We can't get through; not that way. We must make a

103. Carol Travis, "After Great Pain," *New York Times Book Review* (May 12, 1996), 20.
104. C. S. Lewis, *The Four Loves* (New York: Harcourt, Brace & World, 1960), 37.

detour—leave the hills and woods and go back to our studies, to church, to our Bibles, to our knees. Otherwise the love of nature is beginning to turn into a nature religion. And then, even if it does not lead us to Dark Gods, it will lead us to a great deal of nonsense.[105]

Christians do not seek comfort from an impersonal creation but from a personal Creator, who also creates a community. The living Lord, who is the source of new life, is experienced in the worship and activity of his living church.

Redemption in Christ alone. The language of estrangement in 1:21 implies a relationship gone seriously awry. Sin makes a shambles of created harmony and gives battle to God's restoration work. Above all, sin lays waste our critical relationship to God in an infinite variety of tangled ways. We are hostile in mind to God, malicious in our actions to everyone.

It is amazing how quickly sin can take control of something intended for good and corrupt it. The advent of computers have changed many lives for the better, but they have also been used by persons to spread more quickly and more widely malicious rumors, conspiracy theories, racial hatred, and deadly electronic viruses aimed at destroying data. Others have used them to entice young children with pornography or to recruit weak and wavering souls into mind-control cults. Attempts to control abuse with legislation are well-intended but never get to the root of the problem. Sin is not just what we do; it is who we are. Roberts, in his review of Plantinga's excellent book on sin, perceptively observes:

> The practices and ideas of modern psychologies have been so liberally and indiscriminately mixed with the Christian understanding of persons that many churches now propagate spiritualities quite alien to their own traditions. The practices and ideas of show business and marketing so dominate some congregations and public ministries that serious Christian ministry of word and sacrament looks fuddy-duddy, and a penitential, disciplined spirituality of grace looks morbid and certainly not cost-effective. Uniting both these polluters is the idea that all religion is (or ought to be) in service of *us*: It ought to make us wealthy, happy, amused, functional, creative, integrated, high in self-esteem.
>
> One of the first concepts to get neutralized in this mushy mixture is that of sin—the idea that we regularly corrupt ourselves and our fellow human beings, that we have vandalized the beautiful order that God has placed in creation, that we are not just victims of wrong-

---

105. Ibid., 38.

doing but, one and all, perpetrators of it, that we have offended God and cut ourselves off from his fellowship and blessings.[106]

The theme of human rebellion and sin is an unbroken scarlet thread that runs through the entire Bible to the foot of the cross. There it has been severed. Paul proclaims in the opening words of Colossians that Christ has brought hope to a desperate situation, rescue from darkness, and the forgiveness of sins, which separate us from God and from one another. Our response in faith to what Christ has done grounds us firmly in God's grand purpose to remake us into what we were intended to be, holy and blameless.

Paul's statement in 1:23 also contains an implicit warning, "if you continue in your faith." If we understand that through Christ we gain a new relationship with God, we also recognize that relationships can never remain static. They either grow or die. We enter a new relationship when we marry. Most who have experienced marriage understand that a successful marriage takes work. We may remain in the state of marriage, but the relationship can die if we do not work at it. The same is true of our relationship with God. If we neglect it or flirt with other attractions, we endanger it.

---

106. Robert C. Roberts, "Review of *Not the Way It's Supposed to Be: A Breviary of Sin* by Cornelius Plantinga, Jr." *Int* 50 (1996): 324.

Colossians 1:24–2:5

NOW I REJOICE in what was suffered for you, and I fill up in my flesh what is still lacking in regard to Christ's afflictions, for the sake of his body, which is the church. ²⁵I have become its servant by the commission God gave me to present to you the word of God in its fullness— ²⁶the mystery that has been kept hidden for ages and generations, but is now disclosed to the saints. ²⁷To them God has chosen to make known among the Gentiles the glorious riches of this mystery, which is Christ in you, the hope of glory.

²⁸We proclaim him, admonishing and teaching everyone with all wisdom, so that we may present everyone perfect in Christ. ²⁹To this end I labor, struggling with all his energy, which so powerfully works in me.

¹I want you to know how much I am struggling for you and for those at Laodicea, and for all who have not met me personally. ²My purpose is that they may be encouraged in heart and united in love, so that they may have the full riches of complete understanding, in order that they may know the mystery of God, namely, Christ, ³in whom are hidden all the treasures of wisdom and knowledge. ⁴I tell you this so that no one may deceive you by fine-sounding arguments. ⁵For though I am absent from you in body, I am present with you in spirit and delight to see how orderly you are and how firm your faith in Christ is.

Original Meaning

THIS SECTION, WHICH begins the body of the letter, fits Paul's pattern of updating the recipients of his letters with details about his personal missionary endeavors and concern for them after his thanksgiving section (see Rom. 1:11–15; 2 Cor. 1:8–2:4; Phil. 1:12–26; 1 Thess. 2:17–3:11). Not all of the recipients of this letter know Paul personally, so this section functions as a sort of introduction. He is not trying to establish his authority for what he is about to say by outlining his calling as an apostle of Christ.[1] His authority is a given. He simply expands on his

---

1. Jerry Sumney, "Those Who Pass Judgment: The Identity of the Opponents in Colossians," *Bib* 74 (1993): 368, among many, contends that Paul establishes his authority in preparation for his attack on the opponents.

last statement in 1:23, "of which I, Paul, have become a servant," and emphasizes the divine revelation of God's mystery, which he preaches.

Paul wants to restore the Colossians' confidence in their hope and to arm them theologically against the glib arguments of those who sell short the Christians' claims (2:4, 8) or vaunt their own superiority (2:16, 18).[2] All the treasures of wisdom and knowledge are to be found in Christ, and no beguiling pamphleteering by others should persuade them to look elsewhere. He also wants to show his care for them. Physically absent from them, he is present with them spiritually. He suffers for them (1:24); his commission is for them (1:25); and he struggles for them (2:1).

While Paul may not have intended any chiastic structure in 1:24–2:5, it may help us to follow his train of thought better by mapping it out in chiastic fashion.[3]

A The apostle's sufferings for them for the sake of Christ's body (1:24)
  B The apostle's commission: To present the word of God in its fullness (1:25a-c)
    C The apostle's message: The glorious riches of the mystery of Christ in you, the hope of glory (1:25d–27)
  B' Carrying out the apostle's commission: Proclaiming, admonishing, and teaching with all wisdom to present everyone perfect in Christ (1:28)
A' The apostle's toil and struggle empowered by Christ (1:29)
A The apostle's struggle for them even though many have not met him personally (2:1)
  B The apostle's commission: To encourage and bring complete understanding (2:2a)
    C The apostle's message: The mystery of God, namely, Christ (2:2b–3)
  B' The apostle's commission: To prevent them from being deceived by fine-sounding arguments (2:4)[4]
A' The apostle's presence with them in spirit though absent in the body (2:5)

---

2. Dunn, *The Epistles to the Colossians and to Philemon*, 114.

3. See F. Zeilinger, *Der Erstgeborene der Schöpfung. Untersuchungen zur Formalstruktur und Theologie des Kolosserbriefes* (Vienna: Herder, 1974), 44–46.

4. The phrase "I say this" in 2:4 does not start a new paragraph but refers to what has been said. The sentence anticipates the topic of the next section, 2:6–23, as 1:23 ("of which I, Paul, have become a servant") prepared for the next section, 1:24–2:5.

This chiastic outline helps us see how Paul focuses on his apostolic commission, and it sheds light on his conception of that commission. Key ideas emerge:

- His suffering (1:24), toil, and struggle (1:29; 2:1)
- His commission as God's servant (1:25, 28; 2:2, 4)
- The mystery he proclaims (1:26; 2:2)

The Apostle's Suffering and Struggle (1:24, 29; 2:1)

THE "NOW" OF our reconciliation (1:20, 22) and the revelation of the mystery—Christ's lordship over all creation (1:26)—has not changed the "now" of Paul's imprisonment. But the word "now" in 1:24 is probably logical, not temporal: Now Paul rejoices in his sufferings because of the truth he has outlined for them.[5] Paul links his suffering directly to his labors for Christ. The connection between his suffering and his calling from God is stated explicitly in Acts: "But the Lord said to Ananias, 'Go! This man is my chosen instrument to carry my name before the Gentiles and their kings and before the people of Israel. I will show him how much he must suffer for my name'" (Acts 9:15–16; see 1 Cor. 4:9–13; 2 Cor. 11:23–33; 13:4; Gal. 6:17).

But complex exegetical questions immediately confront us in trying to interpret Paul's statement on his suffering in 1:24. A literal translation helps reveal the problems: "Now I rejoice in the sufferings on your behalf and I fill up what is lacking in the afflictions of Christ in my flesh in behalf of his body, which is the church." Several questions need answers. How can Paul connect his sufferings to the afflictions of Christ? How can these sufferings be understood as for the sake of the Colossians, a church he did not found and may not have visited? How does Paul dare to think that he can suffer in behalf of others as Christ did? More specific questions concern the meaning of various words and expressions: What does the verb "fill up" mean? What does the phrase "Christ's afflictions" mean? What is the "lack" in Christ's afflictions that his sufferings fill up? We will deal with the specific issues of what the terms mean first and then come back to the larger questions.

Some argue that the preposition *anti* in the verb "fill up" (*antanapleroo*) makes it mean "instead of," so that Paul refers·to a "vicarious filling up." That is, he fills up the suffering that the Colossians, and all Gentiles, would have otherwise had to endure.[6] Others argue that the prefix signifies that the supply comes from an opposite quarter for the deficiency; the filling replaces the

---

5. Barth and Blanke, *Colossians*, 253, cites 1 Cor. 5:11; 12:20; 2 Cor. 7:9.
6. Moule, *Colossians and Philemon*, 78–79; O'Brien, *Colossians and Philemon*, 80.

lack.[7] But the prefix is not decisive for interpreting the meaning of the verse, and the verb *antanapleroo* is no different in meaning from *anapleroo*.[8] It means that Paul "fills up" the lack that Christ cannot. But this meaning leads to another question: What was lacking in the afflictions of Christ? The "still" in the NIV is not in the text and is misleading.

Interpreters have massaged the varied uses of the genitive case in *tou Christou* ("of Chist") to come to a satisfactory answer. Some interpret it as an objective genitive, sufferings "for the sake of Christ." Others describe it as a genitive of quality, sufferings like those of Christ. The question in both cases is how can it be said that Christ's sufferings are lacking. Lightfoot interprets it to mean the afflictions "which Christ endured." He makes a distinction between the sacrificial efficacy of his suffering and its exemplary impact. We do not share in his sufferings that reconciled us to God, but we do share in his repeated acts of self-denial that build up the church.[9] Lightfoot contends that those sufferings we endure for the building up of the church are incomplete. The problem with this view is that the New Testament does not differentiate the sufferings of Christ, and Paul does not suggest that his sufferings serve to build up the church. He simply says that he suffers for the sake of the body.

Other scholars have argued that the "afflictions of the Messiah" (Christ) is a technical term that refers to the messianic woes (or birth pains) of the last days that are antecedent to the new age. It refers to a measure of afflictions that had to be completed before Christ would return in glory.[10] The use of the definite article in the phrase "*the* afflictions of Christ" also might suggest something well known, such as the birth pains of the Messiah.[11] Jewish apocalyptic writings foretold disasters coming on the world as a prelude to the end time ushering in the new age.[12] If one assumes that the people of God had to

---

7. Lightfoot, *Saint Paul's Epistles to the Colossians and to Philemon*, 162–63; see Bruce, *The Epistles to the Colossians and to Philemon*, 215. W. R. G. Moir, "Colossians 1,24," *ExpTim* 42 (1930–31): 480, contends that the prefix means "one after another," "in quick succession."

8. Barth and Blanke, *Colossians*, 255–56.

9. Lightfoot, *Saint Paul's Epistles to the Colossians and to Philemon*, 163.

10. See, for example, Best, *One Body in Christ*, 132–36; R. J. Bauckham, "Colossians 1:24 Again: The Apocalyptic Motif," *EvQ* 47 (1975): 168–70.

11. Scholars argue that Paul's choice of words for "afflictions" (*thlipsis*) is not the normal word to describe the sufferings Jesus endured in his Passion (*pathemata*). But Heinrich Schlier, "θλίβω, θλίψις," *TDNT*, 3:143–44, and Wilhelm Michaelis, "πάσχω, κτλ," *TDNT*, 5:933, show that the two words are synonymous; see 2 Cor. 1:5. Andrew Perriman, "The Pattern of Christ's Sufferings: Colossians 1:24 and Philippians 3:10–11," *TynB* 42 (1991): 67, n. 15, also points out that the "sufferings have been transferred from Christ to Paul; he is referring to his sufferings, not Christ's."

12. See Dan. 7:21–22, 25–27; 12:1; Jubilees 23:13; 4 Ezra 13:16–19; 2 *Apocalypse of Baruch* 25–30; Mark 13:20; Rev. 7:14; 12:13–17. Later rabbinic texts refer to the woes of the Messiah (*Mekilta Vayassa* 5 to Exod. 16:25; b. *Šabb.* 118a; b. *Pesah.* 118a; b. *Sanh.* 97a).

endure a certain quota of suffering before God's purposes were complete (see Rev. 6:11; see 4 Ezra 4:33–43), then Paul rejoices because he believes his sufferings add to the grand total and speed up the coming of the end.

Several problems make this interpretation unlikely. The Colossians must infer all this from a presumed knowledge of Jewish apocalyptic expectation, because Paul does not say it explicitly and does not expand on end-time speculation elsewhere in the letter.[13] How would the Colossians have recognized that "the afflictions of the Messiah" was a technical term? No text contemporaneous or predating the New Testament specifically refers to the "the afflictions" or "the woes of the Messiah." Nowhere else in Colossians does "Christ" refer to "the Messiah," but it appears consistently as a reference to the historical person, Jesus Christ (see 2:11, 17; 3:15–16; 4:3; see also 1:1; 4:12).

In addition, Paul believes it is the lot of all Christians to suffer (1 Thess. 3:3; see Acts 14:22). He never argues that his suffering cuts down on the sum of suffering his fellow believers must endure. Paul tries to help the Corinthians recognize that he has been afflicted so that they might be comforted; but since they share the same sufferings, his afflictions do not help them escape it (2 Cor. 1:5–7). How could Paul have thought that his suffering, even as the apostle to the Gentiles, would make a significant dent in the universal tribulation of the end time?[14] If he did believe that his suffering was filling up a quota of affliction and hastening the dawning of the future glory, why would he not want as many Christians as possible to suffer to hasten it even more? When Paul talks about his suffering elsewhere, he does not relate it to some divinely set number of afflictions. Suffering comes with the territory of serving the gospel: "For we who are alive are always being given over to death for Jesus' sake, so that his life may be revealed in our mortal body" (2 Cor. 4:11; see 1 Cor. 4:9–13; 1 Thess. 2:1–2; see Mark 13:10–13).[15] Paul's expressed goal is not to complete a quota of suffering but to make the word of God fully known (Col. 1:25). His struggle to accomplish this goal brings

---

13. Unlike modern scholars, the Colossians did not have the advantage of having the relevant texts collected in a compendium of apocalyptic expectations and were probably not even familiar with Jesus' eschatological discourse recorded in the Gospels.

14. Perriman, "Program," 64–65. If this interpretation were correct, Paul would more likely say that he "fills up the measure of the afflictions of Christ" (see Rev. 6:11), not "fills up what is lacking."

15. Michaelis, "πάσχω," 933, n. 20, argues that "the idea of a foreordained amount of suffering which has yet to be met is present neither in Paul . . . nor elsewhere in the NT, nor is it suggested by contemporary assumptions." The New Testament contains references to a quota of wickedness (Matt. 23:32; 1 Thess. 2:16), a quota of Gentiles (Rom. 11:25), and a quota of martyrs (Rev. 6:11), but not a quota of sufferings.

suffering in its wake, and he understands that suffering "in some strange sense, as not his own, but Christ's."[16]

More ominously, this interpretation reopens the door to the false doctrine of a store of merits from which others can draw indulgences. It mistakenly implies that Paul's suffering gives others a bye from travail. Paul rejoices, instead, because he bears his share of suffering for the benefit of the church, which all those joined to Christ must bear.

A more reasonable case can be made for a literal translation that connects the phrase "in my flesh" with what immediately precedes: "I complete what is lacking *in the afflictions of Christ in my flesh.*" Houlden comments: "It is not Christ's sufferings which are being completed but Christ's sufferings-*in*-*Paul.*"[17] What is lacking or incomplete is Paul's own experience of Christ's afflictions, not something defective in Christ's suffering. This interpretation contends that Paul rejoices because what he now suffers on behalf of Christ's church allows him to pay off the balance of his own debt.

In my opinion, Paul's thought reflects his sense of unity with Christ, something he stresses in the letter. Christians have been buried with Christ, raised together with him, and made alive together with him (2:12–13, 20; 3:1, 3).[18] As Christ's body, the church has a corporate personality. If Christians share in dying and rising with Christ, they also share in his sufferings (Rom. 8:17; 2 Cor. 1:5–6; 4:10–12; Phil. 1:29; 3:10; see 1 Peter 4:13) and he with theirs.[19] Christ, therefore, continues to suffer in his body, the church (see Acts 9:4–5). This statement reflects Paul's deeply held conviction that he ministers as Christ's representative (2 Cor. 5:20). Christ lives in him (Gal. 2:20), and he serves in Christ's place as one who died with him and who lives for him (2 Cor. 5:14). He describes "our present sufferings" as sharing in Christ's sufferings (Rom. 8:17–18). It is no great jump, then, for him to label the suffering he endures on Christ's behalf and as a member of Christ's body as "the afflictions of Christ."

---

16. Wright, *Colossians and Philemon*, 86.

17. Houlden, *Paul's Letters from Prison*, 180. So also Edwyn C. Hoskyns and Noel Davey, *The Riddle of the New Testament* (London: Faber and Faber, 1958), 158; L. P. Trudinger, "Further Brief Note on Colossians 1:24," *EvQ* 45 (1973): 36–38; W. F. Flemington, "On the Interpretation of Colossians 1:24," in *Suffering and Martyrdom in the New Testament* (Cambridge: Cambridge Univ. Press, 1981), 84–90; Perriman, "Pattern," 62–79.

18. C. H. Dodd, *The Epistle to the Romans*, Moffat New Testament Commentary (New York: Harper & Row, 1932), 86, attests that Christ is the inclusive Representative of redeemed humanity. "That which Christ did and suffered on behalf of mankind is the experience of the people of God as concentrated in Him." Noted by Henry Gustafson, "The Afflictions of Christ: What Is Lacking?" *BibRes* 8 (1963): 29.

19. Paul also insists that if one member of the body suffers, all members suffer with it (1 Cor. 12:26).

But what is lacking in Christ's sufferings? The word "lack" (*hysterema*) appears nine times in the New Testament and is used to refer to "need" or "poverty" (Luke 21:4; 2 Cor. 8:14; 9:12; 11:9), "what is lacking" (1 Thess. 3:10), and "making up for a group's absence by representing them" (cf. 1 Cor. 16:17; Phil. 2:30). The latter usage fits our passage because the same root verb "fill up" (*anapleroo*) appears with the noun "lack." Paul tells the Corinthians that he rejoiced when Stephanas, Fortunatus, and Achaicus arrived, "because they have supplied what was lacking from you" (1 Cor. 16:17). He tells the Philippians that Epaphroditus risked his life "to make up what was lacking in your service to me" (Phil. 2:30; lit. trans.).

The modern reader might imagine that Paul was ungraciously complaining that the Philippians' service (their gift to Paul) was somehow deficient, and that Epaphroditus had to dip into his pockets to make up for a stingy offering. The NIV correctly alleviates the harshness of the literal translation. Paul is not complaining that they have failed to supply anything material. What is lacking is their personal presence with Paul, which Epaphroditus, as their representative, supplied. This same meaning applies in our text. What is lacking is Christ's bodily presence. Paul's physical suffering as a member of Christ's body represents Christ's continuing suffering for the world through his servants.

We can now give the answers to the questions. This conclusion explains how Paul connects his sufferings to the afflictions of Christ. He suffers as the representative of Christ, who is absent in body but present in spirit (see 2:5). "What is lacking" has nothing to do with some measure that must be filled but is an idiom for representing Christ bodily (see Phil. 1:20). Paul's suffering for the cause of Christ is emblematic of his ministry, which conforms "to the pattern of Christ's suffering that was worked out on the cross."[20] He presents himself as an example of the indwelling mystery of Christ's cross working itself out in a human life, and he makes the astonishing claim that he is suffering for them as Christ would suffer were he present bodily.

How can these sufferings be understood as "for the sake of" the Colossians? Paul's suffering, unlike Christ's death on the cross, does not save them from their sins. Instead, it is connected to his Gentile mission and comes as the byproduct of preaching the gospel to a hostile, pagan world. Paul was in prison because he proclaimed the gospel (see Eph. 3:1), and that struggle on their behalf (Col. 2:1) has brought the benefits of the gospel to them.[21]

---

20. Wright, *Colossians and Philemon*, 88. To use imagery from the Synoptic Gospels, Paul drinks the same cup and is baptized with the same baptism of suffering that engulfed Jesus (Mark 10:38–39).

21. Lightfoot, *Saint Paul's Epistles to the Colossians and to Philemon*, 171, points us in the right direction: "If St Paul had been content to preach an exclusive Gospel, he might have saved himself from more than half the troubles of his life."

These sufferings did not hinder the proclamation of the gospel but were part of furthering it (see Phil. 1:12–14). Paul also firmly believes in the solidarity of Christians with one another. He can be present with them in spirit (2:5) because both live in Christ. He also believes that when one member of the body suffers, all members suffer with it (1 Cor. 12:26); when one member is comforted, all members are comforted (2 Cor. 1:3–7). Both suffering and joy spread from one member to the whole.

Paul's Commission As Servant of the Church (1:25, 28; 2:2, 4)

PAUL AGAIN IDENTIFIES himself as a "servant" in 1:25 (see 1:23). He was a steward commissioned to carry out an assignment for his Master.[22] The stewards of estates in the ancient world were usually slaves. Paul therefore does not view his commission as an appointment to high office but as the exalted privilege and duty of bringing the gospel to the Gentiles. He does recognize it as a divine gift that brings divine power to fulfill it.[23] The same divine force that raised Jesus from the dead (2:12) gives him the stamina to carry out his mission, to endure its toil and strain, and to accept suffering joyfully (see 1:11; 1 Cor. 15:10; Phil. 2:12–13; 4:13).

Paul's mandate is "to present to you the word of God in its fullness" (lit., "unto you to fulfill the word of God"). This phrase may mean that Paul was charged with preaching the whole counsel of God (Acts 20:27), with finishing an assignment by making the word of God fully known (Acts 14:26; Rom. 15:19; see Col. 4:17), or with proclaiming the word of God and setting in motion the full effect of its power (2 Tim. 4:17). Paul believed his first responsibility—what God commissioned him to do—was to "proclaim" Christ as Lord (Col. 1:28). This central task is linked to a twofold emphasis on "admonishing and teaching."

The goal of the preaching, teaching, and admonishing is to "present everyone perfect in Christ" (see 1 Thess. 2:19–20). The Greek idea of *perfection* as something without a flaw or as some self-acquired moral virtue has influenced our understanding of the term. For most, then, perfection is some

---

22. "The commission God gave me" can refer to the office of administrator (steward, see Luke 16:1–3) or to the activity of administrating. See 1 Cor. 4:1–2; 9:17; Gal. 2:9 (the "grace" given to me); Eph. 3:2, 9. On the term *commission* see John Reumann, "OIKONO-MIA 'Covenant'—Terms for *Heilsgeschichte* in Early Christian Usage," *NovT* 3 (1959): 282–92; "OIKONOMIA—Terms in Paul in Comparison with Lucan *Heilsgeschichte*," *NTS* 13 (1966–67): 147–67.

23. In the Greek Paul uses cognates: "according to his energy that is energized in me in power." Caird, *Paul's Letters from Prison*, 187, comments: "The *toil* is Paul's, but *the energy* is Christ's. He is most himself when least reliant on his own resources."

impossible ideal that no one will ever attain. For the Hebrew, however, something was "perfect" if it fulfilled its purpose. Those who are wholehearted, sincere, and in right relationship to God are described as perfect in Scripture. Christ's work is "to present you holy in his sight, without blemish and free from accusation" (1:22). This holiness is connected to being "established and firm" in one's faith (1:23). To "present everyone perfect in Christ" (1:28) is similar. Paul does not offer a ten-step program that leads to some kind of spiritual quintessence. Whoever belongs to the exalted Christ and has unwavering trust that he is Lord over all other powers and forces will be "perfect in Christ."[24] Perfection can be found in nothing else, and the Colossians should not allow others to dampen their faith in this hope or to entice them with enchanting arguments to try another way.

"Everyone" is repeated three times in 1:28 (in the Greek text, only twice in the NIV) to emphasize the gospel's inclusiveness. As no part of the universe is left untouched by Christ's redemption, so the church's saving mission extends to all humankind. The gospel bursts through all ethnic discrimination, all sectarian exclusivism, and all intellectual hubris, denying entry into this perfection to no one who submits to Christ. The emphasis on "everyone" also means that no portion of Christian teaching is earmarked only for the initiated. "All the truth of God is for all the people of God."[25] Everyone, not just a charmed circle, is to become mature in Christ.

Christians were not to be picky about who could respond to God's grace and, in theory, could not exclude anyone who repented and confessed Jesus as Lord. This blanket acceptance of potential converts from any race or strata of society contrasts with the apparent exclusivism of their Jewish critics and may have evoked their derisive censure. The gospel teaching is not some arcane doctrine that is to be kept inviolable under the seal of secrecy, as was true of the mystery cults. It is like computer shareware, free to anyone who wants to download it. God commissions servants to broadcast it worldwide in the public squares and from the housetops.

Paul's purpose is to bring others to maturity in Christ so that they can fend off false teaching (2:2). (1) In this task, he struggles for them so that they may be encouraged and comforted in heart.[26] Discouragement may cause the Colossians to look for answers elsewhere, and Paul wants to assuage troubled minds and pump up deflated spirits.

(2) Paul wants to strengthen the bonds of love that hold them together. Conviction and understanding that is not leavened by love is barren and

---

24. Lohse, *Colossians and Philemon*, 78.

25. Bruce, *The Epistles to the Colossians and to Philemon*, 87.

26. The English words "encourage" and "comfort" are both used to translate the same verb in Greek, *parakaleo*; see Rom. 15:4–5; 2 Cor. 1:4, 6; 13:11; 1 Thess. 3:2; 4:18.

empty (see 1 Cor. 13:2). Love binds everything together in a perfect unity (Col. 3:14). Wright aptly comments: "Living in a loving and forgiving community will assist growth in understanding, and vice versa, as truth is confirmed in practice and practice enables truth to be seen in action and so to be fully grasped (cf. 1:9–11)."[27]

(3) Paul wants to lead the Colossians to "the full riches of complete understanding" of God's mystery. Such understanding is not simply an intellectual exercise, like comprehending a mathematical theorem. It involves the heart as well as the head. Paul has in mind the full assurance that understanding brings. A greater grasp of God's saving purposes in and through Christ will enable his readers better to fend off false teaching. If they are firmly rooted in understanding the rich mystery of their faith, the Colossians cannot be deceived or deluded by arguments no matter how persuasive or plausible.

The Mystery Kept Hidden for Ages and Generations (1:26; 2:2)

PAUL WANTS THE Colossians to know "the mystery of God" (2:2; cf. 1:26–27; 4:3).[28] In modern parlance, a "mystery" refers to a whodunit or some impenetrable puzzle. In the Colossians' pagan religious environment, the word "mystery" referred to information about initiatory rites and symbols—things that had to be kept hidden from the uninitiated. Paul's use of this word accords with Jewish usage. The mystery is something related to God's purposes, which can only be imparted by divine revelation. Humans cannot know or discover this mystery on their own, no matter how clever they might be. For ages no one, not even generations of faithful Jews, guessed the course that God was heading, although there were signposts along the way (Rom. 11:33–36). All that God intended to do was quite inconceivable to human minds. The mystery went against all human reason simply because it was above all human reason.

In the New Testament, the mystery refers to a secret once hidden but which has now been revealed and understood (Matt. 13:11, 17; Rom. 16:25–26). In fact, God calls apostles to make it known to all who have ears to hear

---

27. Wright, *Colossians and Philemon*, 94–95. The verb translated "united" (*symbibazo*) can also mean "taught" or "instructed" (see 1 Cor. 2:16). Beare, "The Epistle to the Colossians," 184, comments that "Paul instructs them *in love*, not as a spiritual dictator, but as a friend and partner (cf. 2 Cor. 1:24); and he trusts that they will receive his instruction in the spirit in which it is offered, not in resentment at his intervention."

28. The fifteen textual variants to 2:2 attest to the awkwardness of the last phrase, literally, "the mystery of God, of Christ," which has given rise to attempts to clarify it. The NIV correctly opts to render *Christou* as an epexegetic genitive, "the mystery of God, namely, Christ." See 1:27, where the mystery is explained with a relative clause, "which is Christ in you."

and eyes to see. Abraham received a preview of the gospel (Gal. 3:8), and the prophets caught glimpses of it (Eph. 2:17; Heb. 1:1; 1 Peter 1:10); but the apostles lived in the time of its fulfillment and were the first to unveil its glory fully.[29] Instead of guarding this secret from others, they proclaimed it to the entire world. God did not call Christians to control a monopoly on the truth but to share it with others.

The key element of the mystery that is stressed in this text is that the riches of God's glory are among the Gentiles—"Christ in you" (1:27). What made this so mysterious to many Jews was their conviction that the "adoption as sons ... the divine glory, the covenants, the receiving of the law ... and the promises" belonged to Israel and to Israel alone (Rom. 9:4). The "Christ" also belonged to the race of Israel (9:5), and most took for granted that his purpose in coming was to restore glory and privilege to Israel (see Acts 1:6). Christ among the Gentiles and for the Gentiles seriously undermined most Jewish expectations. It seemed at best to be a betrayal; if true, God was acting in contradiction to an agreed course of action. Gentiles were "separate from Christ, excluded from citizenship in Israel and foreigners to the covenants of the promise, without hope and without God in the world" (Eph. 2:12), and many presumed that God intended to leave things that way. When, therefore, Gentiles began to respond to the gospel, it outraged many Jews and created a serious identity crisis for many Jewish Christians. It also brought into question the integrity of God. Had God reneged on his promises to Israel and abandoned her for the Gentiles?[30]

The mystery revealed to Paul was that God intended to save the Gentiles *from the very beginning*. Christ "among the Gentiles" was not Plan B after the gospel had been rejected by Jews. Rather, it was God's eternal purpose. The letter to Ephesians develops this idea more fully: "His purpose was to create in himself one new man out of the two, thus making peace, and in this one body to reconcile both of them to God through the cross, by which he put to death their hostility" (Eph. 2:15b–16). Christ "among the Gentiles" and "the hope of glory" for them was startling news to many Jews. For Gentiles, it was the good news that should cause them to rejoice. Paul rejoices because God has chosen him to make this mystery known to Gentiles everywhere. Even though it has cost him an enormous toll in suffering, Paul rejoices to be an active participant in God's astounding plan for creation.

---

29. Radford, *The Epistles to the Colossians and to Philemon*, 203, helps us to understand why the mystery was hidden. "Human experiences and historical processes must first develop and converge upon the point in time and space at which the revelation would be appropriate and apprehensible, and from which it could travel over the whole range of civilization."

30. Paul grapples with this issue in Romans (esp. Rom. 9–11).

IN BRIDGING THE contexts we need to look at how misinterpretations of the phrase "filling up what is lacking in Christ's sufferings" have caused serious theological errors. We will then examine the biblical roots of the word "mystery," which carries a different connotation in our culture.

Filling up what is lacking in Christ's sufferings. Misinterpreting the difficult reference to "filling up what is lacking in regard to Christ's afflictions" can lead to problems. Some might mistakenly infer that Paul suggests that Christ's redeeming work was insufficient and needed supplementing. Nothing could be further from Paul's mind. (1) Such a view would lend credence to the arguments of the opposing "philosophy" that cast aspersions on the Christian hope and would undermine his whole argument in chapter 2. (2) Paul is not referring to Christ's redeeming work in this passage. When he does refer to it elsewhere, he points to his "blood," "cross," or "death," not to his afflictions. (3) Paul has just concluded praising Christ for reconciling all things to himself on the cross (1:20, 22). He understands this redemptive work to be finished, completed, perfected. Nothing remains to be done, and the suffering of Christ's followers does not put the finishing touches on the triumph of Calvary. (4) Paul does not believe that suffering has any atoning benefit for himself or for others. It does, however, "serve to increase Paul's living knowledge of Christ."[31]

The classic misinterpretation of this verse appeared in the church's doctrine of a treasury of merits. The papal bull *Unigenitus*, issued by Clement VI in 1343, drew from this text for support.[32] Such a mistaken view should be rejected out of hand. It contradicts Paul's view of the full achievement of Christ's death and misdirects worship from Christ to worthy saints.

Today, most people view pain and suffering as a curse. They resent it when it invades their lives and make every effort to keep it at bay. Inadvertently perhaps, the medical community has led us to believe that physical suffering can be alleviated if we spend enough money for the right treatment. But no one is immune to it. Many popular self-help authors wrestle with the question: Why does an all-powerful God allow good people to suffer? If we ask instead a question that is implied in the previous one, "Why did God not make a world where we can all enjoy endless pleasure?" the answer becomes more obvious.

Willimon speculates that "suffering is part of the price we pay for our humanity and our freedom."[33] This is all the more true in a fallen world where

---

31. Best, *One Body in Christ*, 134.

32. Noted by Beare, "The Epistle to the Colossians," 177.

33. William H. Willimon, *Sighing for Eden: Sin, Evil and the Christian Faith* (Nashville: Abingdon, 1985), 161.

sin runs amok. But the New Testament has no interest in answering questions about why people suffer, and the suffering that Paul speaks of in 1:24 is not the sort that indiscriminately overtakes any human. Paul offers no help for the questions we have about suffering. His focus is only on suffering that is willingly chosen because of an earnest commitment to preach the gospel. Whenever we choose to confront the many manifestations of evil in this world for the sake of the gospel as Paul did, persecution and suffering inevitably follow. Paul's devotion to his commission as Christ's servant, assigned with the task of carrying the gospel to the Gentiles, meant that he was willing to take on himself Christ's suffering. He did not try to explain it. Instead, he met it and rejoiced in it.

In today's world we expect people to rejoice in their accomplishments, their blessings, their peace, their health and wealth. Consequently, Paul's rejoicing over his suffering jolts a worldview that values comfort and ease as the highest good. We should note that Paul does not say that he rejoices in spite of his sufferings but *in them*. He does not rejoice after the trials are over but *during* them. The apostle obviously did not view his suffering as a problem or as something to be escaped, as we moderns might. Nor did it engender the resentment, hatred, despair, hopelessness, or cynicism that so often accompany travail. Paul accepted suffering as the call of God, and this call led him to look at things from a new perspective.

Paul recognized that Christ had reigned from a tree on Golgotha and that God raised him from death. After Jesus' death and resurrection by God's power, the suffering of his followers took on a new dimension of meaning. Paul understood Christian suffering as a divine necessity (1 Thess. 3:4) in the apocalyptic struggle between God and evil and as the continuation of the afflictions Christ himself suffered. He understood that his apostleship involved "work to be done and sufferings to be borne if the body of Christ is to be built up and the life of Christ to be diffused to new members."[34]

The mystery. Paul's use of the term *mystery* may cause confusion for modern readers who think in terms of a puzzle or something unintelligible. The term derives from Paul's Jewish tradition, but his usage differs from it in three significant ways. (1) In the Old Testament, the mystery is revealed to "the wise." By contrast, Paul says that it has been "disclosed to the saints." He may have in mind specific saints, such as the holy apostles (Eph. 3:2–6); but it is more likely that he refers to all believers (Eph. 3:9).

Paul declares in this letter that Gentiles have learned this mystery because God wanted to make it known to them (1:27). He understands

34. Barnabas Mary Ahern, "The Fellowship of His Sufferings (Phil 3,10): A Study of St. Paul's Doctrine on Christian Suffering," *CBQ* 22 (1960): 28.

himself to be God's appointed servant who was commissioned to publish this mystery for everyone. The mystery is, therefore, open to the public. Anyone, regardless of race, class, gender, intellect, past virtue, or age, may apprehend it.

This universal publication of the mystery makes Christianity disagreeable to anyone who wants to be part of an elite group with exclusive prerogatives—whether as a special, holy people that excludes Gentiles or as exceptional individuals with unique knowledge kept hidden from the vulgar herd. Ferguson writes, "To find that the experience of God reported by a rocket scientist or a saint may to a significant degree be consistent with the experience of God reported by an illiterate farm labourer, a punk rocker, or Miss America is jarring to our sense of the appropriateness of things."[35] Jarring as it may be to some, God's mystery is no arcane puzzle that only highbrow prodigies can crack. It has been revealed to everyone (see Matt. 11:25–27; 1 Cor. 1:18–2:5).

(2) The term *mystery* was used in Jewish apocalyptic tradition for God's secret plans for the last days.[36] Paul does not apply the term to the cryptic timing of end-time events but to a person, Christ (2:3).[37] His incarnation and death on the cross are the heart of the mystery. In Ephesians and Colossians, the mystery applies to God's saving purposes for the redemption of humankind in Christ, which includes the incorporation of Gentiles and Jewish believers together into the body of Christ. Paul defines this mystery as "Christ in [or among] you" in 1:27 (see Rom. 8:10; 2 Cor. 13:5; Gal. 4:19). The mystery, therefore, also involves the inclusion of Gentiles with Jews in salvation.

Ephesians develops this idea more fully.[38] Gentiles are not incorporated into the Messiah's community as temporary guests or as an auxiliary people. They are equals with Jewish believers. Paul appeals to this mystery in Romans

---

35. Kitty Ferguson, *The Fire in the Equations: Science, Religion, and the Search for God* (Grand Rapids: Eerdmans, 1994), 244.

36. C. C. Rowland, *The Open Heaven: A Study of Apocalyptic in Judaism and Early Christianity* (New York: Crossroad, 1982), 160–76. See, for example, Dan. 2:18, 19, 27, 28, 29, 30, 47; 4:9; 1QpHab 7:4–14; 4 Ezra 14:5; 2 *Apocalypse of Baruch* 81:4. Pokorný (*Colossians*, 102) comments: "In apocalypticism the revelation of the mystery of God does not occur until the eschatological cataclysm (1 Enoch 104:11–13). In this age the mysteries are only known to the wise (4 Ezra 14:26)." According to the New Testament, that eschatological cataclysm has already occurred in Christ, and the new age has broken into the present so that the mystery, hidden from eternity past, is now being proclaimed.

37. Wright, *Colossians and Philemon*, 91.

38. Paul refers to "hope" a third time in Col. 1:27 ("the hope of glory," see 1:5, 23). Here it clearly refers to the glorious destiny God plans for human beings despite their falling short of the glory of God (Rom. 3:23).

15:8–12 (citing Isa. 49:6) to encourage his readers to accept each other as Christ accepted them so that they will bring praise to God.[39]

(3) Paul affirms that in Christ "are hidden all ... treasures." The adjective "hidden" appears at the end of the sentence for emphasis: "in whom are all treasures, hidden." "In whom" echoes the poetic exaltation of Christ in 1:14, 16, 19. Paul believes that humans cannot know God or God's purposes apart from Christ. In Christ, however, "we have access to unlimited stores of truth, which are by their nature 'secret,' not the public property of the human race, but belonging to the deep things of God (1 Cor. 2:10)."[40] The deep things that lay bare God's heart are not hidden from view, but we cannot see them except though faith in Christ. Everything we can know about God and God's purposes are therefore summed up in Christ. Christ enlightens our eyes to see the riches of God's glory (Rom. 9:23; Eph. 1:18; 3:16; Phil. 4:19), wisdom (Rom. 11:33), and grace (Eph. 1:7; 2:7).

PAUL'S UNDERSTANDING OF his own personal suffering for Christ can help us in coming to grips with suffering in our world. His view of his calling can also help us improve our understanding of the church's purpose in the world.

Suffering with a purpose. Chamberlain contends that the greatest defect in the modern church is its cowardly retreat from the high demands of the Christian faith by seeking refuge in gentle sentiments. Our day is no different from Paul's in requiring heroism, daring, and sacrifice from Christians.[41] Paul's remarkable statement in 1:24 gives us an opportunity to rethink our view of suffering and our commitment to Christ.

(1) The Church is "the body of the crucified Messiah," something Wright contends has been forgotten by the modern church.[42] That body continues to suffer because reconciliation is "a costly business."[43] No one knew that better than Paul, who believed that all Christians must share in the suffering of their Lord. Menno Simons also understood this and wrote: "If the Head

---

39. We may take this for granted today, but for a first-century Jew, the glory of God's revelation stood out most clearly in the transformation of pagans. Caird, *Paul's Letters from Prison,* 186, comments: "If the indwelling Christ can transcend the deepest social, political, and religious divisions which split mankind, no limits can be set to his ultimate accomplishment."

40. Beare, "The Epistle to the Colossians," 186.

41. W. D. Chamberlain, *The Meaning of Repentance* (Philadelphia: Westminster, 1943), 104.

42. Wright, *Colossians and Philemon,* 89.

43. Caird, *Paul's Letters from Prison,* 183.

had to suffer such torture, anguish, misery, and pain, how shall his servants, children, and members expect peace and freedom as to their flesh?"[44] Because the servant is not greater than the Master and because the world has not changed in its hostility to God, Christians can expect no better treatment than their Lord received. Suffering thus belongs to the Christian calling.

Wright's comments again are apt, "Just as the Messiah was to be known by the path of suffering he freely chose—and is recognized in his risen body by the mark of the nails (Lk. 24:39; Jn. 20:20, 25, 27)—so his people are to be recognized by the sufferings they endure."[45] Christ does not promise us immunity from affliction; he promises only that he will be with us in it. Roston rings the bell with this comment:

> In the biblical model in either testament, to be chosen by God is not to be protected from suffering. It is a call to suffer and to be delivered as one passes through it. The election is for *struggling* with and for God, seen in the very etymology of the name Israel, "a limping people."[46]

This truth becomes clear in biblical narrative of the church's early history. As House puts it, "Acts has no purpose, no plot, no structure, and no history without suffering."[47] But all human efforts to thwart the spread of the gospel and to browbeat and terrify Christians backfire. Nothing impedes the gospel's advance, and the Christians' suffering only results in more and greater victories.

(2) Paul did not view his suffering as heroic or as entitling him to join the long line of God's righteous who have always suffered (see Matt. 5:11–12). He believed it bore the imprint of Jesus' suffering on the cross. He said that he always carries around in his body the death of Jesus and was always being given over to death for Jesus' sake (2 Cor. 4:10–11). How so? "In the sense that he reflects in his person the weakness and humility of Christ and so must endure the same—if not exactly in substance at least in principle—sort of ridicule and scorn, and even physical abuse, which Jesus experienced in his dying on the cross."[48] This allows him to become like Christ in his death (Phil. 3:10; cf. 2 Cor. 4:10–11). We know Jesus best when we share his deepest humiliation with him. It is the glass through which we see God most clearly.

---

44. Cited by Timothy George, *Theology of the Reformers* (Nashville: Broadman, 1988), 263.

45. Wright, *Colossians and Philemon*, 88.

46. Holmes Roston III, "Does Nature Need to Be Redeemed?" *Zygon* 29 (1994): 220.

47. Paul House, "Suffering and the Purpose of Acts," *JETS* 33 (1990): 321.

48. Timothy B. Savage, *Power Through Weakness: Paul's Understanding of the Christian Ministry in 2 Corinthians*, SNTSMS 86 (Cambridge: Cambridge Univ. Press, 1996), 175.

Those who think that Paul gladly drew the enemy's fire to keep the Colossians from facing persecution miss this point. Every disciple must take up the cross of Christ, and Paul did not think that he could somehow lighten the load for others. Nor did he want to. Paul bore his suffering joyfully because he knew that he belonged to Christ. His suffering for the gospel confirmed that. Being conformed to Jesus' death resulted in being conformed to the divine likeness and advancing from one level of glory to another (2 Cor. 3:18; 4:11). Paul's scars revealed more of the glory and power of God than his titles and offices, his public recognitions and diplomas.

(3) Paul did not turn in on himself in the midst of his sufferings. He believed that his life had a special purpose for others, and he viewed suffering as a privilege (cf. Acts 5:41). Paul did not suffer as a private discipline that would bring him some personal spiritual benefit. He looked at the benefits it brought to others. He suffered for them (Col. 1:24); he struggled for them (2:1) and for the sake of Christ's body, the church. In Ephesians 3:13, he asks his readers "not to be discouraged because of my sufferings for you, which are your glory" (see 2 Tim. 2:10). He did not expect the churches to serve him; he served the churches (Mark 10:45). He trusted that his suffering would make the faith of others stronger. His joy sprang from the deep well of this willingness to lose his life for others.

Carrigan describes this same spirit in Jean Donovan's response to friends pleading with her not to return to El Salvador, where she courted certain death.

I love life and living. Several times I have decided to leave. I almost could, except for the children, poor bruised victims of adult lunacy. Whose heart could be so staunch as to favor the reasonable thing in a sea of their tears and neediness? Not mine, dear friend. Not mine![49]

We live best when we put the purposes of God and the needs of others first, even if it means that it brings danger and distress to our own lives. We handle suffering in our lives best when, in the midst of it, we reach out to help others instead of focusing on our own private pain and anguish.

(4) Paul saw Christian suffering as part of the toppling of this present evil age. The suffering of Christians is not senseless but has meaning in the grand scheme of things. Those who afflict the apostle belong to the old order and its stunted, enfeebled powers. God's power, which works through him, far outstrips them. When the opposition is through with its scorn, torture, and instruments of death, it is through; but God is not. God's power,

49. Ana Carrigan, *Salvador Witness* (New York: Ballantine, 1984), 212, cited by James McGinnis, "Living the Vulnerability of Jesus," *Weavings* 8 (1993): 40.

which raised Christ from the dead and turned the discarded stone into the precious cornerstone, will raise us to reign with Christ.

(5) Paul knew that his suffering produced greater faith. Savage captures the spiral of faith:

> By faith Paul preaches the gospel, which in turn brings affliction, which then produces in him greater faith, which in turns creates greater boldness of speech, which then provokes additional affliction. For the minister of Christ, the pattern of believing–speaking–suffering is inescapable and perpetual.[50]

Opponents seek to crush this faith through oppression, but oppression backfires on them as it leads to still greater faith. Paul expresses this paradox in Romans 5:3–5: "We also rejoice in our sufferings, because we know that suffering produces perseverance; perseverance, character; and character, hope. And hope does not disappoint us." Understanding the origin of such devotion, courage, and confidence in the face of suffering is more important than understanding the origin of evil.

The identity and purpose of the church. Paul sketches out his understanding of his commission from God. He is a servant, and his concept of ministry provides a good guide for the identity and purpose of local and national church bodies. God has charged him:

- to present the word of God in its fullness and make known its glorious riches
- to proclaim Christ and admonish and teach in all wisdom so that believers are firm in their faith
- to create believers encouraged in heart, united in love, and full of understanding
- to reach out with good news to those whom some may deem unworthy or excluded.

As Paul served others with dedication and sacrifice, so churches today should take seriously their servant role in the world. Churches are not here to serve themselves or even simply to serve Christ. They are to serve *like* Christ as instruments of God's reconciliation.[51] Hanson writes:

> The church is not some curious or pitiable relic of the past seeking to justify itself either by appeal to an archaic golden age or by attempts to appear more progressive and radical than the latest protest movement, but is an agent of reconciliation and healing basing its identity

---

50. Savage, *Power Through Weakness*, 181.
51. Wall, *Colossians and Philemon*, 89.

on its sense of being present where God is present in the world, and for the same purpose.[52]

The church is to fulfill the same tasks that Paul saw were his. The task is not to spread the church's institutional umbrella but to spread the faith.

(1) *To present the word of God in its fullness and make known its glorious riches.* For Paul, "the word of God" refers to the good news of God's promises having been fulfilled in Jesus Christ (Rom. 9:6; 2 Cor. 2:17; 4:2; 2 Tim. 2:9). For us, the word of God has been canonized in the Scriptures. Too often, we read only selected portions of that Word, or we try to reshape it to fit our preconceptions rather than allow it to challenge and judge us. A preacher once titled his sermon cleverly, "This Is the Lord That the Day Hath Made." While we need to bring the world into the church, we must guard against bringing the pagan mindset of the world into the church. The Scripture provides our only weapon against the incursion of culturally based values. Rightly heard, it fends off the danger that we will mistake our false, selfish hopes for divine truth and recast the true Lord into a false one.

The proliferation of ersatz truth in our world today makes it all the more imperative that the church present the world with the truth revealed in Jesus Christ. A popular American science fiction television show intones that the truth is out there. Some wag has responded, "But the lies are in your head." Before we can beware of falsehood, we need to be aware of the truth. Unfortunately, too many Christians are underexposed to the Word of God. We boast that we live in an "information age," but all too many are woefully uninformed about the Bible's contents. When trouble floods their lives, they can call up to memory nothing from Scripture.

My wife is conducting research on families and faith development.[53] She shared with me her surprise that when she interviewed families of faith and asked what character or story from the Bible they would most readily identify with, many could not think of any. The explanation must be that they do not study Scripture and do not hear biblical truth and biblical stories preached with any regularity.

This fact was driven home to me when I visited a congregation on an Easter Sunday. I was greatly disappointed to hear a sermon that consisted only of long summaries of recent movie plots, which were then applied to a recap of the week's news. The Scripture was read but then completely ignored in the sermon. While movies and literature may help illustrate, support, and corroborate the Scripture, they can never be a substitute for it. They may help

---

52. Paul D. Hanson, "The Identity and Purpose of the Church," *TToday* 42 (1985): 342–52.

53. "Families and Faith Development," sponsored by the Lilly Endowment, Inc.

us gain insight into the human situation, but they do not bring us to God. Only the Word of God has the power and authority to do that and to change lives. Another pastor boasted in a national news magazine that he does not preach on old, stale Bible stories but on things like "Bosnia, peace, and justice." Apparently, he does not realize that the old Bible stories define our understanding of peace and justice. We learn how to act toward others from the way God acted toward us in salvation history.

Throughout history, countless persons have attested that a single line of the Bible has changed their lives, sustained them, or consoled them in trying times. Many have attested that the Scriptures not only addressed their fears, needs, and worries but set them face to face with God. The Bible challenges our reprehensible injustice, constant strife, and smug complacency. It also helps us realize a new purpose for our lives. Our task, then, is to present God's Word in such a way that others will see its hidden riches, which we discover more and more as we study. Armed with that Word written on our hearts, Christians will not be vulnerable to imitation truth. The neglect of Scripture for more current fascinations spells doom for the church.

Buttrick tells the story of a boy

> who heard of a hillside from whose rocks, seen from a distance, a massive shield had been carved—as though some giant had left it lying amid sloping meadows. The shield, he was told, was a place of vision and resolve; and he went to seek it. But no sooner had he crossed the valley than, looking back, he saw the shield clearly patterned on his own hillside. One of its quarters was the garden in which he played.[54]

We may be tempted to look elsewhere for words of eternal life, but we already have them in our Scripture. An unreflecting familiarity with it may make it seem like old hat. A casual neglect of it may make it seem inessential. Only presenting the Word of God in its fullness helps us plumb its great riches.

(2) *To proclaim Christ and admonish and teach in all wisdom so that believers are firm in their faith.* Paul links proclaiming Christ to a twofold emphasis on admonishing and teaching (1:28).[55] We understand the task of teaching, but admonishing may suggest an image of reproving wrongdoers. Paul does use the verb (*parakaleo*) with this disciplinary meaning (1 Cor. 4:14; 1 Thess. 5:14; 2 Thess. 3:15; see the noun form in Titus 3:10), but it can also mean "instructing" or "reminding." According to Acts 20:31, Paul spent three years "admonishing" the Ephesians. He did not spend that entire time upbraiding them,

54. George A. Buttrick, *The Parables of Jesus* (Grand Rapids: Baker, 1973), 253.
55. The issue of admonishing and teaching will resurface in 3:16 and will be dealt with again in the Contemporary Significance section there.

but instructing them (cf. Col. 3:16). Admonition therefore involves encouraging, instructing, and prompting, as well as reproving others when necessary. Note too that Paul did not believe that this task was his responsibility alone; it belonged to the entire community (see 3:16 again).

Roehlkepartain reports a number of unorthodox beliefs making inroads among members of mainline denomination churches. He notes that "one-third of adults believe 'that through meditation and self-discipline I come to know that all spiritual truth and wisdom is within me.' Nine percent believe in reincarnation and astrology. And 7 percent believe it is possible to communicate with the dead."[56] The task of teaching and admonishing remains urgent so that Christians have a firm grounding in their faith and its biblical foundations.

(3) *To create believers encouraged in heart, united in love, and full of understanding.* Most people want to experience growth, to feel appreciated and respected. They also want to feel a sense of community—that they belong. They want to develop deeper relationships that will break into the loneliness and isolation that our modern world has seemed to intensify. We are mistaken if we think that people are simply looking for friendly churches; they are looking for friends. They yearn to be connected to others who will give them encouragement and support.

Note how much Paul encourages the Colossians in this letter. He never berates them but tells them, "I am present with you [not watching over you] in spirit and delight to see how orderly you are and how firm your faith in Christ is" (2:5). Most people respond better to encouragement rather than to reproach. Paul provides a model of this in this letter. He publicly affirms the Colossians' strengths and praises them for it. He wants their faith to blossom even more under the rain of the opponents' harsh criticism. Rather than chastise them for error, he sets forth more clearly the truth to which they have given their lives.

The church should be a place of hope, good cheer, and encouragement, the place where others affirm the areas of growth in our lives and help us on the way to maturation, the place where we are fortified for daily battle in the midst of despair and hopelessness, and the place where we do the same for others. In Bunyan's *Pilgrim's Progress,* as the pilgrims cross the river in the final stage of their journey, Christian begins to sink amid terrible fears. His companion, Hopeful, does all he can to keep his head above water:

> Yea, sometimes he would be quite gone down, and then, ere a while, he would rise up again half dead. Hopeful also would endeavour to

---

56. Eugene C. Roehlkepartain, *The Teaching Church: Moving Christian Education to Center Stage* (Nashville: Abingdon, 1993), 45.

comfort him, saying, "Brother, I see the gate, and men standing by to receive us"; but Christian would answer, "It is you, it is you they wait for; you have been Hopeful ever since I knew you." "And so have you," said he to Christian. "Ah, brother," said he, "surely if I was right he would now arise to help me; but for my sins he hath brought me into the snare, and hath left me." Then said Hopeful, "My brother, you have quite forgot the text, where it is said of the wicked, 'There are no bands in their death, but their strength is firm. They are not in trouble as other men, neither are they plagued like other men.' Psalm 73:4, 5. These troubles and distresses that you go through in these waters are no sign that God hath forsaken you; but are sent to try you, whether you will call to mind that which heretofore you have received of his goodness, and live upon him in your distresses."

(4) *To reach out with good news to those whom some may deem unworthy or excluded.* Paul suffered as an apostle to the Gentiles. Most of his opposition came from Jews, who saw his gospel as dangerously undermining their privilege and special identity. But God never intended for the church to be a holy ghetto where "our kind of people" gather. His purpose has now been made crystal clear: The church is to be inclusive of all peoples, drawing in those with whom we may not have much in common and may not much like. We cannot draw limits on who is eligible for God's glory or who is not, and we may not make a test of fellowship what God does not make a condition of salvation.

Paul eventually died a martyr to this vision of God's grace, which swept aside venerable and long-cherished divisions to bring archenemies together in Christ. The church is to embody this reconciliation in its acceptance of all who name Christ as Savior, in its mission to reach every person, and in its teaching to make every person mature in Christ.

Colossians 2:6–15

SO THEN, JUST as you received Christ Jesus as Lord, continue to live in him, ⁷rooted and built up in him, strengthened in the faith as you were taught, and overflowing with thankfulness.

⁸See to it that no one takes you captive through hollow and deceptive philosophy, which depends on human tradition and the basic principles of this world rather than on Christ.

⁹For in Christ all the fullness of the Deity lives in bodily form, ¹⁰and you have been given fullness in Christ, who is the head over every power and authority. ¹¹In him you were also circumcised, in the putting off of the sinful nature, not with a circumcision done by the hands of men but with the circumcision done by Christ, ¹²having been buried with him in baptism and raised with him through your faith in the power of God, who raised him from the dead.

¹³When you were dead in your sins and in the uncircumcision of your sinful nature, God made you alive with Christ. He forgave us all our sins, ¹⁴having canceled the written code, with its regulations, that was against us and that stood opposed to us; he took it away, nailing it to the cross. ¹⁵And having disarmed the powers and authorities, he made a public spectacle of them, triumphing over them by the cross.

THE MIDDLE SECTION of the letter (2:6–4:6) is launched with a theme statement in 2:6–7.[1] Belief that does not have an impact on one's behavior is useless, and the theme statement connects faith to practice. On the faith side, the Colossians' have received Christ Jesus as Lord (lit., "Christ Jesus the Lord") and have been taught the faith. On the practice side, they need to continue to live in him and to be built up in him, becoming strengthened in their faith and overflowing with thankfulness. This theme statement is followed in 2:8 by the first specific warning against being deceived by a hollow and deceptive "philosophy" (cf. 2:4). Paul then estab-

---

1. Wright, *Colossians and Philemon*, 96–97; Dunn, *The Epistles to the Colossians and to Philemon*, 136. Each step in the letter's continuing argument begins with the inferential particle (*oun*): 2:6 ("so then"); 2:16 ("therefore"); 3:1 ("since"); 3:5 ("therefore"); 3:12 ("therefore").

lishes the all-sufficiency of Christ (2:9–15). His argument provides the theological underpinning for the direct rebuttal of the opponents in 2:16–23.

In 2:9–15 Paul affirms that salvation comes only through Christ, something emphasized by the repetition of the prepositional phrases "in him/Christ" (2:6, 7, 9, 10, 11, 15) and "with him/Christ" (2:12, 13).[2] All the fullness of Deity dwells in Christ, and in him believers have been given the fullness of salvation through his death and resurrection.[3] There is nothing we can do or need to do to achieve it for ourselves. No self-imposed discipline, solemn rites, or otherworldly visions will make us fuller members of the community of the saints (1:12), will deliver us more fully from their sins, or will more fully secure a better hope.

Consequently, we do not need to add religious exercises or observances as if such things were spiritual vitamin supplements that can correct some salvation deficiency. To do so betrays our union with Christ. On the cross, Christ has triumphed over everything that stands over against us—the damaging charges against us and the threatening powers and authorities. Christ's victory has defeated and disarmed them, and Christians need not fear, appease, or take any account of them at all.

Loyalty to Christ the Lord (2:6–7)

THE OPENING STATEMENT of this section affirms that the Colossians have "received Christ Jesus as Lord" and distinguishes them from their opponents.[4] They recognize that Jesus is *the* Lord, not a divine hero, or a lesser household god, or a member of a pantheon of lords. Since they are bound to him as Lord, they are also bound to be obedient to him. Jesus requires that their conduct be consistent with his lordship.[5] Being in Christ, therefore, transforms the way Christians live.[6] After warning them in 2:8, 16–23 against the entic-

---

2. The NIV translates the "in him" (*en auto*) in 2:15 as "by the cross" and gives "in him" as an alternative rendering. See below.

3. The foundation of Paul's argument, the Lordship of Christ and the theme of dying and rising with Christ in baptism, is picked up again in 2:20 and 3:1.

4. Wright, *Colossians and Philemon*, 49, comments are apropos: Christ is "no mere empty cipher: it is the Christ of 1:15–20, in whom is true maturity (1:28), who is himself 'the mystery of God' (2:2), God's eternal secret plan for creating and redeeming the world."

5. By contrast, the mystery cults were only concerned with ceremonial activities, not moral behavior.

6. The NIV translation, "continue to live," translates the Greek verb *peripateo* (lit., "walk"), which has to do with ethical conduct. The use of "continue" captures the force of the present tense in this imperative. Dunn, *The Epistles to the Colossians and to Philemon*, 140, contends that this phrase is "equivalent" to "walk in the Spirit" in Gal. 5:16. Against this interpretation, see Pokorný, *Colossians*, 111.

ing detours offered by opponents, which would divert them from their sole allegiance to Christ and mire them in spiritual quicksand, Paul returns in 3:1–4:6 to directions on how believers should live.

In 2:7, Paul lists four characteristics of what it means "to live in [the Lord]" (2:6), each expressed with a participle. The first participle ("rooted") appears in the perfect tense (expressing the continuing results of an action completed in the past); the next three ("built up," "strengthened," and "overflowing") are in the present tense. Paul attests that what believers have been taught (see 1:7) has effectively "rooted" them in the faith. The image in this word recalls Jeremiah's blessing on the one who trusts in the Lord and whose confidence is in him (Jer. 17:8):

> He will be like a tree planted by the water
>> that sends out its roots by the stream.
> It does not fear when heat comes;
>> its leaves are always green.
> It has no worries in a year of drought
>> and never fails to bear fruit.

The next characteristic mixes metaphors, moving from a plant being rooted to a building being constructed in him. The root as a plant's foundation perhaps inspired the merging of the two images (see 1 Cor. 3:9; Eph. 3:17). "Being built" implies that believers are still under construction and not yet a finished product.

The third characteristic, "strengthened in the faith," could mean that the Colossians are strengthened *by* their faith or *with respect to* their faith. The two options are not mutually exclusive. As we are strengthened in the faith, our faith strengthens us. These first three participles are in the passive voice, "implying that divine action is essential in Christian growth."[7] Paul's readers have not rooted themselves, built up themselves, or strengthened themselves; God has.

The fourth characteristic, "overflowing with thankfulness," is in the active voice and means that God's action in the lives of Christians should evoke overwhelming thanksgiving. As luxuriant green leaves are a sign of a healthy plant, profuse thanksgiving is "the unfailing mark of a healthy spiritual life."[8] Those who bubble over with gratitude for what God has already done are not easy prey to anxiety and doubt. They have no need or desire to look for fulfillment elsewhere and cannot be taken in by false promises or shaken by bigoted detractors.

---

7. Harris, *Colossians and Philemon*, 89.
8. Beare, "The Epistle to the Colossians," 189.

The Flawed "Philosophy" (2:8)

THE WARNING IN 2:8 provides the first direct clue in the letter that the Colossian church faces an outside danger.[9] Compared to Galatians, the polemic that follows is relatively mild. This constraint suggests that Paul does not despair that the Colossians are courting disaster as the Galatians were. They do, however, need to hear a word of caution about the dangers of being hijacked.

Paul describes the potential abductor as a "hollow and deceptive philosophy."[10] One should be cautious not to extend this repudiation of a specific vacuous "philosophy" to a rejection of philosophy in general. The term *philosophy* had a broader meaning in the ancient world than it does in ours. It was not limited to the speculative systems of thought familiar to us in Greek and Roman philosophy; it could also refer to all sorts of groups, tendencies, and points of view, including magical practices.[11] This broad meaning of the term and the fact that Paul describes the "philosophy" in terms of religious practices, such as judgments about eating and drinking and observing festivals and Sabbaths, makes the word "religion" a more suitable translation for us.

Paul draws several contrasts between the gospel and this "philosophy." The gospel is the word of truth (1:5–6); the "philosophy" is deception. Christ rescues and liberates hostages (1:13); the "philosophy" takes the gullible captive, makes them slaves of error, and yanks them back into the dominion of darkness (1:13).[12] One may think of the twisted plots in novels and movies

---

9. "See to it lest" (*blepete me*) implies that the Colossians have not succumbed. The use of the singular indefinite pronoun, "no one" (*tis*), does not mean that Paul has some ring leader in mind (contrast Gal. 1:7). It is truly indefinite.

10. Literally, the text reads "through philosophy and empty deceit"; the NIV correctly takes the second phrase as modifying "philosophy." See also the warning in 1 Tim. 6:20–21.

11. Lohse, *Colossians and Philemon*, 94. Günther Bornkamm, "The Heresy of the Colossians," in *Conflict at Colossae*, ed. Fred O Francis and Wayne A Meeks, 126, asserts, "For syncretistic thought it has long since ceased to designate rational learning, but has become equivalent to revealed doctrine and magic." In the introduction we argue that the "philosophy" Paul has in his sights is the Judaism of a rival synagogue in Colosse. Some Hellenistic Jewish writers presented Judaism to the Greco-Roman world as a "philosophy," as Lohse says, "to woo and attract the surrounding world around them" ("Pauline Theology in the Letter to the Colossians," *NTS* 15 [1969]: 211).

12. The picture is that of marauding slave traders carrying off their victims as booty (Caird, *Paul's Letters from Prison*, 189). Such imagery would send shivers up the spines of those in Paul's day who lived in fear of the possibility, although remote, of being abducted and sold into slavery. Today, people still fear being abducted and cruelly violated. The rare word *sylagogeo* ("take captive") occurs only here in the New Testament; and Wright, *Colossians and Philemon*, 100, proposes that Paul uses it because it "makes a contemptuous pun with the word synagogue." The noun *syla* was used for booty or plunder, but the verb does not appear in the LXX or in contemporary literature. Its rarity adds credence to the possibility that Paul resorts to a bitter wordplay to undermine the claims of a rival synagogue.

where the hero or heroine is captured by villains and then rescued only to fall again into their hands. The "philosophy" is defined further in 2:8 by three prepositional phrases with *kata* ("depends on"), but Paul has no intention of providing us with a full description of its features in this section. He only intends to stress the glories that the Colossians already possess in Christ so that they can see how much the "philosophy" falls short.

(1) The "philosophy . . . depends on human tradition." In Paul's world, ancient tradition insured the excellence and sanctity of knowledge. If it was old, then it was considered good and not to be lightly dismissed. Today, we have convinced ourselves that the newest development is better. New, we assume, means improved; consequently we are inclined to be interested in the latest thing. In the Hellenistic period, the ancient age of a religion authenticated it and made it deserving of honor because it had stood the test of time.

There is nothing inherently wrong with human tradition. Paul, however, discredits the "philosophy" as a tradition that derives from humans (see Mark 7:8) and contrasts it with divine revelation that the Colossians have received in Christ. In 2:6, Paul writes that they have "received Christ Jesus as Lord." Paul uses the verb "receive" (*paralambano*) in his letters as a technical term to refer to the transmission of teaching or tradition.[13] The contrast is clear: The Colossians did not receive a tradition created by humans but a person, the Lord Jesus, the regent and reconciler of all creation.

(2) The "philosophy . . . depends on . . . the elemental spirits of the world" ("the basic principles of the world," NIV). The term "elemental spirits of the world" (*ta stoicheia tou kosmou*) does not reflect some important feature of the opponents' teaching but derives from Paul's derisive appraisal of the "philosophy." This phrase meshes with the other pejorative descriptions used to discredit a "philosophy" that "kidnaps," is "empty and deceptive," and "depends on human tradition."[14] Just as the key word in the phrase "tradition of men" (NIV, "human tradition") is "of men," the key word in this phrase is "of the world."[15] Paul debunks the "philosophy" as belonging to the material sphere created by Christ but now alienated from God and in need of redemption and

---

13. 1 Cor. 11:23; 15:1, 3; Gal. 1:9, 12; Phil. 4:9; 1 Thess. 2:13; 4:1; 2 Thess. 3:6; see Mark 7:4.

14. Against Lohse, *Colossians and Philemon*, 99, who claims that "'elements of the universe' must have played a special role in the teaching of the 'philosophers.'"

15. Francis, "Christology," 206, 208, n. 43; see Arnold, *The Colossian Syncretism*, 190. In Gal. 4:3 and Col. 2:8, 20, the genitive *tou kosmou* ("of the world") qualifies the *stoicheia*. In Gal. 4:9 it is absent. *Stoicheia tou kosmou* is, therefore, not a technical term but Paul's characterization of the *stoicheia*. Note that if the South Galatia theory for Galatians is to be accepted, the term only occurs in Paul's letters to churches in interior Asia Minor in relative proximity to one another (Col. 2:8, 20; Gal. 4:3, 9).

reconciling. It belongs to the domain of flesh, sin, and death, where demonic powers still wield their influence.

Exactly what Paul meant by the phrase *ta stoicheia tou kosmou* is much debated. The noun *stoicheion* derives from the verb *stoicheo*, which means "to be in line" (see Phil. 3:16) and refers to the basic components that make up a whole, similar to the links in a chain. The noun appears in ancient literature to designate the letters of the alphabet, the foundation principles of a science or institution, the rudiments or initial basis for something, the physical components of the body (see 4 Macc. 12:13), and the physical elements of the world (earth, air, fire, water).[16] Does the phrase in 2:8, 20 refer to something elementary, as in teaching, or to something elemental, as in the foundational elements regulating the present world? Does it signify impersonal elemental substances or personal powers, such as star-spirits?

The NIV translation settles the matter for the reader by interpreting the phrase to mean elementary (impersonal) principles (see also NASB, JB). These could refer to the basic principles, the religious ABC's, common to all religion. The reference to a "philosophy" and to human tradition suggests some mode of instruction; and circumcision, calendrical observances, and distinctions about food (2:16) can fall under the category of elementary rules. Others make the case that in literature written before Paul the word designates the elemental substances that make up the cosmos.

The word *stoicheia*, however, was extended to refer to the heavenly bodies, which were widely assumed to be either governed by angels or were themselves personified as lesser divine powers (see Deut. 4:19).[17] It could then refer to malevolent, elemental spirit beings (see NRSV, NEB, TEV) and would be another label for the celestial godlings named in 1:16 and mentioned

---

16. Josef Blinzler, "Lexicalisches zu dem Terminus *ta stoicheia tou kosmou*," in *Studiorum Paulinorum Congressus Internationalis Catholicus II* (Rome: Pontifical Biblical Institute, 1963), 427–43. The varied range of meanings appear in the New Testament: the elements of the physical universe (2 Peter 3:10, 12), elementary teaching (Heb. 5:12), and a connection with Jewish and pagan religious practices (Gal. 4:3, 9).

17. Philo recognized that these could be personified as spirits and given names of deities (*On the Contemplative Life* 3; *On the Decalogue* 53; *On the Eternity of the World* 107–9). Wisdom 13:2 condemns such idolatry:

but they supposed that either fire or wind or swift air,
or the circle of the stars, or turbulent water,
or the luminaries of heaven were the gods that rule the world.

See also Judg. 5:20; Job 38:7; Dan. 8:10; 1 Enoch 80:7; 86; Philo, *On the Creation* 73; *Noah's Work as Planter* 12; see Rev. 1:20; 9:1; Hermas, *Visions* 3.1.3.3. Moreover, Jewish texts refer to angels who controlled the elements (see Jubilees 2:2; 1 Enoch 75:1; 43:1–2; 2 Enoch 4:1; 19:1–4; Testament of Abraham 13:11).

again in 2:15.[18] Dunn contends that the phrase *ta stoicheia tou kosmou* alludes to a common belief "that human beings had to live their lives under the influence or sway of primal and cosmic forces, however precisely conceptualized. . . ."[19] These heavenly powers are part of creation and exercise regulatory control over nature and rule a world corrupted by sin.

I understand the term to refer to the quasi-demonic spirits to which humans have foolishly given their allegiance and awe (see Acts 7:42). The contrast between *according to the stoicheia to kosmou* and *according to Christ* in 2:8 may signify that Paul regards them as rivals to Christ. Paul contends that the "philosophy" he is warning against depends on these created, malignant powers, not on the beneficent Creator. It observes set feasts, New Moons, and Sabbaths—divisions of time governed by the movements of the heavenly bodies, which, in turn, are animated by the elemental spirits.[20] The apostle does not dismiss these astral powers as nonexistent or as myths (see 1 Cor. 8:5) but asserts that they are all subservient to Christ (although they may not yet acknowledge it, 15:24–25). Because they are "of the world" they have been created in, through, and for Christ and therefore must be subservient to him (Col. 1:15–17). Paul reaffirms that Christ is "the head over every power and authority" (2:10).

(3) Paul also characterizes the "philosophy" as devoid of truth. This opinion reflects Paul's deep conviction that all Christ-less teaching is empty at its

---

18. This view has been criticized as anachronistic, but Arnold, *The Colossian Syncretism* 158–94, and "Returning to the Domain of the Powers: *Stoicheia* as Evil Spirits in Galatians 4:3, 9," *NovT* 38 (1996): 57–59, compiles evidence that this term was applied to astrological spirits during the time of Paul. The Greek Magical Papyri use the term for "personalized spiritual forces that have significant influence over day-to-day existence" (*The Colossian Syncretism*, 173). The *Testament of Solomon* reflects a Judaism influenced by magic, and it provides recipes for invoking angels to thwart hostile demons. In 18:1, 2 (see 8:2; 15:5), the term *stoicheia* is used to refer to the astral decans, which ruled over 10° of the 360° zodiac and caused physical and mental diseases. They are reduced from deities to evil demons, which can be thwarted through special knowledge and rites. Another Jewish work refers to angels who govern creation by regulating the order of the stars and seasons. They keep watch for evil activity and restore order and harmony to the cosmic order (2 Enoch 19:1–5).

19. Dunn, *The Epistles to the Colossians and to Philemon*, 150. He argues: "It is quite possible, then, to conceive of an essentially Jewish 'philosophy' in Colossae that drew on such traditions as a way of commending their religious practices to their fellow citizens."

20. According to Gen. 1:14–18, God created the heavenly bodies to rule over night and day and to regulate the calendar. T. C. G. Thornton, "Jewish New Moon Festivals, Galatians 4:3–11 and Colossians 2:16," *JTS* NS 40 (1989): 100, reminds us that in Paul's age "the boundaries between astronomy, astrology, and the worship of heavenly bodies were unclear and easily crossed." While most today view the moon, sun, and stars from a neutral astronomical perspective, most in the first century viewed them as "spiritually potent masters," which not only controlled the calendar but human lives.

core. As something "hollow," the "philosophy" cannot fill anyone except with more emptiness. By contrast, the Colossians have received the word of God in its fullness (1:25), have the full riches of complete understanding in Christ (2:2; see 1:9), and have been given fullness in Christ (2:10).[21] Humans, however, are forever taken in by appearances and by high-sounding drivel. The "philosophy" can captivate people and beguile them into thinking that it has truth.

The All-Sufficient Christ (2:9–12)

TO COUNTER THE attraction of the "philosophy," Paul reiterates in 2:9 what he said about Christ in 1:19: He is "the fullness" of God.[22] In the Old Testament, "fullness" refers to God's presence (Isa. 6:3). The basic affirmation of Christianity is that God was fully present in Jesus within history. In later writings, the noun translated "Deity" (*theotes*) is differentiated from *theiotes*, which refers to an attribute of deity (see Rom. 1:20).[23] If that distinction applies here, Paul distinguishes Christ from the hierarchy of intermediary and angelic beings, who possess dashes of divine attributes. The *fullness* of the Godhead dwells in him. Clearly, the Colossians cannot lump Christ Jesus with the galaxy of lesser ranking divine beings. He is uniquely "God's presence and his very self" and not "a second, different Deity."[24]

The word translated "bodily" can have several meanings.[25] It may refer to the incarnation—God taking "bodily form," "with a bodily manifestation." Using this definition, it describes "the corporeality of Christ during his earthly existence" (see 1:22).[26] The word may also refer to Christ's body, the

---

21. One can infer from the emphasis on "fullness" (2:9) that the opposing group promised some kind of fullness through different means, presumably the rites and practices described in 2:16–18. The perfect periphrastic "you have been filled" in 2:10 (*este . . . pepleromenoi*) emphasizes completed action in the past with continuing results in the present.

22. In 1:19 Paul used the past tense, "For God was pleased to have all his fullness dwell." Here he uses the present tense, "lives." It is a timeless present and refers to permanent residence of Deity in the living Lord (Harris, *Colossians and Philemon*, 98).

23. As Lohse, *Colossians and Philemon*, 100, puts it, *theotes* describes "the quality of being divine"; *theiotes* refers to "divine nature." Paul rarely uses abstract terminology such as this to refer to God.

24. Wright, *Colossians and Philemon*, 103. Pokorný, *Colossians*, 122, comments: "In Christ one encounters the true, authentic fulness of God, over against which all other conceptions of God, speculations, and experiences are secondary." The implications are clear: "There is no need for men to spread their allegiance among a variety of manifestations of divine authority, since God's nature and purpose are seen complete in Christ" (Caird, *Paul's Letters from Prison*, 191).

25. Barth and Blanke, *Colossians*, 312–15, discuss seven possible interpretations of this word, *somatikos*.

26. Ibid., 314.

church (1:18, 24; 3:15). The noun, "body," however, is used in 2:17 "to denote the solid reality of the new age in contrast with the shadowy anticipation of it in the legal systems of the age that is past."[27] The NIV translates it there as "reality." That meaning may best fit the adverb in 2:9: "In Christ all the fullness of the Deity lives in solid reality" (or "actually"). The reality of the indwelling of God in Jesus the man is not a shadow reality or, in modern idiom, a virtual reality. It is something solid, genuine, and true.[28]

Paul's main point, however, is that "you have been fulfilled in him" (NIV, "you have been given fullness in Christ," 2:10).[29] Since Christ is the fullness of God and believers are in him, they have all the fullness humans can ever possess. Boastful Corinthians faced the danger of becoming puffed up by their belief that they had already arrived in Christ (1 Cor. 4:8; see Phil. 3:12–16). Paul tried to show them that they were full of themselves instead of Christ (cf. Col. 2:18). The opposite was true of the Colossians. They apparently were in more danger of being deflated. The opponents tried to disillusion them that the fullness they yearned for was unattainable either through Christ or through Christ alone. Paul counters that they have all the completeness they need in Christ and do not need to look anywhere else.

The Colossians have been filled in Christ and have also received a divine circumcision in him. Paul's mention of the "circumcision of Christ" (lit. trans.) was probably prompted by the opponents' claim that the Gentile Christians in Colosse lacked this crucial marker that would identify them as God's people. Paul's discussion of it is marked by exegetical difficulties centering on the meaning of the "circumcision not made with hands," the "putting off the body of flesh," and "the circumcision of Christ" (2:11, all lit. trans.); but it affirms foundational Christian truths.[30]

The "circumcision not done by hands" (NIV, "circumcision [not] done by the hands of men") refers to something done by God as opposed to some-

---

27. Caird, *Paul's Letters from Prison*, 191–92.

28. The adverb has also been interpreted to mean "embodied" in the corporate life of the church and "in organic unity." But the point is that Deity is not parceled out through a hierarchy of powers but is confined to one real person, Christ.

29. The verb "to fulfill" is used by Paul elsewhere to refer to Christians being filled "with all joy and peace" and with "goodness" and "knowledge" (Rom. 15:13–14), "with the Spirit" (Eph. 5:18); and with "the fruit of righteousness" on the day of Christ (Phil. 1:10–11).

30. Paul does not engage in an assault on circumcision for Christians as he does in Galatians, and the letter contains no evidence that anyone was coercing the Colossians to be circumcised. Dunn, *The Epistles to the Colossians and to Philemon*, 156, presents the most plausible scenario: The Colossians faced a vigorous Jewish apologetic that justified and exalted circumcision (perhaps as Philo does in *Special Laws* 1:1–11 and *Questions on Genesis* 3:46–62) rather than any attempt to make them Jewish proselytes. They rejected any claims that Gentiles had any hope for salvation without circumcision. Paul counters that they have the only circumcision that counts, divine circumcision in Christ.

thing done by human beings (see Acts 7:48; 17:24; 2 Cor. 5:1; Eph. 2:11; Heb. 9:11). It therefore stood over against the external rite for which Judaism was infamous in the ancient world.[31] Literal circumcision was a minor operation that removed a small portion of flesh, but it had major significance for Jews as the sign of obedience to God's covenant. It meant that one was incorporated into the people of God and a beneficiary of the covenant promises to Abraham. Circumcision was the sign God gave to Abraham as a covenant in the flesh (Gen. 17:1–14) and signified inclusion in God's chosen nation.

For most Jews in the first century, circumcision had become the fundamental identity badge for membership in God's people. In times of persecution, Jews regarded it as a confession of faith as well as an act of obedience to God's holy law. God had commanded Israel to be separate, and circumcision did just that; it separated Jews from the heathenish idolaters surrounding them. Paul himself uses the terms *circumcision* and *uncircumcision* as shorthand for the distinction between Jew and Gentile (Rom. 2:25–27; 3:30; 4:9–12; Gal. 2:7–8). As a seal of Israel's election, circumcision also assured God's blessing on the people as the designated beneficiaries of the covenant promises.

From Paul's radical perspective, circumcision in the flesh had become little more than a tribal brand. In Romans 2:25–29, he argues that circumcision, the ground of Jewish confidence, is a meaningless sign unless it signifies a cleansed heart; and he goes on to argue that the cleansed heart can only come from Christ.[32] True circumcision (Phil. 3:2) has nothing to do with the slicing off a piece of flesh from the body; it is something related to Christ and wrought by God's Spirit.

The NIV translation of 2:11, "In him you were also circumcised, in the putting off of the sinful nature, not with a circumcision done by the hands of men but with the circumcision done by Christ," is misleading. (1) By translating the Greek phrase "the stripping off the body of flesh" as "the putting off of the sinful nature," the NIV interprets the "body of flesh" as something immoral, "sinful nature."[33] The term *flesh* (*sarx*) does not always have a sinful implication in Paul's

---

31. Tacitus claimed that the Jews adopted circumcision "to distinguish themselves from other peoples by this difference" (*Histories* 5.5); see Dunn, *The Epistles to the Colossians and to Philemon*, 154.

32. The spiritualizing of circumcision is also found in Old Testament tradition (Deut. 10:16; 30:6; Lev. 26:41; Jer. 4:4; 6:10; 9:26; Ezek. 44:7, 9). See also the Dead Sea Scrolls (1QS 5.4–5, 26; 1QpHab 11.13).

33. On Paul's various usages of the word "flesh" and "body," see R. J. Erickson, "Flesh," in *DPL*, 303–6. The verb "to strip off" (*apekdyomai*) appears in 3:9 and has the "old self" as its object. The "old self" does refer to human nature that has been taken over by sin, but it is not synonymous with the "body of flesh." We might add that the phrase "sinful nature" may also lead the reader to infer wrongly that we have an "unsinful nature." When Paul uses "flesh" in a negative sense, it refers to the degenerate person as a whole (including the fleshly passions),

usage. He can use it to refer simply to the physical body without any negative connotations. All of the uses of *sarx* so far in the letter have denoted the physical flesh (1:22, 24; 2:1, 5). The phrase "body of flesh" is an adjectival (Hebraic, qualitative) genitive, in which an abstract noun in the genitive case is used instead of an adjective to modify another noun. "The body of flesh" is another way of saying "the physical body." The only other time this phrase occurs in the New Testament is in 1:22, and the NIV correctly renders it Christ's "physical body." It has the same meaning here and does not refer to a sinful nature.

(2) The second problem with the NIV translation of 2:11 is that it decides for the reader that putting off the flesh refers to the believer's experience. It interprets the Greek phrase "the circumcision of Christ" as a subjective genitive, "the circumcision done by Christ." This translation prevents the reader from interpreting it as referring to anything but a metaphorical circumcision of the heart, which strips off the desires of the flesh (see also REB, TEV).[34] The alternative rendering, which interprets the phrase as an objective genitive, is more likely: It is a circumcision experienced by Christ, thus referring metaphorically to his death.[35]

Paul uses the image of putting off and putting on for death elsewhere in his letters (1 Cor. 15:53–54; 2 Cor. 5:1–4). But the image of *"stripping off* the body of flesh" is far more intense and vivid. Dunn claims that this image was chosen to emphasize the physical nature of Christ's death, and, we might add, its horror.[36] "The circumcision of Christ" is then a graphic metaphor. It refers to the "circumcision" that Christ underwent in his crucifixion when his physical body was violently stripped off in his death.[37] The statement thus parallels 1:22, which also refers to Christ's death: "He reconciled [you] in the body of his flesh [NIV, physical body] through death."

This interpretation that the "circumcision of Christ" is a vivid image for Christ's death also best explains the unusual progression from circumcision

---

which has arrayed itself for rebellion against God. It is what humans become apart from the regenerating grace of God. But in this instance Paul uses the word *sarx* ("flesh") in a neutral sense to refer to the human body. For a quite different interpretation, see Wright, *Colossians and Philemon*, 106, who argues that the "body" refers to a group of people as in "the body of Christ." Stripping off the body of flesh, he argues, refers to breaking with old fleshly solidarities. Arnold, *The Colossian Syncretism*, 296, contends that Paul refers to cutting off "their solidarity with Adam, 'the body of sin' (Rom 6:6), humanity under the rule of sin and death."

34. Elsewhere Paul always attributes circumcision of the heart to the Spirit (Rom. 2:29; 2 Cor. 3:3; Phil. 3:3).

35. Moule, *Colossians and Philemon*, 95, 96; Barth and Blanke, *Colossians*, 364–65.

36. Dunn, *The Epistles to the Colossians and to Philemon*, 157. "Nailing it to the cross" (2:14) is another vivid image in this passage.

37. So Moule, *Colossians and Philemon*, 96; R. P. Martin, *Colossians and Philemon*, 82; O'Brien, *Colossians and Philemon*, 117.

to burial to resurrection in 2:11–12. If the circumcision of Christ refers to Christ's death, then the sequence summarizes the essential affirmations of Christianity: Christ died, was buried, and was raised (see 1 Cor. 15:1–4). In this passage Paul interprets Christ's death as a vicarious circumcision for us (see 2 Cor. 5:14–15).[38]

This paragraph appeals to what Christ accomplished for us in his saving work in the cross, which has laid the foundation for the forgiveness of sins (2:13–14). Christians identify with what Christ has done and accept its benefits through their baptism and faith.[39] "You were circumcised" means that "you died" in his death.[40] The believer's union with Christ in his death, burial, and resurrection is stressed throughout the passage ("buried with him," "raised with him," "made . . . alive with Christ," 2:12–13; "you died with Christ," 2:20; "you have been raised with Christ," 3:1; "your life is now hidden with Christ in God," 3:3). God reveals his power to overcome and overrule death in Jesus' resurrection, and that power becomes available to those who put their trust in him (see Eph. 1:19–23). Christians die with Christ and enter his tomb with him, and the same mighty God who raised Christ from the dead promises to raise us up with him.

What God Has Done (2:13–15)

IN 2:13–15 PAUL balances the triad of Christ's death, burial, and resurrection by specifying three things God has accomplished in Christ.[41] These achievements are expressed by the finite verbs in each statement:

- Dead in your sins, *God made you alive with [in] Christ* (2:13).
- The written code that was against us, he *"canceled"* it (2:14).
- Having stripped (NIV, "disarmed") the powers and authorities, *he made a public spectacle of them* (2:15).

---

38. Roy Yates, "'The Worship of Angels,'" *ExpTim* 97 (1987): 14, comments: "What the mystic tried to achieve by release from the body, Christ achieved for all 'in his body of flesh by his death' (Col 1:22, cf. 2:11)."

39. Lohse, *Colossians and Philemon*, 103, is correct that "the circumcision of Christ which every member of the community has experienced is nothing other than being baptized into the death and resurrection of Christ."

40. O'Brien, *Colossians and Philemon*, 116. Paul does not view Christian baptism as a more efficacious replacement for the Jewish rite of circumcision.

41. This view assumes that God is the subject of all the finite verbs. The aorist participles "having forgiven" (NIV, "He forgave us," 2:13), "having canceled" (2:14), "having nailed" (NIV, "nailing," 2:14), "having stripped," (NIV, "disarmed," 2:15), "having revealed" (NIV, "he made a public spectacle," 2:15) also have God as the subject and use striking metaphors to express what God has done for us in Christ.

The union of believers with Christ in his death means that the Gentiles' physical uncircumcision no longer signifies their present spiritual death (2:13) and future condemnation.[42] Being united to Christ guarantees that the slate of accusations against them has been wiped clean and promises freedom from the death-dealing powers whom Christ has vanquished (2:15).[43] The emphasis falls on what God in Christ has done, which makes any human attempt to propitiate these powers through rituals and self-chastisement look all the more feeble and ridiculous.

Paul portrays the Colossians' life before they were joined to Christ as a kind of nonexistence in the realm of the dead. The epithets "dead in your sins" and "the uncircumcision of your flesh [NIV, sinful nature]" reflect the standard Jewish assessment of the Gentiles' status as aliens to God's covenant. Whether one was dead or alive depended on one's relationship with the one source of life (see Luke 15:24, 32).

The NIV takes the phrase "the uncircumcision of your sinful nature" (lit., "the uncircumcision of your flesh") as another metaphor for alienation from God, something that applies to Jews and Gentiles alike (Rom. 2:25). It is more likely that Paul uses the phrase as an ethnic category (see Col. 3:11; also Rom. 3:30; 4:9, 11; 1 Cor. 7:18; Gal. 2:7; Eph. 2:11). The phrase "dead in your sins" refers to the Gentiles' spiritual condition; the phrase "uncircumcision of your flesh" refers to their bodily uncircumcision. Since Jews interpreted circumcision to be the tangible sign of God's everlasting covenant and favor (Gen. 17:13; Josh. 5:2–9), the Gentiles' lack of this sign denoted their estrangement from God (1:21). It also signified their exclusion from salvation. Paul affirms that their lack of physical circumcision has been rectified by a spiritual circumcision (one not made with hands).[44]

---

42. The Greek for "sins" in 2:13 has "transgressions" (*paraptomata*), which can imply deliberate disobedience. Formerly, they were morally, spiritually, theologically cut off from God.

43. Some scholars claim to spot an inconsistency between 2:12 and 3:1, which affirm the present experience of the resurrection, and 1 Cor. 15, where Paul insists that the resurrection is "not yet." In Colossians, Paul uses resurrection as an image for one's conversion and transformation. He describes a new life coming from dying to sin in baptism, not a resurrection to glory. The hope remains "stored up for you in heaven" (1:5) and a believer's resurrection victory "is hidden with Christ in God." The statement in 3:4 makes it clear: "When Christ, who is your life, appears, then you also will appear with him in glory." But Paul can use an aorist verb ("he ... glorified," Rom. 8:30) to proclaim the present certainty of our future destiny.

44. Dunn, *The Epistles to the Colossians and to Philemon*, 163–64, makes the case that Paul does not try to rebut this Jewish characterization of Gentile status before God:

> On the contrary, he reaffirms the Christian-Jewish starting point, that Israel was in an advantaged position over other nations by virtue of God's choice of Israel to be his special people. The difference is that the disadvantaged state of "uncircumcision" has been remedied by a "circumcision not performed by human hand" (2:11) rather than by "circumcision in the flesh."

God's forgiveness in Christ gives us new life. Here Paul switches from "you" ("when you were dead") to "us": "He forgave us." Paul is acutely conscious that God did not simply forgive Gentiles with their long history of sinfulness and idolatry, but God also forgave Jews with their long history of rebellion and sinfulness (see Rom. 1:18–3:20).

Paul goes on to use a commercial image to describe this forgiveness: God "canceled [the note] ... that was against us." The word translated "written code" (*cheirographon*) refers to an IOU, a note that acknowledges the obligation to pay a debt and is signed by the debtor.[45] The letter to Philemon provides a good example of one: "I, Paul, am writing this with my own hand. I will pay it back—not to mention that you owe me your very self" (Philem. 19).

The NIV translation of 2:14, however, assumes that Paul has in mind the Mosaic Law with its legal decrees, which would parallel the phrase in Ephesians 2:15, "the law with its commandments and regulations."[46] Our problem with the law as humans is its refusal to grade on a curve. Performing at a 99.99 percent rate of obedience still earns us an F minus and a death sentence for our failure (see Ex. 24:3; Deut. 27:14–26). Yates has objected to this interpretation that the essential characteristic of a *cheirographon* was that it was written by one's own hand to authenticate an agreement. He argues that this image would not apply to the law.

We do better, then, not to interpret the *cheirographon* as a metaphor for the written law code but as a reference to the debt both Jews and Gentiles acknowledge before God. In Romans 1–2, Paul makes the case that Jews share the same sinful plight as the Gentiles. The Jews have the advantage of possessing the written law, which, Paul notes, tells them that *none* is righteous (3:9–20). The Gentiles, without the written law, have the inner voice of conscience that bears witness to God's law. Both Jews and Gentiles, therefore, acknowledge in different ways their indebtedness to obey God's law. Both are guilty of the same willful disobedience. As Yates concludes, "The cheirograph is against us because we have manifestly failed to discharge its obligation."[47] Both Jew and Gentile come under the curse of the law (Gal.

---

45. See Roy Yates, "Colossians 2,14: Metaphor of Forgiveness," *Bib* 71 (1990): 248–59.

46. We should rule out altogether the interpretation, which was spun purely from the imagination of Origen, that it refers to some mythical pact with Satan made by Adam. It is also unlikely that Paul has in view a book, kept in heaven by an angel, in which everyone's transgressions are recorded. Although the idea can be found in Jewish apocalyptic literature (see Ex. 32:32–33; Ps. 69:28; Dan. 12:1; Rev. 3:5; and 1 Enoch 89:61–64, 70–71; 108:7; *Apocalypse of Zephaniah* 7:1–8; *Apocalypse of Abraham* (A) 12:7–18; 13:9–14; (B) 10:7–11:7; 2 Enoch 53:2–3; Odes of Solomon 23:5–9; *Gospel of Truth* 19:17), Paul employs an image of the promissory note that everyone in the Gentile audience could readily recognize.

47. Yates, "Col 2,14," 252.

3:13), the death sentence pronounced on those who violate its ordinances. Our breach of promise and our bankruptcy, however, are met by the riches of God's mercy and faithfulness.

Paul then uses another vivid metaphor to describe God's mercy on sinners: God nailed the incriminating list of unpaid debts to the cross. The IOU exacted a penalty for nonpayment—death. The note was not simply torn up and thrown away, however. The full penalty was exacted in Christ's death. The metaphor of nailing it to the cross may allude to the practice of placing the charge against the criminal on his cross (John 19:19–22). The difference is that the guilty parties were not nailed to the cross with it, only Christ. Christ stood in our place, taking our sin upon himself and taking away our guilt. In return, we take away his righteousness. Martin Luther exclaimed: "Thou Christ art my sin and my curse, or rather, I am thy sin, thy curse, thy death, thy wrath of God, thy hell; and contrariwise, thou art my righteousness, my blessing, my life, my grace of God and my heaven."[48] If we die with Christ, who took the verdict of condemnation against us, then our debt has been paid in full.[49] Those who are in Christ are no longer in default (see Rom. 8:1).[50]

A third colorful metaphor describes what was going on "behind the scenes" in Jesus' crucifixion on Golgotha, not visible to any of the spectators.[51] The verb translated "disarmed" (*apekdyomai*) in 2:15 is the same verb translated "taken off" in 3:9 and in the same word group as the noun translated "putting off" in 2:11. I would translate it "strip off." God strips the powers and authorities of their potency, importance, and anything else that would lead humans to honor or fear them.[52]

---

48. Martin Luther, *A Commentary on St. Paul's Epistle to the Galatians*, ed. Philip S. Watson (London: James Clarke, 1953), 283.

49. The verb "took" (*erken*) is in the perfect tense, emphasizing its permanence.

50. Barclay, *The All-Sufficient Christ*, 79, presses the image of the verb translated "canceled" (*exaleipho*) in 2:14. It means "to wipe or to sponge off," something a scribe would do to correct his writing. He points out that another way a bond could be canceled was by marking an X through it. The charge beneath the mark, however, was still readable. Barclay suggests that Paul's choice of verbs implies that the bond has been obliterated.

51. Houlden, *Paul's Letters from Prison*, 188.

52. We take God to be the subject of the verb, and the middle voice as having an active and not a reflexive force (i.e., "stripping them in one's own interest"). If Christ is the subject, the middle voice would be reflexive; and it would mean that Christ stripped himself of the powers that had assailed him, defeating them on the cross. This interpretation was prevalent among the early Greek Fathers. Lightfoot's interpretation, which reflects this view, has been quoted or paraphrased many times: "The powers of evil, which had clung like a Nessus robe about his humanity, were torn off and cast aside for ever" (*Saint Paul's Epistles to the Colossians and to Philemon*, 190; see a variation of it in Dunn, *The Epistles to the Colossians and to Philemon*, 167–68).

This image captures what Paul calls the secret wisdom of the crucifixion (1 Cor. 2:6–8). Jesus' captors dragged him through the city, stripped him naked, held him up to contempt, and nailed the charges against him to his cross; but all along God was doing it to them. God made them a public example by showing how utterly impotent they were before this divine demonstration of love and forgiveness and how utterly helpless they were to deter the divine power that raises the dead.

The final image in the clause is translated "triumphing over them" in the NIV.[53] The verb *thriambeuo* can mean "to triumph over, to march in a triumphal procession, to make known, or to reveal." Paul uses the image of a triumphal procession in Ephesians 4:8, citing Psalm 68:18: "When [Christ] ascended on high, he led captives in his train." If he is drawing on the image of a Roman emperor celebrating his victories by leading a cortege of vanquished enemies, the irony is striking. As Lightfoot puts it, "The paradox of the crucifixion is thus placed in the strongest light—triumph in helplessness and glory in shame. The convict's gibbet is the victor's car."[54] Calvin is no less eloquent in his comments: "For there is no tribunal so magnificent, no throne so stately, no show of triumph so distinguished, no chariot so elevated, as is the gibbet on which Christ has subdued death and the devil, nay more, has utterly trodden them under His feet."[55]

God has triumphed through Christ's death on the cross over every power and authority. The rulers put him to death without knowing that through his death he would conquer them and escape their rule (1 Cor. 2:6–8). They have been disarmed, stripped of their dignity, and consigned to bring up the rear in Christ's victory procession. They sit at the bar like the war criminals who were brought before the Nuremberg tribunal at the end of World War II and are exposed as weak, beggarly, and benumbed. Christ reigns supreme over these rulers and authorities (see Col. 1:16), and all those who are in Christ never need to fear them and ought never to

---

53. The NIV interprets the Greek *en auto* ("in him" or "in it") as a reference to the cross ("by the cross"). If God is the subject of all the verbs in 2:13–15, however, it would be better to translate it "in him," that is, in Christ.

54. Lightfoot, *Saint Paul's Epistles to the Colossians and to Philemon*, 192. Roy Yates, "Colossians 2:15: Christ Triumphant," *NTS* 37 (1991): 573–91, claims that the triumph imagery pictures a "celebratory procession" from the Roman triumph. Those led in triumph were not "defeated captives, who were driven before the victor's chariot, but liberated Romans, dancers, chorus, and adulating crowds. They are the attendants of the *triumphator* celebrating the fruits of victory in the triumph." He claims that the powers are not despoiled or led in triumph but are part of "the celebratory hosts." It becomes a preview of their reconciliation (1:19).

55. John Calvin, *Commentaries on the Epistles of Paul the Apostle to the Philippians, Colossians and Thessalonians*, 191.

venerate them. Christians belong to Christ, who governs the cosmos and secures them from all threats.

THIS PASSAGE COMBINES the first warning to the Colossians about the "hollow and deceptive philosophy" (2:8) they were facing with a forceful reminder of what they have received through Christ when they were baptized in him (2:9–15). The theological emphasis falls on three vital issues. (1) Paul stresses the all-sufficiency of Christ for our salvation. Christ is the one in whom "all the fullness of the Deity lives" (2:9) and who is "head over every power and authority" (2:9). His preeminence over all creation should eliminate any qualms that other deliverers might be required. His death and resurrection are the definitive means by which God has reconciled the world, and Christians who have been baptized into that death will be raised from death with him. We need no other mediator except Christ.

(2) Paul emphasizes that God has provided Christians complete forgiveness and fullness in Christ. All charges against us were eradicated by his sacrificial death. Consequently, Christians need not seek any other nostrums promising salvation or make vain attempts to cancel the debt with something they do themselves. We can only have forgiveness in Christ and need no other "fullness" except the fullness given us in Christ.

(3) Paul affirms that God, through Christ's cross and resurrection, routed all of the threatening powers arrayed against us. This victory should allay any fears that these powers still have any mastery over Christians. We need no other power except the power of Christ.

The message presented in 2:6–15 is central to the Christian faith. Christians need to hear it repeatedly so that it becomes so much a part of our understanding of the world and ourselves that we will not become prey to false religious propaganda from rival religionists or secularists. The problem, however, is that Paul couches this basic Christian message in imagery that is foreign to most modern readers. Our unfamiliarity with his metaphors makes this text more difficult to translate and to interpret. Three issues in this text deserve particular attention in spanning the bridge from the first century to our modern culture: what Paul means by "receiv[ing] Christ Jesus as Lord" (2:6), what he means by "the circumcision of Christ" (lit.) (2:11), and what is the nature of a "hollow and deceptive philosophy" (2:8). After examining these issues, we will then look at the difficult problem of bridging the meaning of *ta stoicheia tou kosmou* ("elemental spirits"/"basic principles") and the fear of "powers and authorities."

Receiving Christ Jesus as Lord. Wright warns of the danger of interpreting the phrase "receiving Christ Jesus as Lord" anachronistically. Today, evangelical Christians use this phrase to mean "to become a Christian." Believers receive Christ by inviting him "to enter their hearts and life." The verb "to receive" (*paralambano*) in 2:6, however, is a technical term taken over from Judaism that refers to "the transmission of teaching from one person or generation to another" (see 1 Cor. 11:2; 15:1–5; Phil. 4:9; 1 Thess. 4:1; 2 Thess. 3:6). This understanding connects it to the clause "as you were taught" (2:7).[56] The phrase refers "to the Colossians' acceptance of the proclamation of Jesus the Lord, to their consequent confession of faith, and to their new status as members of Christ's body (see 2:19)."[57]

Paul's statement in 1 Corinthians 15:3–4, "For what *I received* I passed on to you as of first importance: that Christ died for our sins according to the Scriptures, that he was buried, that he was raised on the third day according to the Scriptures," parallels what Paul says to the Colossians 2:6, 11–12. The Colossians have "received" the proclamation about Christ the Lord: He died for them (Paul uses the image of circumcision and stripping off his physical body), was buried, and was raised. Having received the crucial facts of what Christ has done for them, the Colossians must continue to live (present imperative) in him.

Dunn appeals to this text to argue against the view that Paul had little interest in Jesus' life and ministry apart from his death and resurrection. Modern scholars have reached this conclusion because Paul so rarely refers to events in Jesus' life or to his teaching. Dunn makes an important observation that if the Colossians believed that Christ Jesus was Lord, "it would have been necessary for some information to be given about this Jesus and his ministry in the Jewish homeland."[58] In strong language he declares:

> It is scarcely credible, that a new movement could be gathered round a single name without a story being told to identify that name and explain its significance and thus to provide foundation (note the metaphor used in 2:7) and identity for the movement itself. And to Gentiles living in Asia Minor, but aware of Judaism and perhaps attracted to its practices (cf. particularly 2:16), that story must have included a fair amount about Jesus' life and ministry (which had taken place less than thirty years earlier) and not just the bare fact of his death and resurrection.[59]

---

56. Wright, *Colossians and Philemon*, 98.
57. Ibid., 99.
58. Dunn, *The Epistles to the Colossians and to Philemon*, 141.
59. Ibid., 142.

Paul believed that the historical traditions about Jesus, what he said and did, provided the foundation and the guidelines for the Colossians' life as they must continue to do for ours. The salvation stories behind the popular ancient mystery religions competing with early Christianity were rooted in ahistorical myths. By contrast, the story of Christianity is rooted in history, and it can be summarized in a nutshell: Christ died under Pontius Pilate, was buried, and was raised on the third day by God's power. The Colossians had "received" these facts surrounding the death of Christ and were rooted, built up, and established in the faith. It is one thing to assent to the facts that Christ gave his life for us and was raised by God, however; it is quite another thing for that truth to permeate our whole lives so that it controls all that we think and do.

Paul encourages his readers to understand more fully what those facts mean for their salvation and to allow this new reality to penetrate their soul and being so that it bursts forth in thanksgiving to God. He recognizes that when Christians fully appreciate the significance of the facts of their salvation, they are more thankful to God for all that they have been given and less vulnerable to the "put downs" or "come ons" of competing ideologies. On the other hand, if Christians take for granted, shrug off, or forget what they have received about Christ, they become easy marks for unsound "philosophies" to take them captive with false promises and enchantments. Consequently, the doctrine about what God has accomplished for us in Christ must be engraved on our minds so that it continually inspires and sustains our lives.

The circumcision of Christ. The particular Colossian situation prompted Paul's reference to the circumcision we have received in Christ (2:11). He chose this unusual metaphor to describe Christ's death to combat the opponents' notions about circumcision. Modern readers are likely to find it confusing. As we understand the Colossian situation, the church had been challenged by errant and truculent local Jews, who refused to accept the validity of the Gentile Christians' hope in Christ.

Such Jewish antagonists presumably argued that unless Gentiles converted fully to Judaism and became circumcised, they remained forever "excluded from citizenship in Israel and foreigners to the covenants of the promise, without hope and without God in the world" (Eph. 2:12). From their perspective, Gentiles who did not become full proselytes had no right to claim or, more pointedly, to filch promises that rightfully belonged only to Israel. If we remember what circumcision meant to Jews as the distinguishing mark of God's covenant people, we can understand their pique over uncircumcised Gentile Christians claiming the same hope of glory that had been promised to Israel. How could Gentiles be the beneficiaries of God's promises without going though the proper channels ordained by God in Scripture?

Though Paul did not deny that circumcision might be appropriate for Christians of Jewish descent (see Acts 16:3; Rom. 3:1—2), he vehemently argued that the physical rite was *not* a prerequisite for the Gentiles' inclusion in God's people. He laid his life on the line for his clear vision of the truth of the gospel (Gal. 2:5). All who trust in Christ (2:16) and have been crucified with him (2:20) are now the authentic Israel, the true heirs of God's promises (Rom. 9—11; Gal. 6:16; Phil. 3:2).

In his letter to the Galatians, Paul takes on Christian Judaizers and insists that Gentiles need not and must not detour through Judaism to get to Christ. Such a detour is only a dead end that will leave them dead in their sins. One becomes a child of Abraham and is justified and blessed with Abraham by faith and faith alone (Gal. 3:6—9). Paul takes on external opponents here in Colossians and argues that Gentiles have received a spiritual circumcision. He understands this spiritual circumcision metaphorically to be Christ's death. In our baptism, we accept that death as for us. We have been crucified with Christ by being baptized into his death and become full-fledged recipients of God's salvation. The Colossians do not need a physical circumcision to become heirs of the promises or to receive forgiveness for their sins.

Christ's death has replaced this rite. God's chosen people are no longer identified by a minor physical incision, only applicable to males, but by belief in Christ and incorporation into his death and resurrection life. Membership now requires a major excision of the old—death. Christian baptism represents all of this.[60]

Most important, however, is Paul's affirmation that this spiritual circumcision, received vicariously through Christ's death, takes care of a problem that physical circumcision never could. The physical rite could never deliver Jew or Gentile from the power of sin. One could be circumcised in the flesh and still remain uncircumcised in the spirit (see Rom. 2:25—29). Paul insists that real circumcision is spiritual, "of the heart" (Rom. 2:29). The Colossians have received the real thing from Christ who was "circumcised" (put to death) for them. What is more, it means that believers have been forgiven their trespasses. All the charges against us, which are seared on every conscience alive to God, have been blotted out by Christ's death.

Few, if any, Christians today are bedeviled by opponents who claim that their salvation is deficient because they have not undergone ritual circumcision. But Christians are often pestered by some group within or without the church who allege that they fall short in some area necessary for salvation. These persons contend that baptized Christians still need to do this or that— something, they promise, that will help remedy the fault. In this text, Paul

---

60. Caird, *Paul's Letters from Prison*, 194.

proclaims that everything that ever needs to be done to secure our salvation has been accomplished once for all by God through Christ's death and resurrection. We lay claim to this salvation when we trust what God has done *for us. God gave us* a circumcision not "done by the hands of men" (2:11). *God made us* who were dead in our sins alive in Christ (2:13). *God took away* all the charges that denounced and doomed us to eternal separation from God (2:14). Thus, those who are in Christ lack nothing.

The passive verbs in 2:6 imply that God has even rooted and built us up in Christ and has strengthened us in the faith. Christians have been given everything that God demands from us and everything that God can possibly give to us. Our task is, then, to continue to live exclusively in Christ and to abound in thanksgiving for what God has done for us through Christ. Any religious tenet or philosophy of life that professes to offer forgiveness of sins, "deeper" knowledge, deliverance, or the finishing touches to salvation through any other means than Christ's death and resurrection is fundamentally flawed and dangerous to the spiritual health of Christians. This leads to the next issue: the danger of an enticing false "philosophy" capturing our fancy and pulling us away from Christ.

False philosophies. The discipline of philosophy has often become the object of ridicule. Ambrose Bierce defined philosophy as "a route of many roads leading from nowhere to nothing."[61] People joke half seriously that philosophy turns solutions into problems and the simplest things into the most unintelligible. Some Christians have appealed to Paul's statement in 2:8 to argue that Christians should have nothing to do with any philosophical speculation. They say that we must rely only on faith and not reason.

This text, however, should not be used as a proof text against philosophy. Paul does not reject philosophy in principle, nor does he discount the value of sound learning or intellectual inquiry.[62] He rejects a particular manifestation of "philosophy" in Colosse, a religious position that pretended to a wisdom that it did not possess. The discipline of philosophy is not inherently empty, deceptive, or dangerous. Phillips paraphrased 2:8: "Be careful that no one spoils your faith through intellectualism or high-sounding nonsense."

---

61. Ambrose Bierce, "The Devil's Dictionary," in *The Collected Writings of Ambrose Bierce* (New York: Citadel, 1946), 325.

62. This is not to say that Paul made any attempt to adjust his theology to current philosophical thinking (1 Cor. 1:21–25). Comparing Paul and Philo, Paul's near contemporary from Alexandria, brings out a striking contrast in their use of philosophy. Terence P. Paige, "Philosophy," *DPL*, 718, points out that Paul was aware of the intellectual currents of his era; but, unlike Philo, he had no intention of trying to reconcile his message with the values and aspirations of Hellenistic philosophy. He comments, "Paul holds the gospel to be the only means to divine wisdom (1 Cor 1:21; 2:6–16; Eph 1:15–18)."

There is nothing wrong with intellectualism except that it has a tendency to become high-sounding nonsense.

In Paul's context, what made the "philosophy" worthless was that it was "hollow and deceptive" and opposed to Christ. Religion, for example, is not bad, but hollow and deceptive religion is. MacLeod comments that Christians are not "to despise knowledge, nor the love of knowledge, nor the search for wider knowledge. But they are called upon to approach all knowledge in the light of Christ."[63] Anything that draws us away from Christ or looks for salvation outside Christ is empty and vain.

Paul does not disparage critical thinking or the rational investigation of the truths and principles of being, knowledge, or conduct, as long as it conforms to Christ. Consequently, we put references to the Colossian "philosophy" in quotation marks in an attempt to distinguish it from the discipline of philosophy. In bridging the contexts, "philosophy" applies to any belief system or way of life that competes for allegiance due only to Christ—even if it claims to revere Christ or incorporates elements of biblical teaching. The key is that it is *not according to Christ* (2:8, the literal rendering of the phrase translated "rather than on Christ" in the NIV).

Those "philosophies" of life that are overtly hostile to Christ are easy to recognize. They cast aspersions on his name and harass his followers. How does one detect if some "philosophy" is "not according to Christ" when it may appropriate some or many Christian beliefs? Its bogus character usually reveals itself whenever it proceeds along these lines: "Faith in Christ is fine as far as it goes, but you are not really right with God, accepted by God, or protected by God unless you also...." It makes no difference how the sentence is completed; it is false and not according to Christ.

The elemental spirits and the powers and authorities. Paul affirms in this section that Christ "is the head over every power and authority" (2:10) and that through the cross God has "disarmed the powers and authorities," making "a public spectacle of them [and] triumphing over them" (2:15). In Christ we do not simply have forgiveness of sins and a clean slate with God. God has also delivered us from every power that would try to claim title to our lives, to win possession of us, or generally to bring harm to us. I would include *ta stoicheia tou kosmou* ("the elemental spirits"; NIV, "the basic principles") in this category of oppressive powers, but this interpretation of the phrase is not necessary for the general affirmation in the text to hold true. We have been delivered from the thralldom of evil powers and inflexible forces.

---

63. MacLeod, "The Epistle to the Colossians: Exposition," 190.

The wide disagreement among scholars about what the term *ta stoicheia tou kosmou* in 2:8, 20 meant in the first century presents some difficulty in relating what it applies to today. Crossing the bridge into our context becomes even more difficult when we take a position that disagrees with the translation that people may be using, and the various translations differ significantly. If we refer to "elemental spirits of the world" and people read "basic principles of this world" in their translation, they are likely to be confused. I have concluded that the contextual evidence suggests that the expression referred to the gods of the stars, which the ancients thought controlled the world for good or ill. But this interpretation may create further problems for bridging its meaning to our world.

After the lunar landings and the astounding exploration of our solar system, we might assume that most people in our culture view the moon, planets, and stars as "lifeless matter, moving according to energy forces which are as impersonal as they are unconcerned with our lives and our destiny on earth."[64] The boom in interest in astrology challenges this assumption. A poll conducted near the turn of the twenty-first century reports that 48 percent of Americans believe that astrology is "probably" or "definitely" valid. Heads of states in the United States, Russia, and India have been known to consult astrologers to help guide them in making decisions. Many ordinary citizens believe that the movement of stars and planets determine more than just the calendar; they also reflect our souls and govern our lives. Some carry handy pocket reference cards listing the auspicious times dictated by the movement of the stars for every activity. Most people who buy into astrology today look at the planetary transits and sun signs as a beneficial way to explore their inner lives and yearnings and to prepare themselves for future events. By contrast, many people in Paul's day viewed the stars more ominously as potent spiritual lords who could tyrannize as well as benefit human lives.

The Colossian error may have held out the promise of solving a fundamental human predicament that troubled everyone in the Hellenistic world: How do people survive "in a world filled with hostile supernatural forces"?[65] Whether this view of the Colossian situation is correct, the text does allude to fears that weighed heavily on the minds of many in Paul's day. They believed that the world was beset by hobgoblins of various sorts. These unseen forces were pitted against humans and controlled their lives in capricious ways, and they needed to be propitiated. The villains were everywhere, and many were convinced that they were helpless pawns in the iron grip of

---

64. Stockhausen, *Letters in the Pauline Tradition*, 39.
65. Arnold, *The Colossian Syncretism*, 183.

these powers that ruled the cosmos. A. E. Housman's lines aptly describe the same dis-ease felt by many in Paul's era:

I, a stranger and afraid
In a world I never made.[66]

These pessimistic lines penned in the twentieth century also reveal that no matter how much we progress in science and technology, the problem of human spiritual discomfort has not disappeared.

People in the ancient world fretted about how to neutralize the evil powers and tried to exploit divine champions to their own advantage. At every level of society people resorted to magic (see Acts 19:19). Savage notes that "peasants and senators alike hung amulets round their necks to chase away evil spirits." According to Suetonius's account of Nero, the emperor "solicited rites from the magi in order to escape his mother's ghost" (*Nero* 34.4). Savage concludes, "Astrology, oracles, portents and dreams filled out an atmosphere of enchantment. The abundance of the evidence suggests that vast segments of first-century society were engrossed in superhuman schemes and engulfed in superstition."[67] We can safely assume that the same attitudes prevailed in Colosse.

Most people appealed to subaltern deities, what we might call the small fries in the divine world, to handle day-to-day life. This approach stemmed from vague notions of an organizational flow chart for the divine world that assigned the various powers their roles and level of potency. At the top were the Olympian gods of ancient Greece or the gods and goddesses of the powerful mystery religions, such as Isis, Serapis, Cybele, and Artemis, who spoke with fearsome voices. At the bottom of this pyramid was a vast array of lesser gods and spirits.

Many may have imagined that one deity reigned supreme over this spiritual realm in the same way that the Roman emperor reigned supreme over his earthly empire. But they assumed that the deity or deities at the top of the heap were also like the Roman emperor in that they did not care about or bother with the daily lives of the average person. The lesser deities, they believed, did involve themselves directly in the everyday affairs of life. They had an impact on such things as illness, luck, love, and business success. Consequently, most thought it was more important to curry favor with these subordinate, but more approachable, deities. One could not safely neglect the higher gods, but attention to these more imminent powers was more apt to pay off in day-to-day life.

66. A. E. Housman, *The Collected Poems of A. E. Housman* (New York/Chicago/San Francisco: Holt, Rinehart and Winston, 1965), 111.

67. Timothy B. Savage, *Power Through Weakness: Paul's Understanding of the Christian Ministry in 2 Corinthians*, SNTSMS 86 (Cambridge: Cambridge Univ. Press, 1996), 27.

Others may have insisted that there was only one all-powerful God. But the belief that this supreme God was remote and worked through an assortment of angelic intermediaries or star gods opened the door for a witch's brew of pagan notions to seep in.[68] Even some Jews believed that the planets were God's angels and the rules of astrology were evidence of God's laws.[69]

Christians in Colosse may have been seeking to venerate or appease starry gods in some way. Even if they were not, Paul suggests three key problems with such attempts. (1) By trying to protect themselves from the realm of dark forces, people actually will get caught in their web. (2) Believers waste their attentions on impotent powers rather than focusing on the reality of God revealed in Christ, their Head. (3) People mistakenly assume that the major problems besetting human beings are these spiritual forces that control us. The real problem is human sin, which makes us susceptible to the rulers and powers. Salvation is not redemption from the elemental spirits, from fate, or from the flesh. Instead, it is redemption *from sin*. This passage connects the leverage of the powers in human lives directly to sin. In rebelling against God, humans submit to the forces of darkness.

Paul makes it clear that God is not some impersonal, universal force, uncaring and distant. God does not rule the universe through the stars and planets, nor has he sent lowly intermediaries to redeem us or help us. God has created and sustains the universe through Christ (1:16–17), in whom the fullness of Deity dwells (1:19; 2:9). He took on our flesh and died on the cross for us (1:20; 2:11, 14). Christ now reigns supreme over the powers and authorities (2:10). All were created in him (1:16), and all were stripped of their potency through his death (2:15).

Christ's death does more than reveal to a sinful world how much God loved it. What is most important, Christ's death brings forgiveness of sins (2:13–14) and the defeat of evil, including demonic evil. On the cross the indebtedness from our sins was canceled and the powers were harnessed. Since Christians have died with Christ, we have been set free completely from these adversaries. The consequence of salvation from sin is deliverance from the tyranny of evil powers and so-called inexorable forces. Those who are

---

68. Arnold, *The Colossian Syncretism*, 218, cites the citation in Hippolytus (*Haeresies* 9.11) on the heretical teaching of Elchasai, who lived during the time of Trajan (A.D. 98–117). It mixed Jewish nomism with astrological beliefs and practices and warned against the wicked stars of impiety and their days of the sovereignty. Elchasai taught that the Sabbath needed to be honored since the powers of these stars prevailed on that day.

69. Lester J. Ness, "Astrology in Judaism in Late Antiquity," *ABW* 2 (1992): 47, cites the "Letter of Rehoboam," dating to A.D. 100, which claims to be Solomon's instructions to his son on how to make the angels and demons serve him. It includes prayers asking God to make the planets obedient and prescribes the offerings for each planet.

in Christ are no longer the playthings of forces and powers—however we conceptualize them—that seem beyond our control.

Paul does not specify what the elemental spirits are, and it is sometimes difficult to convey the patchwork of ancient beliefs about the supernatural world to a modern audience. If we conclude that Paul was referring to star gods, that does not mean that we can only understand them in this sense when we apply the passage to our context—particularly when translations such as the NIV offer an alternative view. The best procedure is to examine the text to see what these powers do so that we can spot the parallels and apply it to any contemporary phenomenon that takes on those aspects.

In Colossians, the *stoicheia tou kosmou* are connected to a "philosophy" that makes a prey of people (2:8), passes judgments (2:16), disqualifies them (2:18), and makes legalistic regulations (2:20). We can sketch out the following main characteristics:

- They are things that want to take over the role of lord. They consequently become rivals to Christ. Humans mistakenly give them a god-like status and submit to them, though they are not by nature gods (see Gal. 4:3, 8).
- They enslave and seek control (Gal. 4:3). Obedience to their supposed demands does not lead to human fulfillment but to greater enslavement.
- They thwart God's creative purposes for humans.
- They create a climate of fear and heighten the terror of existence for humans by making us feel that we are at their mercy.
- They heighten the sense of human insignificance and helplessness.
- They heighten a sense of determinism and create the feeling that humans are puppets under the control of some external force.

The *stoicheia*, powers, and authorities come in all sorts of guises, and in different cultures they receive different names and definitions. But they share a common characteristic in that humans take them to be unrelenting forces that suppress us and squelch our happiness. More important, humans open themselves up to their power through sin and ignorance. But to those who are in Christ, these forces, powers, and authorities are completely impotent.

 THE COLOSSIANS FACED theological danger from opponents who offered persuasive religious arguments that undermined their confidence in the truth they had received about Christ. Every generation of Christians faces such threats. The best defense Christians have

against such onslaughts is to be thoroughly grounded in the basics of their faith in Christ and to understand fully the significance of his death and resurrection and our baptism. We will then be better fortified in fending off the seduction of false ideologies and will have no anxiety about external powers controlling or ruining our lives.

Reiterating the truth of the gospel. In this section, Paul counters the attacks on the Christian hope and assuages the Colossians' fears by reviewing what Christ's death and resurrection mean and what God has done in Christ for us. He reiterates the truth of the gospel for them with vivid images.

The teachings about human sin and Christ's death, resurrection, and triumph, which reconcile us to God, were not something new to the Colossians. They had been taught it by Epaphras (1:7) and had "received Christ" (2:6)—that is, what had happened to Christ and what it meant. But Paul recognizes they need to hear it again. This need is particularly pressing when Christians find themselves besieged by those who mock, deride, or try to discredit their faith.

Sometimes pastors and teachers concentrate all their energy on attacking the opposition rather than first bolstering Christians' understanding of their faith and their confidence in its trustworthiness. Pastors may take for granted that their listeners know the basic doctrines of the Christian faith and so neglect to preach regularly on them. The inevitable result is that many in the pews become less familiar with and less certain of the Christian faith's powerful and life-transforming distinctives. This is not to say that preachers should become like broken records, repeating the same things over and over. But they should plan to address the central doctrines of the Christian faith each year in their preaching. Just as Paul needed to expound more than once the meaning of Christ's death for Christians and used vivid imagery that spoke to his day, so preachers and teachers today need to expound the significance of this mystery repeatedly.

We tend to be more adept at attacking others than we are at justifying our faith to them or training believers in the faith. In this section of his warnings to the Colossians, Paul does not combat the error simply with a withering attack against the opposition. In fact, because he spends more time stressing the sufficiency and supremacy of Christ than in berating the opposition, it makes it difficult to pinpoint precisely who the opponents are.

We can learn from this approach. Paul argues that Christ is superior to every power and authority, and the passage concludes with a picture of his triumphal procession, with his prisoners, beaten and disarmed, bringing up the rear. He reaffirms this truth for Colossians, who may be growing less assured of their victory in Christ. Paul also affirms that believers have already attained fullness in Christ and already have the resurrection life energizing them. Schweizer contends:

> It needs to be said today as well to a world no longer convinced in any sense of the absolute and undisputed superiority of the church, but convinced rather of the superior position of every other kind of power. It needs to be said to a world for which heaven is locked away, a world in danger of becoming heavenless. And it needs to be said with complete assurance.[70]

Paul's also uses graphic and colorful imagery in this section to convey the truth of what Christ's death and resurrection meant. He speaks of kidnapping, of Christ's death as a circumcision, of a stripping off of the flesh, of baptism as burial, of canceling an IOU, of nailing charges to a cross, and of leading defeated captives in a triumphal parade. This imagery, which was so fresh and compelling in a first-century context, may frustrate the modern interpreter since the passage of time has blurred its transparency. But the compelling power of such imagery in its original context provides a model for us when we communicate this truth today. We should always be attuned to metaphors that will both grip our contemporaries and convey faithfully what Christ's death and resurrection means so that the gospel message speaks afresh in every generation and culture.

We therefore need to find ways of making the significance of Christ's death and resurrection just as vivid and meaningful as Paul did for his original readers. This task is not easy. How does one convey that we have received "a circumcision [not] done by the hands of men" in language that people will understand today? Most literal-minded people do not want any such thing. But they may feel deep down the need for some atonement on their behalf. They may recognize that they need something from God that they cannot offer themselves. They can then understand that Jesus suffered the most gruesome of deaths *for us* so that we might be set free from the bondage of sin and death.

Besides understanding the significance of Christ's death and resurrection for our lives, the text demands two things of us: that we continue to live in Christ and that we abound in thanksgiving. If the truth of what Christ's death and resurrection mean sinks into the core of our being, we will live with more thanksgiving, and it will expel all our fears and worries over any unknown, unseen, or seemingly implacable forces. Failure to grasp this great truth, however, will only breed anxiety and dissatisfaction with life and make us susceptible to all manner of fraudulent promises.

---

70. Schweizer, *Colossians*, 152–53.

The lure of false ideologies. Albert Camus once wrote, "Truth, like light, blinds. Falsehood, on the contrary, is a beautiful twilight that enhances every object."[71] Paul warns about persuasive opponents who undermine Christian claims to truth with "twilight" delusions. Every generation of Christians faces new assaults on their faith. But these challenges are only a serious problem for those who are not thoroughly grounded and growing in their faith. Those who are uncertain in their faith can easily fall victim to half truths, misrepresentations, pious fables, and outright lies. They also become vulnerable, depending on their personal inclinations, to anything that may pass itself off as wisdom that appears to be more chic, more cut and dried, more profound, or more esoteric.

Pannenberg argues that many in our secularist culture today dismiss Christianity as a conventional religion, and this perception helps explain the widespread enthusiasm for "alternative religions."[72] People, including some who have been raised in traditional Christian homes, are looking elsewhere for novel approaches and more trendy strategies on how to cope with life. They chase after threadbare "philosophies" that promise to unlock the secrets of just about anything. They buy the tapes and books and attend conferences. Some even make treks to Egypt to sit inside a pyramid and soak up its supposed magical powers. All are searching for that something extra that they hope will put them over the top. But most of the answers that attract people today have no doctrine of human sin—or only a flimsy one—and therefore they never address the real problem that plagues human beings, nor do their adherents experience real redemption.

We also live in an era in which many are looking for personal fulfillment. People reject the fullness offered in Christ and search for other ways to fill themselves. "Selfism" is usually the result. Selfism takes the idea that we were created in God's image too far and ignores the idea that we have been corrupted by our sins and are culpable for them. It makes the self god and makes life's ultimate purpose reaching the self's fullest potential and satisfying its utmost desires.[73] Those who fill themselves only with themselves, however, remain empty. Those who are filled by Christ do not feel any chronic dissatisfaction with life or sense of insecurity, and they long only to please God and to pour their lives out for others. They can even rejoice amidst suffering and afflictions (Col. 1:24).

---

71. Albert Camus, *The Fall* (New York: Vintage International, 1991), 120.

72. Wolfhart Pannenberg, "How to Think About Secularism," *First Things* 64 (June/July 1996): 31.

73. See Paul Vitz, *Psychology As Religion: The Cult of Self Worship*, 2d ed. (Grand Rapids: Eerdmans, 1994).

Death and baptism: Receiving the benefits of Christ's circumcision. In Paul's day, a Gentile male became a Jewish proselyte by becoming circumcised, being washed in a ritual bath, and, if possible, offering a sacrifice at the temple. Paul picks up on these three elements of Jewish initiation and redefines them to assure the Colossians of their new status as full members of God's people. His redefinition centers on Christ's death. Christ's death is our circumcision, and we have been baptized (washed) into his death. His sacrificial death supersedes all temple sacrifices by canceling forever the charges that placed us on death row. Davis writes:

> The cross is the point chosen in time where all the evil in time and space, all the defiance against God can be concentrated into one visible decisive action against him. The cross is the wisdom of God to choose this point to make this attempt manifest and to defeat it. The cross is the power of God to absorb the ignorant blind rage of humanity into himself and avert its deadly consequences.[74]

While baptism marks out our entry into the church, Christ's body, it has more wide-ranging significance than simply as an initiatory rite. (1) In the New Testament, baptism is connected more to *death* than *washing*.[75] In Mark 10:38—39, Jesus uses the image of baptism for his death and says that it is something his disciples can and will share. Baptism becomes a performative visual aid in which we symbolically reenact Christ's death and resurrection.[76] In baptism, we voluntarily accept God's judgment on our sin and the sentence of death (Rom. 6:3—5; 2 Cor. 5:14), but we do not die alone. We die with Christ, who died for us. John Donne's "Hymne to God My God, in My Sicknesse" poetically expresses Paul's thought:

> We thinke that *Paradise* and *Calvarie,*
>   *Christs* Crosse, and *Adams* tree, stood in one place;
> Looke, Lord, and finde both Adams met in me;
>   As the first Adams sweat surrounds my face,
>   May the last Adams blood my soule embrace.[77]

(2) Baptism marks a break with the past. We die to the old—the old ways of living, the old alliances, the old powers that formerly held sway over our lives. In baptism we repudiate our sinful members (3:5). This renunciation is more effective than our puny attempts to restrain "sensual indulgence"

---

74. Henry Grady Davis, *Design for Preaching* (Philadelphia: Fortress, 1957), 103.
75. Moule, *Colossians and Philemon,* 96.
76. Caird, *Paul's Letters from Prison,* 188.
77. John Donne, *The Complete Poetry and Selected Prose of John Donne and the Complete Poetry of William Blake* (New York: The Modern Library, 1941), 271—72.

through our own will power and "harsh treatment of the body" (2:23). The reason it is more effective is because it is done *with Christ.*

(3) Baptism is not only the grave for "the old self"; it is the birthplace of the "new" (cf. 3:9–10). It proclaims death to the old order and the old lifestyle, but we do not "remain in the baptismal water." Baptism also proclaims that the new order is inaugurated.[78] Anyone who is in Christ is a new creation (2 Cor. 5:17).

The transformation, however, is not magical. In the movie "Tender Mercies," a former country music star whose career has been ruined by alcohol winds up working at a run-down motel for a widow with a young son. Eventually they marry, and both the son and his new stepfather are baptized on the same day. As they drive home in their pickup truck, the son reflects on the experience and says to his stepfather, "Everyone said I would feel like a changed person. I guess I do feel a little different but not a whole lot different. Do you?" "Not yet," came the reply. The son continues, "You don't look any different. You think I look any different?" "Not yet," came the reply again.

The "not yet" answer reveals that we should not always expect the transformation at conversion to be instantaneous or even dramatic. For some it is; but for others it is not. Braaten quotes Bishop Bergrav of Norway who said, "In baptism we take the old man and put him under. But the old man can sure swim."[79] Yet the death sentence for the "old man" has been pronounced, and the seeds for our transformation have taken root. Jones reminds us that

> baptism provides the initiation into God's story of forgiving and reconciling love, definitively embodied in the life, death and resurrection of Jesus of Nazareth. In response, people are called to embody the forgiveness by unlearning patterns of sin and struggling for reconciliation wherever there is brokenness.[80]

Some experience a dramatic and immediate turnaround when Christ enters their lives, but the process of unlearning years of sinful habits still takes time and struggle. The need for this continuing struggle explains why Paul adds the ethical exhortation that follows in 3:1–4:6. But because a new, divine power has been released into our lives, the struggle is no longer ours alone. The "not yet" will become a reality as God's loving power works in and through us and as we yield ever more of ourselves to God.[81] Baptism attests to the beginning of our transformation.

---

78. Bruce, *The Epistles to the Colossians, Philemon, and to the Ephesians,* 105.

79. Carl E. Braaten, *Christ and Counter Christ* (Philadelphia: Fortress, 1972), 84.

80. L. Gregory Jones, *Embodying Forgiveness: A Theological Analysis* (Grand Rapids: Eerdmans, 1995), 5.

81. The images of bearing fruit (a slow process) and increasing in knowledge (see 1:10) fit this idea of continual transformation.

(4) Baptism marks the defeat of the powers that formerly held sway over us. Those who have died with Christ and have been raised with him no longer live under the old regime, where the authorities and powers hold sway. Baptism is the sign to the world that we are owned, secured, and empowered by Christ. Christians owe the authorities and powers of this world no allegiance; and, in turn, the authorities and powers have no control over our lives.

Our symbolic death in baptism delivers us from real fears and powers. But this message is not always clearly communicated. A child's view about baptism in the novel *A Day No Pigs Would Die* may match the opinion that some adults secretly hold. A matronly aunt remonstrates with her young nephew about his bad grammar and says if he were a "fearing Baptist," he would do better in English. The frightened lad thought to himself:

> That was it! That there was the time my heart almost stopped. I'd heard about Baptists from Jacob Henry's mother. According to her, Baptists were a strange lot. They put you in water to see how holy you were. Then they ducked you under the water three times. Didn't matter a whit if you could swim or no. If you didn't come up, you got dead and your mortal soul went to Hell. But if you did come up, it was even worse. You had to be a Baptist.[82]

Baptism represents more than our death; it proclaims our triumph with Christ. We are raised with Christ, who is head over every power and authority (2:10), who has disarmed every power and authority (2:15), and who sits triumphantly at the right hand of God (3:1).

Deliverance from controlling forces. Most people in our culture do not live in terror of stars or sky gods regulating our fortunes. But even those who dismiss these elemental spirits as silly myths still may regard the world as a chamber of horrors. Many live in fear of the randomness of evil—random violence, random storms, random accidents—that wreaks havoc in their lives. Most want to experience some control over what will happen to them, and they fall victim to all sorts of self-deceptions and scams. We can spot something of the elemental spirits of the world when individuals consult astrologers, palm readers, Tarot cards, channelers, and psychics, and when they try to commune with ancient spirits, purify their auras with crystals, or make pilgrimages to vortex centers and sites of harmonic convergence to get in sync with powerful earth forces. MacLeod also connects the ancient apprehension with modern views that

> our character, personality and behavior are determined not by moral choices, but by the particular combination of genes, hormones, and

---

82. Robert Newton Peck, *A Day No Pigs Would Die* (New York: Alfred A. Knopf, 1972), 56.

glandular secretions that make each individual human body what it is. On any such view, whether ancient or modern, both the sense of guilt and the experience of forgiveness vanish with the lost conviction of moral freedom and responsibility.[83]

Long goes as far as to say that the Myers-Briggs test, so popular in revealing our differing styles, can be misused and comes perilously close to "fortune cookies for the human potential movement."[84] DeMaris critiques the work of Mary Daly as "uncannily" like the Colossian philosophy (as he reconstructs it).[85] She calls for women to tap their elemental potency, to reclaim their "capacity to receive inspiration, truth from the elements of the natural world." MacLeod points out that any quest for harmony with the forces of sheer power ignores that "the power behind the universe is a *moral* power, loving righteousness and hating iniquity."[86]

In our "biologized" world, DNA and the rigid laws of genetics have also taken the place of the tyrannous rule of powers and authorities in our understanding of the causative factors in our lives. Scott maintains that "we still think of ourselves as held in bondage by iron forces, inexorable laws, in the face of which all our struggles and aspirations are futile."[87] Many have become convinced that they are simply the products of the forces of nature over which they have no control or remedy. Everything from criminality, to addictions, to sexual orientation, to shyness is understood as a matter of genetic destiny rather than choice. It results in a sense of helplessness and a lack of moral responsibility—"I cannot help the way I am."

If most do not believe that their fate is written in the stars, many still believe that they do not make moral choices but simply fulfill unalterable genetic traits. If biological explanations lead us to believe that we cannot help ourselves, we are less likely to try to do battle with destructive behavior and more likely to succumb to it. The Christian faith offers the only remedy to this miasmic spiritual worldview. We find deliverance from everything in Christ.

We can also see these elemental spirits at work when the goal of life is to become successful as the world defines success, rather than to become godly as God requires. I received recently an advertisement that offered several enticements to subscribe to a magazine. The publisher promised to send a

---

83. MacLeod, "The Epistle to the Colossians: Exposition," 192.

84. Thomas G. Long, "Myers-Briggs and Other Modern Astrologies," *TToday* 49 (1992): 294.

85. DeMaris, *The Colossian Philosophy*, 149, citing Mary Daly, *Pure Lust: Elemental Feminist Philosophy* (New York: HarperCollins, 1984), 8–9, 11, 19, 155, 169, 178–81, 291–93.

86. MacLeod, "The Epistle to the Colossians: Exposition," 193.

87. Scott, *The Epistles of Paul to the Colossians, to Philemon and to the Ephesians*, 50.

booklet that would list "the secrets of health and better living," "the secrets of shrewd money management," "the secrets of being a smarter consumer," "the secrets of winning at almost anything," and a book entitled *How to Do Everything Right*. Learning these secrets presumably will lead to what they define as a successful life. It will not lead to salvation, however. MacLeod again is on target when he says:

> Moral salvation consists in the response of the moral will to the righteous purpose and the forgiving love of the living God. It is imparted to those who are brought into vital relationship with Christ, by first learning of him, and then committing their lives to him.[88]

Paul declares that all who have been buried in baptism with Christ have been set free from personal and/or impersonal powers that supposedly rule the universe. We have been set free from all those things that would enslave us, whether they be principles (worldly visions of what constitutes success) or principalities (other worldly or earthly forces). An African Christian song from the Transvaal captures the gist of Paul's argument:

> Jesus Christ is the conqueror;
> by his resurrection he overcame death itself,
> by his resurrection he overcame all things:
> he overcame magic,
> he overcame amulets and charms,
> he overcame the darkness of demon-possession,
> he overcame dread.
> When we are with him,
> we also conquer.[89]

It may be a helpful exercise for us to list all of our fears, whatever they may be. In Christ, we can cross them out one by one.

---

88. Ibid.

89. Quoted by Antonie Wessels, *Images of Jesus: How Jesus Is Perceived and Portrayed in Non-European Cultures* (Grand Rapids: Eerdmans, 1986), 94.

Colossians 2:16–23

❧

THEREFORE DO NOT let anyone judge you by what you eat or drink, or with regard to a religious festival, a New Moon celebration or a Sabbath day. [17]These are a shadow of the things that were to come; the reality, however, is found in Christ. [18]Do not let anyone who delights in false humility and the worship of angels disqualify you for the prize. Such a person goes into great detail about what he has seen, and his unspiritual mind puffs him up with idle notions. [19]He has lost connection with the Head, from whom the whole body, supported and held together by its ligaments and sinews, grows as God causes it to grow.

[20]Since you died with Christ to the basic principles of this world, why, as though you still belonged to it, do you submit to its rules: [21]"Do not handle! Do not taste! Do not touch!"? [22]These are all destined to perish with use, because they are based on human commands and teachings. [23]Such regulations indeed have an appearance of wisdom, with their self-imposed worship, their false humility and their harsh treatment of the body, but they lack any value in restraining sensual indulgence.

Original Meaning

PAUL MOVES FROM his assurance of Christ's all-sufficiency and the humbling defeat of the powers and authorities through the cross to specific warnings against the "philosophy." This direct polemic is the key passage for identifying the error threatening the Colossians. Paul repeats and reinforces his negative evaluation (see 2:8). It is "hollow" because it consists of "idle notions" (2:18); it is "deceptive" because it only has the appearance of wisdom and is incapable of producing what it promises (2:23). Its taboos depend on human tradition (2:22) and on the elementary spirits (2:20). The new pieces of information about the "philosophy" contain obscure vocabulary that has confounded interpreters. Our difficulty lies in trying to decide which of the many possible and plausible religious contexts best illuminate the meanings of these words.

The paragraph falls into a threefold structure consisting of two more warnings and a rhetorical question.

Second Warning (2:16–17; see first warning in 2:8)
- A Let no one condemn you (2:16a)
- B The issues they use to condemn others (introduced by preposition *en*): food, drink, feasts, New Moons, Sabbaths (2:16b)
- C Paul's evaluation: Why these issues are meaningless:
  - -They are only shadows of a reality (the body of Christ) already here (2:17)

Third Warning (2:18–19)
- A Let no one disqualify you (arbitrarily) (2:18)
- B The concerns they use to disqualify others (introduced by the preposition *en*): self-abasement, worship of angels, and visions (2:18b)
- C Paul's evaluation: The result of these concerns:
  - -They lead to puffing up of the mind of flesh (2:18c)
  - -They cut one off from the head, the source of growth for the body (2:19)

Rhetorical Question and Answer (2:20–23)
- A Since you died with Christ to the elemental spirits of the world, why submit to their regulations as if you were under their control? (2:20)
- B A sampling of the regulations: Do not handle, taste, or touch! (2:21)
- C Paul's evaluation: These regulations are useless:
  - -These things are destined to perish (2:22)
  - -They ultimately lead to the gratification of the flesh (2:23)

The basic protests against the "philosophy" are that it belongs to this world, which is destined to perish, whereas the Colossians belong to the world above (3:1–4), that it depreciates the work of Christ, and that it is basically wedded to subordinate, vassal powers.

Let No One Condemn You (2:16–17)

SINCE THE WARNINGS begin with "therefore," what follows spells out the relevance of the fullness of the Deity living in Christ (2:9), the Christian's union in his death, burial, and resurrection (2:10–13), and God's victory over the rulers and authorities (2:14–15). No self-appointed arbiters of divine reality have any right to pass judgment on believers or to decide who qualifies for a share in the inheritance of the saints (1:12). Only Christ can be their judge (see Rom. 14:4; 1 Cor. 4:1–5; 2 Cor. 5:10), and he is their deliverer.

Paul addresses the problems of dietary matters, the observance of days, and the temptation to pass judgment on others in Romans 14–15 (compare 1 Cor. 8–10). There he expresses his conviction that Christians are free to do what their conscience dictates—to eat or not to eat, to observe sacred days or not to observe them. He cautions the overly scrupulous from trying to force their regimen on others and encourages the strong to be especially sensitive to the scruples of the weak: "All food is clean, but it is wrong for a man to eat anything that causes someone else to stumble" (Rom. 14:20). All are to be mindful that the kingdom of God does not consist in "eating and drinking, but of righteousness, peace and joy in the Holy Spirit" (14:17).

In contrast, Colossians condemns outright those who use eating and drinking and the observance of feast days to pass judgment on others. Paul connects such rules to the mind of the flesh (2:18; NIV, "unspiritual mind," i.e., the sensuous mind or a human way of thinking), the elemental spirits of the world (2:20), and human commands and teachings (2:22). The differences between the argument in Romans and what we find in Colossians suggest that the latter does not have to do with an internal dispute among Christians. Paul rebuts *outsiders* who are using these issues to disparage Christians. These opponents have apparently arrogated to themselves the role of determining who belong to God's chosen people and who do not. They use the keeping of food laws and sacred days as part of their criteria for deciding this issue.

Paul does not reject these practices outright as idolatry but insists they are only a shadow of what is to come. The shadow/substance schema was a popular theme in middle Platonism, and the term *shadow* did not have the contemptuous connotation it might have for us today.[1] In this Greek system, it referred to an objective and concrete intimation of what is truly real, the archetype.[2] Paul modifies this schema to give it an eschatological and Christological slant by adding the phrases "the things that were to come" and "found in Christ."

The shadow/reality contrast as used by Paul applies to promise and fulfillment. Since Paul would never describe pagan rituals as a shadow or outline of what was to come in Christ, the promise/fulfillment motif is more fitting as an evaluation of Judaism. Religious festivals and New Moons relate to sacrifices in the temple. Caird observes, "Once we see the fulness of the sacrifice in the cross, we understand what the sacrificial worship of the Old Testament was groping after."[3] The phrase "the things that were to come" also connects these practices to Jewish eschatological hopes for the new age (see

---

1. See Philo, *Confusion of Tongues* 190; *Who Is the Heir?* 72–73, 112; *The Migration of Abraham* 12. The writer of Hebrews describes the tabernacle as "a copy and shadow of what is in heaven" (Heb. 8:5) and the law as "only a shadow of the good things that are coming" (10:1).

2. Hebrews 10:1 provides a parallel: "The law is only a shadow of the good things that are coming—not the realities themselves. For this reason it can never, by the same sacrifices repeated endlessly year after year, make perfect those who draw near to worship."

3. G. B. Caird, *The Language and Imagery of the Bible* (Philadelphia: Westminster, 1980), 53.

Isa. 9:6; Matt. 12:32; Eph. 1:21).[4] The implication is clear: Christ fulfills all Jewish sacrifices and hopes.[5] The future yearned for by the prophets has broken into the present.[6]

The emphasis that the reality is found in Christ picks up ideas from 1:15–20 that Christ is the image of the invisible God and the head of the body.[7] Those who are in Christ's body also share in the reality of reconciliation and will be presented to God as holy and blameless (1:20, 22). Paul's conclusion therefore is: Why play in the shadow world when you have experienced the real thing?

Let No Self-Important, Self-Appointed Umpires Arbitrarily Disqualify You (2:18–19)

FRANCIS COMMENTS ON 2:18 that "the interpretation of nearly every word or phrase has been disputed."[8] Giving thorough attention to the various views and their permutations is a daunting task that is best carried out in a monograph. We will therefore allow the NIV translation to set the agenda for our interpretation, which differs with it at several points.

"Do not let anyone who delights in" renders the Greek participle *thelon* ("wishing," "desiring"), and this translation assumes that Paul's expression reflects a Hebraism.[9] Paul pictures the opponent as setting up "humility" as

---

4. O'Brien, *Colossians*, 140, observes that the term *shadow* does not have the Platonic sense of a timeless, metaphysical copy of the heavenly and eternal "idea." It is used in the sense of foreshadowing what is to come. The addition of the phrase "the things that were to come" clearly transforms it from any static Platonic dualism to an expression of Jewish eschatological hope (see also Dunn, *The Epistles to the Colossians and to Philemon*, 176).

5. The NIV captures this meaning by translating it "the things that were to come," making it clear that the realities have come in Christ.

6. A similar thought is expressed in Gal. 3:23–25, using the imagery of imprisonment and minority: "Before this faith came, we were held prisoners by the law, locked up until faith should be revealed. So the law was put in charge to lead us to Christ that we might be justified by faith. Now that faith has come, we are no longer under the supervision of the law."

7. The phrase translated in the NIV "the reality . . . is found in Christ" reads literally, "the body of Christ."

8. Fred O. Francis, "Humility and Angelic Worship in Col 2:18," in *Conflict at Colossae*, ed. Fred O Francis and Wayne A Meeks, 163.

9. The verb *thelo* does not mean "delight," but Hebrew does use the phrase *ḥapaṣ bᵉ* ("delight in," "take pleasure in," or "have a desire for"; see 1 Sam. 18:22; 2 Sam. 15:26; 1 Kings 10:9; 1 Chron. 28:4; 2 Chron. 9:8; Ps. 111:1; 146:10; *Testament of Asher* 1:6). Some argue that this Hebraic idiom is behind the Greek text. Dunn, *The Epistles to the Colossians and to Philemon*, 178, contends that it refers to "what the other sets as *his own* goal or relishes as the means of achieving that goal, not a goal or means of achieving it which he sets before or wishes to impose on the Colossian Christians."

"his own goal." The opponent then insists, "My way is superior to yours; it achieves goals you fall short of."[10] This interpretation has been widely adopted, but it does not seem likely that Paul would resort to a wooden biblicism to express himself here.

The participle *thelon* can also modify the verb "disqualify": "Let no one willfully disqualify you."[11] Beare translates it: "Let no one disqualify you as he wills [not as God wills], in questions of. . . ."[12] This reading has the advantage of preserving the parallelism with 2:16, where the matters the errorists use to condemn the Colossians are introduced by preposition *en* ("in"; NIV, "with regard to").[13] The opponents declare the Colossians unfit because they fail to measure up on issues of humility, worship of angels, and visions.

The verb translated "disqualify for the prize" (*katabrabeuo*) is a rare word.[14] Most assume that it retains the primary meaning of the verb *brabeuo*, which means to act as a judge who decides or rules and awards prizes in contests (see 3:15). These self-appointed referees rule against the believers and rob them of their deserved award (see 1 Cor. 9:24; Phil. 3:14).[15] The errorists are puffed up and have the gall to gainsay the Christians' salvation.

The NIV has the errorists "delight[ing] in false humility." The adjective "false" does not appear in the Greek text in 2:18 or 2:23. Precisely what "humility" refers to is unclear. In such a pejorative context, one may reasonably assume that Paul scoffs at it. He may imply that it is a "false humility," particularly since it results in their becoming "puffed up." On the other hand, "humility" may be connected grammatically to the angels, so that Paul may have in mind the angels' humility and worship, which the opponents observe.[16] Another option is to interpret it as a reference to a specific form

---

10. See James D. G. Dunn, "The Colossian Philosophy: A Confident Jewish Apologia," *Bib* 76 (1995): 171. See Gottlob Schrenk, "θέλω, κτλ.," *TDNT*, 3:46, n. 13.

11. A. Fridrichsen, "Thelon Col. 2:18," *ZNW* 21 (1922): 135–37. The verb can look forward to the "will-worship" (NIV "self-imposed worship") in 2:23; Paul connects it to individual willpower. See Houlden, *Paul's Letters from Prison*, 197.

12. Beare, "The Epistle to the Colossians," 202.

13. The parallelism can be shown in this literal translation:

"Let no one condemn you in [*en*] food, drink, feasts, New Moons, Sabbaths" (2:16b).

"Let no one disqualify you willfully [or arbitrarily] in [*en*] humility [self-abasement], worship of angels, and visions" (2:18b).

14. See further, Arnold, *The Colossian Syncretism*, 225. The verb without the preposition (*brabeuo*) occurs in 3:15 ("rule").

15. The opponents may not intend to rob them of the prize; that is Paul's reading of the situation and the result of any capitulation to their views.

16. Francis, "Humility and Angelic Worship in Col 2:18," argues that the errorists see the humility of angels in their visions. Christopher Rowland, "Apocalyptic Visions and the Exaltation of Christ in the Letter to the Colossians," *JSNT* 19 (1983): 75, contends that Paul

of humility, namely, fasting.[17] The noun is linked to "harsh treatment of the body" in 2:23, so that "mortification" or "self-abasement" may be a better translation. Fasting may have been part of the preparations for the heavenly visions and revelations. In this case, such humility was intended to purge the errorists of the worldly dross that weighed down the soul and kept it from soaring spiritually.[18] Self-mortification, however, can become twisted into a perverse self-exaltation.

The phrase "worship of angels" is the next knot to unravel. The word translated "worship" (*threskeia*) can mean "religion" (Acts 26:5, "our religion"), the practice of religion (James 1:26–27), or the worship of something (Wis. 14:18, 27). The phrase could refer to religion instituted by angels (a genitive of source). Normally, however, the object of religious veneration is in the genitive case. This would mean that Paul accuses the errorists of worshiping angels (objective genitive). Some have claimed that the Colossian errorists understood these angels to be involved in creation and the government of the world, and they worshiped them as their link to God. These angels could be regarded as malevolent and needing appeasement or as benevolent and bestowing blessing. Their so-called "worship" may only have involved propitiating them to ward off their evil effects or beseeching them for protection.[19]

Others have argued that this phrase refers to the worship that the angels themselves offer (subjective genitive). The angels engage in the highest office of all created beings, the adoration of God. The phrases "humility and the worship of angels," "what he has seen," and "goes into" can be taken together to refer to some heavenly ascent.[20] The "philosophy" would not then be advocating the worship of angels but would be aspiring to enter

---

is not referring to "fasting by human beings followed by devotion to exalted angelic beings but entirely concerned with the angels in heaven." He argues (81, n. 24), "It makes better sense of the section to regard the humility not as a reference to the ritual preparations for visions performed by men (e.g., fasting) but as a part of what was seen by the visionary." See also Craig A. Evans, "The Colossian Mystics," *Bib* 63 (1982): 195–96.

17. It may be a Greek translation of the Hebrew *som*, which can mean "fasting" and "affliction." See Ps. 35:13; 69:10; Isa. 58:3, 5; Judith. 4:9; Psalms of Solomon 3:8.

18. Fasting is associated with heavenly revelation in Dan. 10:2–3; 4 Ezra 5:13, 20; 6:35; 2 *Apocalypse of Baruch* 5:7; *Apocalypse of Abraham* 9:7–10; *Testament of Isaac* 4:1–6; 5:4; *Greek Apocalypse of Ezra* 1:2–7; Philo, *On Dreams* 1.35–37; *Life of Moses* 2.67–70. Hermas, *Visions* 3.10.6; *Similitudes* 5.3.7 connects fasting to receiving visions: "All inquiries require humility; fast therefore, and you will receive what you ask of the Lord."

19. Pagan cults of angels existed in the ancient world; see A. R. R. Sheppard, "Pagan Cults of Angels in Roman Asia Minor," *Talanta* 12–13 (1980–81): 77–101.

20. Rowland, "Apocalyptic Visions," 75, notes that "there was considerable interest in the apocalyptic literature in the worship of the heaven court."

heaven to worship as the angels do.[21] The problems with this view make it an unlikely, although widely accepted, option. First, there are no instances where a noun in the genitive linked to the word "worship" functions as a subjective genitive. Second, the "self-imposed worship" (*ethelothreskia*) in 2:23 describes something that humans offer and is treated as something dubious.[22]

Arnold makes the case that Paul does not have in mind some organized cult that worshiped angels in the same way that gods were worshiped with praise, prayers, and sacrifice. The Greek word *threskeia* can be used to denote invocation or conjuration. He argues that Paul is referring to the magical invocation of angels to ward off evil and believes that such a practice had its roots in deeply ingrained folk beliefs and habits. Local evidence confirms that angels did play a prominent role in the religious life of the people. Whatever their primary religious orientation, the people in this area commonly called on angels to protect and help them, to bring success in business, to destroy enemies, or to remove the effects of a curse.[23]

The spiritual atmosphere of magic pervaded the lives of both rich and poor, both educated and uneducated, in the ancient world and may have continued to exert its effects on the Colossian believers even after their conversion. They conjured the angels, as God's powerful agents (see Matt. 27:53), to protect them from the evil powers (identified as *ta stoicheia tou kosmou*, the rulers and authorities, the thrones and lordships, and every other invisible power) that could potentially injure them. They may also have called on angels to help them to make their lives successful or to bring vengeance on their enemies.[24]

---

21. Rowland (ibid., 77) suggests that like Qumran, the "opponents in Colossae may have considered that the activities of angels were not merely of interest to the visionary but important as an example for the righteous to imitate." Consequently, what worried Paul "was that the Colossians were not interested in Christ as the centre of their religious experience, but in the activities of the angels as a pattern for living which might detract from the example of Christ."

22. See Arnold, *Colossian Syncretism*, 92–93.

23. Arnold picks up and develops a suggestion by A. Lukyn Williams, "The Cult of Angels at Colossae," *JTS* 10 (1909): 413–38, who claimed that it refers to a veneration of angels found on the fringes of Judaism in connection to exorcism and magic.

24. Arnold, *The Colossian Syncretism*, 20, shows that magical texts do reflect a "high regard for 'angels' and other supernatural beings that were invoked by the practitioner.... 'Angels' known from Judaism figure prominently in the magical papyri." Magic was syncretistic, and people involved in it would use whatever names and intermediaries that promised power. Regarded as powerful assistants of God, most assumed that angels could help accomplish the same things as God, and they could be more easily manipulated to do whatever one wanted. Angels were also associated with the stars and planets, which were viewed as active in controlling human fate. Consequently, many invoked angels to provide protection from harmful spirits, to become agents in revelatory magic and dream oracles (to give

In the polemical context that expresses Paul's contempt for the arrogance of the "philosophy," the reference to "the worship of angels" may well be a biased description of its practices. If the errorists were actually and actively worshiping angels, we would expect Paul to spew forth a far more passionate denunciation of such idolatry. We may infer from his relative calm on this issue that they are not actually offering worship to angelic beings or invoking them. Thus, Paul may only be disdainfully caricaturing the "philosophy's" ritual concerns and attention to New Moons as the worship of angels.[25] The aspersion would link the "philosophy" unfavorably to the familiar pagan practice of invoking angels.[26]

Such scorn has modern parallels. Those who grew up in conservative Protestant circles may have heard someone accuse Roman Catholics, for example, of "worshiping Mary" or of being guilty of "Mariolatry." Others may have heard someone accuse conservative Christians of worshiping the Bible or being guilty of "bibliolatry." An undue veneration of either lends

---

answers to questions), and to ensure prosperity and success in any kind of endeavor. One example may be cited from the Greek magical papyri (4.3165–76): "Give me all favor, all success, for the angel bringing good, who stands beside [the goddess] Tyche, is with you. Accordingly give profit [and] success to this house."

25. Caird, *The Language and Imagery of the Bible*, 26, suggests that "worship of angels" was Paul's pejorative and emotive term for a practice he wished to ridicule and which the opponents would have resented. Wright, *Colossians and Philemon*, 122, contends that the tone and context suggest that Paul is using "heavy irony: the people he is opposing spend so much time in speculations about angels, or in celebrating the fact that their law was given by them, that they are in effect worshiping them instead of God. . . ." It is a "contemptuous reference" to their worship that may appear to be "heavenly-minded and super-spiritual" but was in fact "bordering on idolatry." See also Michael Mach, *Entwicklungstadien des jüdischen Engelglaubens in vorrabbinischer Zeit*, Texte und Studien zum Antiken Judentum (Tübingen: J. C. B. Mohr [Paul Siebeck], 1992), 294.

26. We have argued that a local Jewish group that dismissed the Christian hope was the root of the Colossian problem; if they actually worshiped angels, then it would have been a very syncretistic form of Judaism. Rimmon Kasher, "Angelology and the Supernal Worlds in the Aramaic Targums to the Prophets," *JSJ* 27 (1996): 168–91, compares the treatment of angels in Targum Jonathan and the Toseftot Targum. Targum Jonathan, which was more heavily influenced by the views of the rabbinical sages, adopted a more cautious, reserved approach to angels, never assigning them any independent power. The Toseftot Targum was never accepted as an official translation, and its unexpurgated renderings offer "valuable evidence of popular Jewish concepts and beliefs as they evolved in synagogues of Antiquity." It had a positive view of angels, mentioning their names and introducing their involvement in events on earth and in the heavens. But even here angels were not independent beings to be worshiped or addressed and took no part in prayer. When one reads some Jewish texts relating to angels, however, one can easily imagine how the elaborate angelology can be caricatured as a kind of worship of angels. As is the case today, the less theologically sophisticated believer may have shown an undue reverence for them.

---

itself to such attacks from critics. In my opinion, Paul dismisses the belief system of the "philosophy" as no better than "the worship of angels." Christ, on the other hand, created these beings and reigns over them (1:16).

The next phrase in 2:18 is no less difficult to decipher: "Such a person goes into great detail about what he has seen." The verb translated "goes into great detail" (*embateuo*) has a wide range of uses that could fit this context.[27] It could be a technical term for the final stage of initiation in local mystery cults, in which the initiate crosses the divine threshold of the sanctuary's inner shrine and receives the new life offered by the god.[28]

The verb may also mean "to enter into the possession of something," in this case, the heavenly realm as part of some mystical journey.[29] Heaven then becomes the unexpressed object of the verb. If this is the meaning to be used here, one can render the phrase as "entering the things he had seen." Wright contends that this may be an ironic dismissal of their claim that they "enter into the worship of heaven itself." In truth, what they are entering are

---

27. Some manuscripts (followed by the KJV) have "what he has *not* seen," so that Paul denies the reality of these visions.

28. William M. Ramsay, *The Teaching of Paul in Terms of the Present Day*, 2d ed. (London: Hodder and Stoughton, 1914), 285–305. Martin Dibelius, "The Isis Initiation in Apuleius and Related Initiatory Rites," in *Conflict in Colossae*, ed. Fred O. Francis and Wayne Meeks, Sources for Biblical Study 4 (Missoula: Scholar's Press, 1973), 61–121, developed his views that this phrase alludes to an initiation into a mystery religion from inscriptions connected to the Apollo temple at Claros, a short distance from Ephesus.

Apuleius, in *Metamorphoses* ("*The Golden Ass*"), 11.19–23, describes such a visionary journey where Lucius, the protagonist, proceeds to different levels in his initiation to the goddess Isis and sees the higher and lower deities subjected to the goddess. He learns the secret and venerable tradition and prepares for his initiation by abstaining from certain foods and wine, by going through purificatory rites, and by obeying several arduous prohibitions. He puts on a linen garment and enters the innermost sanctuary ("the boundary of death"). At midnight he experiences a vision: "I saw the sun flashing with bright light" and "I came face to face with the gods below and the gods above and paid reverence to them from close at hand" (11.23). He passes through the "elements" (11.23) and then gains immunity from and authority over hostile powers.

Arnold, *The Colossian Syncretism*, 231, offers the possibility that the leaders of the errorists had experienced ritual initiation in one or more of the Phrygian cults before their conversion. They "viewed their past visionary experience as giving them authentic and helpful insight into the supernatural realm." What they had seen was "a partial basis for their claim of wisdom and understanding in these matters" and for belittling others.

In my opinion, the existence of such parallels does not necessitate that Paul refers to such initiatory visions; it only remains a possibility. If someone were extolling their initiation into one of the Phrygian cults as providing greater spiritual wisdom and additional protection from the powers, I cannot imagine that Paul would be so docile in his response. Paul does not call for them to reject their pagan past again.

29. F. O. Francis, "The Background of EMBATEUEIN (Col 2:18) in Legal Papyri and Oracle Inscriptions," in *Conflict at Colossae*, ed. F. O. Francis and Wayne Meeks, 199.

only their own visions—"what they have seen." "All they have discovered in their vaunted mystical experiences is a set of imaginary fantasies."[30]

The verb *embateuo* can also mean "to investigate" or "to scrutinize" (2 Macc. 2:30) and may refer to dwelling on ecstatic visions for divine insight. The NIV adopts this interpretation with its translation "goes into great detail." As Barth and Blanke state it, the errorists were "preoccupied with their own religious experiences."[31] Paul does not need to give the Colossians an objective description of the opponents' beliefs and practices and only wants to deflate their false boasts by subverting them with sarcasm. Their exaggerated visions are all smoke and mirrors, much ado about nothing. Their nervy conceit is all folly.

The upshot of these experiences, whatever they may have been, is clear, and this is what provokes Paul.[32] They puff up the worshiper's "unspiritual mind" (lit., "the mind of his flesh") with idle notions. For Paul, the mind of the flesh is something set over against God (Rom. 8:6–7) and lacks any true spiritual enlightenment. MacLeod best summarizes Paul's antipathy for the "philosophy": It was "emotionally elating, ego inflating, and worst of all, brother berating."[33]

The root of the error is one's failure to hold the Head (2:19).[34] The verb "hold" (*krateo*) appears in Jesus' critique of the Pharisees' traditions: They were "holding to the traditions of the elders" and "of men" and "let[ting] go of the command of God" (Mark 7:3, 4, 8; see also 2 Thess. 2:15; Rev. 2:14–15). Paul opened this section in Colossians with a verb used for the transmission of tradition, "you received Christ Jesus as Lord" (2:6). Now, in 2:19, he may be underscoring the contrast between the Colossian Christians and their antagonists, who do not hold to Christ or observe his teaching. They "hold" to something other than Christ. Holding to anything other than Christ, the Head (1:18; 2:10), will cause them to disintegrate and perish.

The head-body metaphor in 2:19 assumes that the head supplies nourishment to the whole body and enables it to grow. Literally, the text reads that "it grows the growth of God" (cf. 1:6, 10). Growth hinges on a close bond with Christ, though God causes it (cf. 1 Cor. 3:6–7). All who do not hold

---

30. Wright, *Colossians and Philemon*, 123. Paul was reticent about his own visionary experiences. When he did mention them to the Corinthians, he used the third person and said that his entering heaven produced nothing he was permitted to repeat and led to his thorn in the flesh (2 Cor. 12:1–10).

31. Barth and Blanke, *Colossians*, 349. This interpretation best explains the present tense of the participle.

32. Dunn, *The Epistles to the Colossians and to Philemon*, 182, claims that what Paul finds "reprehensible" is "the attitude of dismissive superiority" engendered by the interest in angelic worship, not the interest itself.

33. MacLeod, "The Epistle to the Colossians," 205.

34. See Barth and Blanke, *Colossians*, 350.

to Christ and his teachings have cut themselves off from the only source of vitality and unity. The church is the body of Christ (1:18; 3:15) by virtue of confessing him to be the head and of dying with him and being made alive in him (2:11–13).[35] Paul therefore reminds his readers again of Christ's supremacy over all things and their total dependence on him. They will not find growth or fullness in earthly taboos, celestial observances, "worship of angels," or star-spangled visions. Such things can only puff up human beings with the hot air of empty pride and snap the bonds that moor them to Christ.

Why Allow a False Wisdom to Make the Rules? (2:20–23)

THE VERB TRANSLATED "submit" (*dogmatizo*, 2:20) refers to regulations decreed by someone and recalls the noun *dogma* in 2:14 (NIV, "regulations"). There Paul affirms that the IOU that was against us with its regulations has been abolished by Christ's death. The NIV may imply that the Colossians have already submitted to these rules, but Paul does not rebuke them for already acquiescing to these rules; he only warns them against it. They do not need to live by such decrees.[36]

(1) In 2:20, Paul summarizes the main point from 2:11–15. By dying with Christ believers have moved out of the elemental spirits' control.[37] The phrase

---

35. Jerome Murphy-O'Connor, "Tradition and Redaction in Col 1:15–20," *RB* 102 (1995): 240, questions the widely held view that Paul's vision of the Church as a "body" derives from the Greek philosophical reflections on the body politic. He considers it most implausible and "psychologically impossible" for Paul to take over a term used to characterize civil society that was "riven by divisions" (Gal. 3:28; 5:19–20) and to apply it to the church, whose unity was rooted in the love of Christ (1 Thess. 4:9). Rather, he suggests that the image was a reaction to one of the striking features of the temples dedicated to Asclepius that were "widely scattered throughout the eastern Mediterranean; namely, the ceramic representations of parts of the body which had been cured." He argues:

> The sight of legs which were not legs, of hands which were not hands, brought Paul to the realization that a leg was truly a leg only when a part of a body. Believers, he inferred, were truly "alive" only when they "belonged" to Christ as his members (2:6, 13; 3:4). The "death" of egocentric isolation has been replaced by the "life" of shared existence.

36. Morna Hooker, "Were There False Teachers in Colossae?" in *Christ and Spirit in the New Testament*, ed. Barnabas Lindars and Stephen S. Smalley (Cambridge: Cambridge Univ. Press, 1973) 317, offers the translation "Why submit?" She is followed by Dunn, *The Epistles to the Colossians and to Philemon*, 188. The verb translated "submit" (*dogmatizesthe*) can be middle or passive in form. If it is translated as a passive, "Why should you allow yourselves to be subjected to its rules?" (KJV), it is clearer that they have not already acquiesced. Wright, *Colossians and Philemon*, 125, argues that it should be taken as a passive because it is not "a rebuke for a lapse" but "a warning of danger." See also Barth and Blanke, *Colossians*, 354.

37. The implication is that the errorists still live under their dominion.

---

to stoicheia tou kosmou recurs (see above on 2:8). The NIV again translates it as "the basic principles of this world." But the Colossian Christians have died to something far more malevolent and fearsome than "basic principles"; they have died to formidable powers that now can exercise no control over them. As Christ triumphed over these rulers and powers (2:15), so did they when they died with him.

Since Christians have been released from the rulers' and powers' slavery, why would they ever consider giving these powers new life by submitting to their irksome and irrelevant taboos? Baptism into Christ means death to their dominion (2:11; 3:3), though this reality does not mean that we are now free of all rules. In the context, the rules cited are those that belong to this unspiritual world and cut one off from Christ. The Colossians still live in the world, but they do not need to live as if the powers had any control over them, and they do not need to give any regard to their rules. This statement applies to every historical reconstruction of the problem at Colosse.

(2) The sampling of the taboos in 2:21 ("Do not handle! Do not taste! Do not touch!") could fit a variety of situations. The ban could involve not only food and drink but also sexual relations, which, according to some, made persons ritually impure. People abstained from both for a variety of reasons and in a variety of contexts—for initiation into mystery religions, for magical rituals, for receiving mystical visions in Judaism.[38] The succession of what are clearly Jewish issues in this section (circumcision, New Moons, Sabbath), however, points to a critique of Jewish food laws.[39] Paul lampoons these stifling restraints.[40]

---

38. Philo (*Life of Moses II*, 68–69) claimed that Moses cleansed himself of all the calls of mortal nature (food, drink, and intercourse with women) when he entered on his work as prophet so that he would always be fit to receive the oracular messages.

39. See Rom. 14:5–6, which lumps observances of special days together with food and drink. Dunn, *The Epistles to the Colossians and to Philemon*, 172, points out that "traditional Jews" placed great importance on food laws and fiercely insisted on "maintenance of their practice as a vital test case of Jewish identity and faithfulness to God's covenant with Israel." See Lev. 7:26–27; 11:1–23; Deut. 12:16, 23–24; 14:3–21; Dan. 1:3–16; 10:3; Tob. 1:10–12; Judith 12:2, 19; Add. Est. 14:17; *Joseph and Asenath* 7:1; 8:5. Jewish scruples over food were well known throughout the ancient world.

Jews in the Diaspora normally lived with their Gentile neighbors in a state of mutual respect. Why would they denounce Christians for failing to observe such rules? Dunn (174) argues that Christians had taken over Jewish claims and privileges for themselves, and this would have aroused their ire. They could not tolerate their claims to be redeemed by the God of Israel when they rejected the identity markers that set God's people apart from the unwashed hordes.

40. Beare, "The Epistles to the Colossians," 206, cites Chrysostom's comment: "See how he mocks them."

(3) In 2:22–23 Paul draws out four negative implications from these prohibitions. (1) The string of "do not's" implies that to avoid contamination one needs to avoid practically everything and shut oneself up in a purity cocoon.[41] Such prohibitions contrast dramatically with Paul's advice to the Corinthians: "Eat anything sold in the meat market without raising questions of conscience, for, 'The earth is the Lord's, and everything in it'" (1 Cor. 10:25–26). When eating and drinking is done for the glory of God, it does no harm (10:31). Consequently, Paul tells the Romans, "All food is clean" (Rom. 14:20). What matters is belonging to the Lord (14:8), honoring and giving thanks to God in whatever we eat or drink (14:6), acting in love (14:15), serving Christ (14:18), and building up our neighbor (15:2), so that we may "glorify the God and Father of our Lord Jesus Christ" (15:6).

(2) Such taboos focus only on fleeting realities that "perish with use."[42] Jesus gives a more earthy evaluation of such things. Food "doesn't go into his heart but into his stomach, and then out of his body" (Mark 7:19)—a euphemistic translation (the text lit. reads, "It goes out into the latrine"). From Paul's perspective, this is where the opponents' taboos belong as well. What the errorists offer only has to do with perishable things, and their rules only bind them even more to this present evil age. What Christ offers believers has to do with what is eternal, and he delivers them from the power of darkness. Therefore, they should ignore the objections of those whose religious preoccupations are all empty whimsies with no eternal effects.

(3) Paul repeats that these prohibitions are based on human customs (see 2:8; also Isa. 29:13; Mark 7:7).[43] It may appear on the surface that such rigorous discipline and show of pious sentiment must possess great wisdom, but it is only human wisdom.

(4) These restrictions not only fail to achieve what they advertise, they drive persons ever more firmly into the grip of the flesh. Moule reflects the despair of many commentators since the time of Theodore of Mopsuestia that we will never decipher the meaning of 2:23: "This verse is by common consent regarded as hopelessly obscure—either owing to corruption or because we have lost the clue."[44] The NIV takes the phrase *plesmone tes sarkos* (lit.,

---

41. Caird, *Paul's Letters from Prison*, 200. Houlden, *Paul's Letters from Prison*, 199, says he is mocking them "for their pernickety scrupulosity."

42. This phrase is difficult and reads literally, "which things are all for corruption in the using."

43. Dunn, *The Epistles to the Colossians and to Philemon*, 193–94, claims that this text offers further proof that the opponents are Jewish: "The allusion to a rebuke to Israel would only be effective if it came as a rebuke to those who understood themselves as the people of Israel. These regulations of which the Colossian (Christian?) Jews made so much were the very 'commands and teachings' that Isaiah had long ago warned against."

44. Moule, *Colossians and Philemon*, 108.

"gratification of the flesh") in a bad sense to mean "sensual indulgence." One can, however, make better sense of the sentence by punctuating it differently. The main clause could be: "Such regulations [lit., which things] ... lead to the gratification of the flesh." A subordinate concessive clause interrupts it, "though having a reputation for wisdom in [the areas of] self-imposed worship, humility [mortification], and severe treatment of the body." The phrase "without any value" (or "honor") is subordinate to this concessive clause.[45] The punctuation of this complex sentence would then be: "Such regulations—though having a reputation for wisdom in [the areas] of self-imposed worship, humility [mortification], and severe treatment of the body, [but being] without any value—lead to the gratification of the flesh."

This explanation of the grammar of 2:23 means that the errorists suffered from the law of unintended consequences. Their religious aim to serve God and to bridle the flesh only succeeded in serving the flesh and unleashing its power.[46] Self-imposed worship, humility, and harsh treatment of the body built up the importance of the flesh (see 2:11, NIV "sinful nature") rather than putting it off. They became disciplines for their own sake and only led to puffing up the mind of the flesh (2:18, NIV "unspiritual mind"), which first concocted them. Scott summarizes Paul's critique well: "Their professed object is to lift men out of the lower life, while in point of fact they only plunge them into it more deeply—concentrating all thought and effort on purely material things."[47] This "philosophy" will therefore only squire its adherents to their final disqualification.

From Paul's perspective it is all a sham, though it may impress gullible observers. The *Epistle to Diognetus* (second century) disparages Judaism in much the same way as we understand this section in Colossians to do. It first explains why Christians do not worship in the same way as Jews and then denigrates as ridiculous their scruples about food, observance of the Sabbath, pride in circumcision, devotion to fasting, and the feast of the New Moon. "Their attention to the stars and moon for the observance of months and days," it says, is not "proof of piety" but "rather of foolishness," "general silliness," and "deceit."[48]

---

45. Bruce Hollenbach, "Col. II.23: Which Things Lead to the Fulfillment of the Flesh," *NTS* 25 (1978–79): 254–61. The "which things" (*hatina*) refers backward to the "human commands and teachings " (2:22) and forward to the list in 2:23—wisdom, self-imposed worship, humility, harsh treatment of the body (see Arnold, *The Colossian Syncretism*, 200).

46. Hollenbach, "Col. II.23," 261, reminds us of the clear causal connection in Paul's thought between legalism and the fulfillment of the flesh (see Rom. 6:12–14; 7:5, 8–10, 21–23; Gal. 3:21–22; 5:17–21).

47. Scott, *The Epistles to the Colossians, to Philemon, and to the Ephesians*, 61.

48. *Epistle to Diognetus*, 4.1, 5–6.

Paul is no less critical. The mystical experiences and devotional genuflections of the errorists accomplished nothing spiritual and were worth nothing. But he grounds his critique in Christology. All their shadowboxing is surpassed by the bright light of Christ's victory already won for us. Christians do not need to treat the body with severity because they have already cut off the body of flesh in the circumcision of Christ (2:11).

Asceticism is a futile attempt to defeat the flesh and is no match for the cross. Ascending to heavenly realms and beholding visions is no match for the heavenly ascent of Christ, who now sits at God's right hand. Forgiveness, reconciliation to God, new life, and the defeat of the elemental spirits and powers can only be found only in Christ.

THE DIFFICULTY IN pinpointing precisely what "philosophy" Paul has trained his guns on in this section makes it more difficult to bridge into our context. Although we must make some decision—at least when one writes a commentary on the passage—the scanty evidence increases the margin for error. When we try to bridge the contexts, the question arises: Are we even trying to cross the right bridge?

Many scholars contend that the original problem was some syncretistic mélange of pagan, Jewish, and Christian beliefs and practices. If this view is correct, it would bridge nicely into our culture, which is now seeing a resurgence of syncretistic beliefs. Some modern cults try to pass themselves off as Christian because they have adopted selected Christian beliefs, but in reality they are a mishmash of various ideas jumbled together. The danger of Christianity becoming an amalgam of various beliefs and practices is always real as the intellectual and spiritual fashions of the day exert their influence.

Stewart speaks of a less reflective, more popular syncretism that continues to plague us. He calls it "a vague theism, plus a liberal humanist picture of Jesus, plus a dash of Judaic legalism, the whole being compounded with a certain culture consciousness, a considerable infusion of humanitarian benevolence, and perhaps even a secularising of the Kingdom of God." He cites John Baillie, who dubbed this patchwork of beliefs "a sort of Esperanto religion."[49] When such confusion infiltrates the beliefs and practices of churches, it eviscerates missionary zeal and makes Christians look like they are wearing ill-fitting, hand-me-down clothes.

I argued in the introduction that the "philosophy" Paul counters was a local Judaism that challenged the Colossians' hope. If the original rivals were Jews,

---

49. James S. Stewart, "A First-Century Heresy and Its Modern Counterpart," *SJT* 23 (1970): 422–23.

our historical context has changed so much that it would be inappropriate to connect the text in any way to modern Judaism. Christian persecution of the Jews over many centuries should make us extremely sensitive about painting Judaism as the villain. One should note that Paul does not demonize the opponents, though he does take them to task for denigrating the Christian hope.

Paul's primary tactic is to build up the assurance of the Colossian Christians by reemphasizing the truth they have already accepted and experienced in their baptism rather than tearing down the faith of the opposition. He maintains that the opponents live in a shadow world and do not yet realize that the fulfillment of all their hopes has already come in Christ. But he does not see his sole task as belittling their practices and beliefs. Instead, he wants first to build up the confidence of the Colossians in their faith so that they can resist their onslaughts. When the Colossians recognize that they have received everything they need in Christ, they will also recognize more clearly that the rivals have nothing to offer them except a reversion to the slavery of their erstwhile masters.

The same tactic should be employed by Christians in our world, where various ideologies compete for allegiance. More and more Christians are succumbing to the seductions of contemporary "philosophies," sometimes without knowing it. They captivate people with the promise of euphoric experiences and easier ways to explain and control life's uncertainties. When Christians can clearly identify what it is that they have received in Christ, they will be able to identify more clearly the fraudulent "philosophies" and their delusions and reject them.

The "philosophy" that Paul countered diminished the primacy, centrality, and sufficiency of Christ. It was not the first or the last to do so. Until the end of time, rival ideologies will continue to challenge Christians and their beliefs and vie for supremacy. In applying this text to our culture, it may be safest to describe the "philosophy" in broad strokes. We can then mark the parallels with any contemporary ideologies that set themselves up as competitors to Christ.

This "philosophy" that challenges (or perhaps contaminates) the Christian faith takes on the following ten characteristics:

- It judges, excludes, or disqualifies other persons according to arbitrary, human criteria.
- It engenders religious tyranny over people, based on these arbitrary, human criteria. It tries to make people pay homage to supernatural powers, earthly authorities, or rules rather than to Christ, who has set us free from all these things.
- It panders to human pride and egocentrism and results in puffing up and arrogance—attitudes characteristic of an unspiritual mind. It does

this by promoting such things as mystical euphoria, ritualism, and/or ascetic rigorism.

- It makes mystical experiences, rituals, and ascetic rigor ends in themselves by placing so much emphasis upon them.
- It attaches too much importance on what is ephemeral or perishable— things that pass away.
- It cuts persons off from Christ by substituting something else for a deep personal relationship with Christ. It may take on a pious guise by insisting on obedience to a particularly rigid code of behavior, strict belief in certain doctrines, or an uncompromising devotion to a religious institution. The result, however, is that the commitment to such things "based on human commands and teachings" supersedes commitment to Christ.
- It cuts persons off from the body of believers in Christ.
- It pretends to offer greater wisdom than the wisdom found in the cross of Christ. Its wisdom focuses on fulfilling the self rather than giving one's life to God and for others.
- It places limits on or rejects the efficacy of Christ's work in every area of life, suggesting that it is inadequate or that it needs to be augmented by other experiences, additional spiritual agents, or a regimen of ritual or ascetic observances.
- It is basically a do-it-yourself religion and refuses to believe that all we can hope to attain has already been accomplished *for us* by Christ.

These characteristics continue to reproduce themselves in secular and religious ideologies, and we can therefore find many parallels in our modern context. Paul professes that baptism into Christ's death means death to all this "stuff"—however and whenever it manifests itself. The key defense for Christians against such error is to hold fast to Christ, "the Head," and to recognize that we have died with Christ to the elemental spirits reigning over this world with their various rules and ordinances. When we recognize that we are secure in Christ, we will not be bumped off course by the judgments of others who want to disqualify us in some way.

WE MAY NOT be absolutely certain about what "philosophy" Paul was attacking in the letter to the Colossians, but the text does provide warnings against any "religious" or secular phenomena with similar features that may resurface in our setting. Of the ten characteristics of the "philosophy" identified in the previous section, we will discuss five as having particular contemporary significance. We should be on our guard against any religious practice or worldview that promotes any or all of the following things:

- anything that judges and disqualifies others according to arbitrary human measures
- anything that substitutes sham battles with asceticism for the real struggle with sin (3:5–11), which Christ has already won for us
- anything that makes subjective feelings or mystic states the norm over the historical event of Christ's crucifixion and resurrection
- anything that places more importance on divine intermediaries, such as angels, than on the divine reality in Christ
- anything that cuts people off from Christ, the Head, or Christ's people, the body

(1) **The danger of a religion that judges and disqualifies others.** Beare sums up Paul's statement in 2:18: "Let no one impose upon you his arbitrary standards of Christian conduct; do not feel yourself inferior because your own life is not governed in the way that he declares to be necessary."[50] The Colossian errorists' attempts to squelch fleshly desires and establish their purity let loose a more deadly strain of sin, namely, pride.[51] Many Christian groups want to draw the circle of acceptability ever tighter around themselves and reject others because of some failure to conform to their narrow vision of the truth. They only tolerate or accept their religious clones. They claim the high ground of exceptional piety or exemplary orthodoxy from which to lob a barrage of criticism against others who also claim the name Christian.

Wall comments on one example of this phenomenon:

> In order to draw more sharply the social borders that distinguish the orthodox from all others, evangelical believers tend to draft creeds of right belief and codes of right conduct that oblige them to abstain from certain foods (such as alcohol) and practices (such as dancing or extravagant dress) that mainstream believers consider spiritually harmless. Ascetic and austere expressions of one's devotion to Christ are thought by evangelicals to be useful in bearing witness to Christianity as an alternative to values and convictions of the surrounding secular order. And to a certain extent this is a correct perception.[52]

---

50. Beare, "The Epistle to the Colossians," 201.

51. David H. Stern, *Jewish New Testament Commentary* (Clarksville, Md.: Jewish New Testament Publications, 1992), 612.

52. Wall, *Colossians and Philemon*, 120.

The problem is that we can worship the rules or our theological constructions more than we worship Christ. This process inevitably results in an ugly,
smug arrogance and exacerbates the divisions between us rather than working to bring about reconciliation. Wall rightly contends that Christians have
only one social marker, their "faith that Jesus Christ is Lord."[53] I would add
another social marker: our behavior in accordance with that faith. Those who
have been qualified by their baptism into Christ's sacrificial death cannot be
disqualified by unfit, self-appointed umpires blinded by their own prejudices.

(2) **The danger of a do-it-yourself religion.** Paul does not sneer at a genuine interest in trying to maintain moral standards. Instead, he challenges the
errorists' method of achieving moral behavior. Their system does not work.
Obedience to rigorous rules may earn one a reputation for holiness, but it is
ultimately ineffective in dealing with human sinfulness. Our "moral needs are
too grave to be satisfied by any system of rules which endeavours merely to
regulate the old life and control its unruly impulses."[54]

(a) Someone has said, "Having rules in the head is no substitute for obedience from the heart." Rules do not create morality, but they are attractive
to humans, who may fool themselves into thinking that they do. Baggott
comments, "The 'régime of ordinances'—'handle not, taste not, touch not'—
will always possess a power of attractiveness to men, especially to reformers
in a hurry."[55] Apparently the "philosophy" in Paul's day had its allure because
it provided a clear set of rules and guidelines that made the holy life seem so
much simpler and measurable. It offered specific things to do and to refrain
from doing. A poem captures the basic attitude:

> All jowls and rules,
> that woman. As if
> the motives of God
> were true-false, multiple
> choice or kindergarten simple.[56]

With a list of rules, devotees may feel a greater sense of security. The
rules work like religious training wheels in that they may keep us from tip-
ping over. But they are also confining, for they will keep us from breaking
free. Rules also help us gauge whether we are making any headway in our religious quest or not. This is the rub. They lead us to regard our obligations to
God as a checklist, which, when we have completed the duties, mislead us

---

53. Ibid.
54. Caird, *Paul's Letters from Prison*, 203.
55. Baggott, *A New Approach to Colossians*, 86.
56. Bill Stadick, "Regarding a Co-Worker's Kindergarten Report Card," *First Things* 64
(June/July 1996): 32.

into thinking we have done all that God requires. Paul recounted his former religious vanity to the Philippians based on this record-keeping mentality. He claimed that he was blameless according to the righteousness that derives from obedience to the law (Phil. 3:6).

We can compose a list of observances—things that we believe God requires or will admire—and comply with them to the letter. But such obedience does not make us more devoted to God. Rigorous self-discipline is hardly up to the task of taming the human will, which chronically resists God's will. The law cannot produce inward motivation. That can only be generated by the Spirit. Self-mortification cannot drive out the demons that our sin invites in.[57] Caird points out that

> Christianity offers a more radical and effective solution to man's ethical and spiritual problems than an ascetical legalism. It allows the old human nature, with its unruly passions and bad conscience, to die, nailed to the cross of Christ, so that it may be raised with him to a new life.[58]

In Colossians, being in Christ and holding fast to the head is the only thing that will bring moral growth and inspire moral behavior.

(b) Abstinence may have its appeal because many confuse cause and effect in the holiness they see in others. The asceticism of John the Baptist, for example, did not make him a holy man except in reputation. His holiness came from his complete devotion to God in heralding the coming of the kingdom. That devotion may have led to his abstemious lifestyle, but his austere diet was not the cause of his holiness. Some, however, may mistakenly believe that separating themselves from the material world and stifling its appetites will draw them closer to God or prepare them to receive divine insight. They wrongly infer that a *via negativa* is the only way to God. It may instead drive one further away from God and produce only delusions. One can only come close to God through Christ, not through a regimen of spiritual exercises.

(c) A do-it-yourself religion puts "self" at the center and consequently is doomed to failure. If we set as our goals self-discipline, self-awareness, self-fulfillment, self-esteem, self-actualization, or self-help, we usually wind up with a worship of the self.[59] Such aims focus on the "here and now" and turn human purposes and desires into idols. If the aim is to defeat the flesh, it only

---

57. Rebecca Owanikin, "Colossians 2:18: A Challenge to Some Doctrines of Certain Aladura Churches in Nigeria," *African Journal of Biblical Studies* 2 (1987): 89–95, reports that a certain church group "subjects all its members to periodic beatings with whips as a process of penitence."

58. Caird, *Paul's Letters from Prison*, 201.

59. See Paul C. Vitz, *Psychology As Religion: The Cult of Self-Worship*, 2d ed. (Grand Rapids: Eerdmans, 1994).

gives it new power. Self-denial may give the impression that it checks the desires of the flesh, but it may be simply another way of indulging the flesh. Frye observes:

> Man's attempt to sacrifice for himself does not bring him the ultimate freedom he seeks, however, because it represents an increasing reliance upon the self and it is precisely from self-reliance that man must be freed. . . . Indeed, the attempt to work one's way into favor—whether it be God's favor or one's own—represents a form of the problem itself, rather than its solution.[60]

The letter to Colossians declares that Christ has already accomplished for us all that we might attempt to earn by our own puny efforts. The opponents rely on human attainment; Christians rely on Christ's atonement. Francis comments:

> Asceticism is worldly in the sense that its very rigor presupposes the reality of the world. If one has died with Christ from the world then such disciplined efforts are beside the point. Christ has already accomplished for the saints what the ascetics are seeking to effect.[61]

(3) **The danger of a religion of the eyes.** Many in Paul's world had an unquenchable yearning for the transcendent and were captivated by those who could manufacture vivid visions of it. Meyer notes that in the ancient mystery religions the experience of seeing was primary. The worship was literally geared for eye-opening experiences. One of the priests was called a *hierophant*, the one who shows sacred things; and the initiate into the mystery was called a *beholder*. The adherents would stage initiation ceremonies at night so that "the contrast between light and darkness, made the primal experience of enlightenment that much more vivid to the eyes and emotions."[62]

However one identifies the nature of the "philosophy," Paul opposed it as something fixed on visions that were illusory and resulted in hollow vanity. The cherished visions they claimed opened the divine world to humans amounts to little more than Alice's fantasy trip through the looking glass.

"I see nobody on the road," said Alice. "I only wish I had such eyes," the king remarked in a fretful tone. "To be able to see Nobody! And

---

60. Roland Mushat Frye, *Perspective on Man: Literature and the Christian Tradition* (Philadelphia: Westminster, 1961), 117–18.

61. Fred O. Francis, "The Christological Argument of Colossians," in *God's Christ and His People: Studies in Honor of Nils Alstrup Dahl*, ed. Jacob Jervell and Wayne Meeks (Oslo/Bergen/Tromsö: Unversitetsforlaget, 1977), 204.

62. Marvin Meyer, *The Ancient Mysteries: A Sourcebook* (San Francisco: Harper & Row, 1987), 5.

at that distance too! Why, it's as much as I can do to see real people, by this light."[63]

The direction of this religiosity is inward and upward and only results in narcissistic selfishness. Having such experiences can become an obsession that can undermine our commitment to Christ. Paul did not "take his stand on mystic visions, but on the message of the divine voice to his life, directing and guiding him in paths of moral obedience and loving service."[64] Paul recognizes that the direction of Christianity is downward in the Incarnation and outward in sacrificial labor for others.

Today, Christians face a more insidious "philosophy" that infiltrates our homes and subconscious—the media culture with its emphasis on surround sound and visual marvels. This may not seem to be an obvious threat because it does not usually label itself as a rival religion nor does it overtly malign the salvation offered by Christ. Michael Medved, a noted film critic, warned of the moral corrosiveness of movies and TV in a speech at Gordon College in 1996. He contended that television and all mass media "contradict the fundamental messages of the Judeo-Christian tradition" in the following ways:

- They emphasize the new and the latest instead of what is true and eternal. Only new truth is true. Old truth can only be old-fashioned and obsolete.
- They harp relentlessly on material gratification, which makes it hard for those hooked on it to realize that they cannot always get what they want. "There is only this minute and this hour; appetites to satisfy and desires to be filled." The message is "Go for the gusto"; "You deserve it"; "Have it your way"; "Get yours while there is still some left." Sacrifice becomes something laughable.
- The visual and superficial beautify what is not beautiful. Having attractive people do horrible things or immoral things in sumptuous surroundings tends to make those activities look attractive.
- "The whole emphasis of the media is on the eyes—on the eyes connecting with the heart, connecting with the emotions." It appeals to the senses but does not sustain the soul. He concludes, "Religion does not ask us to follow our hearts or be guided by our eyes. It enjoins us to look below the surface; to believe what is *true*, not merely what is seen."

A religion of the eyes leaves one dazzled; but when the reverie is over, nothing is left. Paul recognizes this truth, which may explain why he never dwelt on his own visions or shared them with others until he was forced to

---

63. Lewis Carroll, *Through the Looking Glass* (New York: A. L. Burt, n.d.), 277.
64. MacLeod, "The Epistle to the Colossians," 206.

by the Corinthian situation. Even then, he related being caught up to the third heaven in such an ambivalent way that he made clear that such glorious experiences paled beside learning that God's grace is sufficient to overcome every thorn in the flesh (2 Cor. 12:1–10). The danger for us is that we will want to keep up with our entertainment culture and its focus on the eyes by turning our worship into a religious stage show. We must walk a fine line between offering worship that is appealing and engaging without becoming simply a splashy performance, and worship that has depth without becoming tedious and flat.

We have glorious riches to offer in Christ, but these riches "are hidden" (Col. 2:3). Since we live in a society accustomed to eye-catching presentations and instant gratification, many are susceptible to the enticements of those who dangle riches that they can have right now for the taking. Packaging can fool us. For example, when we buy a couch, the construction, materials, and workmanship hidden beneath what we can see with our eyes may not enter into the decision. We may buy it simply because it looks good and feels comfortable. Some people choose their faith in the same way. They seek out what looks good and feels comfortable. The cross will have no attraction for them. But the cross is the only thing that can save them.

(4) **The danger of a religion that fills the gap between ourselves and God with divine intermediaries.** I have argued that Paul counters a local Judaism that has contested the Colossian Christians' status as heirs to the promises of Israel and that the reference to "the worship of angels" is a scornful dismissal of their beliefs and practices. But the warning about venerating angels has a contemporary application because of the renewed interest in angels today.

The early church had problems with some who placed angels on too exalted a spiritual pedestal, leading believers to venerate them too highly.[65] Evidence from church decrees in the early centuries reveals that Christians were involved in unseemly magical practices and veneration of angels. Theodoret, writing in the first half of the fifth century, commented on Colossians 2:18: "[This disease] long remained in Phrygia and Pisidia. Chapels were dedicated to the archangel Michael." He explains that this problem prompted the fourth-century synod convened in Laodicea of Phrygia to write their thirty-fifth canon, which "forbad by a decree the offering of prayer to angels; and even to the present time oratories of the holy Michael may be seen among them and their neighbours."[66] The warnings given to John not

---

65. Houlden, *Paul's Letters from Prison*, 165, cites Justin Martyr showing too great an esteem for angels in his *First Apology* 6. The object of Christian devotion is "the Father of righteousness . . . and the Son who came from him . . . and the army of the other good angels, who follow him and are made like him, and the prophetic Spirit."

66. Cited by Lightfoot, *Saint Paul's Epistles to the Colossians and to Philemon*, 68, n. 2.

to worship the angel guiding him on his tour of heaven (Rev. 19:10; 22:8–9) remained relevant.

The curiosity and obsession with angels that were so widespread in the ancient world in paganism, Judaism, and Christianity have intensified in our contemporary setting. McColley contends that "in popular media angels incline to be sentimental, comical, or even raffish, and angelology has largely been replaced by strictly secular and allegorical, psychological, and anthropological explanations which drain them of spiritual power."[67] This renewed fixation on angels crosses religious and secular lines. Angels that regularly intervene in the lives of individuals form the plots of many movies and television series. Bookstores are filled with glittering books and dazzling calendars on angels. The glut of such publications suggests that the angel industry has become quite profitable.

What is the attraction? Bush offers that "angels seem more accessible than God, and more attractive. And while there is only one God, there are many angels—so many that we can each have a private angel devoted to our welfare."[68] This interest reflects hunger both for the spiritual and the miraculous and for some sign that God cares enough to intervene directly in our lives. The comments of Nora Ephron, the writer and director of the movie "Michael," a story of a flawed angel who acts like Cupid in bringing star-crossed lovers together and even raises a dog from the dead, are revealing:

> What people can't stand is, everyone wants to believe God notices you, that He notices the details. ... The horrible truth is that He probably doesn't notice. He's got more important things to do. But angels do notice. You know, they make the tow truck come when you have a flat tire.[69]

These popular sentiments about angels pander to our egocentrism in declaring that "an angel watches over me." People crave the attention and rescue of beneficent angelic beings devoted to our personal happiness and well-being. Biblical angels, by contrast, do not say much, only impart privileged information about divine activity that is otherwise inaccessible to humans and do not remain around for long. Some authors of popular books insist that angels come to pour blessing on us, to play with us, to look after us, to heal us, "and always they try to give us what we want."[70] The explanation for the renewed

---

67. Diane McColley, "Angels," in *A Dictionary of Biblical Tradition in English Literature*, ed. David Lyle Jeffrey (Grand Rapids: Eerdmans, 1992), 41.

68. Trudy Bush, "On the Tide of the Angels," *Christian Century* 112 (1995): 237.

69. James Sterngold, "A Fellowship of Angels and America," *New York Times* (Apr. 6, 1997), H 41.

70. Ibid.

interest in angels is, therefore, likely to be found here: Angels give us what we want without demanding much religious commitment or sacrifice in return.

The angels who appear on Christmas cards and in Christmas pageants have also left the impression that they are all helpful, serene, and unthreatening—announcing tidings of good cheer. Many people are ignorant of or have forgotten the angels' more fearsome roles in Scripture (see Gen. 19:1–29; 2 Sam. 24:15–17; 2 Kings 19:35; 2 Chron. 32:21; Ps. 78:49; Isa. 37:36; Acts 12:23). But the modern-day angels have nothing to do with fighting evil or sin; they simply help to prevent bad things from happening to us. They serve us, not God, and work to improve life for us here and now. People exult in angels who stroke us gently with their wings and whisper sweet religious nothings in our ear, "Don't worry! Be happy!" These angels never challenge us to look out for others, to wrestle with the sin in our life, or to struggle with evil and injustice in the world.

The ancient magical papyri reflect a similar stance toward angels. These records of ancient heathenism show suppliants making direct commands to various angels: "Protect me, preserve me, hear me, give me, come to me, serve me, fulfill me, perform for me."[71] This attitude corresponds to the lapel pins I saw for sale in a bookstore. There were five different beatific figures with confident descriptions of their angelic roles. One was identified as the angel of protection, who "provides protection and guidance." The angel of success "provides the energy to be successful." The angel of happiness brings on "good times and joy." The angel of love brings "romance, love, great relations." The angel of wisdom brings "knowledge and helps us make good decisions." These modern charms may have some kind of "placebo effect" on their wearers, but they are no different from the ancient amulets that wearers hoped would bring good luck and ward off evil goblinry. They have the negative effect of turning us away from looking to Christ for help and guidance.

Another thing that makes angels so attractive today is that they are nondenominational—transcending creed, religion, and philosophy. They offer generic, inspirational stuff with little or no religious content. Since angels are also disembodied spirits and are presumed to function as intermediaries between God and humans, many assume that they are spiritually advanced. Some in New Age religions maintain that we can soar with the angels who are pure spirit and develop the same "angel consciousness." Pope wrote:

Men would be Angels, Angels would be God.
Aspiring to be Gods, Angels fell,
Aspiring to be Angels, Men Rebel.[72]

---

71. Arnold, *The Colossian Syncretism*, 31.
72. Alexander Pope, *An Essay on Man*, ed. Maynard Mack (London: Methuen, 1950), 31.

The problem is that God did not create human beings to become angels, nor angels to become gods.

This preoccupation with angels is a sign of serious spiritual confusion. The reference to the "worship of angels" in our text and Paul's concern that it undermines the supremacy of Christ provides an ideal opportunity to confront this phenomenon, which fosters serious theological error. People have tried to fill the gap that they may sense has grown between themselves and a hidden and faraway God with divine intermediaries like angels.

Speculation about angels in Israel burgeoned during the Exile and later foreign dominance, when many Jews felt abandoned by God. It was also a time when in Jewish thought God became more exalted and correspondingly more distant. The more transcendent God became, the more people thought that celestial attendants were required to sing God's glory and to communicate divine messages to the world. They could not portray God directly but could portray God's assistants, the angels.

When we humans feel that God is removed from our world, we become more attracted to more accessible, more useful, and more user-friendly emanations of deity. The grave peril is that these divine figures will become little more than functionaries whom we can bend to our will. The even graver peril is that they will become rivals to Christ. People will turn to them instead of Christ for protection, for help, and for assurance. Our interest in divine intermediaries whom we can more easily control and manipulate through rites and incantations can easily displace the more demanding requirements of our relationship with God and Christ. Paul affirms that our relationship with Christ is the only one that matters. We must guard against the encroachment of any rival mediators of salvation. When Christians know Christ as the risen Lord forever in our midst (Matt. 28:20), the ministry of angels dwindles in significance.

In Colossians, Paul reminds us that while Christ and the angels are divine agents, only Christ is God's beloved Son (1:13) and the full embodiment of Deity and God's purposes (1:19, 2:9). Only in him do we have a share in the kingdom of light, redemption, the forgiveness of sins (1:13–14; 2:13–14), and the hope of glory (1:27). Only in Christ are we reconciled to God (1:22), because only Christ died for us (1:20; 2:11). Only Christ reigns supreme over all created beings, visible and invisible (1:16; 2:10). We triumph over all the powers and authorities only in Christ, who defeated them on the cross (2:15; see Rom. 8:38–39; 1 Peter 3:22). Only Christ offers the promise of a risen life and the power to live morally in this life (Col. 3:1–3).

The movie director cited above referred to the horrible notion that God does not notice us. The horrible truth is quite the opposite—that we have ignored God and that our sins put the Son of God on the cross. The

Christian message proclaims that God noticed us enough to send his Son into our dark ghetto to bring reconciliation and redemption. The horrible truth is that many continue to reject this offer of love and turn to gods of their own making.

(5) **The danger of losing connection with the Head.** The New Testament affirms that we cannot truly experience God or salvation apart from Christ. Paul reinforces this point with the metaphor of the head and body in 2:19. The Head gives the body everything necessary for life. Without the Head, the body would wither and die. As no member of a physical body can live by itself, no individual can live apart from the body of Christ.

The errorists were wrong in thinking that they could gain access to the heavenly realm apart from Christ. Paul declares that the church is the place where Christ's headship over the cosmos should be most evident, precisely because it is the church that is most fully "'plugged into' (connected with) the source of supply and growth."[73] "The life-giving presence of Christ makes all the difference between an empty inflation and a true growth, such as God intended when He called the world into being."[74] Consequently, we can only experience and grow in our salvation only within the church, where we are dependent on Christ as "Head" and source of our nourishment and inter-connected to one another (see John 15:4–5). Lewis writes, "We are summoned from the outset to combine as creatures with our Creator, as mortals with immortal, as redeemed sinners with sinless Redeemer."[75]

Connection to Christ is decisive for growth. But Paul's use of the image of the body shows that he does not have in mind simply an individualistic union with Christ. We can only know the Head as a member of his body. When we are joined to Christ as part of his body, we are also joined to other members. The New Testament also affirms that our experience of God and salvation does not reach us independently from the church. We cannot grow on our own without Christ; we cannot grow on our own without other Christians. Therefore, we only fool ourselves if we think we can find our meaning, purpose, and significance for God through an isolated contemplation of religious truths. That comes only in a community of believers bound to Christ and to one another. Jones points out that if we are to break the habits of sin, we need supportive friendships in the church and teachings that help us to unlearn destructive habits and to cultivate holy ones.[76]

---

73. Dunn, *The Epistles to the Colossians and to Philemon,* 187.

74. Scott, *The Epistles to the Colossians and to Philemon, and to Ephesians,* 56.

75. C. S. Lewis, *Transpositions and Others Addresses* (London: Geoffrey Bles, 1958), 38.

76. L. Gregory Jones, *Embodying Forgiveness: A Theological Analysis* (Grand Rapids: Eerdmans, 1995), 76.

Lee scores the many modern Americans who "regard Christianity that is inextricably bound to a physical community as a lower stage of faith, compared to Christianity as a way of thinking." They prefer, he says, "the disembodied spirit of Christianity" without the church body dragging it down. He writes:

> Gnostics of all periods take one look at the Church and say to themselves, "You mean this is it? You mean this is all there is? Only what the simple-minded woman or that acned kid can understand; only what that half-educated preacher is saying?"[77]

Bellah calls this trend in American spirituality "Sheilaism." The name derives from a person he interviewed about God who said, "I am religious but don't go to church. I believe that God is inside me, my own little voice." Being religious for her does not mean being connected to anyone else. It is the flight of the alone to the alone. Sociologists tell us that nine out of ten people in America believe in God, but only a fraction worship regularly with others. If these persons are members of a church group, they may regard it "in individualistic terms" as a place in which to discover their own private understanding of the faith. The church becomes little different from a health club, where one goes to work out to fulfill some individual body-building or weight-loss goals.

The church is, instead, to be the place where we work out *God's goals* for creation. When we are severed from Christ and his community, we guarantee our spiritual malnourishment. If we could ever visualize physically the souls of those cut off from the Head, they would look like the heart-wrenching pictures of enfeebled bodies starving to death.

---

77. Philip J. Lee, *Against the Protestant Gnostics* (New York/Oxford: Oxford Univ. Press, 1987), 192.

Colossians 3:1–17

SINCE, THEN, YOU have been raised with Christ, set your hearts on things above, where Christ is seated at the right hand of God. ²Set your minds on things above, not on earthly things. ³For you died, and your life is now hidden with Christ in God. ⁴When Christ, who is your life, appears, then you also will appear with him in glory.

⁵Put to death, therefore, whatever belongs to your earthly nature: sexual immorality, impurity, lust, evil desires and greed, which is idolatry. ⁶Because of these, the wrath of God is coming. ⁷You used to walk in these ways, in the life you once lived. ⁸But now you must rid yourselves of all such things as these: anger, rage, malice, slander, and filthy language from your lips. ⁹Do not lie to each other, since you have taken off your old self with its practices ¹⁰and have put on the new self, which is being renewed in knowledge in the image of its Creator. ¹¹Here there is no Greek or Jew, circumcised or uncircumcised, barbarian, Scythian, slave or free, but Christ is all, and is in all.

¹²Therefore, as God's chosen people, holy and dearly loved, clothe yourselves with compassion, kindness, humility, gentleness and patience. ¹³Bear with each other and forgive whatever grievances you may have against one another. Forgive as the Lord forgave you. ¹⁴And over all these virtues put on love, which binds them all together in perfect unity.

¹⁵Let the peace of Christ rule in your hearts, since as members of one body you were called to peace. And be thankful. ¹⁶Let the word of Christ dwell in you richly as you teach and admonish one another with all wisdom, and as you sing psalms, hymns and spiritual songs with gratitude in your hearts to God. ¹⁷And whatever you do, whether in word or deed, do it all in the name of the Lord Jesus, giving thanks to God the Father through him.

HAVING ARGUED THAT the Colossians have been set free *from* the powers, Paul now contends that they have been set free *for* living a life above moral reproach. The next paragraph (3:1–4), with its *Leitmotif* "with Christ," serves as a transition from the negative warnings to positive exhortation. They have been raised "with Christ" in the past (3:1), are hidden "with Christ" in the present (3:3), and will be revealed "with Christ" in the future (3:4).

A catalog of vices and virtues follows in 3:5–14. As he does in the list of the works of the sinful nature and the fruit of the Spirit in Galatians 5:19–23, Paul first enumerates the vices of the old morality, which need to be renounced (3:5–9a). He then lists virtues of the new morality, which need to be embraced (3:12–14).[1] A statement about the new creation in 3:9b–11 provides a bridge from the vices to virtues—virtues made possible because God has created in Christ a new humanity "being renewed in knowledge in the image of its Creator." The new creation enables the new morality, which, in turn, leads to the new worship in 3:15–17. Thanksgiving, an emphasis throughout the letter (1:3, 12; 2:7; 3:15, 17; 4:2), climaxes this section.[2]

New Life with Christ (3:1–4)

THE OPENING STATEMENT in 3:1, "Since (*ei*), then, you have been raised with Christ," parallels the statement in 2:20, "Since (*ei*) you have died with Christ." Dying with Christ symbolizes the drastic split with the old life (3:2) and forms an essential part of Paul's warning against the rules of a hollow and deceptive philosophy. Being raised with Christ emphasizes the new status of believers, which requires a new way of life.[3] It refers to the power source for living the new life. This transitional paragraph reaffirms the previous theological arguments and lays the foundation for the following ethical admonitions.

(1) The new life gets under way with a new orientation as Christians set their hearts on (lit., "seek") the things above. "The things above" is clarified

---

1. Craig A. Evans, "The Colossian Mystics," *Bib* 63 (1982): 194.

2. Lars Hartman, "Code and Context: A Few Reflections on the Parenesis of Col 3:6–4:1," in *"Understanding Paul's Ethics": Twentieth Century Approaches* (Grand Rapids: Eerdmans, 1995), 189–90, points out that Paul draws contrasts with the description of the "philosophy" in the previous section. The catalog of vices and virtues identify in negative and positive terms how Christians are to relate to our fellow human beings. It differs from the solitary "humility," "worship of angels," and mystic "visions" of the "philosophy." The Christian worship described in 3:16 differs from the observances in 2:16, which are determined by the movement of the celestial bodies. The list of household duties in 3:18–4:1, with their realistic worldliness, differs from the prohibitions against handling, tasting, and touching in 2:23.

3. Paul refers to being raised with Christ as a past occurrence. With the exception of Eph. 2:5–6, he refers to the resurrection elsewhere in his letters as a future event. Some have appealed to this seeming contradiction to argue that Colossians could not have been written by Paul. The "already" of 3:1, however, is balanced by the "not yet" of 3:4, where appearing with Christ looks toward the glorious future. He does not refer in 3:1 to the final resurrection (see 2 Tim. 2:18) but to a spiritual resurrection from the dead (2:12).

as "where Christ is, seated at the right hand of God."[4] This affirmation thrums again a key chord in the letter, and Paul will now draw out its ethical implications.

(a) Since believers are in Christ, they already belong to the world above, where he is. Lincoln's comments are helpful:

> The heavenly realm centres around the one with whom they have been raised and since he is in the position of authority at God's right hand, nothing can prevent access to this realm and to God's presence and there can be no basic insecurity about the salvation they have in him and its final outcome.[5]

(b) Christians already have knowledge of that realm through their faith (2:12) and do not attain it by using other mediators, by pursuing visionary sideshows, by submitting to legalistic decrees, or by mortifying their bodies.[6]

(c) Since Christ is not one of the serving angels but reigns over all, all of our lives should be ruled by him. Every thought, aim, value, aspiration, and striving should come under his lordship.

(2) Paul's second affirmation is that the believer's life is "hidden with Christ in God"; it seals the previous warnings and also has ethical implications.

(a) A believer's life in the One who reigns over the whole cosmos has yet to become unmistakably evident to all observers (see 1 John 3:2); one's glorious appearance with Christ lies in the future. This reality explains why those who adhere to the "philosophy" and base their judgments only on what is seen have dismissed and ridiculed the Christian's hope.[7] Paul reassures

---

4. A comma should be inserted after the phrase "where Christ is." "Seated at the right hand of God" has a separate meaning and echoes Ps. 110:1, the most quoted Old Testament passage in the New Testament. Christ's being seated at the right hand of God (Ps. 110:1) expresses the church's eschatological conviction that the age to come had arisen with Christ. Paul calls believers to allow the things above, where Christ is, to direct their lives. These are the things that are ultimate and transcendent and contrast with the "philosophy's" dependence on "the basic principles of this world" (2:8, 20), "human tradition" (2:8), and things "destined to perish with use" (2:22).

5. Andrew T. Lincoln, *Paradise Now and Not Yet: Studies in the Role of the Heavenly Dimension in Paul's Thought With Special Reference to His Eschatology*, SNTSMS 43 (Cambridge: Cambridge Univ. Press, 1981), 125.

6. They also do not attain it through astrology. The celebrated astronomer and astrologer Ptolemy wrote: "I know that I am the creature of a day; but when I search into the multitudinous revolving spirals of the stars my feet no longer rest on the earth, but, standing by Zeus himself, I take my fill of ambrosia, the food of the gods" (*Greek Anthology*, "Epigrams" 9 § 577).

7. Caird, *Paul's Letters from Prison*, 202, comments, "The Christian life is a process in which, through constant fellowship with the risen Christ and through the operation of his Spirit, the believer is transformed into his likeness, from one stage of glory to another (2 Cor. 3:18). But it is a secret process, invisible both to the outsider and to the believer himself, known

the Colossians that they already have completeness in Christ, but its full demonstration awaits Christ's return. Consequently, they can shrug off the opponents' challenge to them.

(b) A life hidden in the One who is seated at the right hand of God is completely secure. No menacing powers can ever bring them to ultimate harm. They have no need to placate any such powers.

(c) The emphasis on the believers' incorporation into the life of Christ (see Gal. 2:20; Phil. 1:21) leads into the ethical exhortation that follows. The new life of obedience does not depend on their own feeble moral resolve but comes from being united with him.

The Old Morality (3:5–9a)

PAUL ATTESTS THAT one is either dead in sin (2:13) or dead to sin (3:5). Believers, however, are still works in progress, which explains the need for the commands "to put to death ... your earthly nature [lit., the members upon the earth]" (3:5) and to "rid yourselves of all such things" (3:8).[8] A believer's "members" (NIV, "the parts of your body") can be offered to sin as instruments of wickedness or to God as instruments of righteousness and holiness (Rom. 6:13, 19). The "members" can also be taken captive: "But I see another law at work in the members of my body, waging war against the law of my mind and making me a prisoner of the law of sin at work within my members" (Rom. 7:23).

The restrictions listed earlier, "Do not handle! Do not taste! Do not touch!" (2:21), were a futile attempt to protect one's members from sin's domination; but such efforts failed to get at the problem's root, the inner cravings and obsessions. It did not even scratch the surface of the problem. One may putty and paint over termite damage in a house, but unless the termites are eradicated and the damaged boards replaced, the house is doomed to collapse. Paul demands the complete "extermination of the old way of

---

only to faith." He points to the evidence in 2 Corinthians that this invisible process causes even Christians to draw the wrong conclusions about the reality of the transformation. The Corinthians judged Paul on the basis of what could be seen (2 Cor. 4:18), and his battered condition apparently did not match their ideal of a true apostle. Paul confesses that before his conversion he used the same superficial, external standards to misjudge Christ, but his conversion changed his perspective on everything (2 Cor. 5:16).

8. "Put to death" is an aorist imperative. Grammarians usually distinguish the aorist imperative from the present imperative by maintaining that the aorist imperative commands, "Start to do something," whereas the present imperative urges, "Continue to do something." K. L. McKay, "Aspect in Imperatival Constructions in New Testament Greek," *NovT* 27 (1985): 203–8, challenges this assumption. He argues that aorist imperative urges activity as a whole action "without dwelling on its internal details," while the present imperative urges activity as an ongoing process "without focus on its progress or development." "Put to death" refers to a complete action.

life."[9] The danger of an ethical relapse endures if the old is not obliterated. Caird likens the situation of believers to immigrants who have moved to a new country but have not yet become habituated to the new ways of life.[10] Paul insists that Christians eradicate any persisting marks of the old pagan lifestyle—its values, customs, and practices.

Lists were commonly employed in ethical exhortations in the ancient world, and the overlaps between the lists in the New Testament with moral exhortations from the Greco-Roman world reveal that pagans recognized that certain kinds of behavior were debased (see Rom. 2:14–15) and others were praiseworthy.[11] Key differences, however, should be noted. (1) Paul has no interest in simply recording ethical ideals worth pondering. He fully expects Christians to abandon the vices and to live out the virtues. (2) He grounds his exhortation in Christology. Christians are being transformed into Christ's image (3:10). Because this is so, they are asked to be true to themselves.

Sexual sins. The vices are heavily weighted toward sexual sins: "sexual immorality, impurity, lust, evil desires." Paul considered sexual relationships outside of marriage to be sinful, and the term *sexual immorality* runs the gamut of forbidden sexual acts. Paul's frequent warnings against it in his letters (see 1 Cor. 5:1, 9–10; 6:9; 2 Cor. 12:21; Gal. 5:19; Eph. 5:3; 1 Thess. 4:3) suggest that the society's lax sexual mores were not easily weeded out from the habits of converts in his churches. Sexual desire is hardwired into the human psyche and is not evil in itself. But the moral indifference of the age fueled uncontrolled erotic passion, misdirected sexual desire, and bred sexual excesses.

The list is capped off by "greed, which is idolatry." Greed refers to the haughty and ruthless belief that everything, including other persons, exists for one's own personal amusement and purposes. Essentially it turns our own desires into idols. It is the overweening desire to possess more and more things and to run roughshod over other persons to get them. It stands opposed to the willingness to give to others regardless of the cost to self. Greed can crave after persons and is never satiated by its conquests but always lusts for more.

In Hellenistic Jewish literature, all of the sins of the pagan world were epitomized by references to their sexual immorality and their idolatry (see Rom. 1:18–32), and the two were interconnected. Idolatry had as its chief purpose to get some material advantage from the gods, and idol worshipers tried to manipulate them to that end. The lust for worldly possessions quickly elbows God from the center of our lives as it captivates our total allegiance. We

---

9. Caird, *Paul's Letters from Prison*, 205.

10. Ibid., 204. Lohse, *Colossians and Philemon*, 137, comments that it means, "Let the old man, who has already died in baptism, be dead."

11. See Rom. 1:29–31; 1 Cor. 6:9–10; Gal. 5:19–23; 1 Tim. 1:9–10; 6:4–5; 2 Tim. 3:2–5; Titus 3:1–3.

cannot serve both God and mammon, and those who serve mammon cannot serve God (Matt. 6:24). Our desires sit on the throne of our hearts rather than God.

Paul concludes this first list of vices by attesting that such behavior will incur God's holy wrath (Rom. 1:18–32; Eph. 5:6).[12] Moule cites the even more heinous list of sins in 1 Corinthians 6:9–11 and comments that it "reveals the kind of life from which Christianity rescued people."[13] They used to live that way because that lifestyle was normative for their society. People tend to live the same way that others around them live, adopting their standards, values, and ways of thinking. The uncompromising morality of Judaism and Christianity probably attracted many Gentiles who were repulsed by the moral corruption in their society.[14] Christianity demands that Christ's followers live worthily of him. If avowed Christians behave no differently from their surrounding culture, they betray their calling and defame their faith.

Sins of anger. Paul next turns his sights on various manifestations of anger, which destroy community: "anger, rage, malice, slander, and filthy language from your lips." "Anger" refers to a chronic feeling as opposed to outbursts of "rage." More subtle expressions of anger ooze out in the "malice" we bear others and the spiteful potshots we take to defame their reputations. "Filthy language from your lips" does not simply refer to curse words. It has in mind the abusive language we use to hurts others. Christian speech is not determined solely by whether it is true or false but by whether it helps or harms another.[15]

"Do not lie to each other" surprisingly caps the list.[16] Adlai Stevenson, a U.S. senator and presidential candidate, once said, "A lie is an abomination unto the Lord and a very present help in trouble." In Ephesians 4:25 putting off falsehood and speaking the truth are linked to all being "members of one

---

12. God's wrath manifests itself in a variety of ways in our lives, but should not be mistaken for the vindictive bursts of temper imputed to the pagan deities. The verb "is coming" need not point to some distant future (see Rom. 2:5, 8; 3:5; 9:22; 1 Thess. 1:10; 5:9). In Rom. 1:18–32, Paul maintains that the consequences of God's wrath are already at work. The phrase "on those who are disobedient" (see NIV note) is a text variant, and it may have been inserted into the text from Eph. 5:6.

13. Moule, *Colossians and Philemon*, 117.

14. Dunn, *The Epistles to the Colossians and to Philemon*, 218.

15. Wright, *Colossians and Philemon*, 137, aptly comments on how spiteful words injure. They "do not merely convey information or let off steam. They change situations and relationships, often irrevocably. They can wound as well as heal. Like wild plants blown about by the wind, hateful words can scatter seeds far and wide, giving birth to more anger wherever they land."

16. One wonders if some form of lying was not at the root of Onesimus's problem, causing him to run away.

body," and lying is rooted in an attempt to gain advantage over others. It therefore is at odds with Christian love even though Christians have been known to concoct lies to deceive others (see Acts 5:1–11). Such deceit reveals a lack of mutual trust, undermines community, and breeds anger.

The New Humanity (3:9b–11)

THE IMAGE OF having stripped off old filthy rags and put on new clothes (see Gal. 3:28; Eph. 4:20–25; cf. Job 29:14; Isa. 61:10) marks the transition from the list of vices to the list of virtues. It helps us look beyond the individual ethical admonitions to see the basis of our moral transformation. The vices make indiscernible the image of God in a person. Who can see that image in those who misuse their sexuality or who try to destroy others in malicious anger? Christians have discarded the old solidarities and its behaviors like a set of shabby clothes and have joined themselves to a new solidarity, which renews the image of God in them and creates new behaviors.

The phrasing of 3:10 in Greek, "the new that is being renewed in knowledge" (lit.), conveys the following ideas. (1) It means that the new life does not come as the result of a successful, daily battle with temptation. Rather, the new life marks the starting point.[17] Paul does not urge the Colossians to amend their lives for the better, to reform their ways, or to make minor modifications in the direction of their lives. As Schweizer points out, it is a matter of a new creation (cf. 2 Cor. 5:17), "not just giving up a few vices and accepting a few virtues."[18] One's whole nature must be exchanged, not just revamped.

(2) Since the new *"is being* renewed," we are always needing more renewal (see Rom. 12:2)—Paul's use of the present participle suggests continuous improvement (see 2 Cor. 3:18; 4:16–17; Phil. 3:21). Moule's comments are helpful: It requires "a continual 'mortification' of what is, in fact, already dead, a continual actualization of an already existing new creation."[19] This enduring process explains the use of the imperative. The believer "has been made Christ's own" and "set on course," but all must run the race tirelessly for themselves.[20] Theological indicatives are the basis of the ethical imperatives: "You are, now be!"

(3) The passive voice indicates that the renewal does not result from our own efforts. The renewed person becomes the creative handiwork of God. The new nature comes as God's gift, not as the result of our will-worship (see 2:23), our will power, or our self-actualization. What we must do is to work out the salvation that God has worked in our lives (Phil. 2:12–13).

---

17. Wright, *Colossians and Philemon*, 131.
18. Schweizer, *Colossians*, 197.
19. Moule, *Colossians and Philemon*, 120.
20. Victor Paul Furnish, *II Corinthians* (AB; New York: Doubleday, 1984), 290.

(4) Knowledge of God, of God's Son, and of God's ways are crucial for living a life pleasing to God. This fullness of knowledge comes as a byproduct of our renewal. Radford cites Dawson Walker: "The more we are like Him the more we shall understand Him."[21]

(5) The renewal comes from being joined to Christ, who is the image of the immortal God (1:15–16), in whom we have been created.[22] No system of "dos and don'ts" can create the image of God in humans.[23]

Verse 11 proclaims that the new humanity re-created in Christ erases all the old sinful divisions that segregated humans from one another. The first two pairs in the list, "no Greek or Jew, circumcised or uncircumcised" (see 1 Cor. 7:18–19; Gal. 5:6; 6:15), forcefully eliminate the Jew/Gentile division, which was primarily a religious distinction.[24] The presence of these contrasting pairs is best explained by the fact that outside Jewish opponents have threatened the congregation's assurance that they fully belong to God's people.

The second two pairs, "barbarian, Scythian, slave or free," eliminate cultural distinctions. The prejudice against barbarians was based on culture, not on the grounds of "blood" or "race." "*Barbaroi*" originally referred to those who spoke what sounded like gibberish to the Greeks.[25] In our culture, the term *barbarian* has a pejorative ring, but it did not always have an unflattering connotation in Paul's day. In 1 Corinthians 14:11, Paul says that using unintelligible speech in worship makes a visitor "a foreigner [barbarian] to the speaker, and he is a foreigner [barbarian] to me." The term could also apply to the native inhabitants of a region (Acts 28:2, 4) or to Gentiles in a non-Greek culture. Paul tells the Romans that he is indebted to "Greeks and [barbarians]" (Rom. 1:14), which the NIV correctly translates as "non-Greeks." He would not sabotage the tactful opening of his letter by insulting them as lowly barbarians, without culture.

---

21. Radford, *The Epistles to the Colossians and to Philemon*, 268.

22. In other letters, Paul describes the Spirit as enabling this new life.

23. Image recalls the creation of Adam, who was made in the image of God (Gen. 1:27). Christ is the new Adam, who is the image of the invisible God (Col. 1:15) and in whom the fullness of Deity dwells permanently (1:19; 2:9). Moule, *Colossians and Philemon*, 120, comments that when "God re-creates Man, it is *in the pattern of Christ*, who is God's likeness absolutely." That image is restored for others when they are baptized in him.

24. See also 1 Cor. 12:13, "Jews or Greeks, slave or free"; Gal. 3:28, "Jew nor Greek, slave nor free, male nor female." Dunn, *The Epistles to the Colossians and to Philemon*, 225, argues that "the distinction between Jew and Greek, as marked out by circumcision, has been removed by Christ; the privileges of the Jewish people which have kept them separate from the other nations have been opened up to the Gentiles by the Jewish Messiah."

25. It is an onomatopoeic word that makes fun of their speech (it sounded to Greeks like they were muttering bar-bar-bar).

Though the term does not always have a pejorative meaning, it still reflects the tendency of human groups to lump foreigners together and does have a strong tinge of cultural chauvinism.[26] For Greeks, the rest of the world were barbarians. For Jews, who considered themselves to be *the* nation, the rest of the world were "the nations" (the lit. trans. of the word for "Gentiles" in the New Testament) or "the uncircumcision," which is the euphemistic translation of a word that literally means "foreskin."

The "Scythians" were Mongol pastoral nomads, who moved from one seasonal pasture to another in the trackless steppes of the north. Most have assumed that "barbarian" and "Scythian" are not contrasting pairs but that the second term intensifies the idea of first one. Since we find literary stereotypes of the Scythians as a particularly brutish and savage people, "Scythian" could represent a worse form of barbarity (or "especially strange form or kind of barbarian").[27] The TEV even translates it "savages." But "barbarian" does not have a negative connotation here, and a complementary arrangement ruins the contrasting pattern and is not found elsewhere in Paul.[28]

Campbell solves the problem by suggesting that the listing of the groups fits a chiastic structure:

Greek
   Jew
      circumcised
uncircumcised
barbarian
   Scythian
   slave
free[29]

---

26. Thales is said to have given thanks to Fortune that he was born a human being and not a brute, a man and not a woman, a Greek (cultural supremacy) and not a barbarian (Diogenes Laertius 1.33). Among the Jews, a similar prayer to be recited every day is attributed to R. Judah ben El'ai: "Blessed art thou who did not make me a *goy* (Gentile, heathen), blessed art thou who did not make me a woman, blessed art thou who did not make me a boor (brutish man; variant, slave)" (*t. Ber.* 7:18; *y. Ber.* 9.2, 13d; *b. Menah.* 43b).

27. Josephus says, "They delight in murdering people and are little better than wild beasts" (*Against Apion* 2.37 § 269). See also 2 Macc. 4:47; 3 Macc. 7:5; 4 Macc. 10:7. Otto Michel, "Σκύθης," *TDNT*, 7:448, notes that "Scythian" was turned into a verb to mean "to behave like a Scythian," which suggested crudity, excessive drinking, or shaving the head (from scalping fallen enemies).

28. Troy Martin, "The Scythian Perspective in Col 3:11," *NovT* 37 (1995): 249–61, recognizes the problem but tries unconvincingly to relate it to Cynic opponents.

29. Douglas Campbell, "Unravelling Colossians 3:11b," *NTS* 42 (1996): 120–32; particularly 127–28.

In this structure, "Scythian" correlates with "slave." Campbell argues that our interpretation of the term has been biased by the limited literary data. He provides evidence that the word "Scythian" was used to "denote slaves procured from the north of the Black Sea."[30] Paul may be alluding to the Scythian heritage of some Colossian Christians. If this is correct, Paul does not perpetuate the racist cliché that Scythians were monstrous and untamed brutes. On the contrary, he undermines "the *social* antithesis between slaves and owners" who come from "diverse geographical and cultural backgrounds."[31] Paul places slaves on an equal footing with masters before Christ because both are in Christ together.[32] This statement has significant implications for the letter to Philemon.

The gospel breaks down man-made walls. It does not classify people by race, tribe, nationality, or class; nor does it calculate their worth from the various permutations of these divisions. Jew, Greek, circumcised, uncircumcised, barbarian, Scythian, slave, free are subsumed under one word, "brothers" (1:2). Paul expounds on this idea powerfully in Ephesians 2:11–22. While cultural differences may continue to exist—"Jews demand miraculous signs and Greeks look for wisdom" (1 Cor. 1:22)—each group deserves equal respect (10:32). These distinctions, which arbitrarily set humans over against one another, evaporate when a person becomes joined to Christ's body. The gospel shatters an "us" versus "them" mentality. It also dashes the presumption of any special entitlement, which explains why so many who are already privileged react to it with such hostility.

Paul's conclusion is that being in Christ, not being from a certain race or class, is the only thing that matters. Dunn comments: "If 'Christ is everything in everything,' then nothing can diminish or disparage the standing of any one human in relation to another or to God."[33] We can discern how this equality works itself out from Paul's list of his coworkers in 4:7–12 and in Philemon 1, 11. They include a wealthy householder, a slave, a physician, Jews ("of the circumcision"), and Gentiles. As far as Paul is concerned, they are fellow workers, fellow captives, fellow slaves, and all brothers in Christ.

---

30. Ibid., 129–31.

31. Ibid., 132. Philemon as a Phrygian would fall into the category of barbarian. Campbell (132, n. 39) offers the engaging suggestion that Onesimus was a Scythian, but such speculation is not susceptible to proof.

32. Paul would certainly reject the theory of "natural slavery" propounded by Aristotle (*Politics* 1.13). According to Aristotle, slaves were naturally intended to be slaves because of some inherent inferiority. It followed that inferior barbarians, who were naturally slaves, should be the slaves of the superior Greeks. Today, people still believe that just as there is a ruling alpha male in a wolf pack, there is an "alpha" race destined to rule over others, who must submit.

33. Dunn, *The Epistles to the Colossians and to Philemon*, 227.

The New Morality (3:12–14)

PAUL NEXT LISTS five virtues covering Christian deportment that is particularly important for community relations. Since it is possible that the letter to Philemon accompanied the letter to the Colossians, the list of virtues may intentionally complement Paul's appeal to Philemon for Onesimus. They are not airy, ethical ideals, because Paul asks Philemon to put them into practice in the concrete situation that confronts him with the return of his slave Onesimus.

Paul first addresses the Colossians as "God's chosen people, holy and dearly loved." The image of being "chosen" reminds them that their election comes at God's initiative, who has embraced them with the gift of unmerited favor. God's love confers value on the elect, but the idea of election can be misunderstood if we are not mindful that we have been elected for service, not for our personal benefit. Christians have been chosen in Christ (Eph. 1:4), who is the Chosen One (Luke 9:35; 1 Peter 2:4, 6); and, like Christ, they have been chosen for the benefit of "the world whose welfare they are to serve."[34]

This image also takes over terms from Jewish self-identity. Old Testament designations for Israel as elect, holy, and beloved (Deut. 4:37; 7:6–8; 14:2; 26:18–19; Ps. 105:43; 135:4; Jer. 2:3) appear in the New Testament and include Gentile Christians. Jews and Gentiles in Christ represent what God intended Israel to be. The language reminds the Colossians that they are full partners in the heritage of Israel, an Israel without racial and ethnic divisions. But being God's chosen people brings with it ethical responsibilities (see Ex. 19:5–6; Deut. 7:6–10). As those who are chosen by God, they must choose their behavior. They are to be the living advertisements of what God's grace does in human lives.

The graces listed are similar to "the fruit of the Spirit" (see Gal. 5:22–23). All these qualities characterized Jesus' life, and they are vital for a harmonious life with our fellow human beings. "Compassion" (see Rom. 12:1; 2 Cor. 1:3) is all the more crucial when societies become consumed by the race to outdo others and become callous to the needs of the down-and-out.

"Kindness" (goodness, generosity; see Rom. 2:4; 11:2) is gracious sensitivity toward others that is triggered by genuine care for their feelings and desires.

"Humility" (see Phil. 2:8) checks the incessant quest to attain honor and to rise in the pecking order. In the ancient world, honor—what we would equate today with prestige and dignity—was considered to be a scarce commodity. People constantly vied with others to attain elusive glory and engaged in a constant game of one-upmanship. This pursuit of honor coaxed

---

34. Radford, *The Epistles to the Colossians and to Philemon*, 277. See further, Klyne Snodgrass, *Ephesians* (NIVAC; Grand Rapids: Zondervan, 1996), 48–50, 57–59.

outward expressions of egotism and arrogance. Self-boasting, for example, was considered an act of honor; but it creates discord and, in the church, should be regarded as an act of dishonor. Humility allows us to serve others without caring whether it is noticed or not.

"Gentleness" (courtesy, meekness; see 2 Cor. 10:1) betokens the willingness to make allowances for others. Lindemann defines it as the power which, in a situation of conflict, enables us to criticize another's conduct so that they experience it as help and not as condemnation.[35]

"Patience" (Rom. 2:4; 9:22) refrains from exacting revenge or reprisals against enemies and is willing to endure wrongs.

These virtues lead to the action of forbearing and forgiving (3:13; see Eph. 4:2–3). By bearing with and bearing up the brother or sister who sins, we demonstrate this love and our obedience to the law of Christ (cf. Gal. 6:2).[36] Paul's asking believers to forgive one another reveals that he is no utopian dreamer. He recognizes that Christians are not perfect and will sin. They must be conformed to Christ in every aspect of their lives but particularly in the willingness to forgive others.

The final virtue in the list is "love": "As those who are loved by God, they are to be loving of others." The last phrase of 3:14 reads literally, "which is the bond of perfection" and lends itself to a variety of renderings. It may be interpreted to mean "the bond that is perfection" (see Eph. 4:3, "the bond which is peace"), "the perfect bond" (that links all the other virtues together, the option chosen by the NIV), or "the bond that completes or produces perfection." If love is presented as a bond (second option), it ties these other virtues together. We cannot truly exhibit compassion, kindness, humility, gentleness, and patience without love. Love "maintains the balance, but brings each of the other virtues to perfection."[37]

But Paul's main concern is not that these virtues be joined together in a perfect unity. Instead, he is concerned about diverse individuals—Greek, Jew, barbarian, Scythian, slave and free—being joined together in one community. The last option is therefore preferable. Love bonds the community

---

35. Andreas Lindemann, *Der Kolosserbrief*, Zürcher Bibelkommentare (Zurich: Theologischer Verlag, 1983), 60–61.

36. E. D. Martin, *Colossians and Philemon*, 158, notes that the call for toleration is quite different from another's demand "to bear with me." They simply want you to accommodate to their ways and to leave them alone. Jesus had to "bear with" this evil generation (Mark 9:19), but that did not mean he did not confront it with its sins, urge repentance, and offer a new way.

37. Caird, *Paul's Letters from Prison*, 207. Schweizer, *Colossians*, 207, comments: "Love is not simply a further item brought alongside the others; rather it is the source from which all those qualities hitherto mentioned derive their existence."

of believers together into the one body where peace reigns (3:15) and leads to their perfection (see Eph. 4:13).[38]

Harmony and Thankfulness (3:15–17)

THE KEY WORD in each sentence of the last paragraph of this section has to do with Christ: "the peace of Christ" (3:15), "the word of Christ" (3:16), "the name of the Lord Jesus" (3:17).

The verb "rule" in the phrase "let the peace of Christ rule" recalls the athletic metaphor of the umpire used in 2:18. The opponents have decided *against* the Christians (*katabrabeuo*, "disqualify"); Christ's peace, which broke down the dividing wall of hostility (Eph. 2:14), decides *for* them (*brabeuo*). It has two consequences. (1) Christ's peace should characterize relationships in his body (see Rom. 14:19; 1 Cor. 7:15; 2 Thess. 3:16; see John 14:27).[39] Internal harmony in the church is critical. (2) Christ's peace brings thanksgiving. Believers should be as thankful as refugees who have escaped the grim bondage of a repressive culture and have found refuge in a land of freedom and opportunity.

The peace of Christ rules where the word of Christ dwells. The "word of Christ" refers to the message about Christ. It contains the wealth of God's wisdom, which should guide the church's teaching and admonishing. Believers do not need special visions to enhance the wisdom they already have in the word of Christ. We should note that Paul does not assume that he or Epaphras are the only ones who can teach and admonish (1:28). The whole church—no hierarchy of teachers is mentioned—bears that responsibility.

Thanksgiving to God again surfaces and is expressed through "psalms, hymns and spiritual songs." Any distinction among these three words (see Eph. 5:19) is merely guesswork, since we have no direct evidence.[40] They do

---

38. O'Brien, *Colossians and Philemon*, 204, contends that

   Paul is concerned with the reader's corporate life and the perfection he sets before them is not something narrowly individual. It is attained only as Christians, in fellowship, show love to one another. It is by this love, one of the graces of Christ, that his body is built up.

39. This does not refer to some sentimental feeling. The heart was the center of the inner life and the seat of feelings and emotions, desires and passions, thoughts and reflections, moral resolves and religious inclination (Johannes Behm, "καρδία κτλ," *TDNT*, 3:611–13; see further on 2:2).

40. The Greek words for "psalms" is used in 1 Cor. 14:26; for "hymns" in Acts 16:25; Heb. 2:12; and for "songs" in Rev. 5:9; 14:3; 15:3. Lohse, *Colossians and Philemon*, 151, n. 148, cites Gregory of Nyssa (*In Psalm.* 2,3): "For a psalm is a melody produced by a musical instrument, a song is a melody sung with words ... a hymn is a song of praises sung to God for the good things he has given us." A *"spiritual* song" may be one prompted by the Spirit (1 Cor. 14:16).

attest to "a variety and richness of Christian singing" and how central it was to their worship.[41]

The final admonition in this section, "Whatever you do . . . do it all in the name of the Lord Jesus" (2:17),[42] recalls the beginning in 2:6, "So then, just as you received Christ Jesus as Lord, continue to live in him." It prepares the reader for the next set of instructions in 3:18–4:1, which mentions "the Lord" (*kyrios*, trans. "master" in 4:1) seven times. Communal worship is not the only time Christians do things in the name of the Lord and express their thanks to God. Singing and gratitude should be the distinctive feature that embraces all of a Christian's life. We live under Christ's name and are enmeshed in his death and resurrection. Therefore, everything that we do should be done conscious of his calling, his commands, his promises, and his sustenance.

THE ETHICAL LISTS bridge easily into our culture because sin and virtue have not changed, though perceptions of them have. We will look at what it means to set your hearts (minds) on things above, the problems in interpreting ethical lists, and the meaning of the wrath of God.

Philo describes the Therapeutae in Egypt in the early first century as composing "hymns and psalms to God in all sorts of metres and melodies which they write down in solemn rhythms as best they can" (*On the Contemplative Life* 28–29; LCL marginal reading). He also describes their worship:

> Then the President rises and sings a hymn composed as an address to God, either a new one of his own composition or an old one by poets of an earlier day who have left behind them hymns in many measures and melodies, hexameters and iambics, lyrics suitable for processions or in libations and at the altars, or for the chorus whilst standing or dancing, with careful metrical arrangements to fit the various evolutions . . . . They all lift up their voices, men and women alike (*On the Contemplative Life* 80).

Philo relates that they form choirs, one of men and one of women, and then "they sing hymns to God composed of many measures and set to many melodies, sometimes chanting together, sometimes taking up the harmony antiphonally, hands and feet keeping time in accompaniment" (*On the Contemplative Life* 83–89). They sing until dawn. This description of the Therapeutae may also shed light on the worship of the early Christians, who may have done similar things.

41. Wright, *Colossians and Philemon*, 145.

42. It is a remarkable transformation that the Old Testament phrase "the name of the LORD," which referred to God, can now represent for Christians the Lord Jesus Christ (see Hans Bietenhard, "ὄνομα," *TDNT*, 5:259–61). Christians believe that "God has shared his sovereign role with Christ" (Dunn, *Colossians and Philemon*, 240). "Do everything in the name of the Lord Jesus Christ" (see Eph. 5:20) may have an apologetic edge and imply "and not through any other so-called mediator—even angelic ones."

Sets your hearts on things above. Paul has used the word "heaven" in 1:5 ("the hope that is stored up for you in heaven ") and now uses a spatial term, "above," as a synonym (see Ezek. 1:26; Gal. 4:25–26, "the Jerusalem that is above").[43] Our culture is familiar with thinking of the divine world in spatial terms as being "above." Paul's expression, however, has a different twist, which needs some explaining. For Paul, the world above also had an eschatological dimension. He drew a contrast between the present and future ages with spatial language, the upper and lower worlds. When he tells the Colossians to set their minds (hearts) "on things above" and to put to death "the members of the earth" (NIV, "earthly nature"), he wants their moral vision to be controlled by the divine reality that is coming.

There are three pitfalls for interpreting this command in our context. (1) We need to be careful to avoid injecting any potentially gnostic ideas that the world above is the pure realm and that the earthly dimension of our lives is somehow impure, evil, or useless. Paul does not mean that our spirit must escape our earthly nature and ascend to spiritual heights. Lincoln's comments offer a helpful check: "The heavenliness of Christian existence does not mean that real life is in some other realm and human life on earth is doomed to be a shadowy unauthentic existence." If that were true, Paul would not devote so much attention to "the personal, domestic, communal and societal aspects of Christian living." Believers live in the exalted Christ and he in them; therefore, he calls them to live out in earthly structures and relationships "the life of heaven within them."[44] Christians are not called to escape the world but to be obedient to God within it, allowing the transcendent dimension where Christ reigns to set the priorities for our lives.

(2) We must not overemphasize otherworldliness. Paul is not calling for spiritual escapism or encouraging believers always to be dreaming of heaven. Lightfoot's comment on this passage, "You must not only *seek* heaven, you must also *think* heaven," captures Paul's thought; but it can easily be misunderstood when communicated today.[45] Many in our culture are predisposed to dismiss religious commitment as too otherworldly, and they tend to regard the devout as too heavenly minded. Paul does not advocate a monkish withdrawal from the world so that we live with our heads in the clouds. Bonhoeffer's disdain for such otherworldliness is an appropriate critique.

Whenever life begins to become oppressive and troublesome, a person just leaps into the air with a bold kick and soars relieved and

---

43. Colossians 3:1 is the only place where Paul uses this word as a substantive; contrast Gal. 4:26; Phil. 3:14.

44. Lincoln, *Paradise Now and Not Yet*, 130–31.

45. Lightfoot, *Saint Paul's Epistles to the Colossians and to Philemon*, 207.

unencumbered into so-called eternal fields. He leaps over the present. He disdains the earth; he is better than it. After all, besides the temporal defeats he still has his eternal victories, and they are so easily achieved. Other-worldliness also makes it easy to preach and to speak words of comfort. . . . However, Christ does not will or intend this weakness; instead, he makes man strong. He does not lead man in a religious flight from this world to other worlds beyond; rather, he gives him back to the earth as its loyal son.[46]

The aim of a heart fixed on God is to avoid becoming ensnared by the world's lures and entanglements. But we are on the wrong track if we think that we can or should cut ourselves free from the duties of practical living. The next segment of Paul's exhortation addresses how we are to live in the everyday world of the household, a practical concern. Consequently, when he talks about setting your minds "on things above," he refers to our orientation in life, the direction in which our lives are aimed. Scott is correct; the gospel aims "to raise men above the lower interests altogether and make them partakers of a higher kind of life."[47] Our allegiance to Christ should monitor all of our earthly concerns and attachments and make sure that we do not lose our spiritual balance.

(3) The final trap is to overcompensate for the criticism of the cultured despisers of Christianity by adjusting our religious language to conform to secular opinion. Pannenberg argues:

> The absolutely worst way to respond to the challenge of secularism is to adapt to secular standards in language, thought, and way of life. If members of a secularist society turn to religion at all, they do so because they are looking for something other than what that culture already provides. It is counter productive to offer them religion in a secular mode that is carefully trimmed in order not to offend their secular sensibilities.[48]

Christians should not shy away from the fact that our lives are centered on the divine things. We offer a different way of making sense of reality and a different way of living, which go against the grain of what modern society offers as the norm. We also should not shy away from referring to the wrath of God against human sin even though most moderns ignore, disbelieve, or sweeten the pill with deceptions about God's complaisance over sin.

---

46. Dietrich Bonhoeffer, "Thy Kingdom Come," in *Preface to Bonhoeffer*, ed. J. D. Godsey (Philadelphia: Fortress, 1965), 28–29.

47. Scott, *The Epistles of Paul to the Colossians, to Philemon and to the Ephesians*, 61–62.

48. Wolfhart Pannenberg, "How to Think About Secularism," *First Things* 64 (June/July 1996): 31.

The wrath of God. A survey of faith maturity in Christians discovered that most believe that God is forgiving (97%) and loving (96%), but far fewer believe that God is judging (37%) or punishes those who do wrong (19%).[49] These Christians probably doubt that a God of such inclusive love could judge with such inflexible wrath. They may also recoil at an anthropomorphic view of God who, in a burst of temper, would lash out at sinners like an annoyed and frustrated parent swatting an unruly child. Jonathan Edward's famous sermon, "Sinners in the Hands of an Angry God," would fall on skeptical ears today.

The best-selling book *Conversations With God,* by Neale Donald Walsch, represents the current opinion on God's wrath.[50] It portrays a chummy God who patronizes sin, since there is no objective right and wrong. According to Walsh, God smiles on all that we do and only asks that we do our best. Paul's mention of the "wrath of God" presents an opportunity to help people recognize the reality of God's wrath and to disabuse them of common misunderstandings of it.

In 3:6, Paul pictures God's wrath as coming because of the sins listed; in Romans 1:18, he asserts that this wrath is already being revealed. Romans 1:18–32 is the only place in the New Testament where God's wrath is discussed at length. That passage makes clear that we must be careful not to project the emotion of human anger on to God. God is not like the Olympian gods, who petulantly and capriciously punished humans for the slightest offenses. Paul does not portray God's white hot anger erupting in a tantrum against sinners and forcing them to pay for their sins. This image, however, is ingrained in popular consciousness by comic strips that picture God's delivering lightning bolts that zap sinners in their tracks. This common image has nothing to do with the New Testament picture of God's wrath.

In Romans, Paul portrays God's wrath as his turning sinners over to themselves. Three times he repeats the verb "he gave them over" (*paredoken*).[51] "God gave them over in the sinful desires of their hearts to sexual impurity for the degrading of their bodies with one another" (Rom. 1:24). "God gave them over to shameful lusts" (1:26). "Since they did not think it worthwhile to retain the knowledge of God, he gave them over to a depraved mind, to do what ought not to be done" (1:28). Since Paul repeats the verb three

---

49. Eugene C. Roehlkepartain, *The Teaching Church: Moving Christian Education to Center Stage* (Nashville: Abingdon, 1993), 44.

50. Neale Donald Walsch, *Conversations With God: An Uncommon Dialogue. Book 1* (New York: G. P. Putnam's Sons, 1996).

51. See C. H. Dodd, *The Epistle of Paul to Romans,* Moffat New Testament Commentary (New York: Harper & Row, 1932), 21–23; G. H. C. Macgregor, "The Concept of the Wrath of God in the New Testament," *NTS* 7 (1960–61): 101–9.

times, it suggests that he sees this "giving over" as a deliberate act of God. People have willfully deserted God, who, in turn, leaves them to themselves; God allows them to self-destruct.

If we choose chaos for our lives, the wrath of God allows it to work itself out.[52] Consequently, there is no escaping his wrath for any sinful behavior. God does not interfere with our free choice and its consequences but turns us over to ourselves and our sin when we choose to go it alone. If someone wants to drink poison, he can drink poison. God does not break in and say, "I can't let you do it." Dodd adds a corollary to Hebrews 10:31—"It is a dreadful thing to fall into the hands of the living God." He notes that it is also a dreadful thing to fall out of the hands of the living God, "to be left to oneself in a world where the choice of evil things brings its own retribution."[53]

This concept reveals that most people's doctrine of sin is too shallow. They think that the problem with sin resides only with God: "Don't push God too far, or God will get you." The result is that people tend to treat sin as something to be dreaded only if it is detected. They fear getting caught and hope that maybe God is not looking, or that perhaps God can be propitiated in some way to spare them from any retribution. But sin is like cancer that grows out of control and destroys other healthy parts of ourselves. The cancer is the deadly thing, not its detection. Only after the cancer has been diagnosed can treatment begin. The problems come when it goes undiscovered and untreated. Like cancer, sin carries with it its own destructive force. It is something that ruins lives. It distorts and destroys our human relationships as well as our relationship with God.

The surprising thing about Paul's understanding of God's wrath in Romans is that the immorality and the foolishness *is* the punishment, not simply the cause for punishment.[54] Moral perversion and mental pollution are the result of God's wrath, not the reason for it.[55] This means that we are punished by the very sins we sin. If we shut our eyes to the light, we go blind; if we decide to shut our ears to the truth, we go deaf. If we exchange the true God for a false one, we become like the gods we serve.

---

52. Caird, *Paul's Letters from Prison*, 85, voices the opinion of many commentators on God's wrath:

> The principle of retribution [is] built into the structure of God's ordered universe. It may operate through the functions of the state (Rom 13:4), through political disaster (1 Thess 2:16), or through the moral deterioration that ensues upon a rejection of God (Rom 1:18–32; Eph 4:17–19). But the essence of it is that God allows men to reap the harvest of their own disobedience.

53. Dodd, *Romans*, 29.
54. Ernst Käsemann, *Commentary on Romans* (Grand Rapids: Eerdmans, 1980), 38.
55. Ibid., 47.

A perversion of our relationship with God leads to a perversion of all human relationships, and we become less than human. If we do not see fit to have the true God influence our knowledge, we wind up with unfit minds. Such minds become so corrupted that they no longer can think straight and are totally untrustworthy as a guide in moral decisions. This situation leads to a religion based on falsehood, a body that is defiled, and a society where hate and war are at home. The inevitable price of having our way with God is spiritual poverty, spiritual blindness, spiritual deafness, and passions running riot.

At the same time, Paul also indicates that God's wrath is redemptive in intention. When we compare sin to cancer, we realize that we hate the cancer and not the person with the cancer. God hates sin, not the sinner. Paul's reminder to the Colossians that they "used to walk in these ways, in the life you once lived" (3:7) reveals that such behavior does not automatically bring wrathful damnation (see Eph. 2:3). God wishes to redeem us from our sinful destructive ways and allows us to go our own way in the hopes that our eventual wretchedness will cause us to wake up.

Once again, Jesus' parable of the prodigal son helps us see this truth. When the son informed his father that he wanted to depart with his inheritance, the father did not put him under a twenty-four hour guard to keep him home and prevent him from ruining his life in a far country. The boy did not want the father or the father's ways, and there was nothing he could do to force him to obey as a loving son. He let him have his freedom, even if it led to a pigsty. But in that sty he finally snapped out of it: "He came to his senses" (Luke 15:17).

Human beings are trickier to fix than machines. When an engine does not work, it can be repaired, even if it means putting in a whole new set of parts. We cannot deal with human envy, lust, and greed that way. More than once, people have had to plummet to the depths of degradation before they awoke to their condition and turned back to a loving, forgiving Father.

This understanding of God's wrath lies behind Colossians 3, but this text directs us to another dimension of God's wrath. It points to something beyond the reality that we live in a moral universe and that our sins have inevitable consequences. Paul makes clear that sinners will be held accountable to God in a final judgment. This idea is outlined in 1 Peter 4:3–5:

> For you have spent enough time in the past doing what pagans choose to do—living in debauchery, lust, drunkenness, orgies, carousing and detestable idolatry. They think it strange that you do not plunge with them into the same flood of dissipation, and they heap abuse on you. But they will have to give account to him who is ready to judge the living and the dead.

Again, we must be careful to communicate that God does not delight in taking revenge on sinners. Cranfield points out that God's wrath is an expression of his goodness. Humans who are not angry at injustice, cruelty, and corruption cannot be thoroughly good persons.[56] If God is holy, God cannot tolerate willful transgression, indifference to the moral law, or the abuse of others. God honors our freedom to make all the wrong choices, but we will pay the price for snubbing God's love and mercy. Expunging God's holy wrath from our faith drains God's loving grace of any meaning. People need to hear more than the soothing message that God cares about you and "will bless you real good." God will also judge.

Christian ethics. God's desire is not to judge but to reconcile all things to himself in Christ (1:19–20). In the previous section (2:6–15), Paul underscores the gracious act of God in making it possible for humans to come to fullness in Christ, to be alive together with him, and to receive forgiveness of their trespasses (see also 1:12–14, 21–23) without any regard to their own moral or religious successes or failures. This gospel of grace exposed Paul to the charge that he promoted an insidious moral indifference among his converts (Rom. 3:8; 6:1–2, 15). If God forgives all trespasses and justifies the ungodly regardless of their moral character, right and wrong no longer seem to matter.

The ethical exhortation sections in Paul's letters make it clear that he firmly believed that right and wrong and moral character matter a great deal for the Christian. Sinful conduct will face the wrath of God (3:6). Christ's reconciled us in his body to present us before God as "holy in his sight, without blemish and free from accusation" (1:22). Paul differs, for example, from the Colossians errorists in how we become holy in God's sight. Our holiness will not come from our futile attempts to comply with an arbitrary list of observances and taboos. Our godliness is not measured by the things we do not do. It comes from being in Christ, dying with Christ, and being raised with Christ. We should note that his ethical instruction begins with the confession that Christ has been raised from the dead and is seated at the right hand of God (3:1), and with the confident assurance that he will reappear in glory (3:4). Paul's ethics issue from the person of Christ and our being united "with [him]" (3:1, 3–4; see 2:6–7, "rooted and built up in him").

When we interpret ethical passages, we face the temptation of reverting back to the approach of the Colossian errorists. We may want to issue edicts, develop strict rules, and engage in diatribe in order to rein in immorality. But Paul's ethical exhortation immediately follows a refutation of just such an

---

56. C. E. B. Cranfield, *A Critical and Exegetical Commentary on the Epistle to the Romans* (ICC; Edinburgh: T. & T. Clark, 1975), 1:109.

approach. He lampoons the errorists' narrow constrictions and their "don'ts" (2:20–22). He counters that being joined to Jesus Christ is the foundation of the new life and enables changes in our behavior. When Christ becomes our life (3:4), Paul believes we not only die to the human precepts and doctrines (2:22); we die *to sin*. Our motivation to sin completely changes because we have a new motivator in our lives.

But we are not transformed so that we can simply become morally upstanding citizens. Christ puts us under an immeasurably more exacting norm, that of love (3:14; see Rom. 13:8–10; Gal. 5:14). Law codes cannot produce the fruit of the Spirit (Gal. 5:22–23) or the virtues listed in Colossians 3:12–13. A tree, for example, does not produce fruit by an act of Congress. It is the nature of a good fruit tree to produce good fruit. In the same way, living according to the standard set by Christ will not come from any demands to live that way. It is the fruit of a new nature that God gives to us through Christ. Consequently, Paul does not offer a "detailed code of what constitutes proper and improper behavior."[57] Living a life pleasing to God comes spontaneously when we put on Christ. Those who are being renewed in the image of Christ will produce Christlike conduct because that is now their new nature.

We would do well to follow Paul's example rather than that of his opponents with their ledger books and lists of prohibited behavior. Hill astutely recognizes that Paul "focuses on what a believer *is* rather than on what he *must* do. In a sense, the apostle's ethics are more descriptive than prescriptive— he simply encourages readers to act consistently with their status in Christ."[58] Ethical behavior comes as a by-product of putting to death the old and of living in Christ, not from dutifully following a rigorous set of rules.

Schweizer aptly comments on this passage: "In the gospel the call to obedience is *because* one has already been saved and created anew, while in the law, by contrast, it is *in order that* one may become so."[59] Paul is telling the Colossians to live out ethically what they have become in Christ! Believers are to set their hearts on things above, to put to death the things on the earth, to rid themselves of past wicked practices, and to clothe themselves with the new. They are to work out the salvation that God has worked in us (Phil. 2:12–13).

The danger for us in applying this text is to turn Paul's lists into a program of requirements, and to become sanctimonious by engaging in a crusade against others' deplorable vices while ignoring our own. By giving a section

---

57. Alexander D. Hill, "Christian Character in the Marketplace: Colossians and Philemon and the Practice of Business," *Crux* 30 (1994): 30.

58. Ibid.

59. Schweizer, *Colossians*, 172.

of his commentary on this passage the title, "Moral Teaching That Doesn't Go Out of Date," E. D. Martin recognizes that "the items are generic in nature rather than culturally specific."[60] Too often, when we deal with the issues of sexual sins, for example, we get lost in peripheral issues—the length of skirts, the prohibition of skimpy bathing suits, the use of makeup. Rules and policies may be necessary to rein in excesses, but we should never forget that morality is more than obeying rules. And more rules do not make people more virtuous. On the contrary, Paul attests that the introduction of rules may create a greater desire to break them (Rom. 5:21; 7:7–8).

A rabbinic tradition taught that if a man wants to keep his mind on the Law, he should not walk on a road behind a woman, even if she is his own wife.[61] This advice ignores the fact that walking alone on the moon or making everyone wear floor length gunny sacks will not solve the problem of lust that lies buried deep within our hearts. The lustful look begins in the mind's eye. The real solution for male lust is not to avoid women, segregate them, or cover them up, but to transform completely the way a man looks at a woman. He must see a person for whom Christ died, not an object for his own physical gratification. The same solution applies for female lust.

Wall helpfully argues that if we define morality by certain rules of conduct, then we view the person who obeys these rules as moral. The elder brother in Jesus' parable of the prodigal son disproves this assumption. He stayed home with his father, faithfully worked the fields, and never disobeyed a single one of his father's commands (Luke 15:29). But he was no less prodigal than his younger brother, who had skipped out to a far country and wasted his property with a dissolute lifestyle. The elder brother stayed home, but his heart wanted to be in the far country, making merry with his friends while begrudging his father's joy at recovering his lost son. Wall correctly argues that "Paul's ethical teaching flows from a moral vision rather than moral rules. He is less interested in 'doing' codes of rules, although he provides them, than he is in 'being Christian.'" He goes on to say, "The moral issue, then, is not whether one complies with some prescribed code but whether one is the sort of person who is able to be moral. If one has moral character, then one will act morally."[62]

A Tennessee farmer once said, "What comes up in the bucket is usually what's down in the well." The sexual immorality, malevolent bursts of anger, and loathsome speech in Paul's list are all tokens of an inner wickedness. No

---

60. E. D. Martin, *Colossians and Philemon*, 167.

61. *b. 'Erub.* 18b; *b. Ber.* 61a. The text continues: "Whosoever crosses a river behind a woman has no share in the life to come."

62. Wall, *Colossians and Philemon*, 134.

somber list of prohibitions will ever change that wickedness; they may only suppress the ways we overtly express it. The inner wickedness remains and will probably express itself covertly or publicly in ways that may be more socially acceptable but are no less evil. The only solution is to change what is down in the well of our very souls. Only giving ourselves completely to Christ and allowing his transforming power to fumigate and permeate our thoughts and actions will solve the sin problem in our lives. Because we have been raised with Christ and renewed by Christ, living a life pleasing to him is the fruit of our new nature.

 PAUL'S ETHICAL EXHORTATION is based on the Christian's transformed life in Christ. It is a life hidden with Christ and put to death with Christ. It produces a completely changed lifestyle— stripping off old vices and putting on new virtues. Christians give thanks to God for this new life in our corporate praise and worship. We will deal with each of these themes in turn.

A life hidden. Bengel's comments on the affirmation in 3:3 are frequently cited: "The world knows neither Christ nor Christians, but neither do Christians really know themselves."[63] For some Christians their life in Christ is too much hidden from the world. They are at best closet Christians. It is no surprise that the world does not know they belong to Christ because they do not act or think like it. Their "lives sometimes do not measure up even to the lives of those who make no religious claims: they speak of the new life but they do not seem to have gotten as far as the best of the old."[64] But Paul refers here to the paradox that Christians claim to be now what they have yet to become.[65] This new reality may be hidden from others.

Occasionally, a story surfaces in the media describing someone who died leaving millions of dollars. No one had a clue that the person was so rich because he or she led such a simple life, shunning all luxuries. The same may be said about the glorious future of Christians. Outsiders may mistake them for weak, insignificant, dishonored fools for Christ, little knowing that they are tied to the ruler of the universe and destined to reign with him in glory.

This hiddenness—the discrepancy between reality and appearances—can also cause tension within Christians. They may also doubt the reality of God's transforming power in their lives. Like an athlete who has had suc-

---

63. Cited by Schweizer, *Colossians*, 176.
64. Ibid.
65. C. F. D. Moule, "The 'New Life' in Colossians," *RevExp* 70 (1973): 481.

cessful knee surgery but still favors the knee because he remembers the past pain and doubts whether it has fully recovered, a Christian may continue to limp through life. Believers may not believe that God is renewing them, or they may be unwilling to allow God's renewing power to take hold.

The new life is not something automatic, which occurs without any effort on our part. As Moule observes: "The process of fully becoming detached from the old and fully belonging to the new remains to be painfully and laboriously completed."[66] But it must be a "relaxed and confident strenuousness." He contends that if Christians do not experience "growing pains" in their new life, "it is doubtful whether the new life has begun."

Paul's account of his own struggle is helpful:

> Not that I have already obtained all this, or have already been made perfect, but I press on to take hold of that for which Christ Jesus took hold of me. Brothers, I do not consider myself yet to have taken hold of it. But one thing I do: Forgetting what is behind and straining toward what is ahead, I press on toward the goal to win the prize for which God has called me heavenward in Christ Jesus. (Phil. 3:12–14)

Paul visualizes himself in a race in which he has charged off the starting blocks, but there is no reason to gloat over a successful beginning until the race is over. Like a runner, he does not congratulate himself on the laps he has finished but concentrates only on what lies ahead. He refuses to be spiritually self-satisfied, to rest on his religious laurels, or to be distracted by other things, but he presses on to finish the race. On the other hand, in athletics "pressing" can have a negative connotation. Athletes in a slump may get down on themselves and "press" by trying too hard. The extra effort only mires them deeper in the slump. Paul's image is that of a runner in full stride giving his all, but great runners usually make their running look so effortless and natural. They also run with joy and abandon.

When Christ takes hold of us and when we give our striving wholly to Christ, something happens without our even noticing: Transformation occurs. Dorothy Canfield Fisher's short story "The Pragmatist" captures the essence of this hidden transformation. It describes a man on his deathbed, shuddering as he reflects back on his life. He was much praised by others, but he thought of his life as one of unbroken duplicity, in which he had always worn a mask. Soon, he thought, death would make known to him who he really was and how God saw him. He lamented that he had always pretended to a courage he did not possess and counterfeited a serenity and faith he did not feel, all to help strengthen other weak and wavering souls. He gave

---

66. Ibid., 483.

heartening cries for battle against a foe whom he believed in his heart to be invincible. His whole life, he lamented, was a web of falsehood.

And now he was come to the end of it. He was an impostor, through and through. The very face which lay on the pillow was not his, since it was calm from a long habit of hiding his base and real passions, hardened into a mask of meek courage above his fainting heart and weak, despairing soul.

A deathlike chill crept upon him. This was the beginning of the dissolution, he thought. Soon the mask would be torn from him, and his true face of agonized doubt disclosed. In the unsparing mirror, which death was about to hold before him, he would at last see himself as he really was . . . and he trembled with an awful terror.

. . . yet those who were with him at the last, say that at the end he cried out in a voice of exceeding joy.[67]

Sometimes it is those who walk most closely to God who are most acutely aware of how much they have fallen short of God's glory. They still see themselves as poor, wretched sinners. Others may see more of God's transforming presence in their lives than they do. Our assurance is that those who are in Christ are being transformed. John's promise in 1 John 3:2–3 is most fitting for those struggling with their human frailties and accords with the truth in Colossians:

Dear friends, now we are children of God, and what we will be has not yet been made known. But we know that when he appears, we shall be like him, for we shall see him as he is. Everyone who has this hope in him purifies himself, just as he is pure.

A life put to death. Paul insists that the old nature is not renewed or reformed; instead, it is put to death. This forceful image means that Christian renewal is not some cosmetic overhaul of our sinful personalities. We do not simply add on a veneer of Christian values that only laminates our old nature and its value system. Paul does not tell us to put on new clothes over the old; the old must be stripped off and thrown away. We need more than a few minor adjustments and cannot skip over the key element of dying with Christ.

Anne Lamott recalls hearing Marianne Williamson speak about this dying-renewal process:

. . . when you ask God into your life, you think he or she is going to come into your psychic house, look around, and see that you just need

---

67. Dorothy Canfield Fisher, "The Pragmatist," in *The Questing Spirit*, ed. Halford E. Luccock and Frances Brentano (New York: Coward-McCann, 1947), 140–41.

a little cleaning—and so you go along for the first six months thinking how nice life is now that God is there. Then you look out the window one day and see that there's a wrecking ball outside. It turns out that God actually thinks your whole foundation is shot and you're going to have to start over from scratch.[68]

The commitment to get rid of sin, Paul implies, cannot be accomplished by gradual degrees and with minor repairs. The whole foundation must be replaced, and the sooner we allow God to tear it down and start the rebuilding process, the sooner we avert the catastrophe of having the whole house come crashing down around our heads when the weight of sin becomes too much.

The problem is that we may not want to put away our sins quite yet. Augustine admits he had prayed: "Give me chastity, but not yet." We are far more tolerant of sin polluting our lives than we are of bacteria polluting our drinking water. Our family has stayed in a mountain cabin with a shallow well. One year the water did not pass the purity test; the bacteria level in the water was just above the acceptable level. But we were assured by neighbors that it would not hurt us. Despite these assurances, we decided not to drink that water and risk getting sick.

If we felt the same way about the sin in our lives as we do about the water we drink, we probably would not comfort ourselves that the pollution level is only a fraction over the acceptable level. We would ignore the assurances from our culture that a little sin does not do that much harm. In Christ there is zero tolerance for any pollution, and radical measures need to be taken to eliminate the problem. Jesus also used vivid imagery to communicate the seriousness of sin:

> If your hand causes you to sin, cut it off. It is better for you to enter life maimed than with two hands to go into hell, where the fire never goes out. And if your foot causes you to sin, cut it off. It is better for you to enter life crippled than to have two feet and be thrown into hell. And if your eye causes you to sin, pluck it out. It is better for you to enter the kingdom of God with one eye than to have two eyes and be thrown into hell, where

> "their worm does not die,
> and the fire is not quenched." (Mark 9:43–48)

The new life, therefore, calls for more than jettisoning a few vices and augmenting our spiritual lives with regular church attendance. Nor is it simply

---

68. Anne Lamott, *Bird by Bird: Some Instructions on Writing and Life* (New York: Doubleday, 1994), 167.

a matter of trying to do better or making piecemeal progress. Paul clearly says that what gets "renewed" is the "new self," not the earthly nature (3:10). To quote E. D. Martin: "The process as described is not a matter of gradually changing the old into something better, but of progressively actualizing the already-existing new creation."[69]

The Christian cannot move in and out of Christ's lordship whenever it becomes convenient or inconvenient. Holy living is rarely convenient, and we should never forget the looming wrath of God, which brings certain punishment. Even when it seems that we have gotten away with our sin, it gestates within us. Consequently, Paul insists, our unethical behavior, which belongs to our old life, must be discarded like old rags or cut out like a cancerous tumor before it destroys us.

We may wonder if this transformation is possible. Can we really put to death the earthly nature? We can see clear evidence of the opposite process, in which persons have put to death "compassion, kindness, humility, gentleness and patience." Those who have interviewed convicted serial killers and child molesters have testified that something inside these men was dead. They were dead to love, dead to empathy, dead to compassion for their victims or their victim's family. If it is possible for individuals to kill virtue in their lives, it must also be possible for individuals to kill such things as lust, evil desires, greed, anger, rage, malice, slander, and abusive language. We do not do it through our own will power, however. The power comes from our having been raised with Christ and from the one who raised him from the dead. The irresistible compulsion to sin is replaced by the irresistible power of God.

Virtues and vices. Paul's insistence on putting off sin and putting on the new life with its concomitant virtues ran against the grain of his culture. It also runs counter to ours. An attack on sexual sins, for example, is quickly dismissed as prudish, puritanical, or Victorian. Chastity is seen as outmoded or imposed by physical unattractiveness. A character in Oscar Wilde's play *Lady Windemere's Fan* says, "A man who moralizes is usually a hypocrite, and a woman who moralizes is usually plain." H. G. Wells quipped that moral indignation is only jealousy with a halo.

Many today resist any appeal to an objective moral authority. Our culture increasingly questions clear distinctions between right and wrong and good and evil that were taken for granted by earlier generations. Many assume that as independent human beings we are each free to live by whatever standards we choose, and we resent any challenges to our lifestyle choices.

---

69. E. D. Martin, *Colossians and Philemon*, 152–53.

Our moral sensitivity has been deadened by crudity and violence, which make up a regular intellectual diet for many in our culture. In the movie *Broadcast News*, a character expresses disgust over a devious coworker. He asks, "What do you think the devil's going to look like?" and answering his own question, he says that the devil will be attractive to many and influence them "and will just, bit by bit, lower our standards."

The popular media seem to be the best weapon in lowering standards. In our culture, fornication, impurity, passion, evil desires, and greed are treated as "free expression." It has become more acceptable to use God's name in profanity or in exclamations than to use God's name in prayer. Vile pornographers are hailed as great defenders of free speech guaranteed in the United States Constitution. Those who speak out against their odious publications are ostracized and ridiculed. People get rich portraying these things in the movies, making music about violence against women, and slowly, bit by bit, undermining our standards so that many cannot tell right from wrong, impurity from purity, or evil desires from good. Others are lauded for behavior that, as one has said, years ago "would have gotten them arrested or institutionalized."

Sadly, immoral producers wield a powerful and subtle influence over our children. The average child in America is submitted to countless hours of TV, and the influence of the secular dream-weavers cannot easily be countered by an hour or two of Christian teaching in the church or at home. Hanson laments:

> Popular videos, which are just a finger touch away from the youngest, most impressionable minds, revel in the sordid and the satanic. Impermanence, violence, and irreverence have thus become habits of mind. And even as a whole economy has come to be based upon the principle of built-in obsolescence, we tend to treat the reality of beliefs and morals with a corresponding impatience.[70]

Such impatience with Christian morality ignores the ample evidence of the fallenness of humankind and mistakenly assumes that human nature is basically good and that whatever we do is okay. A celebrity tried to explain away his affair with his stepdaughter by saying, "The heart wants what it wants." The problem is that the human heart is easily corrupted and debased, and the debauched human mind then excuses its wanton ways because it cannot tell right from wrong.

In Bill Watterson's comic strip, "Calvin and Hobbes," Hobbes, a stuffed tiger, takes on lifelike proportions when he is alone with six-year-old Calvin.

---

70. Paul D. Hanson, "The Identity and Purpose of the Church," *TToday* 42 (1985): 342.

In one panel, he asks Calvin how he is doing on his New Year's resolutions. Calvin responds that he did not make any and explains:

> See, in order to improve oneself, one must have some idea of what's "good." That implies certain values. But as we all know, values are relative. Every system of belief is equally valid and we need to tolerate diversity. Virtue isn't "better" than vice. It's just different.

Hobbes, the embodiment of a greater wisdom, replies that he does not think he can "tolerate so much tolerance." The indomitable Calvin will not budge: "I refuse to be victimized by notions of virtuous behavior." Calvin represents our shallow, relativistic values.

Many today believe that we should be left to ourselves to create our own morals from a smorgasbord of equally valid choices. In Colossians, Paul makes it clear that there are objective standards that Christians are expected to meet. The church should muster all its energy to instill these values in its members. Martin puts it well: "These teachings constitute an inescapable call to make the ethics of the Savior the ethics of the saved."[71]

Lifestyle issues for Christians. We should never confuse being moral with being Christian, but we cannot claim to be Christian if we ignore morality. A lukewarm morality can hardly damp down the scorching flames of heathenism. Our behavior as Christians becomes an advertisement for what being in Christ does to a person's life. In the words of Lohse, "It is precisely in the Christian's everyday life, where he toils and sweats, that he is placed under the command to prove his allegiance to the Lord."[72] Unbelievers look at Christians and ask how are they any different from anybody else. They should see a clear difference in the way Christians handle their sexuality and anger, how they treat others who are different from them, and how they are forgiving and free from avarice.[73]

Christians and sexuality. If Malcolm Muggeridge is right that "the orgasm has replaced the cross as the focus of longing and the image of fulfillment," it explains the gaping void in many people's lives. God intended the sexual union to promote caring, giving, and intimacy; in every age, humans have perverted what God intended for good. We can see that perversion in modern slang, which uses gutter terms to describe the sexual union in terms of acts of hostility, assault, and abuse. We can also see it in our description of sex as a commodity—as something we "have." And, in a consumerist society, we are conditioned to want to "have" the "best" of something and the "most." Our culture has also developed the daring attitude that anything

---

71. E. D. Martin, *Colossians and Philemon*, 161.
72. Lohse, *Colossians and Philemon*, 153.
73. On the meaning of forgiveness, see the Contemporary Significance section to Philemon.

goes as long as no one gets hurt. It fails to take into account the wrath of God. Buechner's comments are apropos:

> Maybe the injuries are all internal. Maybe it will be years before the Xrays show up anything. Maybe the only person who gets hurt is you.[74]

The emphasis nowadays is on safe sex, but there is no prophylactic for the soul.

The New Testament understands that our sexual expression is not just something we do; it reflects who we are. Christians are those who always put the rights and needs of others first. They act from love. Many discover too late the difference between lust and love. Lust seeks quick fulfillment and is just as quickly sated. Love takes work and deepens over time. Lust focuses only on the senses, but love uses the senses to cherish the other and to nourish the soul. Today, people talk about their individual rights, but in the New Testament the emphasis is on responsibility. Mitton comments that Christian sexual behavior must be controlled by

> responsibility for the true welfare of the other person involved in the relationship, and for any child who may be born in consequence of it. The Christian insight which was evolved from this deep respect for the personal life of others, and for lives yet unborn, has led to the Christian standard in sexual behavior which is normally summed up as chastity before marriage and faithfulness within marriage. The use of the sexual relationship for pleasure or excitement without any real sense of responsibility degrades personal life and personal relationships.[75]

Habits are things that we do that are automatic, unconscious, and comfortable. Many in our culture have become habituated to looking at and thinking about persons of the opposite sex as if they were objects for our gratification and not persons. The church should not ignore this problem but speak out clearly against these tendencies and provide serious help so that people can unlearn and put off these destructive habits.

---

74. Frederick Buechner, *Wishful Thinking: A Theological ABC* (New York/Evanston/San Francisco/London: Harper & Row, 1973), 87–88.

75. C. Leslie Mitton, *Ephesians* (NCB; London: Oliphants, 1976), 161. In the same vein, Helmut Thielicke, *Theological Ethics Volume 3: Sex* (Grand Rapids: Eerdmans, 1979), 201, writes:

> Since premarital and extramarital sexual intercourse is sought mostly for pleasure and relaxation of tension, as satisfaction of libido, those indulging in it are generally little inclined to make the corresponding sacrifices and accept the responsibilities that go with it. To this extent there is here a denial of one of the essential purposes of sexuality, namely personal relationship designed to be permanent and the willingness to accept the office of parenthood.

The dangers of anger. The church is supposed to be a different place from a world where people are at war with one another. It is to be a place where the destructive effects of anger fade. Therefore, we must learn to defuse our anger before it blows up in our face and destroys our fellowship. Anger becomes dangerous when it is fed, justified, encouraged, and nurtured. It eats away at the soul like a cancer and shrivels our gratitude to God and others.

The danger for Christians is not that they might get angry. If they are humans and not vegetables, they will get angry. The issue is how we handle our anger—in constructive or destructive ways. We face the danger of mis-using the anger and engaging in various kinds of warfare: the cold war when we refuse to talk about the issues; guerrilla warfare when we snipe at the other in public; atomic warfare when the anger wells up inside until it explodes like an atomic bomb and everyone around us gets wiped out by the fallout.

Schweizer lists several perils that unchecked anger poses in our lives.[76]

- Gnawing anger can strain lifelong relationships.
- Wrath can explode, throw off all constraints, and utter ill-considered sentiments that cannot be taken back.
- Malice leads one to do and say things that harm one's neighbor.
- Wickedness hurls abuse at someone without caring how much distress it causes.
- Gossip spreads like wildfire behind people's backs. It is frequently impossible to control its damage, so that it makes life virtually unlivable for the victim and proliferates anger.

A life filled with thankfulness for what God has done for us and for what God promises will be ours in Christ drives out the anger caused by petty slights or by perceived threats.

The dangers of prejudice. Christians believe that all have equal value to God and that God offers salvation equally to all. As the children's song has it,

Jesus loves the little children,
All the children of the world—
red and yellow, black and white,
they are precious in his sight;
Jesus loves the little children of the world.

What we believe in theory, however, is not always lived out in practice. Prejudice and suspicion of others who are different endures and can take virulent forms. Our stubborn hearts override our enlightened minds. Even the one

---

76. Schweizer, *Colossians*, 202.

who drafted the Declaration of Independence, declaring that all human beings are created equal, could write later about the racial inferiority of Negroes.

Paul gave his life to proclaiming a gospel that broke down the walls of ancient prejudices. We should not fool ourselves into thinking that we are better than others or more favored by God than others, or that God will skip over us in the judgment because we belong to a chosen people. Colossians 3:11 presents another opportunity to subvert the prejudices that so many of us have. Our birth, race, gender, language, and social class are not barriers to God's love, and they should not be allowed to become barriers in the loving fellowship of God's people. The happenstance of our being born into this world does not cease to exist, but those circumstances should not define what it ultimately means to be human or put any limits on God's love.

(1) Prejudice victimizes both the one who holds the prejudice and the object of the prejudice. Alan Paton's novel, *Cry the Beloved Country*, set in apartheid South Africa, clearly shows how this is true. Two fathers, white and black, both lose their sons to a brutal system. Racial discrimination destroys the victims and the perpetrators of racism.

(2) Prejudice hardens the arteries of the heart and cuts off mercy. It closes around us like a fist so we can neither give mercy or receive it. In one of Barbara Kingsolver's novels, in a chapter entitled "How They Eat in Heaven," a character named Mrs. Parsons is described as particularly mean-spirited. If that same spirit expressed itself in a dog, the narrator says, you would "give it away to somebody with a big farm." This thought was evoked by several snide comments from Mrs. Parsons about "aliens." She was at a meal where two Salvadorans given illegal sanctuary in the United States also were guests. She insensitively yammered on: "Before you know it the whole world will be here jibbering and jabbering till we won't know it's America." When told by her more kindly companion to mind her manners, she said, "Well, it's the truth. They ought to stay put in their own dirt, not come here taking up jobs."[77] All such heartlessness and contempt for others are forbidden to the Christian.

(3) Prejudice is a denial of our justification by faith. Markus Barth writes:

> Justification in Christ is ... not an individual miracle happening to this person or that person, which each person may seek or possess for himself. Rather, justification by grace is a joining together of this and that person, of the near and the far, of the good and the bad, of

---

77. Barbara Kingsolver, *The Bean Trees* (New York: HarperCollins, 1988), 106–7.

the high and the low, liberal and fundamentalist. It is a social event. No one is joined to Christ except together with a neighbor.[78]

It bears repeating: Those who are joined to Christ are also joined to one another. We therefore have no basis for any hatred toward others or feelings of superiority. These feelings must be obliterated—as they were when the slave girl Felicitas and her lady Perpetua faced death together in the arena hand in hand, sisters in Christ; as they were when Philemon presumably accepted Onesimus back as a brother in Christ.

The gospel opposes the use of human criteria to exclude others or to make them second class. It opposes ostracizing others on the basis of external and human distinctions that do not matter to God—race, sex, denomination, class, education, geography, culture, politics, or church rites. These are all "flesh" categories and part of the old order that is under sentence of death. Paul excludes no one except on the basis of flagrant ethical violations—what is referred to in the Old Testament as sinning "with a high hand" (Num. 15:30, RSV; NIV, "defiantly").

Any group that shuts out others on the basis of human differences is not of God. To apply these distinctions to exclude people from salvation and to label them as unworthy until they change their condition is to deny that God is impartial, that we are justified by faith alone, and that Christ's death atones for our sins. Such an attitude insists that God loves us because of who we are, not in spite of who we are. All of these distinctions were rejected by Christ in his earthly ministry, when he treated the sinners, Samaritans, and centurions the same as he treated the so-called righteous Jews.

The dangers of greed. Greed is the hankering to get more and more.[79] Niebuhr argued:

> Man's sense of dependence upon nature and his reverent gratitude toward the miracle of nature's perennial abundance is destroyed by his arrogant sense of independence and his greedy effort to overcome the insecurity of nature's rhythms and seasons by garnering her stores with excessive zeal and beyond natural requirements. Greed is in short the expression of man's inordinate ambition to hide his insecurity in nature.[80]

Humans grasp after power and an overabundance of goods in a vain attempt to shelter themselves from the precariousness of life—inevitably at the

---

78. Markus Barth, "Jews and Gentiles: The Social Character of Justification in Paul," *JES* 5 (1968): 259.

79. E. D. Martin, *Colossians and Philemon,* 168.

80. Reinhold Niebuhr, *The Nature and Destiny of Man* (New York: Charles Scribner's Sons, 1964), 190–91.

expense of other life—or to try to fill up a spiritual emptiness. We fool ourselves into thinking that the more we have, the more secure we are. But
greed provides no defense against the vicissitudes of life or death.

Nevertheless, greed seems to be the engine that drives our lives at home
and at work. Hill asks, "What relevance do the golden rule and Jesus' *agape*
commandments have to a business environment which often seems so Dar-
winian in character?"[81] How does our being in Christ affect our lives in the
marketplace and workplace? Some employers have gone on record saying
that "naive," "idealistic" religious commitments have no place in the cutthroat
world of business competition. Business experts have argued for a dual morality, whereby we compartmentalize and separate our religious loyalties from
our business dealings. It is fine to be honest and loving in our private lives,
they say; but in the dog-eat-dog world of business, the goal is to win at all
costs. They claim that we are not morally culpable for whatever we do to pad
the bottom line of a corporation—lying, bluffing, cheating, hawking deadly
products, and so on.

Paul, however, insists that no activity can fall outside Christ's lordship
for the Christian. The Wall Street sharpie who crows, "Greed is good," would
laugh at Paul's advice to the Corinthians. "Why not rather be wronged? Why
not rather be cheated?" (1 Cor. 6:7). Greed gives a completely different set
of questions: "Why not wrong others? Why not cheat?"

The answers to these questions have been complicated by the premium
placed on material success in our contemporary setting. Modern advertisers have done a superb job in making us want things we might not otherwise have wanted and in fooling us into thinking that we desperately need
them. They have turned us into "the grand acquisitors." The grave danger
is that wanting and getting things can become the driving force of our
whole lives. Worse, our materialistic society may teach us not only to calculate our financial net worth from our possessions but our self-worth as well.
We can be consumed by our consuming ways, wanting more and better of
everything.

Such drives lead to craving what is not ours, and the objects of our greed
can also be persons who attract us sexually. The plague of greed is painfully
evident in the newspaper headlines reporting that a mother-in-law con-
tracted a hit man to kill her son-in-law because she did not think he was
good enough for her daughter, that a mother tried to insure a spot for her
daughter on the cheerleading squad by having her rival's mother killed, and
that an athlete conspired to disable a competitor to better the chances for

---

81. Hill, "Christian Character in the Marketplace," 27. I am indebted to Hill's insights
in the following discussion.

winning an Olympic medal. Such headlines reflect the pervasive idolatry of "me" over others and "me" over God that plagues our world.

The following description of the German composer Richard Wagner is a perfect example of what Paul has in mind when he caps off the first list of vices in 3:5 with "greed, which is idolatry."

> He was a liar, a cheat, and a hypocrite, without the slightest regard for ethics, morality, generosity, or personal honor. He had no sense of responsibility. He borrowed money with no intention of repaying it, and he did not hesitate to use the borrowed funds for extravagances— for he always lived beyond his means, usually in regal style. "The world owes me what I need," he said proudly, because he was convinced that he was the greatest musician, the greatest dramatist, the greatest poet, and one of the most profound minds the world has known. He made love to women without thought of possible consequences or hurts; they were solely for his pleasure and necessities. He could be as callous to the pain of others as he was neurotically preoccupied with his own. And he was filled with hate for everybody around him as he was filled with self-adoration.[82]

Abhorrent examples of greed, however, allow us to be self-righteous and overlook our own desires to have more than we should, to exploit others, and to make our own passions the most important thing in the world. We convince ourselves that, unlike others who are greedy, we need these things or deserve them. We also justify our avarice by convincing ourselves that since "everybody" else has these desired things, we should too. We fail to see that we have turned even our trifling cravings into gods as greedy as the jaws of hell.

Christian worship. Worship is our response to what Christ has done and continues to do. It shapes our faith and makes it meaningful for our daily lives as we respond to the God who has saved us and calls us to be his people. The presence of Christ and our joining together in offering up prayers and songs to God establishes and strengthens our mutual bonds. Our worship provides guidance for our lives in hearing the Word of God applied, brings to our awareness the needs of others in our intercessory prayers, and presents the opportunity for expressing our repentance. It prepares us for the spiritual battles we must often face alone during the week.

Examples in the New Testament of how the first Christians worshiped are slim. We find only a few hints. The first Christians "devoted themselves to the apostles' teaching and to the fellowship, to the breaking of bread and to

---

82. Milton Cross and David Ewen, "Richard Wagner," *The Milton Cross New Encyclopedia of the Great Composers and Their Music* (rev. ed.; Garden City, N.Y.: Doubleday, 1969), 2:1104.

prayer" (Acts 2:42). At Corinth, "everyone has a hymn, or a word of instruction, a revelation, a tongue or an interpretation" (1 Cor. 14:26). Paul's concern in 1 Corinthians was that their worship should build up the whole church, not the egos of the ones who turned it into a performance. In Colossians 3:16, he identifies two key elements of worship: teaching and admonishing that centers on the word of Christ, and singing praise. He couples that with two norms for worship: wisdom and thanksgiving.

Teaching and admonishing the word of Christ. Paul affirms that Christ is among them through their ministry of the word. The worship of the early Christians placed a premium on the spoken word in contrast to perfunctory rituals or mysterious ceremonies. Words are important. Through them Christ engages us, and we learn of his character and will for us. Crichton writes:

> Words play a peculiarly important role (in contrast to primitive worship where the action is dominant and the word seems to have little role at all), first because faith comes by hearing—the word must be proclaimed—and secondly because response in words is the specifically human way by which man makes himself known to himself and to others that he has received the word.[83]

We are to rely on the revelation from God's Word instead of our revelations.

Dawn incisively criticizes what she calls "entertainment evangelism," which has become an ominous trend in the church. Her thesis is that we have "dumbed down" the truth of God that reveals God's splendor and grace in the face of human depravity with false efforts to feel better about ourselves.[84] She observes, "To attract people from our culture, some Christian churches depend on glitz and spectacle and technological toys, rather than on the strong, substantive declaration of the Word of God and its authoritative revelation for our lives."[85] The danger is that worship becomes simply a performance, an exhibition that focuses on us instead of God. It may give people the false impression that the chief purpose of God is to glorify humans rather than vice versa.[86]

For many, worship becomes the time when God is supposed to meet our needs rather than a time when we give glory to God. If it fails in that regard, then we do not have any use for it. The following quote typifies such an

---

83. J. D. Crichton, "A Theology of Worship," in *The Study of Liturgy*, ed. C. Jones, G. Wainwright, and E. Yarnold (London: SPCK, 1978), 10.

84. Marva J. Dawn, *Reaching Out Without Dumbing Down: A Theology of Worship for the Turn-of-the-Century Culture* (Grand Rapids: Eerdmans, 1995), 91.

85. Ibid., 50.

86. Robert Wuthnow, "Small Groups Forge New Notions of Community and the Sacred," *The Christian Century* 110 (Dec. 8, 1993): 1239.

attitude: "Just in terms of allocation of time resources, religion is not very efficient. There's a lot more I could be doing on a Sunday morning."[87]

Worship is not to be about us but about God. The word is God's, the wisdom is God's, and thanks are due God alone. Keck complains:

> We have blown up balloons, danced in the aisles, marched behind banners; we have turned to jazz and sung ditties whose theological content makes a nursery rhyme sound like Thomas Aquinas. But it is not enough to make things livelier, or to set to music our aspirations and agendas. We can do better than that, and we must, for then the truth of God as made actual in Christ and attested in the gospel evokes the truthful praise of God. Christian worship enacts an alternative to the secularism which otherwise deludes us with its promises.[88]

Worship that resembles a three-ring circus may attract many people and result in many responses, but the people who respond may only have a superficial relationship to Christ. Such shallowness is captured in a character from Sinclair Lewis' novel *Main Street*:

> He believed in the church but seldom attended its services. He believed in Christianity but seldom thought about it. He was worried about Carol's lack of faith but was not sure what she lacked.

Dawn asks:

> If people are saved by a spectacular Christ, will they find him in the fumbling of their own devotional life or in the humble services of local parishes where pastors and organists make mistakes? Will a glitzy portrayal of Christ nurture in new believers his character of willing suffering and sacrificial obedience? Will it create an awareness of the idolatries of our age and lead to repentance? And does a flashy, hard-rock sound track bring people to a Christ who calls us away from the world's superficiality to deeper reflection and meditation?[89]

Worship that centers on the word of Christ should lead to a more mature faith. Roehlkepartain isolates eight marks of faith maturity, and we may use them as a guide to test the "wisdom" in our worship and whether our worship generates this kind of maturity.[90]

---

87. Walter Isaacson, "In Search of the Real Bill Gates," *Time* 149/2 (Jan. 13, 1997): 51.

88. Leander Keck, *The Church Confident* (Nashville: Abingdon, 1993), 42, noted by Dawn, *Reaching Out Without Dumbing Down*, 88.

89. Dawn, *Reaching Out Without Dumbing Down*, 50.

90. Eugene C. Roehlkepartain, *The Teaching Church: Moving Christian Education to Center Stage* (Nashville: Abingdon, 1993), 36–37.

(1) Trusting and believing. Mature Christians believe "the basic theological affirmations: Jesus' humanity and divinity, God's unconditioned love, God as both transcendent and immanent; and the reconciling of human suffering and God's love." These truths are communicated through words, and they require more than intellectual assent. They are to become the guide for our daily lives. As Dietrich Bonhoeffer said, "Only he who believes is obedient, and only he who is obedient believes."[91] Our worship should convey our fundamental faith about God and pass it on to others.

(2) Experiencing the fruits of faith. Mature Christians experience a sense of well-being, security, and peace. Our worship should foster these feelings even if life may seem to be caving in on us. Anna L. Waring's hymn captures this spirit:

In heav'nly love abiding, no change my heart shall fear;
And safe is such confiding, for nothing changes here.
The storm may roar without me, my heart may low be laid;
But God is round about me, and can I be dismayed?

(3) Integrating faith and life. Mature Christians filter all aspects of life—what they see, hear, and think; their family, vocation, relationships, finances, politics, and ethical decisions—through their faith in Christ. They do not confine their religious faith to some isolated niche in their lives and take it out now and then, but they allow their faith in Christ to shape all of reality and inform all that they do.

(4) Seeking spiritual growth. Mature Christians move beyond childhood understandings of faith and "seek to grow spiritually through study, reflection, prayer, and discussion." Worship should lead to greater understanding of theological truth. If we contrast the theological depth of the prose hymn in Colossians 1:15–20 with examples from modern praise choruses, we can see more clearly how trivial and insubstantial some of what we sing in our worship is.

Praise choruses can, of course, benefit our worship since they are usually directed to the triune God and glorify his worthiness, name, and majesty. But we must guard against surrendering intellectual and spiritual depth in our music. Dawn argues, "Shallow music forms shallow people."[92] Music makes deep impressions in our minds. Alzheimer patients who sadly can no longer recognize their loved ones can sometimes still remember favorite hymns or songs. We should fill our souls with hymns that convey the full depth of our great faith in Christ.

---

91. Dietrich Bonhoeffer, *The Cost of Discipleship* (New York: Macmillan, 1963), 69.
92. Dawn, *Reaching Out Without Dumbing Down*, 175.

(5) Nurturing faith in community. Mature Christians witness to their faith and nourish one another in community. Many unchurched people who call themselves Christians like to boast that they can lead a good Christian life without the "hypocrisy" of church membership. They believe that God is everywhere, and they can worship God just as well at home. Emily Dickinson sounds their credo:

> Some worship God by going to church
> I worship him staying at home
> with a bobolink for a chorister
> and an orchard for a throne.

They also probably assume that the Christian faith amounts to little more than belief in God and respect for Jesus and the Golden Rule. Home alone, it is unlikely that they will hear the Word that informs them otherwise. They will not learn what God is doing in our world or receive direction for how they are to live. They will also miss out on the communal dimensions of faith—the encouraging friendships and the teaching in the church that help us unlearn harmful habits of sin and develop holy ones.

(6) Holding life-affirming values. Mature Christians believe that life is good and should be affirmed, and they take responsibility for the welfare of others. They care about the plight of those in faraway places or those who are closer to home but tucked away in bleak ghettoes.

(7) Advocating social change. Mature Christians believe "that faith demands global concern and that the church belongs in the public sphere." They struggle with how to be prophetic and create justice for those who cannot speak or act for themselves.

(8) Acting and serving. Mature Christians are not simply advocates, they become "personally involved in serving." They do not say that they are too busy and hire others to do their tasks. Their circle of concern is much larger than their own family and friends and give their time to minister to those who need it most and can never repay.

Singing praise. Christian worship should be marked by joy and gratitude. H. L. Mencken scoffed, "The chief contribution of Protestantism to human thought is its massive proof that God is a bore."[93] This thought was recorded in a collection of his notebooks entitled *Minority Report;* unfortunately, his curmudgeonly opinion may not be a minority report. Many people have been turned off by dour services and droning congregants. This criticism explains why so many churches have perhaps overcompensated by trying to spice up their worship with a variety of gimmicks.

---

93. H. L. Mencken, *Minority Report* (New York: Alfred A. Knopf, 1956), 214.

Times occur that call forth a deep sadness. Christians are not called to be perpetually happy, and worship that ignores the travails of life can only promote a superficial faith. Life does not always come up roses. Our worship should acknowledge that God is God even in the gloom of pain, suffering, and failure. Paul says that they sing "psalms"; and if the Old Testament Psalms are a model, it leaves plenty of room for bitter lament and complaint.[94] Times occur that require us to repent with sackcloth and ashes. H. H. Farmer lamented half a century ago that so often we hear the comment, "We *enjoyed* the service." Would it have not been better to hear, "I saw the Lord high and lifted up; woe is me! I am a man of unclean lips" (cf. Isa. 6:5)? He writes:

> The supreme test for them really is whether they have found the hour in church enjoyable, whether the music being good, the singing hearty, the decorations no offense to the eye, the curtains the right shade, the building beautiful, they come away "feeling" better. The sense that truth, saving truth, the truth that liberates, is at once infinitely valuable and infinitely difficult to come by is almost completely absent. I have sometimes caught myself wondering whether aspirin would not have served as well.[95]

On the other hand, Christianity offers good news, and worshipers are not well served by a steady diet of melancholy. God has broken into our sorrows and bestowed on us such a glorious destiny that it should evoke a joyous thrill. Our worship should reflect the good news that we have been redeemed, and we should express our deepest gratitude to God. Some Christians have been restrained in openly expressing their delight in God, perhaps because they think that too much exuberance can become frivolous and subject to delusion. Some may see their task only in terms of getting people to walk the straight and narrow, and they fear that any hint of holy intoxication will lead instead to people getting out of hand. The letters of Paul, which exude such joy in the direst circumstances, make clear that Christian faith rouses the deepest joy; and Christians need to express this joy in their worship of God.

Dawn recalls an address by James Nestigen based on Psalm 51:15, "O Lord, open my lips, and my mouth will declare your praise," which showed how God's presence opens up lips to proclaim his glory. He claimed that "sometimes these days it is hard to distinguish praise from schmooze." Real

---

94. Most hymnals, unfortunately, do not include many laments, if any, to help worshipers express grief in a context of song.
95. Herbert H. Farmer, *The Servant of the Word* (New York: Charles Scribner's Sons, 1942), 54.

praise occurs when we open our hearts and cry, "Speak your Word so strongly that we can't hear anything else."[96] Jones remarks:

> Every great spiritual revival in the Christian Church has been accompanied by a corresponding outbreak and development of Christian hymnology, and this phenomenon was a conspicuous feature in the first age of the Church's history, with its vivid enthusiasm and its never-ceasing consciousness of the wonder and delight produced by the marvelous achievements of the Spirit of God.[97]

---

96. Dawn, *Reaching Out Without Dumbing Down*, 87.
97. Jones, *The Epistle of St. Paul to the Colossians*, 99.

Colossians 3:18–4:1

WIVES, SUBMIT TO your husbands, as is fitting in the Lord. [19]Husbands, love your wives and do not be harsh with them.

[20]Children, obey your parents in everything, for this pleases the Lord.

[21]Fathers, do not embitter your children, or they will become discouraged.

[22]Slaves, obey your earthly masters in everything; and do it, not only when their eye is on you and to win their favor, but with sincerity of heart and reverence for the Lord. [23]Whatever you do, work at it with all your heart, as working for the Lord, not for men, [24]since you know that you will receive an inheritance from the Lord as a reward. It is the Lord Christ you are serving. [25]Anyone who does wrong will be repaid for his wrong, and there is no favoritism.

[4:1]Masters, provide your slaves with what is right and fair, because you know that you also have a Master in heaven.

Original Meaning

HOW DOMESTIC LIFE should be ordered was not considered a trivial matter in the ancient world, and household management was a topic of discussion among philosophers.[1] Christians probably reflected on this topic because of the widespread interest in household management and because the household was so vital to the life of the church.[2] Since they affirmed that all believers had become equals in Christ, they were

---

1. Aristotle regarded the household as the basic unit of the state. "As part of good ordering, therefore, it was necessary to deal with its basic relationships" (*Politics* I.1253b.1–14). Seneca, in his "On the Values of Advice," reflects on the department of philosophy, which tells how a husband should deal with his wife, how a father should bring up his children, and how a master should rule his slaves. He concludes that we need many precepts to see what we should do in life (*Epistles* 94.1). Today, advice on such things does not come from philosophers but from popular manuals on manners and newspaper advice columns.

2. James D. G. Dunn, "The Household Rules in the New Testament," in *The Family in Theological Perspective*, ed. Stephen C. Barton (Edinburgh: T. & T. Clark, 1996), 53. See further D. Schroeder, "Lists, Ethical," *IDBS*, 546–47. In his Small Catechism, Martin Luther dubbed these instructions regarding family relations *Haustafeln*, "household rules."

forced to deal with the question of how members of the family in various stations, such as masters, slaves, and freedmen, were to relate to one another in the household. They may also have desired to reverse popular opinion that Christians fomented social turmoil.[3] The household rules show that Christians did not oppose the commonly shared moral norms of their culture concerning a well-ordered family life.

Comparing these instructions in Colossians on the responsibilities of wives and husbands, children and fathers, and slaves and masters with its parallel in Ephesians 5:22–6:9 reveals that they are considerably abbreviated. The commands to the slaves and masters in Colossians, however, receives roughly the same length of treatment as in Ephesians and is almost twice as long as the commands to husbands and wives and children and fathers. The extended treatment of the slave/master relationship probably stems from Paul's intercession for the runaway slave Onesimus. The potential backlash from that intervention prompted the more protracted attention to the slave/master relationship in his letter to all the house churches in Colosse.[4]

If, as we believe, Paul wanted Philemon to grant Onesimus his freedom so that he might continue in his service to the gospel, the emphasis on the slave's obligation to obey the master in all things deflects any criticism that Paul encourages disobedience among slaves. Becoming a Christian does not cancel the requirement for them to show respect for authority and to fulfill their duties. Those under the Christ's lordship serve others more gladly and faithfully.

The situation with Onesimus may have been the immediate backdrop that explains the inclusion of these instructions on domestic life in the moral

---

3. Dunn, "Household Codes," 54–55, writes that as a foreign religion Christianity would have been viewed by outsiders with suspicion. This suspicion that Christianity subverted good order would have been deepened by the claim that in Christ there was neither male or female, slave or free (Gal. 3:28), by allowing women to take an active part in the leadership (at least in the churches, see Rom. 16:1–2, 3, 6, 7, 12; Col. 4:13), and by encouraging slaves to regard their masters as "brothers"(Philem. 16). Dunn claims that such a situation would have rendered irresistible the desire to demonstrate responsible household management among Christians. See further, David L. Balch, *Let Wives Be Submissive: The Domestic Code in 1 Peter*, SBLMS 26 (Chico, Calif.: Scholars Press, 1981).

4. John Knox, "Philemon and the Authenticity of Colossians," *JR* 18 (1938): 154–59, isolates parallels with the letter to Philemon that commend this judgment. Particularly significant is the phrase, "anyone who does wrong" (*adikeo*), in 3:25, which appears in Philem. 18, "if he has done you any wrong" (*adikeo*). Houlden, *Paul's Letters from Prison*, 210, argues that "the insertion of this apparently ill-fitting list of household duties is another blow in the campaign of which *Philemon* is the main attack." If this view is correct, Paul typically administers the blow "obliquely." His main point would be that *both* slaves and masters have duties, and now they have a grand opportunity to put them into practice.

---

exhortations, but they also have a function in the letter's theological argument. At first glance, they may seem out of place following, without any transition, the more rarefied atmosphere of counsels on life in the new age and the spiritual songs of the worshiping church. Yet the presence of these household rules in this context draws attention to two truths.

(1) The sequence suggests that "putting the age of the new life into practice begins at home."[5] Christ's lordship finds conclusive expression in the day-by-day, routine experiences of life. The peace of Christ (3:15) is also to rule in the home, and the command to do everything in the name of the Lord Jesus (3:17) applies to the everyday world of family life, where we are most likely to show our cloven hoof. Nothing is more difficult than living in a family where the virtues of compassion, kindness, gentleness, patience, forgiveness, and professions of love (3:12–14) are tested daily.

(2) These directives counter any spiritualistic misinterpretation of the gospel that pursues an otherworldliness (3:1–2) or some spurious interest in visions and ascetic rules (2:18, 21). It makes clear that the call to the Colossian believers to set their minds on the things above (3:1–4) does not mean that they can brush aside their family obligations below.

Wives and Husbands (3:18–19)

THE INSTRUCTION THAT the wife submit to her husband fits the norm of what was regarded as becoming conduct for a wife in Paul's culture. Plutarch argued, "If [wives] subordinate themselves to their husbands, they are commended, but if they want to have control, they cut a sorrier figure than the subjects of control."[6] Husbands congratulated themselves on having an obedient wife.

Paul does not overtly dispute this cultural assumption. The change in women's status in our age and modern sensibilities lead many today to wish that he had. The command for wives to submit, however, was not inappropriate in his context. (1) It reflects the legal state of affairs. The husband as the *paterfamilias* (the head of the household) was the only fully legal person in the family and had power over all property and almost absolute authority over every member in it. They were all obligated to obey him, and Paul does not challenge the existing legal order.

(2) The verb "submit" (*hypotasso*) does not convey some innate inferiority but is used for a modest, cooperative demeanor that puts others first. It was something expected of all Christians regardless of their rank or gender (Mark 10:41–45; 1 Cor. 16:16; Eph. 5:21, 24; Phil. 2:3–4; 1 Peter 5:5). According

---

5. Wright, *Colossians and Philemon*, 145.
6. Plutarch, *Advice to Bride and Groom* 33 [142E].

to the *Letter to Aristeas* 257, God welcomes this attitude, and "the human race deals kindly with those in subjection." The command therefore promotes a demeanor that was believed to help elicit kindness from the husband.

(3) The command addresses wives directly as "ethically responsible partners."[7]

(4) The directive is not one-sided; demands are also made of the husband.

Some nuances may also help to mitigate the command's harshness to modern ears. In contrast to the commands to children and slaves, Paul does not tell wives to "obey" their husbands.[8] In the commands to children and slaves, he uses the active imperative. The verb "submit" (*hypotassesthe*), however, is in the middle voice and can imply a voluntary submission. It makes the wife's submission her willing choice, not some universal law that ordains masculine dominance.

Paul also qualifies this submission further with the phrase, "as is fitting in the Lord." Lohse comments that what is regarded as "fitting" (*aneko*) is determined entirely by custom and tradition. Those who have ever lived in another culture for any length of time soon learn that things "fitting" in their own culture are unseemly in another. But Paul does not just say that it is culturally proper or correct but "fitting *in the Lord*." The Lord determines what is fitting or not. Some things may be culturally acceptable, but reflection on them "in the Lord" leads to the realization that they are unfit for a Christian. This qualification recasts the wife's submission to her husband by turning it into allegiance shown to Christ (cf. Eph. 5:22–24).

Husbands are presented with a much more demanding task. (1) They are told to love their wives. This command reveals that Paul is not writing to prop up the authority and rights of husbands, which everyone took for granted. Instead, he reminds husbands of their obligations "in the Lord." Most in the ancient world did not expect a marriage to be grounded in love. It was considered to be an accord, albeit an unequal one, between a man and a woman to produce legitimate heirs. Soranus contended, "Since women are married for the sake of bearing children and heirs, and not for pleasure and enjoyment, it is totally absurd to inquire about the quality or rank of the family line or about the abundance of their wealth, but not to inquire about their ability to conceive children."[9] Veyne observes that "love in marriage was a stroke of

---

7. O'Brien, *Colossians, Philemon*, 220.

8. Barth and Blanke, *Colossians*, 434–35, remark that Paul cannot have "blind obedience" in mind since he would not condone a wife married to a non-Christian husband yielding to his demand that she venerate his pagan gods.

9. Soranus, *Gynecology* 1.34.1. Exceptions to this attitude can be found, most notably in Musonius Rufus, who argued that marriage should also lead to perfect companionship, mutual love of husband and wife, since it was desire for this as well as having children that

good fortune; it was not the basis of the institution." The many epitaphs recording the husband's affection for his "very dear wife" attest that loving relationships developed, but just as many others simply say that the wife "never gave me any reason to complain."[10]

In a Christian marriage, the husband knows himself to be dearly loved by God (3:12) and is commanded to love his wife in the same way. He is not to exercise his rights over his wife but his love, which means he never thinks in terms of rights and is always willing to forego them. Caird states it well: "If a wife is asked to submit, it is to the husband's *love*, not to his tyranny."[11] Love in the New Testament context means more than having affection or romantic feelings for a wife (see the fuller explanation in Eph. 5:25–33, where Christ is the model).

The NIV translates the next command that husbands are not to "be harsh with [their wives]." If this is the correct rendering, it rules out any overbearing, tyrannical, or intimidating behavior toward the wife. But the verb *pikrainesthe* is in the passive voice and may be translated, "Do not become embittered [or resentful] toward her." Anyone can refrain from harsh treatment of others; Christians must do more, however. They must refrain from becoming flushed with rage or petulant when others treat them or respond to them in ways that irritate them. This directive addresses the eventuality that the wife might not always be properly submissive, which in turn would likely trigger bitterness in her husband.

Sirach, who regarded a "silent wife" as "a gift from the Lord" (Sir. 26:14), advises: "If she does not go as you direct, separate her from yourself" (i.e., divorce her; 25:26). Paul's advice is quite different. Any defiance or insolence on the wife's part does not cancel the husband's absolute obligation to love her.[12] Sulking, fuming, grumbling, or worse, lashing out in verbal or physical violence, regardless of the provocation, real or imagined, is strictly forbidden.[13] Paul recognizes that if bitterness is allowed to taint the relationship between husband and wife, the whole household will suffer.

---

both entered upon marriage. Each was to strive to outdo the other in devotion. They were not to look each to his own interests and neglect the other, looking outside the marriage (Cora E. Lutz, *Musonius Rufus: "The Romans Socrates"* [New Haven: Yale Univ. Press, 1947], 88–89). Clearly, the companionate ideal for marriage is not a modern invention.

10. Paul Veyne, "The Roman Empire," in *A History of Private Life I. From Pagan Rome to Byzantium*, ed. Paul Veyne (Cambridge, Mass./London: Harvard Univ. Press, 1987), 40–41.

11. Caird, *Paul's Letters from Prison*, 208.

12. Dunn, *The Epistles to the Colossians and to Philemon*, 249.

13. Sirach 25:16–26:4 lists all the things about a wife that makes her husband miserable or happy, and they still apply today. How husbands might make their wives unhappy, however, was not one of Sirach's concerns.

Children and Parents (3:20–21)

CHILDREN WERE LEGALLY regarded as their fathers' property, and their status, theoretically, was little better than that of slaves.[14] A slave in one of Dio Chrysostom's works responds to the taunts of a freedman: "Perhaps you do not know that in many states which have exceedingly good laws fathers ... may even imprison or sell them [their sons]; and they have a power even more terrible than any of these; for they actually are allowed to put their sons to death without any trial or even without bringing any accusations at all against them."[15] Epictetus observes that the duty of a son is "to treat everything that is his own as belonging to his father, to be obedient to him in all things, never to speak ill of him to anyone else, nor to say or do anything that will harm him, to give way to him in everything and yield him precedence, helping him as far as is within his power."[16] The command for children to obey their parents, therefore, fits a universal expectation.

It was unusual, however, to address children directly, as if they were independent, responsible subjects. Children are told here to "obey your parents in everything," a variation of the command to honor one's mother and father (Ex. 20:12). This command assumes that parents will not demand anything unseemly from their children (cf. Mark 6:24–25). The command also takes for granted that the parents have the best interest of their children at heart. When their children ask for a fish, they will not give them stones (Matt. 7:7–9; Luke 11:11–13).

But the children's duty to obey their parents is transformed into obedience "in the Lord."[17] Paul emphasizes a child's pleasing the Lord, not just the parents. He or she owes obedience above all to the Lord. The child's independent relationship with the Lord surpasses the relationship with parents, and Christ's obedience to his Father in all things serves as the model.

Fathers are addressed in the next command, not mothers or the inclusive "parents," because the father had absolute control over the lives of his children even after they were grown and married. Dionysius of Halicarnassus remarked:

> The law-giver of the Romans gave virtually full power to the father over his son, whether he thought proper to imprison him, to scourge him, to put him in chains, and keep him at work in the fields, or to put

---

14. The father decided whether a newborn child would be raised or exposed to die, granted permission for his children to marry, decided whom they could marry, and could even force a divorce.

15. Dio Chrysostom, *Dialogues* 15.20.

16. Epictetus, *Discourses* 2.10.7.

17. The Greek text reads literally, "for this is pleasing in the Lord."

him to death; and this even though the son were engaged in public affairs, though he were numbered among the highest magistrates, and though he were celebrated for his zeal for the commonwealth.[18]

This power only ended when the father emancipated his son or he died.[19]

The attitudes toward disciplining children in the ancient world varied, just as they do today. For some, ruling with an iron hand was the norm. Quintilian, however, contended that "physical punishment inflicts shame" and "breaks the heart."[20] Others complained—as they have throughout the ages—about permissiveness which allows the younger generation too much latitude.[21]

Paul identified himself as the father of the Corinthians and had to deal with their arrogant disobedience (1 Cor. 4:14–21). He drew a contrast between the slave guardian (*paidagogos*) and the father, telling them that they had "ten thousand guardians in Christ" but just one father. The *paidagogos* was a trustworthy slave charged with supervising the life and morals of upper-class boys. He led the child to the schoolhouse and back home and protected him from trouble. He became a comic type caricatured for his severity as a stern taskmaster. In pictures on Greek vases he is frequently recognizable by the rod in his hand, and in Greek plays he is often portrayed as harsh and stupid. Paul picks up on this image by contrasting the proverbial pitiless discipline of the guardian with the milder discipline of the father. "What do you prefer? Shall I come to you with a whip [lit., rod], or in love and with a gentle spirit?" (1 Cor. 4:21). As a father, Paul expected obedience, but he believed that a father's discipline should be tempered by love, compassion, kindness, and patience (see Col. 3:12).

Paul therefore comes closer to Quintilian's view on discipline and cautions fathers against alienating their children by being too austere. The causes that provoke a child's resentment are countless but usually involve nagging, belittling, and overly harsh punishment. Pliny wrote to a friend cautioning him about his severe rebuke of his son:

> I was reminded by this example of excessive severity to write to you, as one friend to another, lest you on some occasion treat your son too harshly and strictly. Remember that he is a boy, and that you were once a boy, and perform your duty as a father always remembering that you are a human being and the father of a human being.[22]

---

18. Dionysius of Halicarnassus, *Roman Antiquities* 2.26.4.
19. Gaius, *Institutes* 1.55.
20. Quintilian, *Institutes* 1.2.7.
21. See, for example, Tacitus, *A Dialogue on Oratory* 29.1–3.
22. Pliny, *Letters* 9.12.

Paul has a greater concern that overly stern and heavy-handed parents might drive their children away from the faith.

Slaves and Masters (3:22–4:1)

THE COMMAND THAT slaves must obey their masters in everything is jarring to those who now consider the institution of slavery to be abhorrent. In the first century, however, it was an entrenched reality that the early Christians could neither change nor ignore. Paul does not sanctify slavery with these commands but subtly undermines its very premises while encouraging obedience as an expression of loyalty to the family group.[23]

(1) Paul addresses slaves as responsible human beings when most regarded slaves as little more than animated machines (see commentary on Philemon). One does not impose moral obligations on animals or farm implements. By assigning them moral duties, Paul treats them as morally responsible individuals. One of the things that slaves lacked was what Vincent calls "the first element of manhood—self respect."[24] By issuing them commands, he gives them a measure of respect: I am commanded; therefore, I am.

(2) Most took for granted that slaves were morally incapable of deciding to do good. They assumed slaves were helplessly controlled by their passions and steeped in villainy. Consequently, they needed to be handled as if they were witless children. But Paul treats Christian slaves as morally independent individuals fully capable of Christian virtue. God will not overlook their wrongdoing just because they are slaves who are supposedly not responsible for themselves.[25] They *are* responsible for themselves. Being in the miserable condition of slavery and even being a victim of injustice does not excuse returning evil for evil, or even halfheartedness for evil.

(3) Crouch points out the contrasts with contemporary parallels that only advised masters on how best to handle slaves.[26] Since Paul begins with commands to slaves and then addresses masters, he has no interest in how to help masters run their slaves more efficiently. He is concerned to enhance the mutual solidarity between slaves and masters.

The expectation that slaves would obey their masters conformed to the societal norms. "In everything," however, complicates matters. A slave might not have a Christian master, and slaves were frequently helpless victims of what

---

23. See also the discussion of slavery in the Bridging Contexts section of the commentary on Philemon in this volume.

24. Vincent, *A Critical and Exegetical Commentary on the Epistles to the Philippians and to Philemon*, 163.

25. Scott, *The Epistles of Paul to the Colossians, to Philemon and to the Ephesians*, 81.

26. Crouch, *The Origin and Intention of the Colossian Haustafel*, 116–17.

today we call sexual harassment and abuse.[27] Paul's command assumes that the master's demands were reasonable and appropriate; but the question does arise, How does one serve two masters, one on earth, the other the Lord of heaven and earth? The following commands deal with behaviors that might arouse a master's ire, but they also keep in full view the greater obligation to the Lord.

(1) Slaves are warned against "eye service" (lit. trans.; cf. Eph. 6:6). This phrase may refer to performing tasks only superficially and doing only what can be seen—"going through the motions" of service. It may also refer to doing something only to catch the master's eye, that is, to please those in authority. Or it may refer to working only when one is being watched ("not only when their eye is on you," NIV). Such performance deserves the fitness report: "Works well when under constant supervision."

(2) Slaves are not to beguile their masters ("to win their favor, " lit., be "man-pleasing"). This command proscribes working with ulterior motives and keeps slaves from becoming hypocrites, fawning before their masters. Christians, no matter what their station in life, are always to give sincere, wholehearted service.

(3) Positively, slaves are to serve with "reverence for the Lord" (lit., "fearing the Lord"; see 2 Cor. 5:11; 7:1; 1 Peter 2:18). Paul transforms the motive of their service. If Christians are to do everything in the name of the Lord (3:17), then Christian slaves must work for their earthly master as for the Lord. The master is not a substitute for the Lord, but slaves are encouraged to work "as if" for the Lord. Their deference to their earthly masters is therefore elevated to obedience to Christ, whom they must obey and serve with all their hearts (see Deut. 6:5). The slave's most humble task then becomes a high calling and brings benefit to God.[28]

The three commands to slaves are coupled with a promise of reward and with a warning. Slaves were more accustomed to hear the phrase "you will receive" in connection with some kind of punishment; Paul uses it with the promise of a reward, an inheritance.[29] Slaves who had no legal standing and

---

27. Salvian reflects the problem: "We can imagine how heinous this filthy uncleanness was when women were not permitted by their shameless owners to be chaste, even if they had wanted to" (*The Governance of God* 7.4.17–20, cited by Thomas E. J. Wiedemann, *Greek and Roman Slavery* [Baltimore: Johns Hopkins Univ. Press, 1981], 179).

28. The backdrop of this statement is Seneca's debate over whether a slave can bestow a benefit.

29. In Roman society, many domestic slaves were set free in their master's wills. Wiedemann, *Greek and Roman Slavery*, 101, includes a will, dated in A.D. 156, in which a master sets free some of his "slave bodies" "because of the goodwill and love they have shown towards me." Paul does not encourage them to be good slaves on the chance that they will earn the master's favor and their eventual manumission. The motivation behind their obedience is on a higher level.

could not inherit according to this world's laws are promised an inheritance from the Lord of the universe—the same hope that all Christians have (1:12).

Paul's next comment to slaves is interpreted by the NIV as a statement, "It is the Lord Christ you are serving," which basically repeats what has been said in 3:23. The verb can also be an imperative and the sentence punctuated as a command: "Serve the Lord Christ!"[30] This alternative best explains the "for" (*gar*) that follows (omitted in NIV) and makes it parallel to the imperative "work" in 3:23. It reminds slaves who the true Master is, Christ, and leads into the warning in 3:25: "Anyone who does wrong will be repaid for his wrong"— a kind of measure for measure.[31] The "anyone" may refer only to slaves or to both masters and slaves. Since masters are specifically addressed in 4:1, it is more likely that it refers to slaves. Just because society might consider slaves to be morally incompetent or slaves might consider themselves to be victims of oppression, it does not absolve them from any wrongdoing.

Comparing these instructions to the slaves in Colossians with the parallel in Ephesians 6:5–9 points up several differences. (1) In Colossians it is clearer that slaves are to fear the Lord, not their masters. (2) The reward they receive is the "inheritance from the Lord." (3) The slave, not the master, is reminded that there is no favoritism with God. In Ephesians, by contrast, the matter of receiving a measure for a measure is phrased positively: "The Lord will reward everyone for whatever good he does, whether he is slave or free" (Eph. 6:8).

This phrasing may seem to make more sense to us. Why do slaves need to be warned that God shows no partiality? Knox argues that "slaves are not accustomed to expect favor or partiality. Surely it would appear more fitting to say to them, 'The one who does good will receive his reward, and there will be no discrimination against you because you are slaves.'"[32] Consequently, this statement might seem more appropriate as a warning to those in the superior status, the masters. Slaves, by contrast, need encouragement.

---

30. It also matches the command in Rom. 12:11, "Serve the Lord!"

31. Literally, "he will get back that which he did wrong." The same verb (*adikeo*) appears in Philem. 18: "If he has done you any wrong [*adikeo*] or owes you anything, charge it to me." Alan Watson, *Roman Slave Law* (Baltimore: Johns Hopkins Univ. Press, 1987), 1, writes:

> Slavery is the most extreme form imaginable of exploitation of one human by another, but the exploitation need not always proceed in one direction alone. As a class and as individuals slaves are always exploited, but the individual slave is frequently in a good position to provide the master with a poor return on his investment, to cheat him, rob him, damage his property, or make him liable to others for property damage, to make disastrous contracts for him, to give damaging reports of him, to exploit him sexually, and even to assault or kill him. Moreover, the slave, exploited himself, has the clearest reason to exploit the master.

32. Knox, *Philemon Among the Letters of Paul*, 37.

The differences, however, are best explained by the recent business involving Onesimus. The pronouncement makes clear that becoming a Christian does not nullify past wrongs against others; the wrongs must be paid back. In Onesimus's case, Paul assumes the obligations owed to his master: "If he has done you any wrong or owes you anything, charge it to me" (Philem. 18). With these instructions, Paul may want to forestall any unrest among other slaves who might misinterpret the leniency shown to Onesimus. If Philemon yields to Paul's request, it may appear that running away brings a reward. With the warning of verse 25, Paul dissuades any slave from trying to take advantage of a Christian master's forbearance and willingness to forgive.[33]

The commands to masters is startling in the context of ancient slavery laws. Paul demands that slaves be treated "with what is right and fair" (4:1). Other humanitarians urged slave owners to be good masters and moderate in their punishment. Most pundits advised slave owners on how to get the most out of their slaves. Xenophon records a purported conversation of Socrates concerning how a master handles a slave "who brings no master any profit" and reflects the normal way slaves were treated.

> Is it not the case that they control any inclinations toward lechery by starving them? And stop them from stealing by locking up the places from which they might take things? Prevent them from running away by putting them in chains? Force the laziness out of them with beatings?

Aristippos, his dialogue partner, agrees that as a master he inflicts every kind of punishment on his useless slaves to get them to serve properly.[34]

The hard work and devotion of the Christian slave should avert such punishment. But Paul specifically puts limits on the master's dominance over his slaves. Aristotle had said that it was irrelevant to talk about justice in the master/slave relationship because there can be no injustice relating to things that are one's own.[35] Everyone took for granted that justice has nothing to do with how one treats one's belongings. Paul makes bold to dissent and defends the rights of slaves, who had no legal rights: They should be accorded justice and fairness. That is, masters are not free to set their own standards on how to treat their slaves; rather, it must match what any would regard as "right and fair." The word translated "fair" (*isotes*) is related to equality (see 2 Cor. 8:13) and suggests "even-handed, impartial treatment."[36]

---

33. Beare, "The Epistle to the Colossians," 228–29.
34. Xenophon, *Memorabilia* 2.1.15–16.
35. Aristotle, *Nicomachean Ethics* 5.1134b.
36. Lightfoot, *Saint Paul's Epistles to the Colossians and to Philemon*, 230.

The theological dimension, "because you know that you also have a Master in heaven," explains the Christian peculiarity. The cosmic perspective fills the whole letter, and masters in particular should remember that no one is exempt from accountability to the Master in heaven, regardless of one's station in life. This implied threat punctures any presumption of superiority in the master/slave relationship (see 3:11). If masters are mindful that God has not dealt with them from a strict code of rightness and fairness but by grace, they will be more forgiving and gracious toward those under their charge (see 3:13!). The commands to masters and slaves attempt to minimize the most egregious evils of the system.

CAIRD IDENTIFIES A key problem in bridging this material to our contemporary context:

The modern readers may feel a sense of disappointment that Paul's lofty ethical principles should prove to be reducible to such humdrum instructions, and may find it hard to square this passage with the sweeping declaration that in Christ, "there is neither slave nor free, there is neither male nor female" (Gal 3:28).

We may feel particularly squeamish today about the demands placed on the so-called "weaker" parties in the pairs, the wives and the slaves. The rules strike many as not only antiquated but anti-Christian. Telling slaves to obey their masters upholds the interests of slave owners and seems to give an odious, oppressive institution divine sanction. Modern developments in women's legal rights and in the relations between husbands and wives also make the call for the wife to submit to her husband sound outdated, if not outlandish.

Times have changed. Sir William Blackstone's legal observation on marriage that "husband and wife are one person in the law; that is, the very being or legal existence of the woman is suspended during the marriage," is no longer presumed to be the case today.[37] Many, already suspicious that Paul was a male chauvinist or perhaps even a misogynist, regard his advice on family with a jaundiced eye or even embarrassment. Those who take these commands seriously may be disdained for wanting to take us back to the days when wives were expected to be dutiful drones, bowing their necks to the yoke of their husband's authority.

Paul's culture and ours. Our culture is quite different from Paul's. Today, slavery is outlawed; and most modern wives do not take for granted that

---

37. William Blackstone, *Commentaries on the Laws of England* (New York: W. E. Dean, 1849), 2:355.

they owe their husbands absolute, unquestioning obedience, as they did in the first century. Wives assume that they enter marriage as their husbands' equals. A pastor testifies that when he plans the marriage ceremony with couples, many brides insist, "I don't want anything in the vows about obeying my husband."[38] Paul does not tell wives to obey their husbands, but he usually gets blamed for it. His call for submission also receives a chorus of boos in a culture that glorifies individual rights.

The question for us is: Does Paul have anything relevant to say about family life for people living two millennia later with different social norms? How does it apply to the dual-career marriage, which has become the norm for most American families? Is Paul too out of date? Is his advice too culturally bound to the patriarchal ways of the first century to be useful today? Or does he convey God's intentions for how humans should live together in families, which will always have relevance?

Lohse represents those commentators on Colossians who believe that the instructions in this section can be safely ignored:

> They do not offer timelessly valid laws, nor do they endow a particular order with ageless dignity. As times change so does the general estimation of what is fitting and proper. Christian exhortation, however, must constantly impress on new generations the admonition to be obedient to the Kyrios. How this obedience is to be expressed concretely at any given time, will always have to be tested and determined anew.[39]

According to this view, these time-bound rules cannot be relocated to our dissimilar situation. Elizabeth Schüssler Fiorenza goes even further, arguing that we can only preach on the household codes "critically in order to unmask them as texts promoting patriarchal violence."[40]

Melick, on the other hand, represents those who find no problem with Paul's words in these verses. He asks, "By what standard is the culture to be measured?" and concludes, "The end result is an authority [the Bible] which is no authority since at any place where the culture differs with express biblical commands the Bible will be perceived as secondary to culture."[41] He asks an important question: Is "cultural acceptability" an acceptable hermeneutical key?

Before we resolve these questions, we must first cross over to Paul's side of the bridge to understand the cultural context in which he gave these rules.

---

38. Brian J. Dodd, *The Problem with Paul* (Downers Grove, Ill.: InterVarsity, 1996), 59.
39. Lohse, *Colossians and Philemon*, 157.
40. Elizabeth Schüssler Fiorenza, *Bread Not Stone: The Challenge of Feminist Biblical Interpretation* (Boston: Beacon, 1984), 145.
41. Richard R. Melick Jr., *Philippians, Colossians, Philemon* (Nashville, Broadman, 1991), 309.

Culture in many ways is like water. We usually do not notice that the water we drink every day has any taste. Only when we travel somewhere else does it strike us that the water there tastes "funny." When we get a taste of these commands on family living from a foreign culture two thousand years distant, our initial reaction may be that they taste funny or bad. We cannot fault Paul, however, for living in a different culture from ours, and we should appreciate how apt these instructions were in his context.

(1) Women did not usually receive any kind of formal education in Paul's day except in the domestic arts. Consequently, they were forced to rely on their husbands for a wide range of things.[42] In a culture where spouses are equally educated and have equal legal standing, however, things may be quite different.

(2) Patriarchal hierarchy was firmly entrenched. Ulpian's *Digest* defined the family as follows: "In the strict legal sense we call a *familia* a number of people who are by birth or by law subjected to the *potestas* [power] of one man" (50, 16.195).[43] It was the father's legal duty to guard the welfare of those under his authority—his wife, children, and slaves—and it was their duty, in turn, to show him total obedience and deference.

Shelton points out that the Latin word most often used to express this family relationship is *pietas*, which referred to duty combined with affection: "A Roman was expected to be devoted and dutiful to his family, friends, fellow citizens, country, and gods."[44] In a more self-centered culture such as ours, the focus is more on my individual rights and what the rest of the family owes me. In Paul's world, the question was framed differently: What is my duty to the family? The family was the main basis of economic production, and Paul gives a list of mutual obligations that each member had to shoulder to maintain its smooth functioning.

(3) In contrast to what we today call "the nuclear family," the household in the ancient world consisted of the father, mother, and children, plus any foster children, slaves, unmarried relations, freedmen, or renters. Sometimes brothers with their families lived together under the same roof. We need to keep in mind "that Romans regarded with admiration the large household run on frugal lines by an inflexible *paterfamilias*."[45] Such a large group needed

---

42. Musonius Rufus protested that women should also study philosophy and that daughters should receive the same education as sons (Lutz, *Musonius Rufus*, 38—49).

43. Quoted from J. F. Gardner, and T. Wiedemann, *The Roman Household: A Sourcebook* (London: Routledge, 1993), 3—4.

44. Jo-Ann Shelton, *As the Romans Did: A Sourcebook of Roman Social History* (Oxford: Oxford Univ. Press, 1988), 4.

45. Suzanne Dixon, *The Roman Family* (Baltimore/London: Johns Hopkins Univ. Press, 1992), 31.

some kind of ordering lest it slip into anarchic chaos, and the universally accepted pattern was that all came under the authority of the father of the family (*paterfamilias*).

Paul had no intention of turning that world upside down.[46] Instead, he focused on how to live within one's cultural framework in obedience to Christ. If we read Scripture sympathetically, using a hermeneutic of trust as opposed to suspicion, we can see how Christ's lordship subtly deconstructs the old habits of domination and exploitation. These instructions do not simply parrot the social conventions of the culture, they work creatively on them. The cultural norms are filtered through a Christian sieve, which both critiques and transforms them. On the other hand, if one reads Scripture with overt hostility or with a particular agenda, one is likely to reject or scoff at Paul's counsel.

An apologetic aim? While we are on Paul's side of the bridge, we should also remind ourselves how strange and threatening this new Christian faith would have seemed to his contemporaries. The Roman historian Tacitus maligned the Jews as a seditious source of trouble: "Those who converted to their ways follow the same practice, and the earliest lesson they receive is to despise the gods, to disown their country, and to regard their parents, children and brothers of little account."[47] The same charges were leveled against Christians. Tacitus accused them of a "hatred of the human race," a charge based on the assumption that Christians forsook their familial and social obligations.[48]

Loyalty to Christ did create domestic problems for some married to unbelievers (see 1 Cor. 7:12–16). Christian wives, children (who continued under the authority of the father after they reached adulthood), and slaves would not consent to do certain things that went against their faith. Their religious scruples and their antagonists' malicious gossip combined to give Christianity a sinister reputation for inflaming family tensions and wrecking homes.[49]

---

46. Christians did not set as their primary agenda the transformation of society. Baggott, *A New Approach to Colossians*, 111, argues, "Modern revolutions (even in Russia) may turn things upside-down, and, to a limited extent, avenge the wrongs of an outrageously suppressed and offended proletariat; but it can never of itself create the new world of absolute and equal justice, or even provide adequate compensation for all the cruelty and bloodshed which are involved." Only God can bring the transformation of society and true justice. Until that happens, Paul asserts, the whole creation is subject to frustration and awaits the final revelation of children of God, when it will finally "be liberated from its bondage to decay and brought into the glorious freedom of the children of God" (Rom. 8:18–21). In the meantime, Christians must seek to demonstrate good order in their family lives.

47. Tacitus, *Histories* 5.5.

48. Tacitus, *Annals* 15.44.

49. Dunn, "Household Codes," 54–55, comments that in the first century Christians lived in a context that regarded foreign religions with suspicion. Having wives and slaves embrace this new religion would only add to that suspicion. Christianity seemed a threat to good

---

Today, we worry about the meltdown of the nuclear family as a sure sign of the decay of our civilization. It was no different in the first century, and people did not look with favor on anything they perceived as ripping the fabric of the family, which held society together. Insofar as the Christian movement was thought to disrupt the family, which Aristotle maintained was the basic unit and pattern for the whole political order, it boded ill for them and their message.[50]

Family life was also far more public in Bible times, particularly in the close quarters of the tenement building. Since everyone shared the same set of measures, everyone knew who were the "good" wives and the "good" husbands and who were the "bad" wives and "bad" husbands. A well-ordered household where love ruled was both a significant concern and a compelling witness.

Some have argued that Paul's instructions on family life had an apologetic aim. If others did not perceive Christianity to be disruptive of society's basic building block, they might be more willing to listen to the gospel.[51] We find such an approach in Titus. Slaves are told "to be subject to their masters in everything, to try to please them, not to talk back to them, and not to steal from them, but to show that they can be fully trusted, *so that in every way they will make the teaching about God our Savior attractive*" (Titus 2:9–10, italics added; see also 1 Peter 3:1–2). Irreproachable conduct became a missionary tool as Christians sought to persuade others by their behavior. Christians might worship exclusively a different Lord, but they did not incite insubordination, disloyalty, or disorder; and they did not upset family stability.

While an apologetic purpose may have been in the back of Paul's mind, it certainly was not the key factor in these instructions.[52] If there was any apologetic purpose, it was more likely directed against the asceticism and airy mysticism of the opponents (2:16–23). It will not do, therefore, to treat, and perhaps dismiss, these instructions as simply an apologetic attempt to show that Christianity was not a slippery slope that would cause the family to

---

order with its manifesto that there is no difference in Christ between slave and free, male and female (Gal. 3:28), with women becoming leaders in the churches (Rom. 16:1–2, 3, 6, 7, 12; Col. 4:15), and with slaves permitted to regard their masters as "brothers" (Philem. 16). He concludes that such pressures would make irresistible the desire to "demonstrate responsible household management." See further, David L. Balch, *Let Wives Be Submissive*.

50. Wayne A. Meeks, *The Moral World of the First Christians* (Philadelphia: Westminster, 1986), 113.

51. Dunn, "Household Codes," 58, contends that the concern for well-ordered households was "an integral part of being the church and of effective witness to the wider community." Note how moderns cringe over modern cults that practice unorthodox family patterns, such as open marriages.

52. See Balch, *Let Wives Be Submissive*, 81–116.

slide into chaos. Paul was not giving the Colossians tips on how to curb criticism but telling them what was fitting in Christ. Most important was his conviction that a harmonious, well-regulated household promised a harmonious, well-regulated church. As Lampe has pointed out: "The early church did not exist as an independent body *beside* the private households; it exclusively existed *in* them."[53] The church, founded on egalitarian ideals, needed some rules to guide relationships.[54]

In bridging contexts, we should be sensitive to contemporary impressions of how Christian faith affects family life. Opponents continue to vilify Christianity. Instead of accusing it today of sapping the foundations of family order with its egalitarianism, however, they accuse it of perpetuating the subjugation and ill-treatment of women. We should be careful not to interpret these texts so that it sounds like we are leading a march back to the gender caste system of the first century. We should also be careful not to dismiss or ignore the wisdom they contain that applies to relationships in any social pattern. These texts do not prescribe a hierarchy or endorse patriarchy or slavery, but they do prescribe attitudes that must govern a Christian's relationships in the family.

How these instructions apply to us. These commands counter attitudes that create strife and alienation in relationships: the insubordination of wives and the bitterness of husbands, which lead to brutal mistreatment; the disobedience of children and the harsh discipline of parents; the malingering, hypocritical ways of slaves and the cruel injustice of masters. The principles underlying these instructions—submission, love, service, obedience, conscientious work, and fairness—transcend cultural limits and are applicable in any age.

(1) The instructions show a special concern for the weaker or powerless members of the pair: wives, children, and slaves. The rules cited do not simply reinforce the prerogatives of husbands, parents, and masters, for the stronger parties are given duties in addition to rights. In turn, those who are expected to submit or obey are given rights as well as duties. The commands therefore recognize that reciprocity exists, so that the entitlements are not

---

53. Peter Lampe, "'Family' in Church and Society of New Testament Times," *Affirmation* 5 (1992): 13.

54. The difficulty of how slaves and masters could relate in the household church setting may be compared to the relations between military officers and enlisted personnel in churches today. Christians are supposed to be able to admonish fellow Christians when they are overtaken in a sin (Gal. 6:1). How could a slave admonish a master (see 1 Tim. 6:2; Titus 2:9)? Similarly, how can an enlisted person admonish a superior officer? How can a master or an officer follow the instructions "through love become slaves to one another" (Gal. 5:14, NRSV) without breaking down completely the master/slave, officer/enlisted relationship?

all on one side and the obligations on the other. Schweizer observes that comparable instructions from other literature usually address only the male, adult, and free person. He comments, "The idea that women, children and slaves could also act in an ethically responsible way is scarcely considered. Indeed, the master is recommended to treat his slave well because it is in his own interests."[55]

The gospel in which there is no Greek or Jew, slave or free, male or female recognizes each individual as a full person and is concerned to protect each person's rights, not to enforce his or her subordination. Wives are to be treated with love, children with understanding, and slaves as human beings deserving of justice in a time when slaves were not legally regarded as human. These commands also address wives, children, and slaves as responsible, moral beings, full members of the body of Christ. The commands acknowledge the authority of the husband, parent, and master; but those with power must exercise it with love, sensitivity, and justice, and must be willing to take the role of servant, just as Christ did.

(2) The motivation for the behavior becomes distinctively Christian. The text does not ground its advice in the created order, natural law, or reason, as if to say: "This is the way the world is; accept it and live in harmony with it." Nor does it say that the husband is the natural ruler and the wife the natural subject.[56] Paul bases his appeal not on the laws of nature but on "the law of the *new* nature: Christ releases you to be truly human, and you must now learn to express yourself according to the divine pattern, not in self-assertion but in self-giving."[57] These commands do not tell us how to order families but focus on the Christian motivation behind our family relationships—how we relate to others. Every member of a family, no matter the station, must allow Christ's lordship to control his or her interpersonal relationships.

Paul has no intention of defying all the norms of first-century society in which Christians lived. He adapts the accepted pattern of households in the Mediterranean world of antiquity but transforms it by appealing to the Christian's loyalty to Christ as Lord. The "Lord" (Gk. *kyrios*) appears seven times in this section: It is fitting *in the Lord*. Do what is pleasing *in the Lord*. Fear

---

55. Schweizer, *Colossians*, 213–14.

56. An example of this kind of thinking can be found in Josephus: "The woman it [the Law] says, is in all things inferior to the man. Let her accordingly be obedient, not for her humiliation, but that she may be directed; for the authority has been given by God to the man" (*Against Apion* 2.24 §201). In 1616, William Whateley argued similarly: "Thy husband is by God made thy governor and ruler" (*A Bride Bush*, 192; cited by Anthony Fletcher, "The Family, Marriage and the Upbringing of Children in Protestant England," in *The Family in Theological Perspective*, ed. Stephen C. Barton [Edinburgh: T. & T. Clark, 1996], 110).

57. Wright, *Colossians*, 147.

the Lord. Work as you were working *for the Lord*, not just human masters. *The Lord* shows no partiality and will render judgment and reward. Serve the *Lord*. Know that you have a *Lord* in heaven. The motivation behind each of Paul's commands is charged with the phrase "in the Lord." Christ's lordship imposes itself on all aspects of our lives. Stern comments that the Lord becomes a third partner: "Like a magnet over iron fillings he orients things in the right direction."[58]

Thus, what is fitting in the Lord is the hermeneutical key for bridging these instructions to our modern context. This phrase is not a pious platitude attached to the prevailing cultural pattern to bless the status quo. Putting our family relationships under the microscope of what is fitting in the Lord always challenges and renews them. Our model is how Christ submitted himself to God.[59]

Some reject such a positive, sympathetic reading of the text. Horrell, for example, argues that this section contains an implicit domination and exploitation ideology. It intends "to convince the dominated, the subordinate, that it is right and proper, or inevitable, or in everyone's best interests for them to remain willingly and voluntarily in their place and to fulfill their duties." He maintains that " 'everyone's best interests' may actually mean 'in the ruling class's interests.' "[60] The ideology legitimates hierarchy, domination, and exploitation.

If one chooses to read the New Testament in this way, one is likely to reject the domestic codes entirely. But since our world, including families, needs some kind of ordering unless it breaks down into a free-for-all, what order will be substituted? The record of the modern family with its sky-rocketing divorce statistics and the betrayal of vows, or the increasing avoidance of any vows at all, does not offer an attractive solution. Gilley cites the beginning of Tolstoy's novel *Anna Karenina*, which deals with adultery: "All happy families are more or less like one another; every unhappy family is unhappy in its own particular way." He interprets it to mean that we can go wrong in all sorts of ways, "but there is only one way of going right."[61] Christians can only go right in their families when they are subject to Christ, when the family becomes a place where faith is lived and nurtured, and when each member submits to the lordship of Christ.

---

58. David H. Stern, *Jewish New Testament Commentary* (Clarksville, Md.: Jewish New Testament Publications, 1992), 591.

59. Wall, *Colossians and Philemon*, 156.

60. David G. Horrell, "Theological Ideology in Paul," in *Modelling Early Christianity: Social-Scientific Studies of the New Testament in Its Context* (London/New York: Routledge, 1995), 232–33.

61. Sheridan Gilley, "Chesterton, Catholicism and the Family," in *The Family in Theological Perspective*, ed. Stephen C. Barton (Edinburgh: T. & T. Clark, 1996), 147.

Human beings require institutions as well as some kind of order for the distribution of power among persons. The Christian doctrine of human fallenness reminds us that our sinfulness will corrupt any order and create disorder. C. S. Lewis writes: "Since the Fall no organization or way of life whatever has a natural tendency to go right."[62] Following these instructions in Colossians to the tee will not automatically make one holy or happy. The danger always lurks that they will be misused by the selfish who say: "Serving me is to serve Christ." The next principle rules out this perversion.

(3) Domination of others is prohibited. We cannot eliminate the exercise of power from human relationships, nor can we eliminate the need for guidelines in relationships. The basic premise is that every Christian member of a family is equal as a recipient of God's grace, which makes each a part of God's family. But some have different roles and different power. Someone needs to take a leadership role as a necessary dike against complete turmoil. Others need to yield their freedom of choice to others. The power is given to them by the yielding parties, not taken from them. The freewheeling family where each does his or her own thing, refusing to give or assume power when necessary, will eventually fly apart.

The New Testament has definite views on how power is to be used. Each set of instructions addresses the use of power by the dominant partner and forbids any injustice, exploitation, or mistreatment. The controlling ethic of the gospel is that the greatest should become the servant of all, the one with the towel and basin who stoops to wash the feet of the others (Mark 10:42–45; John 13:1–17; 1 Cor. 9:19; Phil. 2:3–11). Paul served as a model of this service. In his dealing with the various house churches he founded across the empire, the apostle assumed the role of *paterfamilias* (1 Cor. 4:15; 1 Thess. 2:11), but he did not lord over them (2 Cor. 1:24). He also pictured his relationship to them as a mother (1 Cor. 3:2; Gal. 4:19), a wet nurse (1 Thess. 2:7), and a slave (2 Cor. 4:5).

Paul's instructions do not appoint the husband as the overlord of his wife. Parents are not to domineer and crush their children's spirits. Masters are not advised on how best to handle slaves to squeeze the most work out of them. The key is love, justice, and fairness. Ancient patriarchy had nothing to do with love or justice.

Anyone who reads the New Testament will quickly discover all that love entails. What it means to love your wives is explained more fully in Ephesians 5:25–33: Husbands are to imitate Christ's sacrificial love. This kind of love does not love others because of the pleasure or utility they bring to us.

---

62. C. S. Lewis, "The Sermon and the Lunch," in *Undeceptions: Essays on Theology and Ethics*, ed. Walter Hooper (London: Geoffrey Bles, 1971), 235.

Christ's love was so deep that it cherished us when not a single one of us was worth it. His love was not some sentimental emotion; it was so great that he was willing to pay the supreme penalty to express his love by suffering a slave's death, the unspeakable torture and humiliation of crucifixion. Love is a power that can penetrate the most impenetrable of hearts, but it is also powerless because it can do nothing except by consent. Love means caring more about the one you love than yourself. Love is never coercive and never seeks to wound, humiliate, or domineer.[63]

THE BOOK OF Proverbs assumes that the household, not the temple, is "the primary place of moral formation and social duty."[64] The home becomes even more important as the center of Christian nurture and education when surrounding society becomes so wicked that it accepts and even promotes immorality. These texts are not about who gets the power and authority to run the family but affirm that the family is the primary context for faith formation and for living out one's faith. How we live in our family says a great deal about our faith.

Paul's advice in this section is rather sparse, which makes it clear that he has no intention of providing an advice manual on family relationships. He is affirming the family as the place where we first live out our newness as "God's chosen people, holy and dearly loved" (3:12). In the previous section, he reeled off a list of virtues (3:12–15), but such virtues are empty talk unless they are lived out in the structures and relationships of everyday life.

New life begins in the home.[65] Schweizer observes that Christian wisdom and instruction are not always put to the test in times of suffering, which requires a heroic response, but in the everyday situations of life—like in the home. "The real world is, according to our letter, first of all our husband or wife, our children or parents, our employees or chiefs. Only if and when we take this world seriously may we, perhaps, be called to serve our Lord on a greater scale."[66] One can do heroic battle in the public arena but lose the war in the privacy of the home.

The family is where, under the lordship of Christ, we learn to control our anger, rage, abusive language, and lying so that peace might reign. The

---

63. See C. S. Lewis, *The Four Loves* (New York: Harcourt, Brace, Jovanovich, 1988), 44.

64. Stephen C. Barton, "Biblical Hermeneutics and the Family," in *The Family in Theological Perspective*, ed. Stephen C. Barton (Edinburgh: T. & T. Clark, 1996), 4.

65. Paul rejects the "touch-not" philosophy. Had this been recognized, the church today would not be saddled with a long history of denigrating marriage as a necessary evil for the procreation of the human race.

66. Eduard Schweizer, "Christ in the Letter to the Colossians," *RevExp* 70 (1973): 466.

family is where we first learn to work out the values of "compassion, kindness, humility, gentleness and patience" (3:12). There is no more difficult a
place to exercise these virtues day in and day out than in the home. The new
life enables submissiveness that puts others first, love that refuses to grow
bitter, obedience, supportive and encouraging parenting, devotion to doing
work well, and fairness and justice in our dealing with others.

Marriage. Most fairy tales end with the prince marrying the princess, and
the stories always conclude with the words, "And they lived happily ever after."
After the hero has rescued the heroine, the marriage of the prince to the
princess comes as an anticlimax. But that is not the Christian view of marriage.
The wedding day with the bells and rice is not the arrival point that marks the
end of the story; it is only the beginning. The wedding is the beginning of a
lifelong adventure. It is a journey through uncharted seas, which explains why
so many marriages today end with a shipwreck. We know the problems, but
many today do not think that the Bible offers any help to solve them.

Paul's counsel on the relations between husband and wife is interpreted
by some to mean that the wife must knuckle under and do homage to her husband, who ascends some marital throne. This kind of relationship was lam-
pooned on the legendary Archie Bunker television series. In one episode,
Edith thought that she would experiment with fancier cuisine and fixed her
husband a soufflé instead of his regular bacon and eggs. Needless to say,
Archie turned up his nose at something he couldn't pronounce and demanded
his bacon and eggs. Daughter Gloria watched with disbelief as her mother
dumped the soufflé in the garbage and scurried back and forth trying to
appease her husband's wrath. Gloria snarled indignantly: "Submitting to him
... that's what she is doing. Submitting to her ruler ... her lord and master."
Archie responds, "Ain't that a nice way of putting it?"

For ages the blustering, ill-mannered domination of males has been countered by the subtle manipulation of females. A Greek proverb has it that the
husband may be the head, but the wife is the neck that decides which way
the head will turn. Male jests about marriage over the centuries reveal an interesting point: Many feel it sentences them to a ball-and-chain existence,
where they are ruled and regulated by their wives. Thus we might laugh at
the student's blooper that Socrates died of an overdose of wedlock. In the
novel *The Man in the Gray Flannel Suit*, a wife takes subtle revenge on her successful businessman husband for her own feelings of worthlessness. "She had
a high art of deflating him, of enfeebling him, with one quick, innocent
sounding phrase. ... She was, in fact, a genius in planting in him an assurance of his inferiority."[67]

---

67. Sloan Wilson, *The Man in the Gray Flannel Suit* (New York: Simon and Schuster, 1955),
206.

Marriages fail when struggles for power between the couples get out of hand and one wants to dominate the other, whether by overt means or in more subtle ways. Commenting on Genesis 2:4b–3:24, Vogels writes: "What kills the relationship is the desire to possess, to keep, to hold, to dominate, or to crush the other."[68] The one who dominates with bellicose threats and the one who manipulates with domestic blackmail are motivated by self-interest, and both are wrong. They treat the marriage as if the goal was conquest of the other.

When Paul calls for submission, our "liberated" culture responds snippily: "How dare he tell anyone to submit to anyone." Submission is out of style, though sinful human beings have always been resistant to it. The anthem today is: "Express yourself. Do not repress yourself." Marriage bonds that were once thought to be irrevocable, for better or worse, in sickness and in health, have become limited, contingent, and temporary arrangements. Commitment to my personal welfare supersedes commitment to the welfare of others. The value placed on individual freedom and independence has become nonnegotiable; consequently, when a relationship becomes troublesome, it is scuttled. We do not want to yield control of our lives or our choices to others or to put ourselves at their disposal.

The problem is that when marriage partners get caught in the vortex of thinking, "My needs must be met first," neither have their needs met. The result is divorce, particularly if we have bought into the modern marketing mantra that we should continually upgrade to new and improved versions. The incalculable damage to children and our family and community is considered less important than the pain in the relationship. We have become too devoted to ideas of self-assertion and self-fulfillment to appreciate the concept of servanthood and its very different joys. We may be afraid to trust our happiness to anyone else, so we keep our unconditional commitment to ourselves.

Burtchaell recalls an adaptation of the story of Pinocchio, the self-centered, wooden puppet who was given his growing nose to cure him of his egotism and to bring him to repentance. When that failed to work, he was taken on a tour of hell in hopes of shocking him into virtue. There he saw a ballet dancer and a carpenter so caught up in their dancing and their work that nothing Pinocchio did attracted their attention. "It was at this point that Pinocchio saw, in a flash, that in hell everyone is left to himself, to do only what he wants to do and to take no notice of anyone else."[69] Paul's advice offers a way out of such a hell.

---

68. Walter Vogels, "The Power Struggle Between Man and Woman (Gen 3,16b)," *Bib* 77 (1996): 209.

69. James Tunstead Burtchaell, *Philemon's Problem: The Daily Dilemma of the Christian* (Chicago: Foundation for Adult Catechetical Teaching Aids, 1973), 70.

The instructions to wife and husband focus on how they are to live together responsibly, not on how they can get their needs fulfilled. In our context, "submission" might connote spineless acquiescence, cringing abasement, demeaning servility, and passive resignation. But Paul does not consign wives to servile bondage to their husbands or expect them to become doormats and compulsive pleasers, though this is how he has been misinterpreted for centuries.[70] Submission is not submersion, losing our own personalities in another's. Selflessness can be carried too far and can become detrimental. Submission can only be done with a healthy sense of self. Wall comments:

> For example, if a wife sees herself as subservient to her husband, she will allow him to dominate and even abuse her. If, however, she views herself as Christ's disciple and her husband's equal in Christ, the understanding of submission will be changed: she will submit herself to her husband in the same way that Christ submitted himself to God. . . . Being made equal in Christ will radically alter the way two disciples relate to each other as husband and wife. The result will be the woman's elevation within the Christian home and the end of her abuse there . . . , and this in turn will be a witness to a misogynistic world.[71]

The opposite of submission is not a craven spirit, but the belief that I and my perceived needs are more important than any others. It manifests itself in a variety of ways:

- a lack of consideration for the other
- indifference to the other's needs
- haughtiness
- self-aggrandizement, using the other to get your own way
- living only in the present and promising no future commitment

Submission, on the other hand, is:

- committing one's entire life and all its possibilities to another
- wanting the other person's good (not just wanting the other person to meet my needs)
- being concerned for the ultimate well-being of another without trying to control that person or to win praise for such sacrifice
- accepting the demands of the relationship without bitterness and not tallying the labors and sacrifices to see when I have done enough

---

70. See further, Diana S. Richmond Garland and David E. Garland, *Beyond Companionship: Christians in Marriage* (Philadelphia: Westminster, 1986).
71. Wall, *Colossians and Philemon*, 155–56.

- accepting responsibility for another, accepting his or her problems as our problems
- listening to the other

Examples of such holy submission abound. When C. S. Lewis's wife was dying from cancer, he was convinced that he had the power through Christian love to transfer to his own body his wife's pain and made every effort to do so.[72] The submission of the Samaritan to the needs of the mugged stranger lying helplessly beside the road best captures what submission means. The robbers acted on the principle that "what is thine is mine and I am going to take it." The priest who passed by acted on the principle that "what is mine is mine and I am going to keep it." The Samaritan acted on the principle that "what is mine is thine, and I am going to use it to restore your life."

We live in a culture of violence, which has for too long silently tolerated abuses against women in the home, in the workplace, and through pornography. We must not allow this text to be misused to apply pressure on wives to put up with husbands who abuse them emotionally, sexually, or physically, or who abuse their children in any way. Wives are not called to accept mistreatment without complaint. They should be allowed to express anger and grief and may need to take tough stands to confront their husbands with the consequences of their abusive behavior—what is known today as "tough love." Abusers need treatment; wives and children need protection. Such action may be the greatest sign of love. Wall asks:

> Should a Christian wife continue to submit uncritically to her husband if it results in personal abuse (the vices of 3:5–9) rather than in spiritual maturity (the virtues of 3:12–15)? I think not. Should the measure of a husband's love for his wife be whether her devotion to the Lord Christ is strengthened and God's interests (rather than her husband's) for her life achieved? I think so. In Christ God shows no favorites; God is for both husband and wife, and in equal measure.[73]

Today, we are also more conscious of spouse abuse, and we must recognize that Paul gives a general principle here and does not list possible exceptions. Modern society creates new and different pressures for marriage relationships. We should not neglect to address the stressors, such as unemployment, a high crime environment, financial pressures, and isolation, that

---

72. Perry C. Bramlett, *C. S. Lewis: Life at the Center* (Macon, Ga.: Peake Road, 1996), 46, citing John Lawlor, "The Tutor and the Scholar," in *Light on C. S. Lewis,* ed. Jocelyn Gibb (New York: Harcourt Brace, 1965), 63.

73. Wall, *Colossians and Philemon,* 158–59.

can induce family abuse when we have the least resources within ourselves to resist it. William Aikman (1682–1731) wisely said:

> Civilization varies with the family, and the family with civilization. Its highest and most complete realization is found where enlightened Christianity prevails; where woman is exalted to her true and lofty place as equal with the man; where husband and wife are one in honor, influence, and affection, and where children are a common bond of care and love.

Paul talks about fairness and justice in dealing with slaves. But fairness and justice apply to wives as well. The family is where children learn these things, and any mistreatment of the spouse undermines the discipline and moral nurture of the children.

The successful marriage is based on love. Since love is commanded, it is not simply a feeling. Romantic love may lead to marriage, but it does not sustain it for long. It is much easier to feel romantic love for someone when you do not live with them. The love that Paul commands husbands to have for their wives is something that can be willed. This kind of love is not a feeling but an action. It always puts the welfare of the wife and her needs first. It is never concerned with power or control.

Parental discipline. Sirach offers advice on parental discipline that differs considerably from Paul's. He says the father who loves his son should whip him often (Sir. 30:1). He also tells us:

> Bow down his neck in his youth,
>   and beat his sides while he is young. (Sir. 30:12)[74]

---

74. Philo says that "fathers have the right to upbraid their children and admonish them severely and if they do not submit to threats conveyed in words to beat and degrade them and put them in bonds" (*Special Laws* 2.232). John Pilch, "'Beat His Ribs While He Is Young' (Sir 30:12): A Window on the Mediterranean World," *BTB* 23 (1993): 101–13, provides a helpful summary that shows how the ancient world's approach to child-rearing differed from the predominant American pattern. Sirach focuses only on the son because the father can take pride in him and make his enemies envious, and glory in him in the presence of friends (Sir. 30:3). When he dies, he can take comfort that he is not dead because he leaves behind him "one like himself" (30:4), an avenger against his enemies and benefactor to his friends (30:6). Daughters are a bane because the father constantly worries that she will do something that will bring dishonor to him by losing her virginity, not marrying, getting divorced, proving unfaithful. His solution:
Keep strict watch over a headstrong daughter,
    lest she make you a laughingstock to your enemies,
a byword in the city and notorious among the people,
    and put you to shame before the great multitude (42:11).

Sirach reflects the widespread assumption in the Mediterranean world that obedience does not arise naturally and can only be imparted through thrashings and stern discipline (Sir. 22:6; see Prov. 3:11–12; Heb. 12:7–11). He thinks only in terms of how the pampered, spoiled child, who becomes willful and stubborn, will bring disgrace to his father (Sir. 22:3). The solution is to break the will of the son to prepare him for faithful obedience to a demanding God. Sirach has a spiritual counterpart in the English Puritan, Bartholomew Batty, who argued that God specially created the buttocks for children to receive just correction with stripes and blows without causing serious bodily injury.[75]

While Paul may have agreed with the accepted approach to discipline in his culture, he does not say so. Here he reflects the new insights we find in the New Testament, which appreciate the child's point of view and feelings.[76] The apostle worries more about the discouraged child, the one who is so bowed down that he or she is broken. He knows the danger that the one invested with the final word "in everything" may misuse that authority in destructive ways. His concern is not that children will grow up to disgrace the father by their disobedience, but that the father will hinder the nurturing of his children through discipline at all costs.

Constant criticism and reprimand can be as destructive as none at all and can destroy a child's sense of worth. Beatings are counterproductive and tend only to teach children that physical violence is an appropriate means of handling conflict. It can also produce psychological damage.[77] Shaming children almost guarantees that they will work out their anger in some kind of violence. Parents are to discipline their children in ways that will encourage and guide them into courageous and hopeful living. Parents must wrestle with trying to find the best way of doing this and adjust their approaches as the child grows in understanding and responsibility.

Wuthnow's research on young people to see how they learn to care for others beyond their own families and friends led to some interesting conclusions.[78] Caring is not something innate but learned, and we learn it in our family life from our parents and their everyday small acts of kindness—how

75. Cited by Fletcher, "The Family, Marriage and the Upbringing of Children," 120.

76. See James Francis, "Children and Childhood in the New Testament," in *The Family in Theological Perspective*, ed. Stephen C. Barton (Edinburgh: T. & T. Clark, 1996), 65–85.

77. Fletcher, "The Family, Marriage and the Upbringing of Children," 127–28, contends that it is not coincidental that the flagellant brothels first appeared in London around the 1670s as the legacy of regular and humiliating physical beatings by all powerful schoolmasters.

78. Robert Wuthnow, *Learning to Care: Elementary Kindness in an Age of Indifference* (New York: Oxford Univ. Press, 1995).

they treat one another, their children, and others. These small acts show children that kindness is not something exceptional but a natural part of life. Youth associate their parents' kindness with their personhood; that is just a part of who they are. In a world that is becoming increasingly indifferent and uncivil, parents need to inculcate in their children the spirit of kindness and compassion by setting good examples, beginning with the way they discipline their children.

The workplace. Paul's counsel on slaves and masters has no contemporary significance in our culture, which now considers slavery to be intolerable. The relationship between employees and employers in democratic societies is so completely different from that of master and slave in the first century that we must exercise extreme caution in making any correlations. We cannot make a one-to-one correspondence, where slaves equal employees and masters equal employers. We must look elsewhere in the New Testament for help on such things, but there are certain principles in these instructions that apply in any setting, including the workplace. The statement in 3:17, "And whatever you do, whether in word or deed, do it all in the name of the Lord Jesus," is the hermeneutical key for how this exhortation can be applied to our world.

(1) Many justify their dishonesty, their negligence, or their shoddy work because of perceived mistreatment by their employers. They assume that the injustice gives them a license to be dishonest or to use passive aggressive ways of striking back. One observer says that many people find their jobs futile, boring, and unproductive. When they are plagued by abusive bosses who weigh them down with ludicrous policies and incoherent strategies, they live only for the weekend. Throughout the work week they do as little as possible to get through.

A popular comic strip pillories the inanities of corporate America, draws the hair of the boss to make him look like a devil with horns, and refers to workers carrying their morale in thimbles. Its popularity suggests that many identify with this workplace malaise. Because the boss is a pompous idiot and the company policies unfair, burdensome, and ridiculous, the employees regularly seize every chance to become slack in their duties. The Christian ethic requires an altogether different approach to our assignments. If Christian slaves were expected to work heartily out of reverence for the Lord, every Christian, regardless of the circumstances, must do the same thing. The temptation may be to work only to attract attention or to get by with as little as possible. The Christian, by contrast, must give wholehearted service in the workplace in all circumstances, because our work is something done for the Lord. We work in the confidence that it will not be wasted but that it will be gathered up by God, who brings everything to its successful culmination.

(2) Those who find themselves in a position of control over others should always seek to preserve dignity, fairness, and respect and to avoid treating persons as disposable property. The common assumption that business is a battlefield in which competitors engage in warfare undermines this goal. Employers do not honor employees as persons but treat them merely as subordinates. Some managers use what one has called a "My Lai philosophy of management." My Lai was a Vietnamese village that rogue American troops destroyed and whose inhabitants they massacred as part of the war effort to "save" Vietnam. Some managers, both secular and religious, believe they have to destroy a business or institution to save it. They do not seem to care about fairness or justice or what their strong arm tactics do to the lives of persons involved.

Those who are Christian, however, are held to different standards. Those whose management decisions affect the lives of others should not forget the biblical principle that the measure that you mete out to others will be the measure that you receive. Always trying to enhance the bottom line may lead one to cross the line of what is moral and just.

Colossians 4:2–18

D EVOTE YOURSELVES TO prayer, being watchful and thankful. ³And pray for us, too, that God may open a door for our message, so that we may proclaim the mystery of Christ, for which I am in chains. ⁴Pray that I may proclaim it clearly, as I should. ⁵Be wise in the way you act toward outsiders; make the most of every opportunity. ⁶Let your conversation be always full of grace, seasoned with salt, so that you may know how to answer everyone.

⁷Tychicus will tell you all the news about me. He is a dear brother, a faithful minister and fellow servant in the Lord. ⁸I am sending him to you for the express purpose that you may know about our circumstances and that he may encourage your hearts. ⁹He is coming with Onesimus, our faithful and dear brother, who is one of you. They will tell you everything that is happening here.

¹⁰My fellow prisoner Aristarchus sends you his greetings, as does Mark, the cousin of Barnabas. (You have received instructions about him; if he comes to you, welcome him.) ¹¹Jesus, who is called Justus, also sends greetings. These are the only Jews among my fellow workers for the kingdom of God, and they have proved a comfort to me. ¹²Epaphras, who is one of you and a servant of Christ Jesus, sends greetings. He is always wrestling in prayer for you, that you may stand firm in all the will of God, mature and fully assured. ¹³I vouch for him that he is working hard for you and for those at Laodicea and Hierapolis. ¹⁴Our dear friend Luke, the doctor, and Demas send greetings. ¹⁵Give my greetings to the brothers at Laodicea, and to Nympha and the church in her house.

¹⁶After this letter has been read to you, see that it is also read in the church of the Laodiceans and that you in turn read the letter from Laodicea.

¹⁷Tell Archippus: "See to it that you complete the work you have received in the Lord."

¹⁸I, Paul, write this greeting in my own hand. Remember my chains. Grace be with you.

THE FINAL INSTRUCTIONS in 4:2–6 divide into two units with two imperatives: "Devote yourselves to prayer" (4:2a), and, "Be wise in the way you act [lit., walk] toward outsiders" (4:5). Both pertain to the mission work. Paul wants the Colossians to pray that he will have an open door to speak and that they themselves seize every opportunity and know how to answer others. Both he and they are under a sense of "ought": "how I *must* [*dei*] speak" (4:4; NIV "as I should"); "how you *must* [*dei*] answer" (4:6; NIV, omitted).

In the concluding greetings (4:7–18), Paul introduces the bearers of the letter, Tychicus and Onesimus (4:7–9), and sends greetings to the church from his associates (4:10–14). He then asks them to send his regards to the church at Laodicea and to exchange letters with them (4:15–17). He concludes by writing the salutation with his own hand and asking them to remember his chains (4:18).

Devoting Yourselves to Prayer (4:2–4)

THE IMPERATIVE "DEVOTE yourselves to prayer" is modified by a participle ("being watchful") and a prepositional phrase ("in thanksgiving"). Another participle directs them to pray for Paul and his associates so that a door might open to them.

Devotion to prayer recalls the disciples' early days after the resurrection (Acts 1:14; 2:42, 46; 6:4; see also Rom. 12:12; 1 Thess. 5:17). It implies unrelenting persistence.[1] "Being watchful" may be related to the unknown hour of the Lord's return and the world's end. It will keep the Colossians from being caught off guard or unready (see 1 Thess. 5:4–6). But more likely Paul is warning them against spiritual lassitude so that they can fend off the temptations that can steal upon them. This command recalls Jesus' words to his disciples in Gethsemane: "Stay here and keep watch!" "Watch and pray so that you will not fall into temptation!" (Mark 14:34, 38).[2] Vigilant prayer provides the spiritual fortitude to face down temptation.[3]

Paul knows his dependence on God and asks for intercessory help in prayer, just as he has prayed unceasingly for them (1:9–11).[4] He does not ask them to pray for anything that will bring personal advantage to him; his

---

1. Beare, "The Epistle to the Colossians," 230, cites Jacob's wrestling with the angel in Gen. 32:26 as an example.

2. Dunn, *The Epistles to the Colossians and to Philemon*, 262, argues that the Gethsemane accounts would have been "familiar in all the early Christian churches."

3. The appeal to be thankful recurs throughout the letter (1:2, 12; 2:7; 3:15, 17; 4:2).

4. See 2 Cor. 1:10–11; Eph. 6:19–20; Phil. 1:19; 1 Thess. 5:25; 2 Thess. 3:1–2; Philem. 22.

sights remain firmly fixed on his mission calling (1:25). He therefore asks them to pray that God will open a "door for our message" (lit., "the door of the word").[5] Such opportunities exist even in prison. He tells the Philippians that his imprisonment has helped advance the gospel. The whole palace guard has learned that he is in chains for Christ, and his imprisonment has miraculously emboldened believers "to speak the word of God more courageously and fearlessly" (Phil. 1:12–14).[6]

Paul does not fear imprisonment (see Acts 21:23–24), though the possibility of deliverance (see Philem. 22) is important to him because it will open up unrestricted mission opportunities. His request may then parallel the one in 2 Thessalonians 3:1–2: "Finally, brothers, pray for us that the message of the Lord may spread rapidly and be honored, just as it was with you. And pray that we may be delivered from wicked and evil men, for not everyone has faith." MacLeod notes that God answered the prayer perhaps differently from the way Paul expected: "The letters he wrote from prison are sacred scripture, and have kindled countless flames of Christian devotion from that day to this."[7]

Paul again mentions the content of his message as "the mystery of Christ" (4:3; cf. 1:26, 27; 2:2), which is God's purpose to reconcile the world through Christ and to welcome Gentiles in him.[8] Preaching the gospel does not always win friends and influence people. It can evoke enormous hostility and has led to his current imprisonment. Paul usually qualifies references to his chains with some comment on his commitment to the gospel (see Phil. 1:7, 12; Philem. 13). This subtly notifies his readers that proclaiming the mystery of Christ crucified is more likely to open the door to a prison cell for them instead of the door to financial and social success (see 1:24).[9] The comments in 2 Timothy 2:8–9 are apt:

---

5. The image of the open door is found in Acts 14:27; 1 Cor. 16:8–9; 2 Cor. 2:12; Rev. 3:8.

6. His request to Philemon, however, "And one thing more: Prepare a guest room for me, because I hope to be restored to you in answer to your prayers" (Philem. 22), suggests that he may also hope that the door to his prison cell might open (see Acts 12:5–19).

7. MacLeod, "The Epistle to the Colossians," 231.

8. Lightfoot, *Saint Paul's Epistles to the Colossians and to Philemon*, 231, contends that the mystery of Christ refers to the admission of Gentiles, which provoked Jewish opposition: "It was because he contended for Gentile liberty, and thus offended Jewish prejudices, that he found himself a prisoner." See Eph. 3:1, "the prisoner of Christ Jesus for the sake of you Gentiles."

9. Markus Bockmuehl, "A Note on the Text of Colossians 4:3," *JTS* 39 (1988): 489–94, offers the attractive argument for reading *dio kai* ("as indeed") rather than *di ho kai* ("for which" or "on account of which") in 4:3. He translates 4:3–5: "And pray that God may open for us an opportunity for proclamation, so that we may speak forth the mystery of

Remember Jesus Christ, raised from the dead, descended from David. This is my gospel, for which I am suffering even to the point of being chained like a criminal. But God's word is not chained.

The narrative ending to Acts 28:30 confirms these words: Paul remained under house arrest, but the gospel was proclaimed "unhinderedly" (NIV, "without hindrance").

The NIV translation, "Pray that I may proclaim it clearly" (Col. 4:4), suggests that Paul has the responsibility to proclaim the word so that people will not misunderstand—so that the message is clear to all. This translation may be misleading, because some remain blind to the truth no matter how clearly or simply it is proclaimed. They willfully misunderstand or misinterpret the message. The verb "proclaim" (*phaneroo*, "to make manifest") only means that Paul announces this mystery revealed in Christ intelligibly. "As I should" has to do with making the message appropriate for the audience, but it also implies a sense of oughtness. A better translation might be, "as I am bound to do." Paul is bound more by his commission to preach the gospel (1 Cor. 9:16–23) than by his chains.

Being Wise in Reaching Outsiders (4:5–6)

THE NEXT IMPERATIVE advises the Colossians on how to act toward outsiders in daily life. As a minority in a hostile environment, Christians were concerned about the impressions they made on their neighbors. They were not resentful that they were marginalized in their society. They believed they "have been given fullness in Christ, who is the head over every power and authority" (2:10), and it led them to look at the pagans around them as the deprived "outsiders," aliens to God's kingdom (see Mark 4:11; 1 Cor. 5:12–13; 1 Thess. 4:12; 1 Tim. 3:7).[10] This theological viewpoint can be dangerous if it leads to a false sense of privilege that would shut the door on outsiders rather than flinging wide the gates. The Colossians share the responsibility of evangelizing unbelievers as much as the traveling missionaries. They must blend wisdom (1:9, 28; 2:3; 3:16; see Eph. 4:5) with a sense of reckless urgency that exhausts every opportunity to reach unbelievers.[11]

Christ. For it is to this end that I have been imprisoned, in order that I might manifest it, *as indeed* I am obliged to do" (492). He contends that Paul sees an intrinsic link between his imprisonment and his apostolic manifestation of the mystery. In Phil. 1:12–14, his bonds have become a visible witness to Christ (cf. Eph. 4:1; 6:20).

10. Beare, "The Epistles to the Colossians," 231–32.

11. The verb translated "make the most of " (*exagorazomai*) means "to buy out" or "buy up." See R. M. Pope, "Studies in Pauline Vocabulary: Of Redeeming the Time," *ExpTim* 22 (1910–11): 552–54. "Opportunity" translates the word *kairos*. Believers are to buy up the

Paul does not want the Colossians to be fearful, threatened, or isolated. He wants them to speak openly with others and gives three characteristics that should govern their speech. (1) Their words should always be gracious.[12] Civility and graciousness can overcome the misgivings of neighbors and make them more receptive to the message. Gracious speech forms a stark contrast with the sins of speech listed in 3:8–9 and the cocky arrogance of the opponents who belittle the Christians' faith.[13]

(2) The Colossians' speech is to be salty. In our idiom, salty language is something replete with profanities, but obviously that is not Paul's meaning. "Seasoned with salt" was used to refer to witty, amusing, clever, humorous speech.[14] Their saltiness will prevent them from being ignored as irrelevant bores.

(3) Because believers live in a hostile context, they need to have their answers ready for those who challenge or are curious about their faith (see 1 Peter 3:15–16). To do this they need to be well-grounded in their faith (Col. 1:9–10; 4:12).

Introduction of the Bearers of the Letter:
Tychicus and Onesimus (4:7–9)

PAUL'S LIST OF coworkers in his letters reveals several things about his ministry. (1) It was "a team effort."[15] Paul could not possibly do all that he did without the help and support of others, and he is not stingy in giving them credit and thanks. It is striking that two people on the list, Luke and Mark, are considered to be authors of two Gospels (see 2 Tim. 4:11; Philem. 24).

(2) Paul inspired love and loyalty, and any picture of him as an embattled and embittered loner is mistaken. Dunn makes the interesting observation that persons driven by a "burning conviction and sense of destiny" are often "uncomfortable companions." Many may harbor the suspicion that Paul was just such a person. But the long list of Paul's coworkers suggests that he "was

---

time like determined bargain hunters, lest their opportunity slip away. The parallel in Eph. 5:16, "making the most of every opportunity," offers the reason, namely, "the days are evil." It may have that idea here. The present has fallen under the sway of evil and needs urgent rescuing.

12. The NIV translation, "conversation" (lit., "word"), may convey to us private conversation, but Paul has in mind also our public proclamation ("word" refers back to "the message" [lit., "word"] in 4:3).

13. Paul's speech on the Areopagus in Athens provides a good example (Acts 17:22–31).

14. The parallel in Eph. 4:29 lends weight to the possibility that salt may have a purifying function: "Do not let any unwholesome talk come out of your mouths, but only what is helpful for building others up according to their needs, that it may benefit those who listen."

15. Dunn, *The Epistles to the Colossians and to Philemon,* 271.

evidently able both to retain sufficient equipoise and to inspire tremendous loyalty and commitment on the part of others."[16] Rapske shows that they risked personal danger by staying close to the apostle. They faced the danger of being bullied by the rough characters assigned to guard prisoners, of being too closely linked to someone deemed a danger to national security, and of being betrayed by prison spies.[17] Their physical presence and assistance would have heartened the apostle emotionally and spiritually during the dark days of his confinement and the long wait for some decision about his case.

(3) The early Christians relied much on a network of friends. Without supportive friends and partners throughout the world, Christians could never have succeeded in advancing the gospel across national barriers. All Christians need a community of friends and fellow workers. Maintaining such a network across the empire required much time-consuming, costly, and dangerous travel. The variety of those listed by Paul—a slave, a physician, Jews ("of the circumcision"), and Gentiles—shows how the gospel reached into every sphere of life to recruit committed missioners. For the Colossians, the list of names shows that Paul's interpretation of the gospel is not idiosyncratic. Others (including those from the circumcision) hold to the same gospel and work with him to further it.[18]

Tychicus, as the bearer of the letter, is the first coworker mentioned (see Eph. 6:21–22). He appears in Acts 20:4, along with Trophimus, as a native of Asia.[19] He is mentioned again in 2 Timothy 4:12, "I sent Tychicus to Ephesus," and in Titus 3:12, "As soon as I send Artemas or Tychicus to you, do your best to come to me at Nicopolis, because I have decided to winter there." Perhaps he accompanied Onesimus on his return home, bearing a circular letter along with the letter to the Colossians. He receives the highest praise a Christian can receive: "a dear [lit., beloved] brother, a faithful minister and fellow servant in the Lord" (see 1:7). He comes to encourage the Colossians with news of Paul and his team (see 2:2).

Paul may have judged it too risky to divulge in the letter any information about his circumstances that might jeopardize his case. He consequently

---

16. Ibid., 264.

17. Bruce M. Rapske, "The Importance of Helpers to the Imprisoned Paul in the Book of Acts," *TynB* 42 (1991): 1–28.

18. The emphasis in listing these names is not to endorse their ministry to the Colossians, as some have argued. In 4:8, for example, Tychicus and Onesimus come to tell how Paul and his associates are faring. The emphasis is not on the confirmation of these men but on the Colossians' comfort from their news.

19. Since Trophimus was identified by Paul's accusers as the one he unlawfully brought into the temple area (Acts 21:29), Tychicus may also have accompanied Paul to Jerusalem with the collection. Lightfoot, *Saint Paul's Epistles to the Colossians and to Philemon*, 234, speculates that he is "the famous brother" whom Paul commends in 2 Cor. 8:18.

passes on only innocuous details; Tychicus and Onesimus will supply the full particulars of "the news about me."[20] We might wish that Paul had provided more information about himself in his letters so that we also could learn more of his circumstances, but Paul was not the kind of leader who thought that everything revolved around him. Consequently, he does not readily share how things are going with him personally unless it is directly related to issues in the letter.

Paul identifies Onesimus simply as a "faithful and dear brother" (cf. Philem. 16) and as "one of you," without mentioning any ministerial role. He offers no explanation of how he had contact with him. We can only guess. Was the letter to Philemon written sometime in the past? Paul sent the converted Onesimus to Philemon; Philemon honored his request and sent him back to serve Paul; and now Onesimus returns home again? If this scenario were true, we might expect Paul to explain why he was sending him back again, as he did for the Philippians when he sent Epaphroditus home (Phil. 2:25–30). Paul explains why Tychicus is coming to them but not Onesimus. If Onesimus were a runaway slave returning home, the reason would be obvious enough. The letter to Philemon, which Onesimus brings, fills in the rest of the story. I am inclined to believe that this is his first return to Colosse after his flight and conversion.[21]

Onesimus is not yet a "faithful minister and fellow servant" as Tychicus is, but he is a Christian. This is his new identity in Christ, not as the slave of Philemon. No individual is identified specifically as anybody's slave in the New Testament except where Paul calls himself a slave of Christ (Rom. 1:1; Gal. 1:10; Phil. 1:1) or a slave of God (Titus 1:1). Even the discussion of Onesimus in the letter to Philemon is ambiguous enough for some to argue that he indeed was not Philemon's slave but had some other relationship to him (see the discussion in the introduction to Philemon). He is not described as active in the ministry or part of Paul's fellow workers, but both he and Tychicus come to share news.

---

20. Those who believe that the letter was not written by Paul have argued that the phrase in 4:7, *ta kat' eme* ("all the news about me"), refers to "information relative to the apostle's position and importance" (Pokorný, *Colossians*, 190). But the same phrase appears elsewhere to refer to his imprisonment and legal case (Acts 24:22; 25:14; Phil. 1:12; see Eph. 6:21). Tychicus does not come to confirm Paul's authority but to provide news and comfort concerning everything that has happened to Paul (4:9).

21. Calvin, *Commentaries on the Epistles of Paul the Apostle to the Philippians, Colossians and Thessalonians*, 227, does not think that this is the same Onesimus who is the slave of Philemon, "inasmuch as the name of a thief and a fugitive would have been liable to reproach." He misses the point of Onesimus's restoration. Scott, *The Epistles to the Colossians and to Philemon, and to Ephesians*, 87, is more on target: "He simply introduces him as he might do any other Christian friend of whose honourable standing there is no doubt."

Greetings from Associates with Paul (4:10–14)

ARISTARCHUS IS MENTIONED in Acts 19:29 as a Macedonian from Thessalonica who braved the riotous uproar in Ephesus with Paul. He also traveled with Paul to Jerusalem (20:4, as one of the delegates from Thessalonica?) and then on to Rome (27:2). He may have been one of the other prisoners (27:1). Paul identifies him here as a "fellow prisoner" (see Rom. 16:7). This may be an honorific title using a military metaphor, "a captive of Christ," akin to "fellow servant" (1:7; 4:7) and "fellow soldier" (Phil. 2:25; Philem. 2). In Philemon 23, Paul applies the phrase "fellow prisoner" to Epaphras (cf. Col. 4:12), not Aristarchus. If it is an honorary title, it might explain how Paul could apply it to one fellow worker and then another.

On the other hand, Paul refers to his actual captivity in 4:3, 18, so one assumes that he is referring to the actual imprisonment of his fellow workers. Aristarchus and Epaphras could have rotated in voluntarily sharing Paul's quarters and hence his captivity, though they were not charged with any crime. Taking turns in sharing Paul's captivity would explain why Paul refers to them in this way.[22]

Mark is identified as "the cousin of Barnabas," who was apparently a well-known figure in the ancient church, familiar to the Galatians (Gal. 2:13) and the Corinthians (1 Cor. 9:6). This relationship presumably adds stature to Mark and makes it likely that he is the same John Mark we meet in Acts (Acts 12:12, 25; 13:5, 13; 15:36–41; see also 2 Tim. 4:11; Philem. 24; 1 Peter 5:13). If so, then Onesimus is not the only one who has turned the corner.[23] Mark is no longer a cause for dispute (Acts 15:36–41) but has become a source of comfort as a coworker. We do not know the content of the "instructions" or from whom they came. Paul does not presume to be dispatching Mark as if he were controlling his movements. He may or may not come.

Jesus Justus is mentioned along with Aristarchus and Mark as "the only Jews" (lit., "of the circumcision") among his coworkers. It is unclear who fits

---

22. William M. Ramsay, *St. Paul the Traveller and Roman Citizen* (London: Hodder and Stoughton, 1895) 311, 316, noted that a respectable prisoner was allowed two slaves to serve him as personal attendants, and Aristarchus and Epaphras may have posed as his slaves to serve him during his imprisonment. Brian Rapske, *The Book of Acts in Its First Century Setting. Volume 3. Paul in Roman Custody* (Grand Rapids: Eerdmans, 1994), 374, challenges his reading of the primary sources and whether the Romans would have tolerated such a legal fiction. Lucian, *The Passing of Peregrinus* 12–13, refers to Christians who take great pains to support imprisoned believers, bringing them meals, reading their sacred books, and bribing guards to sleep inside with the prisoner.

23. Dunn, *The Epistles to the Colossians and to Philemon*, 276, believes that Mark was "one of the few effective bridge figures between different strands of the early Christian mission (perhaps having been one of the casualties of the earlier disagreements)."

in this category and how to punctuate the sentence.[24] If it means that they are the *only* Jewish converts among his coworkers, it would appear to exclude Timothy, the coauthor of the letter. Possibly the phrase "of the circumcision" refers to the circumcision party (see Acts 10:45; 11:2; Gal. 2:12) and means: These are the only ones from that group who bring him comfort. If it refers to these three as Jews, it may be a lament (see Rom. 9:1–3)—these are the only ones. In the context of Jewish opposition in Colosse, however, it is more likely that Paul wants to remind them that some Jews, whom they know or know about, have been willing to throw aside their religious entitlements for the sake of the gospel in which there is no Jew nor Greek, circumcised or uncircumcised. They also serve with him in his mission among the Gentiles.

Epaphras, like Onesimus, is identified as "one of you." He is also given the title "servant of Christ Jesus," a title Paul uses for himself in Romans 1:1 and Philippians 1:1 (including Timothy). "Servant" in our idiom implies voluntary service, but the Greek word *doulos* is better translated "slave." To be a "slave of Christ" means that all one's possessions, aspirations, and time belong completely to him. Christ owns him, and therefore Epaphras does not offer service to him only as his time or inclination permit.

Paul again reminds the Colossians of the prayer bond among Christians by telling them that Epaphras "is always wrestling in prayer for you." If Epaphras founded the congregation, he did not forget it when he left but continued to pray for it, perhaps suffering from the same anxiety for the well-being of his church that plagued Paul (2 Cor. 11:28). The verb "wrestling" (*agonizomai*) may allude to Christ's struggle in prayer in Gethsemane (see Luke 22:44), but Paul uses the word in 1:29 to refer simply to his missionary labor (cf. 1 Cor. 9:25; 1 Tim. 6:12; 2 Tim. 4:7). Paul connects prayer with his "working hard" for them, and the battle metaphor pictures prayer as a struggle. Epaphras does not wait for things to grow desperate before interceding for them but continually prays for them, day in and day out (see 2:1).[25]

---

24. The name Jesus Justus reflects the tendency of Jews with Semitic names to have a second Greek or Latin name (see Acts 1:23; 13:9; 18:7).

25. Epaphras's "working hard for you" (4:13) relates to his work for the gospel, not to raising money from wealthier Christians in Rome for disaster relief after the terrible earthquake, as some have speculated (see 1:29–2:1). "You ... Laodicea and Hierapolis" list the cities in their geographical order from Colosse west. Paul omits mention of Hierapolis in 2:1 (see the textual variant) and 4:16. It may be that the positive descriptions of the community in Colosse did not apply to them, or that the ties between Laodicea and Colosse were closer.

Epaphras's goal for the Colossian believers is no different from Paul's: "that you may stand mature and fully assured in all the will of God" (4:12c, lit. trans.; see 1:9–14; 2:2).[26] The prayer fits our reconstruction of the Colossian situation. Outside opponents are assailing the Colossians' faith, and they need to stand firm. The "will [*thelema*] of God" does not refer here to what God wants them to do but to God's plan of salvation: "God has chosen [Gk. *ethelesen*, willed] to make known among the Gentiles the glorious riches of this mystery, which is Christ in you, the hope of glory" (1:27; see 1:9). Epaphras, like Paul, wants the Colossians to become less tenuous in their understanding of all that God has done in Christ so that they will not become easy marks for false teaching that has an "appearance of wisdom" (2:23).

The greetings of Luke and Demas come last, and Paul does not mention their specific mission tasks. Luke is identified only as "the beloved physician" (NRSV).[27] Demas is mentioned only by name with no commendation, which may hint of his future desertion of Paul (2 Tim. 4:10). He did not prove to be faithful in Christ. We have no information about the reasons for that desertion or what happened next.

Greetings to Other Christians in the Area (4:15–17)

PAUL ALSO EXTENDS his greetings in this letter to the Christians in Laodicea and particularly to the church that meets in Nympha's house (4:15).[28] In the Greek, if the accusative *Nymphan* is given a circumflex accent on the last syllable, the name would be masculine (from *Nymphas*). If it is given an acute accent on the first syllable, it would be a feminine name (from *Nympha*). The original and the earliest texts did not employ accent marks, so the key for deciding the gender is the personal pronoun modifying the house, but it has three textual variants. Some texts read "his" house (masculine), others read "her" house, and still others have "their" house, which would include the "brothers."

---

26. The NIV translation places "mature" and "fully assured" after the prepositional phrase "in all the will of God," but they occur before it in the Greek. Paul uses the verb *plerophoreo* to mean "fully assured," "fully convinced," "certain" of Abraham in Rom. 4:21, that he was "fully persuaded that God had power to do what he had promised." See also Rom. 14:5: "Each one should be fully convinced in his own mind."

27. Lightfoot, *Saint Paul's Epistles to the Colossians and to Philemon*, 241–42, contends that the first "we passage" in Acts (16:10) occurred near the time of Paul's malady mentioned in Gal. 4:13–14. He deduces from this that Luke may have joined Paul "in a professional capacity." Lohse, *Colossians and Philemon*, 174, n. 41, dismisses such speculation out of hand.

28. Churches did not have separate buildings in the first century, and Christians met in the home, in the courtyard, or on the roof of someone with a large enough house to accommodate the group (see Acts 12:12; 16:40; Rom. 16:3–5, 23; 1 Cor. 16:19; Philem. 2).

The feminine reading best explains how the others may have developed.[29] It is more plausible that later scribes thought it impossible for Paul to refer to a woman's house church (with its implication of some leadership role for her) than that they would have mistaken a man's house for a woman's. They would know that the householder did more than simply provide space for the church to meet, so they altered it accordingly. The reference to the church meeting "in her house" does not treat it as an unusual circumstance or anything worthy of special comment. She is probably either unmarried or widowed. Either status would give her more independence and flexibility in the ancient world as the *patria* of her household than if she were married and under a husband's legal authority.

The greetings assume that the Colossians will go to Laodicea with their letter and will retrieve a copy of the letter sent to them (4:16). The reference to this Laodicean letter, however, poses an intriguing puzzle: Who wrote it? What happened to it?

Paul does not say that the letter is "to" Laodicea but "from" (*ek*) there. Some contend that the letter was written by the Laodiceans to Paul, to Colosse, or to Epaphras.[30] Others suggest that it was a letter written by Epaphras.[31] Since Paul knows about the letter and can decide who should read it, we can safely assume that he wrote it. The phrase "the letter from Laodicea" reflects an epistolary style that views things from the perspective of the Colossians.[32]

If this reference is not some ruse by a forger composing Colossians to explain the sudden appearance of the letter, three nominees from canonical letters have been proposed for this unknown letter: Hebrews, Philemon, and Ephesians.[33] The letter could have been lost long before Paul's letters were collected, possibly destroyed in the earthquake in A.D. 61–62, or allowed to fall into neglect by a "lukewarm" church. If this were the case, it raises the natural questions: How many more of Paul's letters were lost? Why would the

---

29. One of the core principles of textual criticism of variant readings is to adopt the reading that best explains how the others may have come into being.

30. The forged letter to the Laodiceans containing snippets of Pauline phrases patched together (existing today only in Latin) appeared from the fourth century on and made some inroads in the churches. Lightfoot, *Saint Paul's Epistles to the Colossians and Philemon*, 275, correctly recognized that the motive behind the interpretation that the letter in question was *from* the Laodiceans was connected to the desire to undermine support for this apocryphal letter without having to argue that a letter written by Paul had been lost.

31. C. P. Anderson, "Who Wrote 'The Epistle from Laodicea'?" *JBL* 85 (1966): 436–40.

32. Dunn, *The Epistles to the Colossians and to Philemon*, 287.

33. Philemon is a semiprivate letter. Lightfoot, *Saint Paul's Epistles to the Colossians and Philemon*, 281, is correct: "The tact and delicacy of the Apostle's pleading for Onesimus would be nullified at one stroke by the demand for publication."

letter to the Laodiceans be lost, if an exchange took place, when the companion letter to the Colossians was not?

Lightfoot's argument that the letter was our canonical Ephesians still has merit.[34] Ephesians was a circular letter without specific greetings or advice tailored to a specific setting.[35] Tychicus was sent with a copy of the letter to the churches in the Lycus valley; the reference to him in Ephesians 6:21–22 agrees almost exactly with the one in Colossians 4:7–8. He naturally planned to visit Colosse after Laodicea. He also brought with him Onesimus and the special letter for Philemon. Paul apparently did not think that the circular letter with its more sweeping agenda and poetic expression was adequate to resolve the issues broached in 2:8–23, nor were the issues addressed in the Colossian letter suited for a circular letter. Consequently, Paul wrote a separate letter to the Colossians to deal with the specific problems.[36] Though Paul wrote to particular situations, he fully intended his letters to have wider circulation.

Paul concludes his greetings with a cryptic comment about Archippus's work: "Tell Archippus: 'See to it that you complete the work you have received in the Lord'" (4:17). Is this word to be taken as a warning (cf. the phrase in 1 Cor. 16:10) or as supportive encouragement? The charge to Timothy in 2 Timothy 4:5, "Discharge all the duties of your ministry," is similar in Greek. In Timothy's case, it is "do[ing] the work of an evangelist." This parallel makes it more likely that Paul intends this exhortation as a positive reminder to Archippus.

We can do no more than guess at the nature of Archippus's "work" (lit., "ministry"), but it parallels what Paul says about himself in 1:25. Paul writes that he has become the church's "servant [*diakonos*] by the commission God gave me to present to you the word of God in its fullness" (lit., "given to me unto you to fulfill [aorist infinitive of *pleroo*], the word of God"). Similarly,

---

34. Lightfoot, *Saint Paul's Epistles to the Colossians and Philemon*, 244; 272–300. J. P. Rutherford, "St. Paul's Epistle to the Laodiceans," *ExpTim* 19 (1907–8): 311–14. Marcion was the first to make this connection by giving our canonical Ephesians the title "To the Laodiceans" in his Apostolic Canon. He may have no sound historical basis for this connection other than conjecture that his copy of Ephesians may have lacked an address.

35. The lack of greetings may explain Paul's request for the Colossians to relay his greetings.

36. Wright, *Colossians and Philemon*, 161, reasons that "'Ephesians' may be seen as the author taking a step back, as it were, from Colossians and contemplating in worship the great truths he has been emphasizing. (Conversely, of course, Colossians could be seen as a more sharply focused version of certain themes in 'Ephesians.')" Many scholars assume that Ephesians was written later than Colossians. Leaving aside the question of authorship, Ernest Best, "Who Used Whom? The Relationship of Ephesians and Colossians," *NTS* 43 (1997): 72–96, shows that the two letters were written at almost the same time, if not simultaneously.

Archippus has received in the Lord a ministry (*diakonia*) that he may "fulfill" it (present subjunctive of *pleroo*).[37] We can only guess what it was but should observe that "the whole body of believers at Colossae is asked to share the responsibility for its execution."[38] Ministry and authority are shared obligations in this community (3:16).

Final Greeting from Paul's Own Hand (4:18)

PAUL SIGNS HIS letter with a terse, final request for them to "remember my chains." The apostle customarily dictated his letters, but he takes the pen in hand for the final greeting. His brief benediction may hint at the difficulty of writing with manacles binding his wrists.[39]

The call to remember his chains is not some forlorn plea for pity from a woebegone and disheartened apostle. He does not ask for commiseration. He is glad to suffer for Christ (1:24) and his bonds are the bonds of the gospel (Philem. 13). It is better to regard this call as a note of encouragement for those who may also suffer persecution for their faith as well as another request for their prayer support. Theodore of Mopsuestia interpreted it: "Following my example, do not be ashamed to suffer for the truth."[40] Following Paul's example requires more than a halfhearted commitment to the gospel. The letter itself becomes a means by which believers can see and experience God's grace even when things become difficult.

 IT IS TEMPTING to disregard the concluding greetings and blessing of Paul's letters with the cluster of names as an insignificant postscript to the theological meat found in the body. Here we get a glimpse, however, into the boiler room of the New Testament, those laboring in various capacities in various places. The bits of limited information we get with names are tantalizing, and we should be cautious not to read too much into the references and construct fanciful theories that go beyond the evidence. There is a danger of building up romantic reconstructions from the brief references, and I may be guilty of this in identifying the letter to the

37. Some interpret it as related to Onesimus. Archippus is Onesimus's owner, and Paul asks him in a communal letter to accede to his request about Onesimus, bringing public pressure to bear upon him. See the discussion in Philemon.

38. Beare, "The Epistle to the Colossians," 240.

39. Dunn, *The Epistles to the Colossians and to Philemon*, 290, suggests that the words were kept short because they "were penned under considerable difficulty, so that only the most basic benediction could be given."

40. Noted by Beare, "The Epistle to the Colossians," 241.

Laodiceans with Ephesians. We need to be careful that we not get snared in the web of our historical spinning and miss the theological and practical cues that these concluding greetings offer us.

PAUL'S CONCLUDING WORDS show his driving concern for the advancement of the gospel throughout the world. He does not ask them to pray for his deliverance but that his work might be even more effective. We do not know how the prayers were answered, but we do know that his imprisonment forced him to write letters that have blessed far more lives than he could have reached had he been free to speak in person.

Guidelines for advancing the gospel. Paul's final exhortation and greetings have contemporary significance for our task of advancing the gospel in our world and gaining a hearing for the witness to the mystery of God revealed in Christ. E. D. Martin notes that Paul does not ask them to pray for God "to save lost people," but that they get "new opportunities" for witness.[41] Paul gives guidelines for making the most of those occasions.

(1) *Praying earnestly.* A new technique to increase efficiency in automobile manufacturing is to have materials manufactured as needed. That tactic may work in industry, but it does not work in prayer. If we expect our prayer life to have any effect in our lives and in our world, it cannot be sporadic or haphazard. We cannot fall back on prayer only when we think we need it; we must devote ourselves to it (see Acts 1:14; 6:4; Rom. 12:12).

Prayer requires serious discipline. Paul describes Epaphras's indefatigable prayer for the Colossians as something akin to a wrestling match (Col. 4:12). He prays for them with all his might, straining every nerve and muscle. If Christians prayed with the same zeal that some people manifest to keep themselves physically fit for a longer and healthier life, they might see different results in the life and witness of their church. William Cowper's hymn expresses it well:

And Satan trembles when he sees
The weakest saint upon his knees.

A church in a rural part of a rural state has experienced phenomenal quantitative and qualitative growth, and they attribute it to the Holy Spirit and their prayer ministry. The associate pastor says, "God is doing some unbelievable things at Buck Run because His people are daring to open up the

41. E. D. Martin, *Colossians and Philemon*, 198.

channel for the power of the Spirit to flow. . . . They are paying the price in prayer."[42]

(2) *Cultivating a sense of urgency.* The metaphor of "buying up the time" implies that believers must capitalize on every chance and use every moment to the full. Successful evangelism requires a sense of urgency. Scott states it well: "If men are to be won to Christ before he comes to judgment it must be done now."[43]

Unfortunately, that sense of urgency has faded. Too often we have frittered away opportunities. As someone has put it, the world has been multiplying while the church has been making "additions"—indeed, sometimes "subtractions." Some members in churches that are experiencing a dwindling membership may wonder where all the people are and worry about the decline. But it does not seem to bother them enough to do anything about it. They have no sense that it requires immediate action and no compulsion to reach out to unbelievers.

Jesus' parable of the shrewd manager (Luke 16:1–8) provides an illustration of someone who acted decisively when the urgency of the moment demanded it. Caught in a desperate situation threatening total ruin, the steward deftly and quickly took action to secure his worldly life. When everything was at stake, he staked everything on a bold course of action. He represents the prudence of worldlings who recognize crisis and respond to it promptly with daring. The parable draws a pointed contrast between "the people of this world" and "the people of the light." If worldlings such as this fellow act so astutely in a crisis to protect their self-interests, should not the people of the light seize each moment and act astutely to ensure their interests in the world to come?

In Colossians we might apply the lesson of the parable slightly differently. Others ("the people of this world") face the crisis, and the time is short. But "the people of the light" sit idly by, twiddling their thumbs, as if the time for those living in darkness to decide for Christ were unlimited. If Christians felt the same urgency to reach others with the gospel as they do about securing their own welfare in this world, our churches would see amazing results.

(3) *Acting wisely.* Paul insists that the Colossians should act in the right way as well as at the right time.[44] The message Christians have is clear: Jesus Christ embodies God's good purposes for creation. Creation has come under the bondage of satanic powers and human sinfulness, but Christ's death on the cross defeated these powers and canceled the debt of sin. God raised him

---

42. Thom S. Rainer, *Eating the Elephant* (Nashville: Broadman & Holman, 1994), 115; for a powerful book on the effect prayer can have on a church, see Jim Cymbala, *Fresh Wind, Fresh Fire* (Grand Rapids: Zondervan, 1997).

43. Scott, *The Epistles to the Colossians, to Philemon and to the Ephesians,* 85.

44. E. D. Martin, *Colossians and Philemon,* 200.

from the dead and exalted him, and salvation is now available to all through him. But people listen to our message sometimes more with their eyes than with their ears. Its clarity gets garbled by our boorishness, acrimony, and misbehavior. Paul is acutely conscious that unbelievers watch what Christians do, and the New Testament contains many cautions, warning Christians to do nothing that would bring discredit to the gospel or confirm unbelievers' misgivings about Christianity (see 1 Cor. 10:32–11:1; 1 Thess. 4:11–12; 1 Tim. 3:7; 6:1; Titus 2:5; 1 Peter 2:12, 15; 3:1).

In Paul's world, Christianity was a new and different teaching. In our contemporary world, nations that were formerly overwhelmingly Christian now have a majority who claim to be agnostics or atheists, or who follow another religious faith. Christianity is increasingly becoming an unfamiliar and strange teaching in our world. Many have become skeptical about Christians and their faith, and a few well-publicized scandals involving prominent Christians have substantiated these suspicions. Pokorný recognizes, "In the secularized world of today, when being a Christian is no longer a matter of course, Christian conduct itself takes on a missionary function again."[45]

Making a good impression is not everything, but it is not unimportant. The purpose of acting wisely is not simply to win the good opinion of outsiders but to help win them to God. The gospel message must always be fleshed out by the way believers live. The silent force of righteous living can speak loudly, and the most productive evangelists are Christians who enter the daily mix of life and live their faith. It can cause others who may be dubious or indifferent to become more receptive to hearing the verbal message of God's love. It can lead them to ask why Christians live as they do, and the answer should point them to Christ. Christians are to present the gospel at all times, especially when they do not use words.

(4) *Being gracious.* The experience of grace should make us gracious. Christians must leaven a bold, uncompromising witness with civility, gentleness, kindness, and good humor. Before we can make disciples, we need to make friends and build rapport. Amos Starkadder, a character in the novel *Cold Comfort Farm*, is a caricature of the grim religious fanatic, and he provides a perfect example of how *not* to reach others. The following exchange captures his preaching philosophy: "'They'll all burn in hell,' added Amos in a satisfied voice, 'and I mun surelie tell them so.'"

When his cousin Flora wants to come to hear him preach to his small flock of Brethren, Amos replies:

> "Aye ... ye can come ... ye poor miserable creepin' sinner. Maybe ye think ye'll escape hell fire if ye come along o' me, and bow down and

---

45. Pokorný, *Colossians*, 186–87.

quiver. But I'm tellin' ye no. 'Tes too late. Ye'll burn with the rest. There'll be time to say what yer sins have been, but there'll be no time for more."

When she asks if she needs to confess her sins publicly, he responds churlishly: "Aye, but not tonight. Nay, there'll be too many sayin' their sins aloud to-night; there'll be no time for the Lord to listen to a new sheep like you. And maybe the spirit won't move ye."[46] Probably not, when confronted with this kind of attitude. Amos begins his sermon with scorn.

> "Ye miserable, crawling worms, are ye here again, then? Have ye come like Nimshi, son of Rehoboam, secretly out of yer doomed houses to hear what's comin' to ye? Have ye come, old and young, sick and well, matrons and virgins (if there is any virgins among ye, which is not likely, the world bein' in the wicked state it is), old men and young lads to hear me tellin' o' the great crimson lickin' flames o' hell fire?"[47]

This approach may be "salty," but it is not full of grace. We do well to remember what is was like when we were formerly estranged from God. What was it that we needed to hear? What was it that touched our hearts? It would help our approach if we look at those we consider to be "poor, miserable sinners" the same way we imagine that Christ looked at us when we were once lost in the darkness of our own sin. We should respect others and treat them as reflecting, sensitive human beings who can decide for themselves. The key is to season our witness with liberal doses of the virtues enjoined in 3:12–17: compassion, kindness, humility, meekness, patience, love, wisdom, and thanksgiving.

On the other hand, we can go to the opposite extreme by trying to be so gracious that we never share the gospel with others. This is no less problematic. Some Christians have become so hypersensitive about offending non-Christians that they never present them with their vision of God's truth clearly and directly. Many people never darken the door of a church because they have never been invited in. We are not showing compassion or love if we choose to keep meekly silent and never share the truth about Christ with those who need desperately to hear it.

Helen Keller's poignant reflection on her blindness and deafness resonates with the way many sighted and hearing people feel:

> Sometimes, it is true, a sense of isolation enfolds me like a cold mist as I sit alone and wait at life's shut gate. Beyond there is light, and music, and sweet companionship; but I may not enter.[48]

---

46. Stella Gibbons, *Cold Comfort Farm* (New York: Penguin, 1994), 86.
47. Ibid., 97–98.
48. Helen Keller, *The Story of My Life* (New York: Grosset & Dunlap, 1905), 130.

Her isolation was caused by physical barriers. Others who have both physical sight and hearing may feel a similar isolation induced by their spiritual alienation from God. For these persons, Christians have good news. Christ has broken down the barriers of sin that bar us from God's presence, isolate us from others, and imprison us in our own little hell. Christ invites all to enter his light and sweet companionship, but he invites them through us. Christians should never forget that the grace given to us was intended to be passed on to others (see Eph. 3:2).

(5) *Being lively (seasoned with salt).* Many believe that obedience to God is "tedious, boring, dull"; and many believers "do their part to confirm this attitude by being tedious, boring, and dull, seasoned with nothing."[49] A wearisome, dreary, lackluster, and insipid presentation of the gospel has done immeasurable harm. Godliness is not to be equated with stodginess. Flat formulas or lifeless platitudes do not capture the gospel's excitement. It must be made palatable with a savory combination of charm and wit.

The danger is that we can go overboard in trying to be entertaining. Lively presentations can be as hollow as "fine-sounding arguments."[50] We should not emphasize being colorful at the expense of communicating the basics of the faith. Scott's comment on 4:6 offers a helpful check: "The *salt* with which they are to flavour their talk is not literary allusion and epigram, but the spirit of the gospel."[51] Anything that does not accord with that spirit should be avoided.

What people may regard as "lively" usually depends on their cultural background. Some may find certain styles of speaking or writing disagreeable, while others find them captivating. Regardless of the style we use, if we are to communicate powerfully our message, it will need to be "salted" with images that connect theological truth to everyday life. As most preachers know, people usually remember their illustrations while forgetting the details of the argument.

Jesus provides a classic example of this kind of "salt" in his parables. He captured profound theological truth in homely stories that have captured the imaginations of persons for generations. Paul also wove in different images from everyday life to make his points. Most of his metaphors, so familiar and concrete to his original listeners, have become obscure to us because the distance of time has dissipated their power or because we have so theologized them that we do not even recognize that he is using everyday imagery.

---

49. David H. Stern, *Jewish New Testament Commentary* (Clarksville, Md.: Jewish New Testament Publications, 1992), 614.

50. Wall, *Colossians and Philemon*, 167–68.

51. Scott, *The Epistles to the Colossians, to Philemon and to the Ephesians*, 85.

The result is that it no longer grips us in the same way that it did the first audience.

We spoke earlier of how Paul utilized vivid images in 2:6–23 (kidnapping, death as circumcision, baptism as burial, the head and the body, canceling IOUs, nailing charges to a cross, and leading defeated captives in a triumphal parade) to convey the truth that we have died in Christ's death, triumphed in his victory, and been forgiven our trespasses. Most effective preachers and teachers recognize that communicating the message of timeless truth requires packaging it in time-bound imagery that excites the imagination and opens the eyes of the mind and heart to see the truth more clearly.

(6) *Being well grounded.* Paul tells the Colossians to be ready to answer unbelievers' questions and challenges. The key here is that they are *their* questions. All too often we arm ourselves with pat answers to questions about theological fine points and debates that people never ask. People do not respond well to a canned message and are usually sophisticated enough to see through something that is only slick propaganda. When they quiz us on the issues bothering them, we may be caught off guard and stammer out only muddled replies. If someone asks, for example, "Why do you think Christianity is better than any other religion," many Christians are at a loss to give anything more than pious clichés learned from childhood Sunday school experiences. Some cannot answer their own spiritual questions, let alone the questions the world poses concerning the latest scientific discoveries, personal crises, and moral dilemmas.

Christians must be well grounded and well prepared in advance to answer others' questions whenever they pose them. When the Ethiopian eunuch asked Philip what the passage from Isaiah 53 meant, the evangelist did not ask for time to go home and study and tell him that he would get back to him later. The chance would have been lost forever. He needed to give him the answer right then; and to give an answer, he needed to know what his Bible said and what it meant. Many today may not even know how to formulate their questions. We need sensitivity to reach out to them where they are and wisdom and knowledge to provide answers.

(7) *Cultivating networks (and unity).* Throughout these closing remarks Paul mentions how Christians should pray for one another. Prayer links individuals and churches together into overlapping networks (see Rom. 15:30–32). It keeps us from focusing only on our own immediate group and its concerns. If Epaphras founded the congregation in Colosse, he did not forget it when he left but continued to pray for it. How many pastors continue to pray for the congregations they once served when they moved to different, usually greener pastures? How many Christians continue to pray for the churches

they may have left after moving away? We see the premium Paul put on friends working together and praying together, caring about what was going on in their lives, and offering mutual support.

Paul clearly did not believe that he was self-sufficient; he needed the help of all those listed and appreciated and affirmed each person's contribution. No one works alone. The emphasis is on

- cooperation, not independence or competition
- praying for mission opportunities for others, not just for ourselves
- praying for mission opportunities over the entire world, not just our corner
- praying that every Christian in every circumstance will have the wisdom and courage to communicate the gospel boldly and clearly.

Like Paul, we should never lose sight that God has called us to serve him and has called us to serve with others. We need each other's prayers and support.

(8) *Being ready to accept the consequences of preaching in a hostile world.* Paul preferred to be freed from his chains so that he might carry the gospel to ever more distant climes (see Rom. 15:23–24; 2 Cor. 10:15–16). But he accepted his present chains and continued to preach the gospel and to write encouraging letters to churches. For centuries those letters have blessed those who have studied them. For this reason, Paul's imprisonment may have contributed more to advance the gospel than his freedom. Paradoxically, suffering may abet our mission, and we must be prepared to accept it graciously.

Will Willimon recorded this exchange with Bishop Emilio de Carvalho from Marxist Angola. The struggles with government oppression caused his church to grow stronger.

> The government does what it needs to do. The church does what it needs to do. If we go to jail for being the church, we shall go to jail. Jail is a wonderful place for Christian evangelism. Our church made some of its most dramatic gains during the revolution when so many of us were in jail. In jail, you have everyone there, in one place. You have time to preach and teach. Sure, twenty thousand of our Methodist pastors were killed during the revolution, but we came out of jail a much larger and stronger church.

Willimon remarked that the Bishop saw the drift of the questions directed to him from the audience and responded:

> Don't worry about the church in Angola; God is doing fine by us. Frankly, I would find it much more difficult to be a pastor in Evanston,

Illinois. Here there is so much. So many things. It must be hard to be the church there.[52]

Overcoming failures. If we read the names in Paul's final greeting canonically, we discover three names associated with personal failures in the New Testament—Mark, Onesimus, and Demas. John Mark went along with Paul and Barnabas on their first missionary journey to help them (Acts 13:5). For unspecified reasons, he left the mission and returned home to Jerusalem (13:13). Acts records a later split between the former mission partners Barnabas and Paul over whether to take Mark again on a new mission (15:36–40):

> Some time later Paul said to Barnabas, "Let us go back and visit the brothers in all the towns where we preached the word of the Lord and see how they are doing." Barnabas wanted to take John, also called Mark, with them, but Paul did not think it wise to take him, because he had deserted them in Pamphylia and had not continued with them in the work. They had such a sharp disagreement that they parted company. Barnabas took Mark and sailed for Cyprus, but Paul chose Silas and left, commended by the brothers to the grace of the Lord.

Paul clearly harbored suspicion of Mark. But this breach between Paul and Barnabas did not hinder the gospel's advance. Instead, it meant that there were now two missions. Yet somehow, by the writing of Colossians, Mark redeemed himself in Paul's eyes and become helpful to his ministry (see also 2 Tim. 4:11).

The fascinating and moving story of Onesimus, a runaway slave, will be dealt with in the commentary on Philemon. He also was guilty of desertion but had turned things around when he was converted by Paul. Paul warmly recommends him to his master as a brother in Christ who has served him in the gospel while he was in chains.

Paul mentions the third person, Demas, without any commendation. Perhaps this is a hint of his failure to come: "Demas, because he loved this world, has deserted me and has gone to Thessalonica" (2 Tim. 4:10). In Bunyan's *Pilgrim's Progress*, Demas appears as the halfhearted Christian who beckons the pilgrims to turn aside from their journey to tarry at a silver mine. The judgment of Bunyan's Christian against Demas may be too strong:

> I know you; Gehazi was your great-grandfather, and Judas your father; and you have trod in their steps; it is but a devilish prank that thou usest: thy father was hanged for a traitor, and thou deservest no better reward.

---

52. Will Willimon, "Set Us Free," *Pulpit Resource* 23/2 (1995): 38.

After all, Paul only says that Demas deserted *him*, not Christ. We do not know the rest of the story; but we do know how God can redeem failure, including those who even desert their Lord and deny him with curses (cf. John 18:15–18, 25–27; 21:15–19). The key to overcoming failure is that one turn to God in repentance and trust in God for renewal.

The stories of personal failures connected to these names presents an opportunity for the homilist to investigate the nature of failure. Failure happens, but failure need not be final. Those who have triumphed over their failures or in spite of their failures recognize that they may have had a failure, perhaps many; but they *were not* failures. Failures may simply be underpasses that lead to success. C. S. Lewis wrote:

> *No amount* of falls will really undo us if we keep picking ourselves up each time. We shall of course be v.[ery] muddy and tattered children by the time we reach home. But the bathrooms are all ready, the towels put out, and the clean clothes in the airing cupboard. The only fatal thing is to lose one's temper and give up. It is when we notice the dirt that God is most present in us; it is the v.[ery] sign of his presence.[53]

We can never succeed on our own. The good news of the gospel is that we do not have to. We live in Christ and triumph through him.

---

53. W. H. Lewis, ed., *Letters of C. S. Lewis* (New York: Harcourt, Brace and World, 1966), 199.

Introduction to Philemon

LIGHTFOOT VOICES THE OPINION of many who delight in this brief letter: "As an expression of simple dignity, of refined courtesy, of large sympathy, and of warm personal affection, the Epistle to Philemon stands unrivalled."[1] Knox lauds it as "one of the most charming letters ever written."[2] Guthrie says that it "breathes the great-hearted tenderness of the apostle,"[3] and Jewett calls it "one of the most subtle letters in world history, an expression of Paul's ambassadorial style."[4]

As heartwarming as Philemon is, it does have its frustrations for the interpreter. It leaves us in the dark about several things we would like to know to understand more fully the circumstances behind this letter. Reading Philemon is like coming into the middle of a movie and having to catch up on who the characters are and what has already happened in the plot, and then having to leave before the end. Paul does not tell us where he is imprisoned, what the conditions are like, or, more to the point, how it happened that Onesimus came under his influence long enough for him to be converted. He also does not tell us why Onesimus fled his master, if indeed he did flee. Because of the letter's ambiguity on this point, some have argued that Onesimus had been sent to Paul by his master on some errand and had only overstayed his leave. Paul also does not state precisely what he wants Onesimus's master to do with him except to regard him now as a brother in Christ. A student of ancient papyrus letters observes that he knows of no parallel in the papyri that is as long as this one or "so oblique, so faltering, that one has difficulty in determining what it is, precisely, Paul requests."[5]

From the letter we only know for sure that Onesimus had been converted by Paul during his confinement (v. 10), but there is no hint that Onesimus was a fellow prisoner. We also learn that Onesimus had been useful to Paul and

---

1. Lightfoot, *Saint Paul's Epistles to the Colossians and to Philemon*, 319.
2. Knox, *Philemon Among the Letters of Paul*, 7.
3. Donald Guthrie, *New Testament Introduction* (Downers Grove, Ill.: InterVarsity, 1973), 638.
4. Robert Jewett, *Paul: The Apostle to America: Cultural Trends and Pauline Scholarship* (Louisville, Ky.: Westminster/John Knox, 1994), 64.
5. John White, "The Structural Analysis of Philemon: A Point of Departure in the Formal Analysis of the Pauline Letter," SBLASP (Missoula, Mont.: Scholars Press, 1971), 35–36. John M. G. Barclay, "Paul, Philemon and the Dilemma of Christian Slave Ownership," *NTS* 37 (1991): 175, concludes from the letter's lack of clarity that Paul has deliberately left the request open-ended because he is not sure what is best to recommend.

served him (vv. 11, 13) and that before he had been "useless" to his owner (v. 11) and may have "done [him] . . . wrong" in some way (v. 18). Paul sends him back (v. 12) in hopes that Philemon will do a good thing (v. 14) and will receive him graciously as a brother in Christ (vv. 12, 17). But he also expresses the confidence that he will do even more than he asks (v. 21). When we interpret the letter, we have to fill in the gaps and make some assumptions about the situation. Two important questions need answers: What brought Onesimus to Paul? and, What was Paul requesting Philemon to do?

What Brought Onesimus to Paul?

A RUNAWAY SLAVE. The traditional view is that Onesimus was a runaway slave.[6] As slaves were wont to do from time immemorial (see 1 Sam. 25:10), Onesimus fled from his master, Philemon, and somehow, voluntarily or accidentally, fell in with the apostle Paul, who was able to win him to the faith; he now sends Onesimus back to his master. Scholars in this century have challenged this traditional scenario. They call attention to the absence of any explicit mention in the letter that Onesimus had run away, of his subsequent penitence, or of the need for his master to forgive his slave's offense. They also note that it would have been an astounding coincidence for a fugitive slave to meet Paul, the one person who knew his master, during his imprisonment.

For a slave to run away was a grave crime that the authorities treated seriously. As a Roman citizen, Paul would have been subjected to a looser form of confinement. A captured runaway slave would have been clapped in irons and kept under guard in a slave prison and would not have been allowed free contact with Paul.[7] How then could he have been of much service to Paul (v. 13)?

If Onesimus were not a prisoner and had freedom of movement, he could have done much for Paul. But how and why would he have had contact with the imprisoned Paul? Lightfoot strains his imagination trying to explain what could have drawn Onesimus to Paul's side:

> Was it an accidental encounter with his fellow-townsman Epaphras in the streets of Rome which led to the interview? Was it the pressure of want which induced him to seek alms from one whose large-hearted

---

6. This view is most recently defended by John G. Nordling, "Onesimus Fugitivus: A Defense of the Runaway Slave Hypothesis in Philemon," *JSNT* 41 (1991): 97–119.

7. Brian M. Rapske, "The Prisoner Paul in the Eyes of Onesimus," *NTS* 37 (1991): 191. If Onesimus had been captured, the authorities, not Paul, would have been the ones to send him back to his owner. How did Paul, a prisoner, think he had the authority to send back a runaway slave (v. 12)?

charity must have been a household word in his master's family? Or did the memory of solemn words, which he had chanced to overhear at those weekly gatherings in the upper chamber at Colossae, haunt him in his loneliness, till, yielding to the fascination, he was constrained to unburden himself to the one man who can soothe his terrors and satisfy his yearnings?[8]

Given what we know of human nature, these guesses are possible; but Caird argues that we should not "attempt to conjecture by what chance Onesimus in Rome fell in with Paul."[9] The problem is not so easily dismissed, and it has led others to offer quite different sketches of the situation. Something other than happenstance brought Onesimus to Paul.

A commissioned servant. Winter argues that Onesimus had not run away. He was with Paul in prison because he was sent there by his owner (probably Archippus) on behalf of the church in Colosse.[10] He had been commissioned to bring Paul practical and financial assistance. Winter's suggestive thesis, however, fails to stand careful scrutiny. If Onesimus was not a Christian before he met Paul and was regarded as "useless" (v. 11), he would have been an unlikely candidate for the church to entrust with such a responsibility. Why let an undependable slave run loose across the countryside? Why charge a non-Christian with such an important spiritual mission? Was he the only one who could be spared?

True, the owner might have sent Paul a generally worthless slave as a cost-effective but miserly way, to help Paul or, more positively, in hope that contact with Paul might help to straighten him out. But both options seem most improbable. What rules against this view is Paul's discreet mention of his willingness to reimburse the owner for any wrong that Onesimus may have done (vv. 18–19) and his diplomatic description of Onesimus's separation from his master: "He was separated from you for a little while" (v. 15). If Onesimus had been sent by the church, Paul could simply say that he had been sent and describe him in the same glowing terms as he used for the Philippians' Epaphroditus, "whom you sent to take care of my needs" (Phil. 2:25).

---

8. Lightfoot, *Saint Paul's Epistles to the Colossians and to Philemon*, 312–13.

9. Caird, *Paul's Letters from Prison*, 214.

10. Sara C. Winter, "Methodological Observations in a New Interpretation of Paul's Letter to Philemon," *USQR* 39 (1984): 203–12; "Paul's Letter to Philemon," *NTS* 33 (1987): 1–15. See also Craig S. Wansick, *Chained in Christ*, 175–99. Bruce, *The Epistles to the Colossians, to Philemon, and to the Ephesians*, 197, allows this as a possibility. Houlden, *Paul's Letters from Prison*, 226, expresses his honest doubt that we know anything about how Onesimus came to be with Paul, but he surmises that "he had been lent to Paul over a difficult period. And the reason for Paul's delicacy is simply that he wishes to retain his services longer."

In the letter to Philemon, it sounds as if Paul is gingerly searching in verses 15–16 for some euphemism to describe a getaway rather than a commissioning. He only mentions it to hint that there may have been some divine reason behind Onesimus's departure, "that you might have him back for good—no longer as a slave, but better than a slave, as a dear brother." If Paul could find such a reason, it would help to absolve his guilt in keeping Onesimus so long.

Paul's hesitation in expressing his wish in verse 13, "I would have liked to keep him with me so that he could take your place in helping me while I am in chains for the gospel," is also inexplicable if the church had sent Onesimus to serve him. If Paul wants to keep him longer, why does he need to send Onesimus on a perilous journey home to obtain permission to keep his services only to have him turn around and head back if it is granted? Why not send Tychicus with a letter to make the request and keep his services a while longer while he waits for the reply? What is more important, why does Paul worry how Onesimus will be received (v. 17)? Paul does not seem anxious that his owner will allow Onesimus to continue to serve him but that he may not embrace his slave as a brother in Christ.[11]

The case is based on an argument from silence that fails to consider rhetorical reasons why Paul does not explicitly mention Onesimus's wrongdoing. He employs extreme tact in this letter. Barclay observes: "Indeed, the extraordinarily tactful approach that Paul adopts throughout this letter is a clear indication that he recognises that he is dealing with a delicate situation in which Philemon could well react awkwardly."[12] Yet Paul does allude to past problems that presumably were a major obstacle to any future reconciliation. Onesimus has done something wrong to raise the ire of his master, and Paul must intercede.[13]

A prodigal brother. The letter's ambiguity and our heightened sensitivity in this age to Paul's tacit endorsement of slavery has prompted Callahan to propose another radically different story behind the letter.[14] His arguments raise

---

11. Nordling, "Onesimus Fugitivus,"119, complains that this interpretation turns a heartfelt plea "into a rather dispassionate, non-theological financial transaction between Paul and Onesimus's owner. Yet I doubt that such a routine scrap of business correspondence would ever have become part of the canonical NT."

12. Barclay, "Paul, Philemon and the Dilemma of Christian Slave Ownership," 164.

13. Barclay (ibid., 164) notes that Paul admits that Onesimus had been useless (v. 11) and that he may owe Philemon something (v. 18). He concludes: "It is almost inconceivable that Paul should mention such negative details concerning his protégé unless they were a major obstacle in the relationship between Philemon and Onesimus."

14. Dwight Allen Callahan, "Paul's Epistle to Philemon: Toward an Alternative *Argumentum*," *HTR* 86 (1993): 357–76; "Brother Love," *Harvard Divinity Bulletin* 22 (1993): 11–16.

a contemporary issue we must address. Why is it that Paul does not apply the gospel in the case before him to attack the inherent injustice of slavery? Paul not only does not condemn slavery for Christians but speaks glowingly of a member of the slave-holding class and treats Onesimus's flight as an injury to his master that requires restitution (v. 19).

Callahan notes how problematic this picture was for those African Americans who endured the tyranny and humiliation of slavery and how it remains a sensitive issue for their heirs today. He cites an example from the diary of Charles Colcock Jones, a white Presbyterian minister who preached on Philemon to slaves in Georgia and was startled by their bitter reaction to his sermon:

> When I insisted on fidelity and obedience as Christian virtues in servants and upon the authority of Paul, condemned the practice of *running away*, one half of my audience deliberately rose up and walked off with themselves, and those who remained looked anything but satisfied, either with the preacher or his doctrine. After dismission, there was no small stir among them; some solemnly declared that there was no such Epistle in the Bible; others, that they did not care if they ever heard me preach again.[15]

Callahan solves this moral dilemma by arguing that Onesimus was not a slave but Philemon's estranged younger brother, who ran to Paul to have him intercede in a family dispute. He points out that nowhere in the letter does Paul identify Philemon (or Archippus) as a master.[16] He argues that Paul's plea to welcome Onesimus "no longer as a slave, but better than a slave, as a dear brother" (v. 16) does not refer to Onesimus's actual status as a slave. Instead, it refers to his virtual status in Philemon's eyes.[17] "Slave" was an appropriate metaphor for one who was socially dead, who had "no formal, enforceable ties of blood."[18] Paul simply wants to effect domestic reconciliation, which explains the rich familial vocabulary in the letter. Callahan contends, "If Philemon is hospitable toward his brethren in the Lord, how much more incumbent upon him it is to be so toward one who is a member of his own family as well as the household of faith." He should be able to for-

---

15. Albert J. Raboteau, *Slave Religion: The "Invisible Institution" in the Antebellum South* (Oxford: Oxford Univ. Press, 1982), 139, cited by Callahan, "Brother Love," 14.

16. He traces the traditional interpretation back to the "imaginative and ingenious hypothesis of John Chrysostom," who was countering an antislavery wing in Christianity.

17. Callahan, "Paul's Epistle to Philemon," 362. He argues that in v. 17 Paul asks Philemon to receive Onesimus "as me," as Paul's virtual presence. He considers the "as" in v. 16 to be similar: He is not to treat Onesimus as virtually a slave.

18. Ibid., 370.

give the foibles of his brother in the flesh. Paul's plea in verse 16 is not that he accept Onesimus back as a brother, but as a *beloved* brother.

This carefully argued thesis helpfully raises issues that must be addressed and shows how the issue of forgiveness lies at the heart of the letter, even though it is unstated. Nevertheless, it is a case of special pleading to avoid the unpleasant fact that Paul regarded running away as more wrong than slavery. Paul does not specifically identify Philemon as Onesimus's master because he does not want to reinforce the master/slave relationship when he asks him to accept Onesimus as his brother in the Lord. We should therefore read verse 16 literally to mean that Onesimus was a slave.[19]

A slave seeking Paul's intercession. A fourth option offers a cogent explanation for how Onesimus joined up with Paul and why the latter said nothing of his running away. Onesimus had deliberately sought Paul out, looking for a sympathetic, influential friend of his master to intercede on his behalf. Because of the slave's low estate, it would have been considered impudent for him to plead clemency for himself. Veyne points out that pardon was a free act:

> Because granting the pardon was not a duty, it could not be solicited by the slave himself, but only by a third party, born free, like the master. The intermediary honored himself by persuading the father to substitute clemency for severity. At the same time he honored the authority of masters in general over slaves in general.[20]

Roman law, recorded in *The Digest of Justinian* 21.1.17.1–16, consistently argued over the years that the slave's attitude of mind decided whether he was a fugitive or not.[21] A slave who had no intention of running away but absented himself to ask a friend of his master to intervene was not regarded as a fugitive.[22] Onesimus, according to this theory, had provoked Philemon in some

---

19. Onesimus's name was a typical slave name. See the evidence compiled by Lightfoot, *Saint Paul's Epistles to the Colossians and to Philemon*, 308–9. Callahan, however, points to the evidence in G. H. R. Horsley, *New Documents Illustrating Early Christianity* (North Ryde: Macquarie, 1982), 4:96, that shows the name was borne by free persons and was not necessarily an indication of servile status.

20. Paul Veyne, "The Roman Empire," in *A History of Private Life I. From Pagan Rome to Byzantium*, ed. Paul Veyne (Cambridge/London: Harvard Univ. Press, 1987), 65. Ovid even encouraged clever lovers to use a slave to beg the mistress to intercede with the master on their behalf for what he was going to do anyway, as a ploy to win them over. It cast her into the role of kindly aunt and him into the role of stern father.

21. *The Digest of Justinian*, ed. Theodor Mommsen and Paul Krueger, trans. Alan Watson, (Philadelphia: Univ. of Pennsylvania Press, 1985), 2:606.

22. See Heinz Bellen, *Studien zur Sklavenflucht im römischen Kaiserreich* (Wiesbaden: F. Steiner, 1971), 78–79. Peter Lampe, "Keine 'Sklavenflucht' des Onesimus," *ZNW* 76 (1985): 135–37, cites the judgment of Proculus (first century) that a slave is not considered a runaway

way and was due punishment. He hurried to the apostle, his master's spiritual patron, to entreat him to intercede with his Christian master and assuage his wrath. This story behind the letter may explain why Paul thinks his intercession has such a good chance for success.

In other words, the apostle does not make the case for a fugitive slave but for a slave in hot water, who was seeking Paul's mediation with the master. Verses 10–13 imply that Onesimus has been with Paul long enough for Paul to convert him and to become tenderly devoted to his welfare. Harboring a runaway slave was a serious offense.[23] Paul would not have won Philemon's favor if he had been sheltering his runaway slave during this time.

If Onesimus were not making a daring bid for freedom, what prompted his flight is impossible to know. One can guess that he may have been involved in a business deal for his master that somehow went wrong (see Luke 16:1–8). Or, he may have done something that caused Philemon to renege on an agreement to manumit Onesimus—a reward for loyal service—and he wanted Paul to mediate. We have no evidence.

Conclusion. The best options for explaining the situation behind the letter are the first and the last. Either Onesimus tried to escape the bonds of slavery and by some quirk ended up with Paul, or he deliberately set out to find Paul in hopes that this influential friend would assuage his master's anger with him.[24] It is hard to decide between the two. Slaves frequently ran away but usually because they had been mistreated in some way, had done something to make their masters angry, were about to be sold,[25] or had no prospects of manumission.

---

if he flees to a friend of his master to try to persuade him from punishing him for something (*Digest* 21.1.17.4). Other examples refer to a slave who flees to his mother to entreat the master on his behalf (*Digest* 21.1.17.5). In *Digest* 21.1.43.1 the judgment is: "A slave who takes off to a friend of his master to seek his intercession is not a fugitive; indeed, even if his thinking be that in the event of his not receiving assistance, he will not return home, he is not yet a fugitive, for flight requires not only the intention but also the act of flight"; and in 21.1.17.12 we find this opinion: "A slave who does what it is adjudged permissible to do publicly is not a fugitive."

23. *The Digest of Justinian* 11.4.1 records this opinion: "Anyone who has hidden a runaway slave is guilty of theft." It then records the decree from the Senate that anyone who restores a runaway slave to his owner or brings him before the authorities within twenty days is exonerated. All who apprehend runaways must produce them in public, and the authorities then take responsibility for guarding them, usually with chains.

24. Another slant on the situation imagines that Onesimus was seeking asylum with Paul. It is stretching the point to think that Athenian law would apply in this case or that Paul, if he is under arrest, could provide asylum for anyone.

25. In Mark Twain's, *Huckleberry Finn*, Miss Watson's slave, Jim, runs away because he overhears his mistress say that she was going to sell him down river in New Orleans.

We can assume that mistreatment could have occurred even in a Christian household, just as sexual molestation and violence can occur in Christian families today. But Paul's praise for Philemon's love and compassion (vv. 4–6) and his confidence that he will accede to his request (v. 21) leave the impression that Philemon was not some cruel tyrant who would drive a slave to the desperate act of stealing away.

On the other hand, if one argues that Paul's place of imprisonment is Rome, it seems unlikely that a slave would travel 1,300 miles from Colosse to seek a mediator to smooth over some dispute with his master. If this was what led Onesimus to Paul, then Ephesus, one hundred miles distant, is far more likely as the place of Paul's imprisonment.

In my estimation, it seems more probable that Onesimus was a runaway slave who providentially came under Paul's influence. This means that Paul writes on behalf of a runaway slave—something unheard of in the ancient world.[26] This extraordinary situation required the greatest delicacy and best explains why Paul's appeal differs so much from Pliny's more forthright intercession for a friend's freedman who had offended his patron.[27]

Paul uses euphemisms in his appeal and is careful not to overstep any legal bounds ("without your consent," v. 14).[28] His letter is presumably the first word that Philemon has heard about Onesimus since his departure. Understandably, he would want to avoid mentioning the unmentionable—Onesimus's desertion—which brought shame and also economic loss to his master.[29] He uses a pun to describe Onesimus (a name that means "useful") as being formerly "useless" (v. 11). Instead of plainly saying that Onesimus ran away, Paul describes his absence with a passive voice, suggesting that God's

---

26. Paul believes that *he* is sending him back, not the authorities. It is possible that Onesimus escaped detection as a fugitive slave, and Paul did not let on to the magistrates in hopes that he might escape rough treatment and punishment when he returned home with Paul's intercessory letter in his hand.

27. See the copy of the letter in the Appendix to this introduction.

28. Nordling, "Onesimus Fugitivus," 99, contends: "Paul has deliberately minimized Onesimus's past crimes against his master and softened the frightfully harsh language ordinarily associated with the criminal runaway slave."

29. It caused a master to lose face as one who could not control his slaves or as a brutal master who drove his slaves to try something desperate. It cost him financially in having to purchase or rent a replacement and possibly in hiring a slave catcher. It also cost him status. If one aspired to high status, he needed to have a suitably large retinue of slaves with increasingly specialized tasks. Apuleius had to defend himself in court against accusations that he employed sorcery in getting a wealthy woman to marry him. The accusing lawyer tried to blacken his reputation by charging him with immoderation by manumitting three slaves in one day, with being untrustworthy, and with lacking honor because he brought only one slave with him (*Defense* 17).

hand was involved: "He was separated from you for a little while" (v. 15). He broaches the subject of Onesimus's past misdeeds with a conditional sentence, "If he has done you any wrong or owes you anything" (v. 18). Paul does not explicitly ask Philemon to forgive his slave, but the general tone of the letter assumes that he should adopt a forgiving attitude.

Dunn suggests that Paul's tentative and restrained appeal may be attributable to the necessity of getting the letter past the prison censor. Paul did not want to arouse suspicion among unfriendly officials that he was sympathetic to fugitive slaves or condoned such behavior, and so he avoids any reference to his crime by using "Christian code language."[30]

Wilson, however, offers a more likely explanation for the letter's indirectness.[31] Americans culturally are more accustomed to coming directly to the point and not beating around the bush. We might think that if Paul wants his friend to do something, he should ask him outright. After all, he is an apostle. But social mores required him to use politeness strategies to lessen the perceived cost of Philemon's forgiveness of Onesimus.[32] This conciliatory approach required him to maneuver delicately around Philemon's feelings of anger and betrayal, to establish a level of mutual comfort that will not cause Philemon to lose face publicly, and to promote rapport.[33] Granted, Paul's request to forgive Onesimus may "be regarded as pious by either Christian or Stoic principles," but it would have been costly to Philemon because "it may also be construed as weakness both by society and by the other slaves who may perceive the risk in running away to be diminished."[34]

Using the framework of Geoffrey Leech's interpersonal rhetoric and politeness theory, Wilson maintains that the way Paul expresses his thoughts and makes his request is heavily motivated by the following politeness strategies:

- The generosity maxim: minimize benefit to self; maximize cost to self
- The approbation maxim: minimize dispraise of other, maximize praise of other (in the thanksgiving)
- The modesty maxim: minimize praise of self, maximize dispraise of self (in the salutation and v. 10)

---

30. Dunn, *The Epistles to the Colossians and to Philemon*, 324.

31. Andrew Wilson, "The Pragmatics of Politeness and Pauline Epistolography: A Case Study of the Letter to Philemon," *JSNT* 48 (1992): 107–19.

32. Ibid., 116.

33. Ibid., 108. Dunn, *The Epistles to the Colossians and to Philemon*, 332, comments: "It was important not to provoke a confrontation, in which Philemon might have to choose between accepting Paul's authority (and thus losing face among his own circle of the influential well-to-do) or maintaining his social status at the cost of a rupture with Paul."

34. Wilson, "The Pragmatics of Politeness," 112.

Paul employs these strategies to pour balm on resentment and to dissolve resistance. He recognizes that one does not go about passing judgments on another's slave; "to his own master he stands or falls" (Rom. 14:4). Most parents today would resent someone else, including a close friend, offering unsolicited advice on the discipline of their children. In the first century, everyone accepted as inalienable the right of masters to do as they pleased with their property, their slaves.[35] They would naturally bristle if anyone else tried to meddle in that relationship. Paul's politeness strategy eases the tension and diminishes the cost of yielding to his wishes. There is no disgrace in giving way to a friend who serves God at such cost to himself.

Paul is not simply using clever tactics to defuse a volatile situation and to get Philemon to see things his way. His purpose is swaddled in a basic theological conviction about what it means for us to be in Christ. The key phrase in Philemon is "in Christ" (vv. 8, 20, 23); "in the Lord" appears in verses 16 and 20, and "unto Christ" ("in Christ," NIV) appears in verse 6. This letter shows how Paul applies this abstract, mystical concept concretely to the real world of personal relationships.[36] The caste and honor system that regulated social relations was inimical to Christian ethics. If Philemon yields to Paul's request and does more than he asks, it shows how the truth of the gospel breaks down social barriers and dethrones cultural indoctrination.

What Did Paul Want Philemon to Do?

THE NEXT QUESTION is, What does Paul want Philemon to do? Rather than throwing his apostolic weight around to bend Philemon's will to his own, Paul makes his appeal based on his new relationship with Onesimus, his old relationship with Philemon, and the potentially redefined relationship between Philemon and Onesimus. Philemon is free to do what his conscience dictates, but it is informed by the gospel and his relationship to Paul.

In making his case, Paul first stresses his deep affection for Onesimus. He is his child (v. 10), his heart (v. 12), and his beloved brother (v. 16). Onesimus has served him during a difficult time when he has been encumbered by chains (v. 11). Next, he appeals to his intimate relationship to Philemon. He too is a beloved brother as Onesimus is, but more. Paul describes him as a coworker (v. 1), a partner (v. 17), and one who owes Paul his very life (v. 19). Finally, he mentions the redefined relationship between master and slave created by Onesimus's conversion. As his brother in Christ and equal before God, Onesimus now has eternal worth to Philemon (v. 15).

---

35. Slaves felt much the same way because the evidence is overwhelming that when they were freed, they treated their slaves with no greater consideration.

36. On the phrase "in Christ," see M. A. Seifrid, "In Christ," *DPL*, 433–36.

The only specific request Paul has is that Philemon welcome Onesimus as if he were Paul (v. 17). Paul wants Philemon to accept his formerly troublesome slave as he would his dear friend, who is now in chains for the gospel; the apostle only hints that Philemon should extend the same forgiving love to Onesimus that he had already received from God (see Col. 3:13). Their reconciliation is so important that it overrides Paul's wish to keep the now invaluable Onesimus to help him. Paul appeals to the obligation that friends must reciprocate favors, framing it as a business deal: You owe me, but I will repay whatever is owed you (vv. 18–19). He knows, however, that as a Christian, Philemon's favorable response will spring from his being in Christ and his knowing the fellowship of the Spirit (Phil. 2:1–2).

Does Paul only want Philemon to allow Onesimus to return to his household without punishment? Since Paul never explicitly mentions that Onesimus ran away or was filled with contrition and since he makes no pleas for indulgence and mercy on Philemon's part, John Knox concludes that Paul does not simply want Onesimus's reinstatement. Instead, Knox claims, Paul makes a roundabout request for the owner to give him Onesimus so that he can continue to assist him while in prison. He does not ask *on behalf of* Onesimus but *for* him (v. 10).[37]

In Knox's reconstruction of the story, Archippus is the actual owner of Onesimus and the letter's principal addressee.[38] Paul brings Philemon into the picture because he did not personally know Archippus. As Paul's beloved coworker, Philemon had possibly become the overseer of the churches in the Lycus valley after the departure of Epaphras and, according to Knox, was stationed in Laodicea.

The weakest link in Knox's argument is his conclusion that the letter to Laodicea, mentioned in Colossians 4:16, is the letter to Philemon. He envisions that the letter first came to Philemon in Laodicea, who was then expected to exert his influence on Archippus in Colosse. Since it is a quasi-legal letter, the church is also addressed to increase the pressure on Archippus to consent to the request. Paul's letter to the Colossians was sent at the same time, and it was partially designed to elicit further support for Paul's request. According to Knox, the command to tell Archippus to see to it that

---

37. Knox, *Philemon Among the Letters of Paul*, 22–23, interprets the force of the preposition *peri* in v. 10 to express the content of the request.

38. The antecedent of "your" in v. 2, "the church that meets in your house," is ambiguous. Knox argues that it referred to Archippus, who is the closest noun. Lamar Cope, "On Rethinking the Philemon-Colossians Connection," *BibRes* 30 (1985): 46, appeals to the grammatical rule that the pronoun agrees with its nearest available antecedent unless the context dictates otherwise.

he completes the work he has received in the Lord (Col. 4:17) refers to the request in the letter to Philemon.

Few have accepted Knox's reconstruction. Most interpreters assume that the first person listed in the greeting, not the last, is the primary addressee. It is also unlikely that Paul would identify a semiprivate letter directed to Philemon in Laodicea as the letter to the Laodiceans (Col. 4:16). His use of the second person singular throughout the letter, particularly in the thanksgiving (Philem. 4–7) and the climactic request (vv. 21–22a), indicates that he writes to a trusted friend who has the power to grant his extraordinary request.

But Knox does help us see that Philemon is a personal letter that the church is allowed to overhear.[39] He also points us to a deeper purpose of this letter hidden between the lines. Paul's cryptic statement in verse 21, "Confident of your obedience, I write to you, knowing that you will do even more than I ask," invites us to ask what this "even more" is. Paul's confidence suggests that he wants to accomplish more than reconcile a master and a slave who are out of sorts or to have a master embrace his prodigal slave as a brother in the Lord. Since Paul confesses how gladly he would have kept Onesimus by his side to serve him (v. 11), he allows Philemon to see how valuable Onesimus has become in the service of the gospel.

Possibly, Paul wants Onesimus to be allowed to return so he can continue to minister to his needs, as Knox argues.[40] But Paul is never interested in how he might benefit materially (see Phil. 4:10–20) but how the gospel might benefit. This overarching concern for the mission cause of the gospel drives his request concerning Onesimus, and he never identifies the cause of the gospel with his personal needs.[41] Paul wants Philemon to set Onesimus free for a greater service in the gospel whether he returns to Paul's side to serve him or not. This is the "even more" (v. 21) and the "good thing" (v. 14; NIV "favor") that Paul hopes for but does not dare ask.

Paul's "heart" will be refreshed in Christ when Philemon receives his recalcitrant slave as a brother in the Lord (v. 20b). But he will receive a benefit in the Lord only if Philemon sets Onesimus free for the service of the gospel.[42] Given the social manners and customs of Paul's day and the deferential way Paul must approach the whole problem, this aim is above and

---

39. On its significance, see the commentary on v. 2.

40. Knox, "Philemon: Introduction and Exegesis," 557.

41. This raises questions about what Paul would have done had Onesimus not become a Christian. It is unlikely that he would have identified him as his heart (v. 12) or as his representative (v. 17), but he could only appeal for Philemon to exercise fairness (Col. 4:1).

42. Readmitting him as a slave would provide no real benefit to Paul "in the Lord." Paul can only have a "benefit in the Lord" if Onesimus is free to serve the gospel, not just his master.

beyond anything that could ever be voiced aloud. No other examples of intercession for a runaway slave exist, which shows how remarkable it was for Paul to intervene.

Barclay argues that Paul intentionally leaves things open-ended because the situation was so awkward. If Philemon felt obligated to set free a slave who had run away and returned as a Christian, what would that say to other slaves? Would they not be encouraged to try to get their freedom by following suit? What about those slaves who may already have become Christians and remained slaves? Should not the fundamental incongruity between being a brother in Christ and living as master and slave mean that they should all be given their freedom?[43] Barclay, however, concludes, "Caught in this dilemma, Paul can do little more than offer a variety of different suggestions, none with the certainty of a clear instruction and all leaving unresolved the central tension in the present status of Onesimus as both slave and brother to Philemon."[44] The dilemma is real because of the unavoidable social constraints, and Paul does everything possible to ease the perceived cost involved in forgiving a runaway slave.

Reading between the lines, I get the impression that Paul would like Onesimus to be more than a dear brother (v. 16) and a useful slave to Philemon (v. 11). He wants Onesimus to join the ranks of his coworkers (vv. 1, 23–24). In Colossians, Paul makes it clear that he has authorized Onesimus along with Tychicus to make known to the readers all that has happened to Paul (Col. 4:7–9). In other words, Onesimus has the same responsibility as Tychicus, who is identified as a "dear brother, a faithful minister [*diakonos*] and fellow servant [*syndoulos*, lit., fellow slave] in the Lord." Onesimus is identified only as a "faithful and dear brother," but we learn from the letter to Philemon that he has served (*diakoneo*) Paul faithfully (v. 11). Paul also says that Onesimus is to be received as his ambassador ("as . . . me," v. 17). For Onesimus to become one of Paul's coworkers he needs complete emancipation, not simply his manumission to serve Philemon as his freedman.[45] It was possible to be a slave and a Christian; it was impossible to be a slave and a Christian missionary, who must speak boldly and move freely.[46]

---

43. Such issues related to slavery in the ancient world will be dealt with in the Bridging Contexts section.

44. Barclay, "Paul, Philemon and the Dilemma of Christian Slave Ownership," 183.

45. See below on manumission.

46. From the fourth century we find the following counsel from the *Apostolic Canons* (82) concerning the ordination of slaves (cited in Joseph Cullen Ayer, Jr., *A Source Book for Ancient Church History* [New York: Charles Scribner's Sons, 1949], 388):

We do not permit slaves to be ordained to the clergy without their masters' consent; for this would wrong those that owned them. For such a practice would occasion

Such a goal mitigates some of the social problems mentioned by Barclay that freeing Onesimus would create. But Paul cannot make such an unparalleled request except in coded language. The letter to Philemon reveals Paul's tender, humanitarian concern for a brother in Christ and the premium he places on Christians' reconciling with one another. It also reveals how his desire to spread the gospel to the world (see Col. 4:3–4) dominates his thinking, even in a semiprivate letter about a reformed and reclaimed slave.

What Happened Next?

WE CAN ONLY guess what happened next, but since this letter was included in our canon, we can assume that Philemon complied with Paul's wishes. Had Philemon not acceded to Paul's request, the letter probably would have been suppressed.

We would like to know more, however. Developing a theory first set forth by Goodspeed, Knox proposed the captivating hypothesis that the freed Onesimus eventually became the bishop of Ephesus mentioned by Ignatius in his letter to the *Ephesians* (1:3; 2:1; 6:1–2).[47] Ignatius was the bishop of Antioch and had been arrested by the Romans, who hauled him off to Rome to be thrown to the wild beasts in the arena. The date is traditionally assigned as A.D. 110. On the way, his escorts allowed him to meet with other Christians. Christian emissaries from Ephesus, Magnesia, and Tralles gathered in Smyrna to meet with Ignatius, and he sent them back with letters to their respective churches. If Onesimus were twenty years old when Philemon was written, he could have been seventy at this time.

To make his case, Knox spots many verbal parallels between Ignatius's letter to the *Ephesians* and Paul's letter to Philemon. He concludes that Ignatius knew the letter to Philemon and deliberately made allusions to it, although he never cites it verbatim. Knox infers that the former runaway slave had become bishop of one of the leading churches in Asia. Onesimus may have participated in the collection of Paul's letters, and he included with them this small pearl, his treasured charter of liberty.[48]

---

subversion of families. But if at any time a servant appears worthy to be ordained to high office, such as Onesimus appears to have been, and if his master allows it, and gives him his freedom, and dismisses him free from his house, let him be ordained.

47. Knox, *Philemon Among the Letters of Paul*, 71–108; see also P. N. Harrison, "Onesimus and Philemon," *ATR* 32 (1950): 290–93. The theory is deemed possible by Moule, *The Epistles to the Colossians and to Philemon*, 21; Peter Stuhlmacher, *Der Brief an Philemon*, EKKNT, 2d. ed. (Zurich/Neukirchen: Neukirchener Verlag, 1981), 19; F. F. Bruce, *The Epistles to the Colossians, to Philemon, and to the Ephesians*, 200–2.

48. F. F. Bruce, "St. Paul in Rome. 2. The Epistle to Philemon," *BJRL* 48 (1965): 97.

We are naturally curious to know the rest of the story and want to believe that Paul's intercession was not only wise and justified but turned out with glorious results. The touching story about a wayward slave begotten in chains, becoming a beloved leader in the church, and collecting and publishing the letters of Paul almost makes us wish it were true even if it is not. But we should guard against allowing an interesting theory from becoming a pious romance that persuades only because it brings tears to the eyes. Onesimus was a common name, particularly in Ephesus, and just because the bishop bears the same name as this slave does not necessarily indicate that the two are the same person.[49] Martens has shown that the linguistic ties between the letter to Philemon and Ignatius's letter to the *Ephesians,* which is the linchpin of Knox's theory, fail on careful scrutiny. Ignatius never quotes directly from the letter, and the verbal links are purely happenstance since they reappear throughout the Ignatian corpus.[50]

What happened next, like so many things we would like to know in the New Testament, is lost in the mists of history. This brief appeal reveals something far more important: The power of the gospel transforms lives and relationships.

Provenance

THE QUESTION OF where Paul was confined when he sent this letter (Rome, Ephesus, or Caesarea) turns on two issues in Philemon: How far could Onesimus have ranged from his master's home in Colosse, and Paul's request for Philemon to prepare a guest room for him.[51]

Those who argue for Ephesus point out that it is only one hundred miles from Colosse and much easier for Onesimus to reach than Rome, thirteen hundred miles away, a costlier and riskier journey. It makes much more sense as a closer destination, particularly if Onesimus fled to Paul to beg him to intercede with his master. Paul also would not have scuttled his plans for a mission venture to Spain to return eastward to the Lycus valley (Rom. 15:23–29) if this letter comes from an earlier Ephesian imprisonment.

---

49. The bishop may have taken the name of Onesimus to revere the Onesimus of the letter or for symbolic reasons (Lightfoot, *Saint Paul's Epistles to the Colossians and to Philemon,* 308–9).

50. John W. Martens, "Ignatius and Onesimus: John Knox Reconsidered," *Second Century* 9 (1992): 73–86.

51. The traditional arguments are laid out by G. S. Duncan, *St. Paul's Ephesian Ministry* (London: Hodder & Stoughton, 1929), 72–73; "The Epistles of the Imprisonment in Recent Discussion," *ExpTim* 46 (1935–36): 296, arguing for Ephesus, and by C. H. Dodd, "The Mind of Paul, II," in *New Testament Studies* (Manchester: Manchester Univ. Press, 1953), 95, arguing for Rome.

On the other hand, if Onesimus is a fugitive slave, Rome would provide the best place to hide and lose one's past since it was teeming with people from all over the empire. Slaves were not distinguished from freedmen by their race, dress, or occupation, and they could have easily blended into the crowd. Justinian's *Digest* (1.14.3) records a runaway slave who not only eluded recognition but won election as a magistrate of Rome before he was found out. If one links Philemon with Paul's letters to the Colossians and to the Ephesians, Rome becomes far more likely as the place of writing.

What Philemon Means for Us Today

WE CAN BEGIN to approach this letter's contemporary significance by asking why such a short letter consisting of only 335 words was preserved in our canon. Scholars have guessed that Paul wrote many other personal notes; why was this particular one saved?[52] It provides no dividend for the development of dogma since it contains no grand theological teaching. Jerome and others defended its inclusion in the canon against those who considered its theme to be beneath the dignity of an apostle, but their defense was rather lukewarm.[53] Lightfoot explains:

> In the fourth century there was strong bias against it. The "spirit of the age" had no sympathy with either the subject or the handling. Like the spirit of more than one later age, it was enamoured of its own narrowness, which it mistook for largeness of view, and it could not condescend to such trivialities as were here offered to it. Its maxim seemed to be *De minimus non curat evangelium* ["Concerning what is insignificant the gospel does not pay attention"]. Of what account was the fate of a single insignificant slave, long since dead and gone, to those before whose eyes the battle of the creeds was still raging? This letter taught them nothing about questions of theological interest, nothing about matters of ecclesiastical discipline; and therefore they would have none of it.[54]

Preiss contends that the letter therefore was kept because of one or all three of the following reasons: (1) Church leaders so venerated the apostle that they wanted to conserve everything from his hand; (2) they recognized it to be "an incomparable model of spiritual direction, of tact, of love"; (3) they "relished the quite new and luminous way in which Paul approaches and

---

52. Lightfoot, *Saint Paul's Epistles to the Colossians and to Philemon*, 303, says it was "rescued . . . from the wreck of a large and varied correspondence."
53. So also was that of Chrysostom and Theodore of Mopsuestia.
54. Lightfoot, *Saint Paul's Epistles to the Colossians and to Philemon*, 316–17.

decides a delicate matter arising between a Christian master and slave."[55] These last two alternatives are particularly suggestive for the letter's contemporary significance.

Paul's letter to Philemon serves as a model of Christian compassion. In many ways, it parallels Jesus' parable of the prodigal son, which captures the gospel in a nutshell. The letter speaks of failure, the need for intercession, returning, forgiveness, and restoration. When we read it side by side with the letter to the Colossians, we learn that getting relationships straight is just as important as getting doctrine straight. If we are genuine disciples of Christ, we will relate to our fellow believers with grace, forgiveness, and encouragement.

The atrocities committed by Hutus and Tutsis against one another in Rwanda and neighboring countries during the last decade of the twentieth century are horrific and difficult to fathom. A surprising statistic makes the holocaust even harder to understand: "Ninety percent of Rwanda's people are professed Christians." John D. Roth shares that an InterVarsity leader in the region explained that "missionaries preached a gospel about having a right relationship with God but not necessarily right relationships with one another. This is why we can be 90 percent Christian yet kill in the name of ethnicity,' he says."[56] Philemon helps us put things in proper perspective with its extraordinary emphasis on right relationships based on love and forgiveness. Some people believe that Christianity only needs to change what we believe. This letter makes it clear that it also needs to change how we treat other people.

This wonderful but much neglected missive can also give us a new appreciation for Paul, the human being. It casts Paul in quite a different light from a prevailing view that he is a cantankerous, heavy-handed guardian of the truth of the gospel, who is always on the warpath against theological offenders. Vincent comments:

> We are accustomed to conceive of the apostle as always armed for warfare, sheathed in logic, and bristling with arguments. It is delightful to find him at ease, and for a moment able to unbend, engaged in this friendly intercourse, so full of freedom and even playfulness.[57]

---

55. Theo Preiss, "Life in Christ and Social Ethics in the Epistle to Philemon," in *Life in Christ* (Chicago: Alec R. Allenson, 1954), 32.

56. John D. Roth, "The Mennonites' Dirty Little Secret," *Christianity Today* 40/11 (Oct 7, 1996): 48.

57. Marvin R. Vincent, *A Critical and Exegetical Commentary on the Epistles to the Philippians and to Philemon*, 169.

In this letter Paul is, as Johnson puts it, "unexpectedly diplomatic, urbane, even witty," using several elegant puns.[58] The bitter sarcasm in the pun in Galatians 5:12 differs drastically from the gentle compassion expressed in the pun in Philemon 11. Dodd therefore claims: "Its chief interest is in the light it throws on Paul himself at a moment when he is neither the preacher, the controversialist, the theologian, nor the ecclesiastical authority, but simply a man writing to a friend in the interests of another friend."[59]

The image of Paul as fond of wrangling, determined to blast his opponents off the theological map, a bull in an ecclesiastical china shop, is distorted. In this letter we have a better glimpse of the real Paul, and certainly a Paul more congenial to American sensibilities. He does not project himself as the all-wise and overbearing apostle that people think him to be. He makes no demands and bends over backwards to help others do the right thing, without offending them.

Jewett goes so far as to argue that our picture of Paul as an intellectual warrior derives from a European legacy that has projected its own eristic style (the love of wrangling) on to Paul. He calls it "The Eurocentric Paul—Painted in Blood."[60] This attitude interprets all of Paul's letters as "expressions of theological combat," marked by a "take no prisoners" style. But that picture, which overlays the intense Galatians' dispute on nearly all of Paul's letters, diminishes or ignores evidence where Paul clearly tries to find common ground, is tolerant of differing points of view, is gentle as a nurse (1 Thess. 2:7; see 1 Cor. 4:20; Gal. 4:19–20), and is considered by some to be far too meek (2 Cor. 10:1).[61] We meet in the letter to Philemon a Paul who sees the best in a runaway slave and an irate master and who knows that the gospel takes root and spreads when individuals are joined in Christ.

---

58. Luke Timothy Johnson, *The Writings of the New Testament: An Interpretation* (Philadelphia: Fortress, 1986), 354.

59. C. H. Dodd, "Philemon," in *The Abingdon Bible Commentary*, ed. F. C. Eiselen, E. Lewis, and D. G. Downey (New York/Nashville: Abingdon, 1929), 1292.

60. Jewett gets the imagery from Stuart Miller, whom he quotes (*Paul: The Apostle to America*, 7; citing Miller's *Painted in Blood: Understanding Europeans* [New York: Atheneum, 1987], 224):

"Over and over again, I have found that beneath the polished appearances of culture, if you hold them long enough in your view you will hear among Europeans the grunt and clash of weapon on shield, the bang of egotistical mace on heavy buckler, the harsh splintering of a lance and the puffing into temporary retreats: all the back and forth of the armored conflict of social selves endlessly contending for place and mastery."

61. Jewett, *Paul: The Apostle to America*, 3–12.

Appendix

BECAUSE OF ITS parallels to Paul's letter to Philemon, it has become customary for commentaries on Philemon to include Pliny the Younger's appeal to Sabinianus for a freedman who had fled to him to request his intervention. Pliny enjoyed a prosperous legal and administrative career during the reigns of Domitian, Nerva, and Trajan. He is famous for his carefully articulated personal letters, revealing the customs, perspectives, and activities of the Roman upper class.[62]

To Sabinianus

Your freedman, whom you lately mentioned as having displeased you, has been with me; he threw himself at my feet and clung there with as much submission as he could have done at yours. He earnestly requested me with many tears, and even with the eloquence of silent sorrow, to intercede for him; in short, he convinced me by his whole behaviour, that he sincerely repents of his fault. And I am persuaded he is thoroughly reformed, because he seems entirely sensible of his delinquency.

I know that you are angry with him, and I know too, it is not without reason; but clemency can never exert itself without more applause, than when there is the justest cause for resentment. You once had an affection for this man, and, I hope, will have again: in the meanwhile, let me only prevail with you to pardon him. If he should incur your displeasure hereafter, you will have so much the stronger plea in excuse for your anger, as you shew yourself more exorable to him now. Allow something to his youth, to his tears, and to your own natural mildness of temper: do not make him uneasy any longer, and I will add too, do not make yourself so; for a man of your benevolence of heart cannot be angry without feeling great uneasiness.

I am afraid, were I to join my entreaties with his, I should seem rather to compel, than request you to forgive him. Yet I will not scruple to do it; and so much the more fully and freely as I have very sharply and severely reproved him, positively threatening never to interpose again in his behalf. But though it was proper to say this to him, in order to make him more fearful of offending, I do not say it to you. I may, perhaps, again have occasion to intreat you upon his account, and again obtain your forgiveness; supposing, I mean his error should be such as may become me to intercede for, and you to pardon.

Farewell.

---

62. See Pliny, *Epistles* 9.21 (found in LCL 2:220–23).

The response to this entreaty was favorable, and Pliny writes back to express his satisfaction.[63]

> I greatly approve of your having, under conduct of my letter, received again into your family and favour, a freedman, whom you once admitted into a share of your satisfaction. It will afford you, I doubt not, great satisfaction. It certainly, at least, has me, both as it is a proof that you are capable of being governed in your anger, and as it is an instance of your paying so much regard to me, as either to obey my authority or to yield to my entreaty. You will accept therefore, at once, both of my applause and thanks. At the same time, I must advise you for the future to be placable toward erring servants, though there should be none to interpose in their behalf.
>
> Farewell.

Pliny's appeal differs from Paul's first of all in that he makes it on behalf of a freedman who has incurred his patron's wrath and not a slave. There are other differences. He places an emphasis on the patron's justifiable anger with his freedman. He stresses the freedman's penitence and abject appeal for forgiveness. He tells how he sharply rebuked the man and threatened him with future punishment. The freedman was put in his proper place in the caste system. Finally, Pliny makes an appeal for mercy and forgiveness.

Paul makes an unheard-of appeal for a slave who, in my opinion, has run away—a far greater offense. But he says nothing of anger, penitence, or threats. He does not say that Onesimus has learned his lesson and now accepts his servile station in life and will be properly subservient. He insists instead that he be received as a brother in Christ and as an equal to Paul. Both Pliny and Paul make humanitarian appeals. Christian values and motives, however, govern only one of these appeals.

---

63. Pliny, *Epistles* 9.24 (found in LCL 2:228–31).

Outline of Philemon

I. Salutation (1–3)
II. Thanksgiving (4–7)
III. Main Body (8–18)
    A. The First Mention of Onesimus (8–12)
    B. Paul's Unfulfilled Desire to Keep Onesimus with Him (13–14)
    C. The Request to Receive Onesimus as a Brother (15–16)
    D. The Request Backed by Paul's Pledge (17–18)
IV. Conclusion (19–25)[64]

---

64. Jeffrey A. D. Weima, *Neglected Endings: The Significance of the Pauline Letter Closings*, JSNTSup 101 (Sheffield: JSOT, 1994), 231, argues convincingly that the conclusion begins with the autograph (see Gal. 6:11–18) and recapitulates the purpose of the letter.

Selected Bibliography
on Philemon

Note: See also the bibliography on Colossians for list of commentaries on Philemon that are combined with commentaries on Colossians.

Buttrick, George A. "Philemon: Exposition," in *The Interpreter's Bible*. Ed. G. Buttrick. Nashville: Abingdon, 1955, 11:555–73.

Dodd, C. H. "Philemon," in *The Abingdon Bible Commentary*. Ed. F. C. Eiselen, E. Lewis, and D. G. Downey. New York/Nashville: Abingdon, 1929, 1292–94.

Donfried, Karl P., and I. Howard Marshall. *The Theology of the Shorter Pauline Letters*. Cambridge: Cambridge Univ. Press, 1993.

Kim, Chan Hie. *Form and Structure of the Familiar Greek Letter of Recommendation*. Missoula, Mont.: SBL, 1972.

Knox, John. *Philemon Among the Letters of Paul*. Rev. ed. New York/Nashville: Abingdon, 1959.

_____. "Philemon: Introduction and Exegesis," in *The Interpreter's Bible*. Ed. G. Buttrick. Nashville: Abingdon, 1955, 11:555–73.

Peterson, Norman R. *Rediscovering Paul: Philemon and the Sociology of Paul's Narrative World*. Philadelphia: Fortress, 1985.

Vincent, Marvin R. *A Critical and Exegetical Commentary on the Epistles to the Philippians and to Philemon*. ICC. Edinburgh: T. & T. Clark, 1897.

Wansick, Craig S. *Chained in Christ: The Experience and Rhetoric of Paul's Imprisonments*. JSNTSup 130. Sheffield: Sheffield Academic Press, 1996.

Philemon 1–7

P AUL, A PRISONER of Christ Jesus, and Timothy our
brother,
To Philemon our dear friend and fellow worker, ²to
Apphia our sister, to Archippus our fellow soldier and to the
church that meets in your home:
³Grace to you and peace from God our Father and the
Lord Jesus Christ.
⁴I always thank my God as I remember you in my prayers,
⁵because I hear about your faith in the Lord Jesus and your
love for all the saints. ⁶I pray that you may be active in sharing
your faith, so that you will have a full understanding of every
good thing we have in Christ. ⁷Your love has given me great
joy and encouragement, because you, brother, have refreshed
the hearts of the saints.

PAUL'S BRIEF LETTER to Philemon follows the standard letter form that we find throughout antiquity. It begins with the name of the writer, then
the name(s) of the addressees, and a greeting.
Thereupon follows the body of the letter. At the end Paul appends concluding comments and further greetings, this time from his coworkers, and
he closes with another brief salutation.

The Salutation (1–3)

PAUL BEGINS HIS appeal to Philemon by identifying himself as a prisoner of
Christ Jesus, the only time this epithet appears in a salutation in Paul's letters. He may simply want to inform Philemon of his personal situation.[1] But
he may also wish to engage his readers' sympathy.[2] His prisoner's chains
come up frequently in the letter (see vv. 9, 10, 13, 23; see also Eph. 3:1; 4:1;
Phil. 1:7, 13, 14, 17; Col. 4:18), and the image of a dear friend shackled for
the cause of Christ would have an emotional affect.[3]

---

1. See O'Brien, *Colossians, Philemon*, 194.
2. See Dunn, *The Epistles to the Colossians and to Philemon*, 311.
3. On the use of chains in imprisonment, see Brian Rapske, *The Book of Acts and Paul in
Roman Custody* (Grand Rapids: Eerdmans, 1994), 25–28, 31, 206–9.

Some argue, however, that Paul treats "prisoner of Christ Jesus" as a title of honor, almost as if it were part of his name. Whether this last view is correct or not, Paul would have appreciated the double meaning of the phrase. He is now physically locked up because of his work for Christ, but metaphorically he has been Christ's prisoner for years (see 2 Cor. 2:14–17; Phil. 3:12–13). The love of Christ constrains him far more than his present manacles. He is Christ's prisoner, not Caesar's.

I would challenge the view that Paul had any intention of appealing to some high rank as a prisoner to lend greater authority to his message that the recipients must obey.[4] On the contrary, his imprisonment is something that others might consider a cause for shame (see Phil. 1:12–18; 2 Tim. 1:8).[5] More likely he identifies himself as a prisoner to remove any power issues before he makes his behest. Luther argued that Paul does not use force or compulsion "as lay within his rights; but he empties himself of his rights to compel Philemon also to waive his rights."[6] He diminishes his own status and will boost Philemon's before asking something that can threaten his friend's prestige in the community at large. As a prisoner, Paul shares the social alienation of the slave, and chains were also something used to keep would-be runaway slaves from escaping.[7] He therefore appeals to Philemon as a friend in distressed circumstances, not as his spiritual director.

As the first person listed in the salutation, most assume that Philemon is the principle addressee. Since Onesimus comes from Colosse (Col. 4:9), Philemon must also live in Colosse as a relatively well-to-do host of a church. We do not know how Paul became acquainted with Philemon. They may have met when Philemon was in Ephesus on a business trip. Regardless, Paul regards him as his fellow worker, a title bestowed on those engaged in the same missionary task as Paul.[8] Theophylact perceptively commented on the terms, "dear friend and fellow worker": "If beloved he will grant the favor; if

---

4. See Lohse, *Colossians and Philemon*, 189, who contends that the personal costs from his imprisonment for the gospel "allow him to speak to the community with greater authority." In my opinion, such an interpretation misreads this letter.

5. Later scribes who emended the text to read "apostle" (D*) or "slave" (323, 945) apparently did not attach any honor to the title, "prisoner of Christ."

6. Martin Luther, "Preface to the Epistle of Saint Paul to Philemon," in *Luther's Works* (Philadelphia: Fortress, 1960), 35:390.

7. Andrew Wilson, "The Pragmatic of Politeness and Pauline Epistolography: A Case Study of the Letter to Philemon," *JSNT* 48 (1992): 113, contends that Paul seeks "to emphasize his situation as a prisoner and hence by analogy his social solidarity with Onesimus."

8. Paul's other named fellow workers include Prisca and Aquila (Rom. 16:3); Urbanus (16:9); Epaphroditus (Phil. 2:25); Euodia, Syntyche, and Clement (Phil. 4:3); Aristarchus, Mark, and Jesus Justus (Col. 4:11); and Epaphras, Demas, and Luke (Philem. 24).

a fellow-worker, he will not retain the slave, but will send him forth again for the service of preaching."[9]

Timothy, the cosender of the letter, is identified simply as "the brother" (v. 1); and Apphia is identified only as "the sister." These are normal terms in the New Testament for Christians (see Rom. 16:1; 1 Cor. 7:15; 9:5; James 2:15).[10] Apphia is probably Philemon's wife. As the *paterfamilias*, the male head of the family, Philemon had absolute authority over all others in his household, and Paul need only deal with him. But since wives were charged with running the affairs of the household, Apphia would have a stake in the disposition of the case concerning their slave. Apphia must also be convinced that this is the right thing to do.[11]

Most have assumed that Archippus is Philemon and Apphia's son. Houlden dismisses this possibility as legend taking over when history fails.[12] If Archippus is not a member of Philemon's household, the title "fellow soldier" suggests that he is active in some ministry for the church. Paul uses the same term to describe Epaphroditus in Philippians 2:25, who risked his life to fulfill his mission and to give Paul aid. The image refers more to "dedication and discipline" than "fierceness and warlike behavior."[13] Archippus is a conscript who serves a far more noble King than the sentries assigned to keep watch over Paul. Caird speculates that Archippus exercised a leadership role in the church, perhaps as a replacement for Epaphras, since Paul singles him out in Colossians 4:17.[14] We cannot know for sure.

Paul also addresses "the church that meets in your home."[15] This means that the letter is not an exclusively private note to Philemon; the whole

---

9. Cited by Vincent, *A Critical and Exegetical Commentary on the Epistles to the Philippians and to Philemon*, 176.

10. The term "brother" and "sister" in Greek are distinguished only by a masculine (*adelphos*) or feminine ending (*adelphe*).

11. In the novel *Uncle Tom's Cabin*, the death of his daughter Eva led Augustine St. Clare to read his Bible and decide to free all his slaves. He died before he could put his plans into effect, and his widow had no intention to free them. Instead, she sent Tom to the slave auction.

12. Houlden, *Paul's Letters from Prison*, 228.

13. Dunn, *The Epistles to the Colossians and to Philemon*, 312.

14. Caird, *Paul's Letters from Prison*, 214. The three terms *fellow worker*, *sister*, and *fellow soldier* do not imply different church functions.

15. The "your" in Greek is singular, "thy house," and refers to Philemon. We find mention of other house churches in Acts 5:42; Rom. 16:5; 1 Cor. 16:19; Col. 4:15. See Robert Banks, *Paul's Idea of Community: The Early Churches in Their Historical Setting* (Grand Rapids: Eerdmans, 1980); and V. Branick, *The House Church in the Writings of Paul* (Wilmington, Del.: Michael Glazier, 1989). Dunn, *The Epistles to the Colossians and to Philemon*, 313, suggests that Paul does not address them as "the saints in Colosse" (as in Col. 1:2) because Philemon's house church was not the only one in the city, or because the letter was meant for them alone.

church is included in the appeal. Why does Paul address the whole church on what seems to us to be a private matter? One could argue that by doing so Paul subtly intensifies the pressure on Philemon to comply with his request.[16] I think the explanation lies elsewhere. Paul sees Philemon's two households, the natural and the spiritual, intersecting. Therefore, the whole church, not just his master, must accept Onesimus, particularly if Paul would like him to be set free for ministry.[17] The slave's flight showed disloyalty and jeopardized the harmony and welfare of the household in which he lived, and he needs their forgiveness, welcome, and spiritual support. Consequently, they also need to know what has happened to him since his departure and to accept him back as a brother.

In this context, Paul's greeting, "Grace ... and peace," are not meaningless words. They remind Philemon that he has already experienced God's grace through Jesus Christ. He is now expected to extend grace to a slave, now a brother, who has wronged him. If he does so, he will know more fully the peace of God and of the Lord Jesus Christ. Peace does not just appear out of the blue; Christians must make it. Philemon has an exceptional but difficult opportunity to do just that.

Paul's Thanksgiving for Philemon (4–7)

PAUL MUST HAVE spent a significant amount of time in prayer each day, giving thanks for and interceding on behalf of all his churches, coworkers, and their benefactors. He tells Philemon how he prays for him and lets him know the basis of his thanksgiving to God for him. The "your" in "your faith in the Lord Jesus and your love for all the saints" is singular and indicates that Paul directs his remarks only to Philemon, who alone had the power to grant his request. Paul is not trying to soften up Philemon with praise before broaching the topic of Onesimus's status. He normally offers congratulatory thanksgivings in his letters (Rom. 1:8–9; 1 Cor. 1:4; Phil. 1:3–5; Col. 1:3–4; 1 Thess. 1:2–3; 2 Thess. 1:3–4; 2 Tim. 1:3–5). His tribute to Philemon for his faith and love is identical to his praise of all the Colossians (Col. 1:4).[18]

---

16. See Peterson, *Rediscovering Paul*, 99–102. But the matter of a runaway slave came solely under the jurisdiction of his master's domestic court. The master presided as sovereign judge, and his decision was law.

17. Wall, *Colossians and Philemon*, 215, notes that if Philemon responds the way Paul expects, Onesimus will be "included as a member of the congregation, the equal of everyone in the house he once served as a slave."

18. Dunn, *The Epistles to the Colossians and to Philemon*, 316, comments: "In this case at least the rhetorical technique of the Pauline letters ... seems to be neither contrived nor merely manipulative but a fulsome expression of genuine respect and regard."

The word order of verse 5 in the Greek reads literally, "the love and the faith which you have for (*pros*) the Lord and unto (*eis*) all the saints." It forms a chiasm:

A the love
  B the faith
    C which you have
  B' toward the Lord Jesus
A' and unto all the saints

Since this way of expressing thoughts is unfamiliar to us, the NIV correctly prevents confusion by making clear that the faith is in Jesus Christ and the love is for the saints.[19] The chiasm, however, shows how closely intertwined faith in the Lord Jesus and love for others are. Faith in Christ is the impetus for love for others, and together they make one a Christian. Missing either faith in Christ or love for others renders any claim to be Christian a deadly lie (see 1 John 3:10). Paul notes that Philemon's love is directed to *all* the saints. He does not discriminate, which suggests that he would not exclude from his love slaves who are in Christ.

The opening thanksgiving in Paul's letters always contains a shorthand outline of what will follow in the letter, and Philemon is no exception. Seven words from verses 4–7 reappear later in the letter: "love" (vv. 5, 7, 9, 16); "prayers" (vv. 4, 22); "partnership," "partner" (vv. 6 ["sharing," NIV], 17); "good" (vv. 6, 14 ["favor," NIV]); "heart" (vv. 7, 12, 20); "refresh" (vv. 7, 20); "brother" (vv. 7, 20). Philemon has an exemplary record for showing his love and helping fellow Christians, which gives Paul the confidence to ask him to show his love again for another saint.[20] This particular saint, Onesimus, has done Philemon personal injury. Yet he too has become a brother and more. He has become Paul's "heart" (v. 12). Paul languishes in his chains, and his "heart" now needs refreshing from his partner, Philemon.

Paul moves in verse 6 from thanksgiving to an intercessory prayer.[21] Every Pauline letter contains verses that puzzle interpreters, and what Paul intends to say in this verse is unclear. Interpreters have suggested a dizzying array of

---

19. It matches the thanksgiving in Col. 1:4: "because we have heard of your faith in Christ Jesus and of the love you have for all the saints." See also Eph. 1:15, "your faith in the Lord Jesus and your love for all the saints." Other options ignore the chiasmus and interpret "faith" to mean "fidelity" or "faithfulness" toward Christ and the saints, or they understand it as "confidence" in Christ and the saints.

20. Did Paul hear about Philemon's love for the saints from Onesimus, who spoke graciously of his master?

21. The phrase "and I pray" is not present in the Greek but is supplied from verse 4 to show that this verse is dependent on verse 4, not verse 5.

options, and some even despair of ever fully understanding what Paul means. The text literally reads: "in order that your sharing of the faith ['your' can go with sharing or faith] may become active in the recognition of every good that is in us toward Christ." One wonders if Paul's extreme care leading up to the mention of Onesimus is behind this diffuse expression. The exegetical problems center on the meaning of the phrases "the sharing [fellowship] of your faith" (*he koinonia tes pisteos sou*), "every good" (*pantos agathou*), and "toward Christ" (*eis Christon*).[22]

Regarding the phrase "the *koinonia* of your faith," Paul occasionally uses the noun *koinonia* to refer to a charitable gift for others (2 Cor. 9:13; Phil. 1:5 [4:15–16]; cf. Heb. 13:16). The phrase "the sharing of your faith" could then cite Philemon's generosity that issues from his faith. When a genitive denoting a person follows *koinonia*, it usually means "fellowship" (see 1 Cor. 1:9; 2 Cor. 13:13).[23] The phrase could refer to the fellowship created by your faith. When *koinonia* is followed by the genitive of an impersonal noun, however, it usually means "participation" or "sharing" (see 2 Cor. 8:4; Phil. 3:10). The NIV translation correctly captures this meaning.

But by rendering the phrase, "that you may be active in sharing your faith," the NIV misleads. Paul is not praying for success in Philemon's evangelistic or pastoral work. The phrase does not refer to witnessing to others who do not have faith; instead, it has in view sharing the same faith with other believers. Paul is referring to "the mutuality of Christian life which springs from a common participation in the body of Christ."[24] The NEB captures the meaning best: "your fellowship with us in the common faith." Shared faith in Christ has a bonding character and welds us to others who share the same experience of faith. Paul is praying for Philemon to grow in the faith he shares with Paul and others, including Onesimus. This shared faith will be the basis of his appeal.

The phrase "become active" presents no difficulty: Participation together in the faith is to become productive in promoting thorough knowledge. Knowledge (*epignosis*) refers to moral insight, which knows what is important (see Col. 1:9–10; 2:2). To be worth anything, this knowledge must be acted upon, not simply possessed.[25] The church knows and confesses that "God was

---

22. Harald Riesenfeld, "Faith and Love Promoting Hope: An Interpretation of Philemon v. 6," in *Paul and Paulinism*, ed. Morna D. Hooker and Stephen G. Wilson (London: SPCK, 1982), 251–57, offers an excellent discussion of the various options.

23. Phil. 1:5 is an exception because it is determined by "in the gospel," not by the pronoun.

24. Wright, *Colossians and Philemon*, 175.

25. Lightfoot, *Saint Paul's Epistles to the Colossians and to Philemon*, 336. Riesenfeld, "Faith and Love Promoting Hope," 253, comments: "Thorough understanding is the result and the reward of faith manifesting itself in deeds of love."

pleased to have all his fullness dwell in [Christ], and through him to reconcile to himself all things, whether things on earth or things in heaven, by making peace through his blood, shed on the cross" (Col. 1:19–20). It can only
be the visible witness of Christ's reconciliation of the world to God if its
members actively discern the will of God in their lives and apply it to their
relationships with fellow Christians and fellow human beings.

Several social factors, however, press on Philemon that might sway his
decision in the wrong direction. He will lose face in the community if he
capitulates to a runaway slave. Philemon may have been a figure of some status in the wider society, and he will forfeit that standing if he becomes known
as someone soft on slavery. He must also bear the financial cost of freeing a
slave and cope with possibly throwing his whole household into an uproar
by his extreme leniency. The right decision requires an extraordinary exercise of faith, love, and knowledge.

"Every good" refers to every good deed (NIV, "every good thing"). Moule
contends that the good usually refers to something "which is *done* or *performed* (as in v. 14 below), rather than as a *possession* or the *object of knowledge*."[26]
Paul clarifies what he means by good in verse 14: "But I did not want to do
anything without your consent, so that any favor [lit., good] you do will be
spontaneous and not forced." In the immediate context, then, Paul relates the
good to the granting of his request concerning Onesimus.[27]

The NIV renders the last phrase of verse 6, "every good thing we have in
Christ," referring to what Christians have as a whole. It is more likely that
eis Christon expresses a goal "for Christ" (see NASB, NRSV, JB).[28] Christ is the final
object of the Christian hope and the ultimate goal of the Christian life.[29]

With this enigmatic prayer, which I translate, "I pray that your participation in the faith may become active in the knowledge of every good deed
which is in us [which we may do] for Christ," Paul prepares Philemon for his
request. He intends to entrust the decision about Onesimus to Philemon's

---

26. Moule, *The Epistles to the Colossians and to Philemon*, 143.

27. Lohse, *Colossians and Philemon*, 194, and Riesenfeld, "Faith and Love Promoting Hope,"
255–56, make a strong case that it refers to the content of Christian hope, the salvation
offered in preaching that God is working in us. Lohse comments: "If Philemon recognizes
'the good' that God has given us and that consequently is 'in us' . . . he will also comprehend
the will of God and heed the admonition of the Apostle. . . ." Riesenfeld sees verse 6 as a
parallel to Eph. 1:17–19. He interprets "every good thing we have in Christ" as corre-
sponding to "the riches of the glorious inheritance in the saints" (Eph. 1:18) and notes similar expressions in Rom. 8:28; Heb. 9:11; 10:1 (e.g., "the good things to come").

28. "We have" also may refer to Paul and his work, which is how the NRSV renders it: "I
pray that the sharing of your faith may become effective when you perceive all the good
that we may do for Christ." See Knox, "Philemon: Introduction and Exegesis," 564–65.

29. Riesenfeld, "Faith and Love Promoting Hope," 257.

Christian moral insight. His fellowship in the faith should lead him to express his love and generosity again by welcoming Onesimus and releasing him for the work of the gospel.

Verse 7 gives the reason for Paul's thanksgiving and optimism. Philemon's past benevolence to fellow Christians shows him to be a man filled with Christian compassion, and his past generosity emboldens Paul to make an audacious request for Onesimus.[30] He rejoices because he is confident that one who has shown such love and brought such joy will not refuse to grant his entreaty.

THE SALUTATION AND thanksgiving sections of Paul's letters are usually quickly passed over in the study and preaching of Paul's letters. But they deserve careful attention. The salutation in Philemon is particularly instructive as Paul prepares to ask his dear friend to do something completely unheard of and to show unparalleled generosity.

The opening salutation and thanksgiving reinforces Paul relationship to Philemon and recalls Philemon's vital relationship to others in the church. He has a well-deserved reputation for doing good and being generous—refreshing the hearts of the saints. But the salutation also reveals that Paul believes that our goodness must be encouraged by a supportive community of believing Christians. He addresses this letter concerning a matter over which Philemon had sole legal jurisdiction to the entire church that meets in Philemon's house. Paul expects that the church will also listen in on this private request. He understands that individual moral decisions affect the entire believing community and apparently assumes that the best way to make ethical decisions is in a communal context of faith.

By addressing a seemingly "private" letter to the entire church, Paul insinuates that the church has some say in the personal relationships and business decisions that we may consider being ours alone. Our society prizes individualism, and most would not appreciate our church being allowed to overhear supposedly personal correspondence on how we should dispose of our property or how we should reconcile with another. We would probably resent it as unwanted meddling and an invasion of privacy. Our culture encourages us to regard religion as a purely private matter, which need brook no outside interference or authority.

Paul approached things differently. He assumed that Christians live and act out of a communal context, and the first-century church "functioned in

---

30. The perfect tense refers to something he had done in the past that had lasting results.

some sense as an extended family."[31] Trust and respect governed the community, and no secrets were to be hidden from others (see Acts 5:1–11). Dunn comments on verse 6 that "the corporate character of the shared faith is central to the thought; Paul had no desire to promote the ideal of religious faith as something private, that which a person enjoys alone and practices as a separate individual."[32] He therefore prays that Philemon's faith in Christ, which is shared with others, will help him to appreciate "the important roles that other believers, including Onesimus, have in his spiritual formation in Christ."[33]

 CHRISTIANS ARE NOT alone. When we are joined to Christ, we are joined to others. Recognizing how integrated we are with others who share the faith leads to greater understanding of its truth and to greater understanding of others. A recognition of the blessings we have all received freely by grace should promote our love and forgiveness of our fellow Christians. Wall astutely comments that "the spiritual well-being of the congregation will always be demonstrated publicly by the well-being of its social relationships."[34] The reconciliation of a disloyal slave with his master as brothers in Christ speaks volumes to the community within and without. It demonstrates how Christian faith recasts all relationships and how Christ reconciles all things (Col. 1:20). The letter provides "an opportunity to instruct an entire community in the principle of practical Christianity."[35]

Unfortunately, many have lost a sense of bonding with other Christians and generally see no interconnection between the business they conduct in their private household and their membership in a spiritual household. Many insist that they are free to manage their own lives without any thought to what other Christians might think or how it might affect them. In our culture we see the church more as "a voluntary association of people who happen to hold the same religious views."[36] Paul, however, saw membership in the church as something far more, and in this letter he shows how two households, the natural and the spiritual, intersect. He understood that what Philemon decided

31. Dunn, *The Epistles to the Colossians and to Philemon*, 313.
32. Ibid., 319.
33. Wall, *Colossians and Philemon*, 199.
34. Ibid., 212–13.
35. F. Forrester Church, "Rhetorical Structure and Design in Paul's Letter to Philemon," *HTR* 71 (1978): 34–35.
36. R. H. Strachan, *2 Corinthians*, Moffatt New Testament Commentary (London: Hodder and Stoughton, 1935), 62.

to do with his unfaithful slave, a purely private matter over which he had the final say, would have consequences for his whole house church. Paul allows Philemon to decide completely for himself what he will do, but he expects that he will consider how his decision will have impact on his community of faith. Since the house church meets in his home, his ethical decisions will have immediate repercussions for the whole church.

Things have not changed in this regard. How leaders respond to the demands of love in everyday decisions directly effects the spiritual health of the whole congregation. It matters greatly whether they show love or disdain for others, whether they refresh or drain the hearts of the saints, whether their actions stem from profound spiritual knowledge or from shallow spiritual illiteracy, whether they are motivated by selfishness or selflessness. The cause of Christ has had its reputation blackened by many who have ignored the effect of their business decisions on their church.

It may be helpful to have members of our church advise us in moral decisions that we now consider to be private matters. Left alone, we are more likely to make the wrong ethical decision. Surrounded by those who are committed to Christ and who pray together, we may be more likely to choose God's will. Our fellow Christians may be more toughminded in helping us put God's love to work in our lives.

Philemon 8–25

THEREFORE, ALTHOUGH IN Christ I could be bold and order you to do what you ought to do, ⁹yet I appeal to you on the basis of love. I then, as Paul—an old man and now also a prisoner of Christ Jesus—¹⁰I appeal to you for my son Onesimus, who became my son while I was in chains. ¹¹Formerly he was useless to you, but now he has become useful both to you and to me.

¹²I am sending him—who is my very heart—back to you. ¹³I would have liked to keep him with me so that he could take your place in helping me while I am in chains for the gospel. ¹⁴But I did not want to do anything without your consent, so that any favor you do will be spontaneous and not forced. ¹⁵Perhaps the reason he was separated from you for a little while was that you might have him back for good—¹⁶no longer as a slave, but better than a slave, as a dear brother. He is very dear to me but even dearer to you, both as a man and as a brother in the Lord.

¹⁷So if you consider me a partner, welcome him as you would welcome me. ¹⁸If he has done you any wrong or owes you anything, charge it to me. ¹⁹I, Paul, am writing this with my own hand. I will pay it back—not to mention that you owe me your very self. ²⁰I do wish, brother, that I may have some benefit from you in the Lord; refresh my heart in Christ. ²¹Confident of your obedience, I write to you, knowing that you will do even more than I ask.

²²And one thing more: Prepare a guest room for me, because I hope to be restored to you in answer to your prayers.

²³Epaphras, my fellow prisoner in Christ Jesus, sends you greetings. ²⁴And so do Mark, Aristarchus, Demas and Luke, my fellow workers.

²⁵The grace of the Lord Jesus Christ be with your spirit.

Original Meaning

PAUL BEGINS THE body of the letter with a delicate reference to Onesimus's return as one newly converted to Christ (vv. 8–12). He underscores his great value to him by mentioning that he would have liked nothing better than to keep Onesimus with him (vv. 13–14). He then makes his formal request that Philemon receive Onesimus as a brother (vv. 15–16) and backs up that request with a pledge to pay any damages that Onesimus may have cost his owner (vv. 17–18). He then concludes this brief letter (vv. 19–25) by reminding his good friend again of their close bonds and expressing his confidence that he will do even more than what Paul has specifically asked him to do. Final greetings from Paul's coworkers and a blessing close the letter.

The Return of Onesimus (8–12)

PAUL PREFACES HIS first reference to Onesimus by bringing up his boldness in Christ to command what ought to be done. Many commentators equate that boldness with his authority as an apostle. Lightfoot paraphrases it: "My office gives me authority to dictate thy duty in plain language, but love bids me plead as a suitor."[1]

If this is Paul's meaning, he subtly asserts his apostolic authority by saying that he refrains exercising it. Such a seemingly innocent statement would contain a veiled threat: "Do what I ask freely, but if you don't, I will command you." He cloaks his authoritarian posture with a thin veil of politeness. He then only pretends to be a helpless petitioner and fully intends to lower the boom if he is not obeyed. This interpretation is wrong for three reasons. The word "boldness" is not a synonym for "authority."[2] Paul calls Philemon his partner (v. 17) and treats him as an equal. Third, showing him an iron hand in a velvet glove of humility would undermine all of the politeness strategies that Paul employs to avoid the least hint of compulsion.

Wilson understands Paul's statement quite differently:

> Ordinarily, a request from Paul would have the *prima facie* force of an apostolic command. If Paul genuinely wants to reduce the force of such a command, and turn it into a friendly request, he needs to formulate a new pragmatic principle, and this he can only do by describing the new "rules."[3]

Paul does this by making clear that his request comes from one brother to another. He bends over backwards to avoid any hint of authoritarianism, and we should not read it into the text. He does not pull rank and issues no command but instead humbly "appeals" (vv. 9–10) and offers his personal

---

1. Lightfoot, *Saint Paul's Epistles to the Colossians and to Philemon*, 337. See also Lohse, *Colossians and Philemon*, 198; Ulrich Wickert, "Der Philemonbrief—Privatbrief oder apostolisches Schreiben?" *ZNW* 52 (1961): 230–38.
2. "Boldness" (*parresia*) does not have the meaning "authority" in the New Testament but means "outspokenness" (see 2 Cor. 7:4), "courage, "or "fearlessness."
3. Wilson, "The Pragmatics of Politeness," 115.

financial guarantee as an equal partner (v. 18). Paul does not want to coerce Philemon's decision in any way or box him into a corner so that he will lose face in granting his request.

"Boldness" refers to the right to speak freely, frankly, and fearlessly, which any Christian can do. Paul's right to speak with candor and to command does not derive from his apostolic office but from being "in Christ." Any Christian, apostle or not, bishop or not, can tell a brother or sister in Christ to do what they ought to do. Such people may obey out of deference to the authority of the one who commands or out of fear of punishment (loss of face or position) for failing to comply. Paul would rather that Christians do what is good out of faith and love because they know it is the Christian thing to do (vv. 5–7).

Many have noted how reticent Paul is in this letter, only dropping hints here and there about what he wants his friend to do. Verse 9 explains why. He wants his friend to do what is right but will not command, because he wants Philemon to draw his own conclusions and to make his own decision about what is fitting in Christ to do. Paul understands that interfering directly in a master's relationship with his slave is as impertinent as someone today ordering about another's children or meddling in how they should be disciplined. Most parents do not appreciate unsolicited advice on how they ought to raise or discipline their children; masters in the ancient world did not want to be told what to do with their slaves.

Philemon's culture had conditioned him to view slaves as less than full persons who were deservedly consigned to their lot by fate, and Philemon would have been expected to exact revenge on one who stole away. But what was culturally permissible for dealing with a runaway slave was at odds with what is fitting in Christ.[4] A captured runaway in the first century could expect to receive anything from a brutal flogging to branding, from being sold to work on a farm to being sold to work in the galleys or mines, from crucifixion to being thrown to the wild beasts in the arena.[5] He might also be compelled

---

4. The same word, *to anekon*, is translated "fitting" in Col. 3:18.

5. Heinz Bellen, *Studien zur Sklavenflucht im römischen Kaiserreich* (Wiesbaden: Franz Steiner, 1971) 17–31. A letter (dating from A.D. 298) from Aurelius Sarapammon to a friend reveals how runaways normally were dealt with:

> I commission you by this writ to journey to the famous city of Alexandria and search for my slave, by name . . . about 35 years old, known to you. When you have found him you shall place him in custody with authority to shut him up and whip him, and to lay a complaint before the proper authorities against any persons who have harbored him, with a demand for satisfaction. (POxy 1643; vol. 14)

Since a slave could not be penalized by forfeiting his status, severe physical punishment seemed to be the only alternative. According to Hippolytus (*Refutatio* 9.12.4), a Christian master in the third century punished a runaway slave by sending him to a treadmill.

to wear an iron collar engraved with the name and address of the owner and the command "Catch me for I have fled my master."

Forgiveness was not the norm in Philemon's world, but it is a fundamental requirement for Christians (Matt. 6:14–15; 18:21–22). Paul makes that clear in Colossians 3:12–14, where he tells them that God's chosen people are to be clothed with compassion, kindness, humility, gentleness, and patience, and to be as forgiving as the Lord. Paul seeks to activate Philemon's Christian consciousness to make him aware of what is required for him to do in this situation, and his request puts flesh and bones on the abstract ethical exhortation to have compassion, kindness, humility, gentleness, and patience. He expects Philemon, as a Christian who has been renewed in the image of his Creator (Col. 3:10), to show love and to forgive his grievance against Onesimus, just as the Lord forgave him his sins.

Love becomes the virtue that wraps the community of saints together into a perfect unity and is the touchstone of Christian conduct. It forms the basis of Paul's appeal. In his hymn to love in 1 Corinthians, Paul writes that "It is not rude, it is not self-seeking, it is not easily angered, it keeps no record of wrongs" (13:5). "It always protects, always trusts, always hopes, always perseveres" (13:7). Because we have redemption and forgiveness of sins in Christ (Col. 1:14), Philemon should forgive his repentant and converted slave the wrongs committed against him and give him his earthly redemption.

What is frequently overlooked is that Paul also expects Onesimus to act from love. Paul sends him home with a ringing endorsement, but he has no guarantee that Philemon will honor it. Onesimus must be willing to accept with grace whatever Philemon might decide in his case, which could include severe punishment or being sold to another master.[6] Like the prodigal son returning home, he can only cast himself on the mercy of his master. He has now become his brother in Christ, but he surely knows that brothers do not always act with love toward one another. Paul makes his request with confidence because of Philemon's previous demonstration of a loving spirit (vv. 5, 7), but Onesimus cannot expect an impartial arbitrator to intervene decisively for him. He returns because of love and hopes that he will be received in love.

Verse 9b begins a new sentence (as in the NIV), which highlights Paul's wisdom of experience and his suffering and weakness: "an old man and . . . a prisoner of Christ" (v. 9), though Paul is not trying to augment his authority. "Old man" does not mean that Paul is aged or has one foot in the grave.

---

6. The verb to send back (*anapempo*) is used in Luke 23:7, 11, 15; and Acts 25:21 for sending accused persons (Jesus and Paul) to a judge. In this case, Paul sends Onesimus to Philemon who is the judge making the final decision.

Philo lists the seven ages of man, according to Hippocrates, and the elderly man (*presbytes*) is the next to last stage (from age 50 to 56).[7] What is important for his argument is the implication that he is older than Philemon. According to Leviticus 19:32, the younger should "show respect for the elderly and revere your God" (see Sir. 8:6), and the customary deference shown to elders in ancient cultures gives Paul more leeway to make his extraordinary request.[8]

Paul pulls at Philemon's heartstrings by reminding him of his captivity for preaching the gospel (see v. 13) while appealing to an old man's privilege. The request for Onesimus may seem obvious and natural to those of us who live in societies that consider slavery to be a heinous sin against human decency. In Paul's culture, however, thoughts of abolitionist reform were unheard of and a world without slavery was inconceivable. Paul's plea to welcome Onesimus and his hints that he should be given his freedom were unprecedented. He therefore begs that allowances be made for the quirks of an old man who is now imprisoned.

Before making his actual appeal Paul smoothes the way with four deft touches.[9] (1) He lets Philemon know that Onesimus has become a Christian.[10]

(2) The father/son imagery used to relate this conversion conveys Paul's close relationship to Onesimus.[11] He says he "begot" him (NIV, "who became my son") in chains.[12] Imprisonment did not neutralize the fruitfulness of Paul's ministry in making converts (see Phil. 1:12–14).

Paul then eases the tense situation further with a play on the name of Onesimus, which means "useful" in Greek.[13] Slaves bore the names that either

---

7. Philo, *On the Creation* 105. One may guess from this piece of information that Paul was born sometime in the first decade of the Christian era.

8. See R. A. Campbell, *The Elders: Seniority Within Earliest Christianity* (Edinburgh: T. & T. Clark, 1994).

9. Knox, *Philemon Among the Letters of Paul*, 22–24, interprets the force of the preposition *peri* in verse 10 to express the content of the request (see 2 Cor. 12:8). Paul is delicately asserting a claim on Onesimus; he wants Onesimus to continue in his service. The NIV translation, "I appeal . . . for . . . Onesimus" could be taken as support for this theory. But the *peri* means "concerning him" in the sense of "on his behalf," not in the sense of asking for him to be given to me.

10. In the Greek, Onesimus's name stands last in this verse so that Paul does not bring up his name until after he has affirmed that the runaway slave has become a Christian.

11. Paul refers to his churches as his dear or little children (1 Cor. 4:14; Gal. 4:19; 1 Thess. 2:11); he uses similar language to address his closest associates, Timothy (1 Cor. 4:17; Phil. 2:22; 1 Tim. 1:2, 18; 2 Tim. 1:2; 2:1) and Titus (Titus 1:4).

12. David Daube, "Onesimus," *HTR* 79 (1986): 40, notes that in rabbinic literature a proselyte is likened to a "child just born" (b. *Yebam.* 22a).

13. "Useful" was a degrading name, which one might give to a farm animal.

slave dealers gave them to extol their wares or that their masters gave them to express their hopes. "Formerly he was useless to you, but now he has become useful both to you and to me" (v. 11) contains a wordplay that can be found in other writers, but it becomes more poignant and memorable in this situation.

Paul takes the wordplay to still another level. The word *achrestos* ("useless") and *achristos* ("Christless") would have been pronounced exactly the same.[14] Onesimus was not useful before because he was without Christ![15] When he became a Christian, however, he became useful, *euchrestos*. Onesimus was not useful before because he was without Christ. But now that he is in Christ, he has become truly Onesimus, useful. Philemon's slave returns as the slave of Christ, having found his true identity.

(3) Paul is careful to note that Onesimus had already been useful to him before he sent him back to Philemon (v. 11). As a prisoner, Paul needed others to take care of his needs, fix his food, run errands, and keep him company (see Acts 24:23). Onesimus may have possessed special skills that enabled him to offer Paul even greater service than fulfilling menial chores. Paul's friendship with Philemon allows him to take for granted that he would have done as much as possible to help him.

Unknown to Philemon, Onesimus had represented him ("take your place") in serving Paul in the gospel (v. 13). As Scott points out, Paul gives Philemon full "credit for all this faithful labor. Onesimus had been acting for his master, who would only have been too happy, if he had been near at hand, to comfort his old friend who was suffering for the gospel."[16] As Philemon has refreshed the saints on numerous occasions, Onesimus, his slave, has refreshed Paul. Both have served others in the Lord.

(4) Paul intensifies his request by calling Onesimus his "very heart" (v. 12). He uses the term "heart" (*splangchna*) in all three sections of the letter (vv. 7, 12, 20). Paul has already praised Philemon for "refresh[ing] the hearts of the saints" (v. 7), referring to some benevolence that lifted their spirits, and he cannot imagine that Philemon will be callously indifferent to his own heart. In his conclusion, Paul will make yet another pun with Onesimus's name: "that I may have some benefit [*onaimen*] from you in the Lord; refresh my heart in Christ" (v. 20). He indirectly requests that Philemon refresh his heart as he had other Christians and that if it involves financial generosity on his part; he should not penalize Onesimus.

---

14. On Greek pronunciation, see Chrys C. Caragounis, "The Error of Erasmus and Un-Greek Pronunciation of Greek," *Filologia Neotestamentaria* 8 (1995): 151–85.

15. See Lohse, *Colossians and Philemon*, 200–1.

16. Scott, *The Epistles of Paul to the Colossians, to Philemon and to the Ephesians*, 108.

"Refreshing the heart" rarely appears in other ancient literature, and Clarke argues that its use by Paul (perhaps coined by him) highlights an important feature of Christianity. While other Greco-Roman religions did not think refreshing the lives and spirits of other adherents to be vital to piety, Paul's phrase reflects his Christian conviction that "all of one's actions should be directed to the benefit of others."[17]

Paul's Unfulfilled Desire to Keep Onesimus with Him (13–14)

PAUL EXPRESSES HIS personal preference, "I would have liked to keep him with me" (v. 13), but he puts aside his own wishes out of consideration for Philemon's rights and feelings. The use of the imperfect tense (*eboulomen*) may imply that Paul debated whether to send Onesimus back, but it places the burden of responsibility for Onesimus's delay in returning on Paul: He had kept the slave because of his usefulness. By sending back his child, his heart—someone who had become very useful to him—Paul exemplifies "the kind of selfless love he wishes to instil in Philemon."[18] He waived his own interests out of a sense of duty to Philemon. The implication is that Philemon should do the same for Paul.

There are two reasons why Paul sends Onesimus home. (1) Paul will do nothing without Philemon's specific consent (v. 14), nor will he try to make his ethical decisions for him. He refuses to take his friendship with Philemon for granted and assume that he would be delighted to learn that his slave was an indispensable help during Paul's incarceration and should stay on as long as Paul needed him. Nor did Paul allow Onesimus's conversion to override his sense of duty and assume that Onesimus's conversion now meant that Philemon should let bygones be bygones. The reality was that if Philemon rejected his appeal, Paul could do nothing except break relations with Philemon and perhaps encourage others to do so. That he calls his request a "good deed" (v. 14, NRSV) concedes that Paul and Onesimus are entirely subject to Philemon's goodwill. Goodwill is not something that can be dictated.[19] Philemon must decide for himself to do good.

---

17. Andrew D. Clarke, "'Refresh the Hearts of the Saints': A Unique Pauline Context?" *TynB* 47 (1996): 277–300.

18. Church, "Rhetorical Structure," 27.

19. Paul instructs the Corinthians: "Each man should give what he has decided in his heart to give, not reluctantly or under compulsion, for God loves a cheerful giver" (2 Cor. 9:7). God also loves a master who cheerfully forgives his slave and sets him free for a greater service. See 1 Cor. 9:16–17 and 1 Peter 5:2 for a similar weight attached to something offered voluntarily.

Old Testament law would also have allowed Paul to give Onesimus protection. "If a slave has taken refuge with you, do not hand him over to his master. Let him live among you wherever he likes and in whatever town he chooses. Do not oppress him" (Deut. 23:15–16). Roman law, however, strongly condemned anyone who corrupted another's slave or knowingly offered asylum to a fugitive slave. But the law is not a key factor in Paul's decision to send Onesimus back. Dunn astutely comments: "Paul makes it clear that he is sending Onesimus back not because of such legal obligations, but because of Onesimus's new status: wrongs done among fellow believers had to be sorted out as among fellow believers (v. 16; cf. 1 Cor. 6:1–8)."[20]

(2) The other reason for sending Onesimus home is the premium Paul places on a face-to-face reconciliation between two believers, a slave and an owner. The apostle's personal wishes therefore must yield to this greater end. Essentially he says in these verses, "I would like to keep him, but his reconciliation with you is more important."[21]

I find two indications in these verses that Paul would like Philemon to free Onesimus. (1) The first is his reference to Onesimus's help. He ties that service to the gospel ("helping me while I am in chains for the gospel").[22] Paul uses the verb "help" ("serve," *diakoneo*) elsewhere for Christian service (2 Cor. 3:3; 8:19, 20), and he uses the noun form (*diakonia*) in Colossians for service in the gospel ministry (Col. 1:7, 23, 25; 4:7, 17). From this delicately worded statement, Philemon could infer that Paul would like him to send Onesimus back to work with him or to be allowed to leave with Paul after his visit. Paul's need for help in the gospel was far greater than any need Philemon had of his slave.

(2) The other indication comes from his use of the word *to agathon* (the "good") in verse 14. Translations render it variously: "your good deed" (NRSV), "your kindness" (REB), "act of kindness" (NJB). These are better than the NIV's "any favor," because Paul is not simply asking a favor from Philemon but for him to do "a good thing" as a Christian brother. Philo comments on the law of slavery in Deuteronomy 18:12–85 and its requirement that a slave be set free after six years of service and uses the word "good" for giving the slave his freedom. He encourages that it be done without hesitation: "For a slave can have no greater boon ['good,' *agathon*] than freedom."[23] The "good" that Paul wants Philemon to do is to set free his slave.

---

20. Dunn, *The Epistles to the Colossians and to Philemon*, 329.

21. Paul sends Onesimus home for a face-to-face reconciliation between master and slave, but formal manumission could not be done by proxy. If Onesimus is to know freedom, he and his master must apply in person to a magistrate in the province (see Pliny, *Epistles* 7.16).

22. In Col. 1:23 Paul uses the phrase "the hope of the gospel"; here, the "chains of the gospel." Paradoxically, the gospel can be linked equally well to hope or chains.

23. Philo, *Special Laws* 2.84.

The Request to Receive Onesimus As a Brother (15–16)

PAUL CONTINUES TO speak with reserve and leads into his actual request with a "perhaps." The passive voice, "he was separated from you," is a euphemism for Onesimus's illegal flight. But the passive voice is also used in the New Testament to denote God's agency and further mitigates the seriousness of whatever Onesimus may have done by attributing it all to God's purposes. Gnilka states what many commentators have concluded: "Behind the passive formulation is to be presumed the activity of God, who is involved in the case."[24] Paul would like Philemon to see the hand of God in what has happened by insinuating that Onesimus's flight may have had some divine purpose.

This move is psychologically astute. The less malicious intent we attribute to the person who violates us in some way, the less anger we feel toward them. Couching Onesimus's departure in the grammar of God's purposes can only help Philemon ease his anger at his slave. The basic assumption is that God is the one who transformed Onesimus and that God *"separated the slave from Philemon for a time—in order to effect the transformation."*[25]

If this is so, then Philemon should ponder what God's will is for Onesimus. Why did the slave experience this transformation? Was it only to make him a good slave, or was he intended for something more as a slave of Christ? We can imagine that slaves who became sincere Christians served their masters more industriously (see Col. 3:22–25). But Paul does not revel in the transformation of a useless slave into a useful one, as if conversion's only purpose in such cases is to improve the service that slaves render their masters. God's designs, then, will not be complete until Philemon receives him as a beloved brother and sets him free for service in the gospel—hence Paul's use of "perhaps."[26]

Philemon has lost a slave for a brief time so that he can gain him back forever as a brother. Paul frames this comment as a business deal with spiritual dimensions by using accounting language for receipts (*apecho*; see Matt. 6:2, 5, 16; Phil. 4:18). The NIV translation "have him back for good" literally reads "have him back forever" and may miss a theological nuance. Paul is not saying that Onesimus's new faith will mean that his owner need never worry

---

24. Joachim Gnilka, *Der Philemonbrief*, HTKNT (Freiburg/Basel/Vienna: Herder, 1982), 50. We can see the divine passive at work in the NIV's translation of Col. 1:9. The passive verb in Greek (*plerothete*), "that you might be filled," is correctly translated into English with an active voice, "asking God to fill you."

25. Marion L. Soards, "Some Neglected Theological Dimensions of Paul's Letter to Philemon," *Perspectives in Religious Studies* 17 (1990): 216.

26. Clarice J. Martin, "The Rhetorical Function of Commercial Language in Paul's Letter to Philemon (Verse 18)," in *Persuasive Artistry: Studies in New Testament Rhetoric in Honor of George A. Kennedy*, ed. Duane F. Watson, JSNTSup 50 (Sheffield: JSOT, 1991), 328.

about his slave trying to escape again.[27] He alludes to the new relationship between them. Philemon receives Onesimus back as a fellow Christian, and they will be together in eternity. It is as if Paul says: "He will always be yours but on a different level, not as your possession, but as your brother."[28]

Paul speaks theologically of the transformed relationship between Onesimus and Philemon based on forgiveness and love. The phrase in verse 16, "both as a man and as a brother in the Lord," translates an ambiguous Greek phrase that reads literally, "both in the flesh and in the Lord." Paul may only be asking that Onesimus be treated with love as a fellow Christian. In the flesh, Onesimus remains legally Philemon's slave; but spiritually, he should be regarded and treated as much more—as a brother. Their spiritual union together "in the Lord" transcends the earthly master/slave relationship.

In other words, Paul affirms that Onesimus, the man, is far more than a piece of property. He is Philemon's equal before the Lord. Veyne comments on the master/slave relationship:

> Personal ties were highly unequal, and it was this inequality that was common to all slaves, however different their condition was in other respects. This common condition—involvement in an unequal personal relation with a master—is what makes "slavery" a meaningful word. Whether powerful or wretched, all slaves were spoken to in the tone and terms used in speaking to children and inferior beings.[29]

When love, warmth, care, and respect rule our treatment of others who may be socially, legally, and economically at a lower station in this world, all "flesh" categories eventually fade away.

Paul asks Philemon to consider Onesimus differently.[30] The question is, how differently? Can he still regard him as his slave and as his brother? Does Paul send Onesimus back as a contrite slave who will now resume his duties

---

27. Compare Ex. 21:2–6. The Hebrew law, however, does not govern Paul's discussion with Philemon.

28. Lightfoot, *Saint Paul's Epistles to the Colossians and to Philemon*, 342, writes: "Onesimus had obtained eternal life, and eternal life involves eternal interchange of friendship."

29. Paul Veyne, "The Roman Empire," in *A History of Private Life I: From Pagan Rome to Byzantium*, ed. Paul Veyne (Cambridge, Mass.: Harvard Univ, Press, 1987), 58. Slaves were regarded as nonpersons and treated as if they were invisible, perhaps a consequence of masters and mistresses being constantly surrounded by slaves. Absolute power over others can breed contempt for life. The violence and ruthlessness in the ancient world spilled over into the treatment of slaves, wives, and children. Slaves, in particular, were frequently victims of physical, psychological, and moral tyranny.

30. S. Scott Bartchy, "Slavery [Greco-Roman]," *ABD* 6:71, submits that "Paul confronted Philemon with the choice either of continuing to regard himself as Onesimus's owner or of becoming his brother in a new social reality."

with renewed vigor as a Christian? Or does Paul expect the change in their spiritual relationship to have direct effects on their social and legal relationship? Paul adds a new dimension to the equation in verse 16, well paraphrased by Lightfoot: Onesimus is a dear brother "most of all to me—more than most of all to thee."[31] With this statement Paul makes it clear that the issue does not concern only the relationship between Onesimus and Philemon.[32] It is a three way relationship: Onesimus–Paul–Philemon. Christ reigns over them all and joins them together. If Paul is to have any benefit in the Lord (v. 20), Philemon needs to go beyond what Paul specifically asks (v. 21) and set his slave free.

Receiving him "no longer as a slave" (v. 16) is therefore a subtle but open invitation to free Onesimus. One can take it literally: "Since he has become a beloved brother, he should no longer be your slave." Paul, however, cannot bluntly ask this since it presents Philemon with a ticklish, practical dilemma. Almost everyone would have considered it absurd to manumit a runaway slave immediately upon his return with a letter from Paul. Such an action would have two effects: It would seriously diminish Philemon's reputation among other slave owners in a society where reputation was important;[33] furthermore, it would also have a negative impact on any other slaves in his household.[34] The carrot-and-stick approach that governed slave relations would be dealt a serious blow. Manumission would no longer be a reward for years of hard work but a prize for running away.

If it were explained that Onesimus was freed because he had become a Christian, other slaves would soon feign conversion. What if some of his other slaves were already Christians? Would they not expect the same treatment?[35] Barclay concludes that the social situation was so complex that Paul deliberately left things open-ended, leaving the decision entirely to Phile-

---

31. Lightfoot, *Saint Paul's Epistles to the Colossians and to Philemon*, 343.

32. Dunn, *The Epistles to the Colossians and to Philemon*, 336.

33. Athenaeus argues that "one must punish one's slaves according to their deserts, not admonishing them as one would freemen and so making them conceited. Practically every address to a slave should be a command" (*Deipnosophistai* 6.265a). He goes on to say that failing to discipline slaves and joking with them makes them shoddy servants and difficult to rule.

34. We can assume that since Philemon had a home large enough to accommodate his church, he had other slaves to serve him.

35. To manumit all of his slaves would be an economic burden for Philemon and would diminish his status. John M. G. Barclay, "Paul, Philemon and the Dilemma of Christian Slave Ownership," *NTS* 37 (1991): 176–77, points out: "To urge Christian masters to be rid of their slaves was to require them not merely to demean themselves but also to deprive themselves of important means by which they could serve other Christians." In our culture it would be like asking someone to sell all his cars and rely on public transportation. We live in a world where the car(s) we drive is the clearest indication of our status. In addition,

mon because Paul did not know what to advise.[36] Barclay helps us see how radical a request for Onesimus's freedom would be and how costly it would be for Philemon. The decision must be Philemon's, but Paul does not leave him clueless about what he should do.

The Request Backed by Paul's Pledge (17–18)

VERSE 17 IS the letter's climax: "Welcome him as you would welcome me."[37] Paul not only intercedes for Onesimus but identifies with him. Onesimus, the runaway slave, returns home as Paul's apostolic representative. We would hardly expect Philemon to treat Paul as a slave, but we would also hardly expect him to receive Onesimus as Paul's ambassador and clad in his honor. But Paul asks Philemon to receive his slave not only as a brother but as he would his partner. As Onesimus's service to Paul represented Philemon's service to the jailed apostle (v. 13), so Philemon's reception of Onesimus will represent his reception of Paul.

Again, Paul does not try to throw his apostolic weight around but makes his request as a partner and laces it with accounting terminology: "if he owes," "charge it to me," "I will pay."[38] Paul tries to forestall any possible unwillingness to receiving Onesimus back with open arms by incurring a debt of honor to make restitution for any wrong committed by Onesimus. This sweeping pledge is more than a rhetorical appeal "merely for the sake of argument."[39] Although Paul states the matter hypothetically, "if he has done you any wrong," it is hypothetical "only in form."[40] Paul knows very well that Onesimus has *wronged* his master and may perhaps owe him a considerable sum of money.

Paul is deliberately vague about how Onesimus has wronged Philemon to avoid stirring up unpleasant memories and shifting attention away from the dramatic change in Onesimus. Commentators, however, try to guess what the wrong was. They note how runaway slaves frequently made their

---

most Americans live in areas where public transportation is limited and unreliable, and such a demand would be considered totally unreasonable and unfeasible.

36. Barclay, "Paul, Philemon and the Dilemma of Christian Slave Ownership," 183. He assumes that since Paul could spell out "the practical implications of love" elsewhere, his vagueness here is because he *"did not know what to recommend"* (175).

37. Paul uses the verb "welcome" (*prosdechomai*) in Rom. 14:1 and 15:7 (NRSV) for Christian acceptance of one another. For Paul's other instructions for receiving people, see Rom. 16:1–2; 1 Cor. 16:10–12, 15–18; Phil. 2:19–30.

38. Perhaps since slaves were regarded as property, the whole affair has a commercial dimension (Dunn, *The Epistles to the Colossians and to Philemon*, 336).

39. As Martin, "Commercial Language," 333–34, for example, argues.

40. Caird, *Paul's Letters from Prison*, 222–23.

getaway with their master's silver and jewelry, perhaps to ensure that they could get as far away as possible. Many, such as Lightfoot, speculate that Onesimus pilfered enough money to make his way to Rome:

> He seems to have done just what the representative slave in the Roman comedy threatens to do, when he gets into trouble. He had "packed up some goods and taken to his heels." Rome was the natural cesspool for these offscourings of humanity. In the thronging crowds of the metropolis was his best hope of secrecy. In the dregs of the city of the rabble he would find the society of congenial spirits.[41]

Callahan vigorously challenges this kind of speculation as having no foundation in the text and buying "into the stereotype of the thieving, indolent slave which is part of the mythology of all slave-holding societies."[42] Nothing suggests that Onesimus looted Philemon of his goods except that this was commonly done by runaways. Nevertheless, running away from a master was itself regarded as a form of theft; he has stolen himself.[43] His truancy, like any absenteeism, cost Philemon something. Not only would he lose the value of each lost day's work, Philemon may have had to rent another slave to fulfill Onesimus's duties and may have hired slave catchers to hunt him down. Onesimus may also have brought some loss to his master in a business dealing. Whatever it is, Paul accepts the debt as his own: I'll cover it from my own pocket.[44]

This pledge is astounding when one considers the historical context, and it emphasizes how committed Paul is to Onesimus. Few would be willing to take full responsibility for any debts that others may have incurred, let alone those of a slave, since most regarded slaves as morally irresponsible. Paul's exceptional pledge should not be dismissed as an empty promise that banks on Philemon's reluctance to accept it.[45] The pledge that follows in verse 19 is legally binding. Paul's rhetorical strategy is to shift "much of the perceived cost from Philemon onto himself."[46] He eases Philemon's concession by maximizing the cost to himself and minimizing the cost to Philemon. But this pledge also uses typical Greco-Roman friendship language of debt and credit

---

41. Lightfoot, *Colossians and Philemon*, 310.

42. Dwight Allen Callahan, "Paul's Epistle to Philemon: Toward an Alternative *Argumentum*," *HTR* 86 (1993): 361.

43. Cf. *Digest of Justinian* 47.2.60.

44. Normally, the loss would be made good by taking the amount from the slave's *peculium*, the small savings a slave might have accrued to buy his freedom.

45. Joachim Gnilka, *Der Philemonbrief*, 84, claims that "Philemon must have laughed over the pledge of a man who, as a prisoner, possessed not a penny in the world."

46. Wilson, "The Pragmatics of Politeness," 117.

to express the reciprocal obligations of friends.[47] In modern idiom, Paul is say-ing to his friend, "I owe you one."

Conclusion (19–25)

SINCE THE LETTER is being read aloud to the church (v. 2), it is necessary for Paul to notify the listeners, who cannot see the change in handwriting, that he has taken the stylus to write out his promissory note.[48] This IOU is the same kind of bond that Paul refers to in Colossians 2:14. This bond adds a new twist to Paul's request. Paul never specifically mentions forgiving Ones-imus (contrast the Pliny's letter to Sabinianus), and Koester contends that Paul "is meticulously concerned not to put Onesimus in a situation which would henceforth bind him in thankfulness to his master's magnanimity." The "legal and business-like guarantees" lift Onesimus's personal obligations to his mas-ter.[49] Paul may also be expressing a willingness to bear the cost of the slave's freedom.

With the phrase "not to mention that" Paul uses a rhetorical gambit whereby one mentions what he will not mention. The apostle subtly reminds Philemon of the basis of their relationship and how he could even make such an unheard of request. He suddenly converts Philemon from a creditor, whose debt will be paid in full, to a debtor, who cannot possibly repay the price of his life. "You owe me your very self" means that the debt, unlike the one created by Onesimus, is not monetary but spiritual.[50] The New Testa-ment assumes that monetary obligations can be repaid in full; spiritual oblig-ations cannot (see Matt. 18:23–35; Mark 8:37). This debt owed Paul, therefore, puts Philemon "under a limitless moral obligation to comply with Paul's requests."[51] His letter calls in that debt without seeming to do so.[52]

---

47. See Peter Marshall, *Enmity in Corinth: Social Conventions in Paul's Relations with the Corinthi-ans*, WUNT 2/23 (Tübingen: J. C. B. Mohr [Paul Siebeck], 1987), 160–64; Gordon Fee, *Paul's Letter to the Philippians*, NICNT (Grand Rapids: Eerdmans, 1995), 5–6, 423.

48. Lightfoot, *Saint Paul's Epistles to the Colossians and to Philemon*, 344, claims that Paul "wrote the whole letter with his own hand."

49. Helmut Koester, *Introduction to the New Testament. Volume Two: History and Literature of Early Christianity* (Philadelphia: Fortress, 1982), 135.

50. We can guess what that spiritual debt was. Paul may have "begotten" Philemon as he did Onesimus (10), but he does not use that metaphor here or refer to him as his child. Possibly Paul, as the apostle to the Gentiles (Rom. 15:16; Eph. 3:1–3), has in mind his bringing the gospel to this area and his imprisonment "for the sake of you Gentiles" (Eph. 3:1). He may have considered the work that Epaphras did in establishing the churches in the Lycus valley as work done as "a faithful servant of Christ in behalf of us" (Col. 1:7).

51. Barclay, "Paul, Philemon and the Dilemma of Christian Slave Ownership," 172.

52. Peterson, *Rediscovering Paul*, 74–78.

Verse 20 begins with an emphatic "Yes" (NIV, "I do wish"). Friendship in the ancient world was a reciprocal relationship that continued when friends exchanged gifts, services, and benefits. Philemon's positive response will be a "benefit" to Paul that will "refresh" his "heart in Christ." Paul eases the tension created by the unanticipated "non-mention" of Philemon's indebtedness with another playful pun on Onesimus's name: "that I may have some benefit."[53] That this phrase was used elsewhere does not mean that the pun on the name was not intentional in this situation.[54]

As a Hebrew of Hebrews, Paul comes from a pun-loving background, and he continues his wordplay by saying that his heart will be refreshed. He has already commended Philemon for refreshing the hearts of the saints (v. 7) and has identified Onesimus as his heart (v. 12). By granting his request, Philemon will lift Paul's spirit and alleviate his fears and worries about his child, Onesimus. He describes the benefit, however, as "in the Lord." Simply readmitting him as a slave would provide no real benefit in the Lord to Paul. The apostle will truly have a "benefit in the Lord" if Onesimus is free to serve the gospel, not just his master.[55]

Paul's words in verse 21 exude confidence because he knows his man.[56] Philemon is a beloved coworker (v. 1), a brother (v. 7), and a partner (v. 17), who has already shown his love and faith (v. 5) and hospitality (v. 7).[57] He is not just a good man but one who is in the Lord. Paul knows he will obey. The obedience is not to Paul but to the Lord, whom he has just referred to in verse 20, and to the command of love that undergirds the entire letter.[58]

---

53. The verb is *onaimen* from *oninemi*, from which the name Onesimus derives. It appears only here in the New Testament and in the rare optative mood.

54. Xenophon records a conversation of Socrates with Aristippos: "Why are you so confident that no one will ever enslave you: Is it because you would be thought the kind of slave who brings no master any profit? No one wants to keep in his household a man who does not want to do any work but enjoys an expensive lifestyle" (*Memorabilia* 2.1).

55. See Ernst Lohmeyer, *Die Briefe an der Kolosser und an Philemon*, Meyer Kommentar (Göttingen: Vandenhoeck & Ruprecht, 1961) 191; Knox, *Philemon Among the Letters of Paul*, 25.

56. Wilson, "The Pragmatics of Politeness," 118, compares it to the modern phrase in a letter to a friend, "I am sure that I can count on you."

57. Nordling, "Onesimus Fugitivus," 107, n. 2, cites Luther's pertinent commentary: "We take pleasure in the honor that people trust us. This is good flattery; but it is holy, because it proceeds as in Christ. Whomever I praise, I praise as a Christian; therefore I neither flatter him nor am disappointed in him, because it is impossible to praise Christ enough. If I flatter a Christian man, I do so not for his sake but for the sake of Christ, who dwells in him; and Him a Christian should honor" ("Lecture on Philemon" *Luther's Works*, 29:98–99).

58. See Rom. 1:5; 16:19, 26; 2 Cor. 7:15; 10:5–6; 2 Thess. 1:8; contrast 2 Thess. 3:14. Some (Wickert, "Der Philemonbrief," 233; Lohse, *Colossians and Philemon*, 206; and Peter Stuhlmacher, *Der Brief an Philemon*, EKKNT, 2d. ed [Zurich: Benziger/Neukirchen: Neukirchener, 1981], 36–37) stress the apostolic character of this writing so that Philemon's obedience is to the word

Paul does not exert his apostolic authority in a heavy-handed way. He relies only on the power of moral persuasion by authoritatively presenting the options for Philemon's decision: "This is clearly what you should do as my partner in Christ guided by the rule of love, but you be the judge." Paul has delicately framed his entreaty for Onesimus so that Philemon will not be obeying Paul but his Lord.[59] He fully expects Philemon to meet Onesimus's disobedience to him, his master, with his own obedience to a greater Master (Col. 4:1).[60] Obedience is a matter of faith, and it recalls Paul's grateful prayer for Philemon's "faith in the Lord Jesus" (vv. 5–6).

Paul does not explicitly ask Philemon to do anything more in this letter than to accept Onesimus as his brother in Christ and to welcome him as if he were Paul. To what, then, does the "even more" in verse 21 refer? It could simply be a crowning rhetorical flourish.[61] It might allude to Paul's desire to have "his heart" returned to him so that Onesimus can continue his service to him. It might also imply that Philemon will give Onesimus his freedom. I opt for this last alternative. Paul is hopeful—more than that, confident— that Philemon will set Onesimus free so that he might devote himself fully to serving in the gospel.

Paul makes one last request related to his hoped-for release from prison and his prospective visit. Paul has shrouded his supplication for Onesimus in a guarded indirectness. Now he makes a direct request: "Prepare a guest room for me" (v. 22). In our culture, this may seem a little pushy because many imagine hospitality as a serious imposition. This attitude is reflected in Ben Franklin's witticism (expressed in different forms through the ages) that fish and visitors smell after three days. We can imagine the reaction a pastor might get after informing a spouse that a famous evangelist had called and said that he might be coming to town and planned to stay with them for a while. The evangelist did not say when he would arrive, but he expects the pastor and his wife to get a room ready for him. In our setting, most would not be overjoyed by the news, and consequently few would be so bold to make such a demand of others' hospitality.

---

of Paul. I have argued that this is a misreading that imposes authority issues on the text and that Paul has meticulously avoided imposing his will on his friend so that he responds from his love for Christ and not from compulsion (v. 14).

59. This perspective mitigates the social problem of freeing Onesimus. His pagan acquaintances would not understand why he should treat his mutinous slave as a brother, but they could grasp how it might be prudent to give way to some god who had made claims on his slave.

60. Paul makes no threat about what he will do if Philemon does not obey (contrast 2 Cor. 10:6).

61. Church, "Rhetorical Structure," 30–32.

By contrast, Paul's self-invitation would not have been a serious imposition in his culture. Osiek reminds us that the house was

> not the place to escape from work but the place where much of the work was done; it was not the place to be free of a public role but the place to enhance that role by hospitality. The modern idea of the sacred privacy of the home does not apply.[62]

Wilson argues that since granting such a request was not costly or threatening to Philemon, Paul did not need to express it with the same politeness strategies that he used in making his request for Onesimus.[63] He could bluntly tell him to get a room ready, but he could *not* make his request for Onesimus so artlessly.

Paul's arrival in Philemon's home would be a gracious answer to prayer. Paul again uses the divine passive "to be restored to you" (see v. 15), which reveals that he would regard his release from prison as divine intervention. The plural "your prayers" reminds us that this letter is intended for the entire church. He takes for granted that his prayers for them (v. 4) will be reciprocated with their prayers for him. This verse is, therefore, not an implied threat: "I will be coming, God willing, to see how you responded."[64] If Philemon only complies because Paul threatens to make some inspection tour, then the letter has failed to do its work in motivating him to respond from love.

Paul signs off with greetings from his fellow prisoner, Epaphras, and his fellow workers. The "you" in verse 23 is singular. Presumably, each of these persons would vouch for Onesimus and concur with Paul's request on his behalf.

AT FIRST GLANCE, Philemon may seem to have little practical value to the reader today since slavery has been abolished in most of the world. Worse, the letter may be an embarrassment, since Paul seems to tolerate an institution that we now consider a monstrous abuse of human rights. Paul wrote that in Christ there is no slave or free (Col. 3:11), and he had an opportunity to denounce slavery as a great evil in this letter.

---

62. Carolyn Osiek, "The Family in Early Christianity: 'Family Values' Revisited," *CBQ* 58 (1996): 12. Since inns in the ancient world were notoriously dangerous and sordid, hosting visiting missionaries was vital to the expansion of the gospel in Palestine (see Matt. 10:40–41; Luke 10:5–10; Acts 9:43; 10:6; 21:8, 16) and in the wider Greco-Roman world (Acts 16:14–15, 33–34, 40; 18:2–3; 20:20; Rom. 16:23; 3 John 5–8; Did. 11–12).

63. Wilson, "The Pragmatics of Politeness," 117–18.

64. For example, Wall, *Colossians and Philemon*, 217, maintains that the visit "is not friendly and casual but apostolic and official (although certainly neither unfriendly nor unwelcome)."

He does not make a peep of protest, however. Instead, the letter only seems to reinforce the command for slaves to obey their earthly masters in everything (cf. Col. 3:22). He cajoles rather than castigates a member of the propertied slave-holding class and sends a slave back to face the judgment of his master—a judgment he hopes, but cannot guarantee, will be tempered by love and forgiveness. To bridge the cultural divide from the first century, in which slavery was an entrenched institution, to our world, where it is considered loathsome and immoral, we need to explore three topics. We need first to explain how slavery functioned in the ancient world. Next we need to see how it differed significantly from American slavery, with which we are more familiar. Finally, we must analyze why the early Christians did not lead a crusade against this evil.

Slavery in the ancient world. Roman civilization was based on slavery, and the imperial economy depended on slaves for its basic labor. Originally, the slave population was comprised of captured prisoners of war and the kidnap victims of pirates and bandits.[65] This source of slaves led Romans to fancy that a slave's whole existence was a gift from the master, who had saved him from death.[66]

By the first century, however, the slaves' offspring provided a steady supply of slaves. Their ranks were supplemented by persons convicted of capital crimes, freeborn children who were sold by parents who could no longer feed them, foundlings (children dropped off at temples or dumped in the open), and persons who, for various reasons (such as to avoid starvation or to become a steward in an important family), sold themselves into slavery. Some estimate that slaves comprised a quarter to a third of the population in central and southern Italy. Seneca (died A.D. 65) remarks that a proposal in the Roman Senate to differentiate slaves from free persons by making them wear distinctive clothing failed when the senators expressed fears that the slaves would quickly see how many they were and decide to revolt.[67]

Slaves carried out various functions in the working world, depending on their lot. The imperial slaves managed the daily administrative tasks of governing the empire, and many rose to prominence as freedmen and became

---

65. Josephus's account of the speech of the rebel leader Eleazar, in the final days of the siege of Masada, vividly reveals how some would prefer death to being captured and made slaves (*J. W.* 7.8.6 §§ 323–36).

66. Thomas E. J. Wiedemann, "Slavery," in *Civilization of the Ancient Mediterranean: Greece and Rome*, ed. Michael Grant and Rachel Kitzinger (New York: Charles Scribner's Sons, 1988), 1:578. He notes that Latin writers commonly derived the word *servus* from *servare* and defined the slave as someone "saved" as opposed to killed in war.

67. Seneca, *On Mercy* 1.24.1.

quite prosperous.[68] Other slaves were owned by temples and cities and were charged with assorted roles from treasurer to maintenance work. Some even served as policemen.

Household slaves in urban centers had a variety of tasks. They existed primarily to serve the privileged class, and their owners expected them to make their life more comfortable and to increase their wealth and prestige. Even those with comparatively modest means owned two to three slaves. In an age of conspicuous consumption, the wealthy acquired numerous slaves as a status indicator. Slaves were assigned menial chores as janitors, cooks, dishwashers, gardeners, table servers, musicians, door keepers, litter bearers, couriers, wet-nurses, laundrymen, seamstresses, maids, hairdressers, personal attendants, secretaries, and child minders. Some served as concubines. Those who were better educated received assignments requiring intellect, skill, and culture, working as secretaries, treasurers, clerks, overseers, bailiffs, sea captains, architects, artists, musicians, writers, librarians, doctors, and tutors. Slaves could be found doing every job except serving in politics or in the military.

The greatest drudgery was endured by field workers and labored on farms, many of whom never knew their owners. At the lowest end of the scale were the penal slaves, who worked in mines and slave galleys and died in their slavery.

The legal status of slaves. Everyone took for granted that there were two categories of human beings, free and slaves.[69] The free were regarded by the law as persons; slaves were not legally persons but were defined as things and tallied as living pieces of property. Aristotle classified a slave as a living tool.[70] Cato advised the frugal farmer: "Sell the worn-out oxen, blemished cattle, blemished sheep, wool, hides, an old wagon, old tools, an old slave, a sickly slave, and whatever else is superfluous."[71] One can see this dehumanizing classification of slaves in the bitter lament of the heartless merchants who weep at the destruction of Babylon because they have lost the market for their cargo (Rev. 18:11–13). Last in the inventory of cargo are "bodies," a common

---

68. Marcus Antonius Felix, the procurator of Judea from A.D. 52/53–59/60 (see Acts 23:24–24:27), was a freed slave, probably of the emperor Claudius's mother, Antonia. His brother M. Antonius Pallas, also freed by Claudius's mother, was famous for his fabulous wealth. See further, R. P. C. Weaver, *Familia Caesaris: A Social Study of the Emperor's Freedmen and Slaves* (Cambridge: Cambridge Univ. Press, 1972).

69. Gaius, *Institutes* 1.9.

70. Aristotle, *Politics* 1.2.4; see also Varro, *On Agriculture* 1.17.1, who describes a slave as "an articulate implement." The closest thing to a slave in our culture is the fetus, who also is not regarded as a legal person and has no legal rights.

71. Cato, *On Agriculture* 2.7.

reference to slaves. John's Christian convictions, however, led him to modify it, "that is, the souls of men" (pers. trans.).

The slave experienced "civil death" with no legal or human rights. Seneca characterizes a slave as one who "does not have the right to refuse."[72] As a piece of property, a slave's whole life was completely at the disposal of the owner. The master could even dictate conditions on succeeding owners of a slave by expressly forbidding in his will that a slave ever be sold or manumitted. Slaves did not own their time, labor, or children.[73] The slave owner could keep the children as slaves or sell them at a slave auction, as a farmer might sell calves or piglets. Or he might expose them as one might drown unwanted kittens.

Slaves could not enter into a legal marriage and had no legal kin. If a master wanted to marry his slave concubine, he would have to set her free first. Some slaves probably had common law marriages, but one wonders how stable they would have been. Religion was the one area of life open to slaves. In some cults they could even serve as priests. In Aeschylus's play *Agamemnon*, Cassandra is brought to Greece as a slave, and when she is about to prophesy, the chorus comments: "The gift divine still abides even in the soul of one enslaved" (1084).

Because slaves were a significant investment and asset, many recognized that they would get better and longer service by treating slaves well. A wise master would take care of his slaves, the way one might care for an expensive automobile today. Concern for a slave's welfare was usually utilitarian and motivated by self-interest. It is telling that Gaius's *Institutes* does not give moral compassion as the grounds for intervening in cases of excessive and unreasonable brutality but the "misuse of rights" by those "who waste their own property."[74] Like car owners who never change the oil in their cars, some masters abused their slaves. Absolute power over others can breed contempt for life.

The treatment of slaves. The violence and ruthlessness in the ancient world spilled over in the violation of slaves, wives, and children. Slaves were frequently victims of physical, psychological, and moral tyranny. Some owners were sadistic monsters given to furious tantrums.[75] According to Seneca,

---

72. Seneca, *On Benefits* 3.19.1.

73. Slaves could be rented to others. One surviving rental contract stipulates that if the master needs the slave during the night for baking bread, he can send for her without any deduction from the rental fee. Obviously, this slave would be required to put in long, exhausting hours (cited by Jo-Ann Shelton, *As the Romans Did: A Sourcebook of Roman Social History* [Oxford: Oxford Univ. Press, 1988], 169).

74. Gaius, *Institutes* 1.55.

75. Galen describes the fits of anger that overtake masters: "There are other people who don't just hit their slaves, but kick them and gouge out their eyes and strike them with a pen if they happen to be holding one" (*The Diseases of the Mind* 4). He then relates how the emperor Hadrian put out an attendant's eye with a pen in a rush of anger.

the sadistic Vedius Pollio ordered that a slave who had broken a crystal cup be thrown to his lamprey eels.[76] The boy escaped and appealed to the emperor Augustus to be executed in a less savage way. Outraged by such injustice, the emperor ordered that he be set free and that all of Pollio's crystal cups and his fish pond be destroyed. The hero of Apuleius's novel *Metamorphoses* describes the scrawny and sallow slaves working in a flour mill, with brands on their foreheads, skin embroidered with purple welts, and backs scarred by beatings—all exposed by their shredded clothing.[77] Slaves also could suffer abuse from their fellow slaves or could be rented out to others who would be less concerned about caring for rental property.

All income that accrued to a slave (e.g., through business deals) legally belonged to the master (see Matt. 25:14–30). Because slaves had no legal identity, they could not seek compensation for any injuries or grievances. If a slave was injured, any compensation was assessed at a lesser rate than for a free person and went to the owner, not the slave. Owners could punish misbehavior in any way they chose and were usually not held accountable for any injuries they inflicted. Slaves had no legally recognized way to appeal to anyone in authority with complaints. If they tried to protest, they could be severely punished. Slaves had only limited options if they wished to escape abuse. They could try to remove their masters by murder or magic spells or remove themselves by running away or seeking asylum in a temple.[78]

Running away was a risk that promised little reward. Having taken flight, a runaway could join one of the robber bands that plagued the countryside, but life expectancy in such a group was short. He could sell himself to a slave dealer in hopes of being resold to a more kindly master. A slave who claimed ill-treatment could also flee to a religious sanctuary and find refuge. It did not lead to freedom but only to the possibility of finding a more benevolent owner.[79] If runaways were caught, however, they could be severely whipped, branded on the face, put in chains, forced to wear an iron neck collar to alert others in case they ever tried to flee again, or have their legs broken. They could also be sold to the mines or sentenced to death.[80] Later

---

76. Seneca, *On Anger* 3.40.1–5.

77. Apuleius, *Metamorphoses* ["The Golden Ass"] 9.12.

78. Thomas E. J. Wiedemann, ed., *Greek and Roman Slavery* (Baltimore: Johns Hopkins Univ. Press, 1981), 190.

79. Wiedemann, *Greek and Roman Slavery*, 195, cites one example: "The best thing for me to do is to run to the Temple of Theseus for refuge and stay there until I manage to find someone to buy me."

80. One neck collar that has survived is Christian and inscribed: "I am the slave of archdeacon Felix: hold me so that I do not escape." (G. H. R. Horsley, *New Documents Illustrating Early Christianity* [North Ryde: Macquarie University, 1981], 1:140–41). Another has Chi-Rho symbols on it (cited by Nordling, "Onesimus Fugitivus," 106).

legislation tried to protect slaves from unreasonable abuse, but it was riddled with loopholes, and there was no one to enforce it.

The governance of slaves. The carrot-and-stick philosophy governed the relationship between slaves and masters. To bridle the vast population of slaves, masters made certain that slaves knew swift and harsh punishment would follow for any offenses. They kept their slaves in line with fear tactics.[81] Fear, however, works insidiously, and its tentacles have a way of entrapping those who try to wield it against others. Both masters and slaves lived in fear. The slave feared the master's evil whims and bad temper; the master feared the slave's conspiracies, violence, flight, or resort to sorcery. Lightfoot notes Seneca's expression, "as many enemies as slaves," as showing that the relationship between master and slave was poisoned by "universal distrust."[82]

Memories of past slave uprisings quashed any moral misgivings about the treatment of slaves. Many also worried about losing control over such overwhelming numbers of a potentially explosive group. To increase their sense of security, the oppressors sought to undermine any common bond between their slaves and encouraged them to inform on others, lest they be charged with complicity in any slave's crime. For example, if a master were murdered and the culprit a slave, all of the slaves in the household would be executed.

Tacitus mentions such a case involving a prefect of Rome who was murdered by one of his slaves. All four hundred of his slaves were set for execution. The prospect of executing so many innocent victims sparked a mass protest from the general population and a debate in the senate. In the debate, one senator argued that since household slaves now came from many different nations, with differing customs and religions,

> you will never coerce such a medley of humanity except by terror.—
> "But some lives will be lost!"—Even so; for when every tenth man of

---

81. One should not be misled by Seneca's remarks about the humanity of slaves: "They are slaves," people declare. Nay rather they are men. "Slaves!" No, comrades. "Slaves!" No, they are unpretentious friends. "Slaves!" No they are our fellow-slaves, if one reflects that Fortune has equal rights over slaves and free alike. (*Moral Epistles* 47.1)

Wiedemann, *Greek and Roman Slavery*, 233, contends that Seneca does not write about slavery as a humanitarian crusader but as a pundit. "Seneca is more interested in writing exciting Latin than in improving the conditions of his reader's slaves."

82. Lightfoot, *Saint Paul's Epistles to the Colossians and to Philemon*, 322. The quotation is from Seneca's *Moral Epistles* 47. Pliny's worry that a friend was killed on a trip by one of his slaves reveals a silent fear of slave conspiracies (*Letters* 3.14):

> Do you realize how many dangers, how many injuries, how many abuses we may be exposed to? And no one can feel safe, even if he is a lenient and kind master. Slaves are ruined by their own evil natures, not by a master's cruelty.

---

the routed army drops beneath the club, the lot falls on the brave as well. All great examples carry with them something of injustice— injustice compensated, as against individual suffering, by the advantage of the community.[83]

Fear won the day; the slaves received no reprieve.

Epictetus, who was raised in slavery, wrote: "It is the slave's prayer that he be set free immediately."[84] The carrot held out to the slave was the possibility of manumission as a reward for loyal service. Unlike the false promise on the gates of concentration camps, *Arbeit macht frei* ("Work leads to freedom"), freedom was a real, if fragile, hope for slaves who worked faithfully for their masters. "Home-born slaves" had an obvious advantage over slaves who toiled on faraway farms and did not live in their owner's household. They led rougher lives and most died in their slavery. Domestic slaves who lived with the family had a good chance of being set free. Some masters would transfer property, livestock, or even other slaves to their slaves and also give them small gifts of money and clothing. This *peculium* might accumulate eventually enough to buy the slave's freedom, although it legally belonged to the master and could be taken back at any time.

Such provisions were a matter of enlightened self-interest. They gave slaves something to hope for so that they might serve more faithfully. Manumission, therefore, was regarded as a reward for faithful work, and regular manumissions kept the wheels of slavery well oiled. It encouraged slaves to behave nicely, work hard, and increase their productivity. We should note that the admonitions to slaves in the New Testament never mention the prospect of manumission as a motivation for their obedience. Obeying masters "only when their eye is on you and to win their favor" is condemned (Col. 3:22). Christian slaves do not obey in order to win early release but to please the Lord.

Masters frequently were generous with their slaves to attract the esteem of their peers and a large crowd of mourners at their funerals.[85] Some would give freedom to slaves nearing death so that they might have "the consolation of dying in freedom and being buried as freedmen."[86] Trimalchio, the fantastically rich but exceedingly crude freedman in Petronius's satire, boastfully

---

83. Tacitus, *Annals* 14.44.

84. Epictetus, *Discourses.* 4.1.33.

85. Dionysius of Halicarnassus complained about manumission for the wrong reasons (e.g., slaves who bought their freedom from the profits of criminal acts; masters who had a vain thirst for popularity and released their slaves to win the esteem of others) and related it to the general decline of moral standards (*Roman Antiquities* 4.24.1–8).

86. Paul Veyne, "The Roman Empire," in *A History of Private Life I: From Pagan Rome to Byzantium*, ed. Paul Veyne (Cambridge, Mass.: Harvard Univ. Press, 1987), 86.

announces at his dinner party that in his will he plans to set all his slaves free with sizeable gifts as his master had done for him. He says: "The reason I'm telling all this now so my household will love me now as much as if I was dead."[87]

Dionysius of Halicarnassus writes: "I know of some who have allowed all their slaves to be freed after their death in order that they might be called good men when they are dead and that many people might follow their biers wearing their liberty-caps."[88] Sometimes owners would give slaves their freedom for selfish financial reasons. The slave's *peculium* that was used to buy his freedom might be greater than the cost of buying a new slave to replace him, or the master could save money by using the slave's services as a freedman client without having to house, clothe, and feed him.

Manumission did not mean that slaves were freed from all obligations to their owners and could go or do as he wished (see Pliny's letter to Sabinianus concerning his wayward freedman). Freedmen took on the family name of their masters and were obliged to show due gratitude and pay them regular homage (*obsequium*). The former master could still expect some economic profit from his freedman. The freedman promised to provide a certain number of days of service or work each year (*operae libertorium*), which was enforceable by civil action.[89] Masters might also require gifts (*munera*) from their freedmen. In return, the master, now the patron, would look after the interests of his freedmen, providing some food, caring for health, and offering legal protection.[90]

The difference between ancient slavery and slavery in the new world. Most Americans' knowledge of slavery derives from some awareness of New World slavery, even if it only comes from novels made into movies, such as Margaret Mitchell's *Gone With the Wind* or Alex Haley's *Roots*. Slavery may call to mind a picture of beautiful Southern plantations combined with ugly racism and toil in a cotton field. That image should not be projected onto the slavery of the New Testament world. Slavery in any form corrodes the spirits of all parties involved, but ancient slavery was less beastly than New World slavery and its slave trade.

---

87. Petronius, *Satyricon* 15.71.

88. Dionysius of Halicarnassus, *Roman Antiquities* 4.24.6.

89. Tacitus discusses the two types of manumission. "All, whose patron had not liberated them by the wand, were still, it might be said, held by the bond of servitude" (*Annals* 13.27). He recommended that the owner be slow to grant any freedom that could not be revoked if the freedman got out of line.

90. Because of this arrangement, Dunn, *The Epistles to the Colossians and to Philemon*, 330, contends that if Philemon freed Onesimus, "the latter would almost certainly have had to remain in a state of financial dependence on Philemon as his client ('have back for ever'). . . ."

We should be cautious, however, not to portray ancient slavery as a benevolent, humane institution.[91] It was not. Gordon writes: "The growth of the empire had a background of human suffering which is unimaginable in its degree and extent."[92] We do not know what the average slave experienced or felt about his or her condition since they did not write literature. We see only things from the perspective of their owners; and, if human nature holds true, they probably saw themselves as far more magnanimous than they were in actuality. The number of papyri dealing with runaway slaves suggests that it was not a benign institution. For any who argue that ancient slavery was not all that bad, Abraham Lincoln's remarks are appropriate: "Whenever I hear anyone arguing for slavery, I feel a strong impulse to see it tried on him personally."[93] Nevertheless, crossing the bridge into the first-century world makes us aware of the major differences between New World slavery and the slavery that Paul encountered.

(1) We should not assume that all first-century slaves were poorly treated and desperately wanted to escape their slavery. Slave and freedman in the ancient world were not separated by a vast economic and racial chasm as they were in the New World. Some hapless individuals even sold themselves into slavery to improve their lot. Dio Chrysostom remarked that "great numbers of men, we may suppose, who are free born sell themselves, so that they are slaves by contract, sometimes on no easy terms but the most severe imaginable."[94]

New World slaves, on the other hand, longed desperately for freedom. Frederick Douglass (1818–1895) wrote of the slaves' singing, "Every tone was a testimony against slavery, and a prayer to God for deliverance from chains."[95] This cry for freedom drew heavily from the Exodus for its images and rang throughout the spirituals:

Before I'd be a slave,
I'd be buried in my grave
And go home to my Lord and be free.

(2) Ancient slavery did not have any racial overtones. Ethnic origin played no role in whether one was a slave or not, and slaves came from

---

91. Dale B. Martin, *Slavery as Salvation* (New Haven: Yale Univ. Press, 1990), 1.

92. Mary L. Gordon, "The Nationality of Slaves Under the Early Roman Empire," in *Slavery in Classical Antiquity*, ed. Moses I. Finley (Cambridge: Cambridge Univ. Press, 1960), 180.

93. Address to an Indiana Regiment on March 17, 1865.

94. Dio Chrysostom, *Orations* 15.23.

95. Frederick Douglass, *Narrative of the Life of Frederick Douglass an American Slave*, ed. Benjamin Quarles (Cambridge: Harvard Univ. Press, 1967), 37.

every nationality. If we walked along the crowded the streets of ancient Rome, we could not tell who was a slave and who was a free person. Slaves belonged to no particular race, wore no distinctive clothing, could be well educated, and worked at the same kinds of jobs as free persons. New World slavery, by contrast, was a racist institution. Slaves were Africans. "American slave holders justified their position of authority and control by labeling the African American essentially subhuman and an infantile adult."[96]

In antiquity, slave owners did not invent theories of racial inferiority to justify slavery. They saw no need to justify slavery at all except to say that Fortune inexplicably brought such degradation on unlucky individuals. They assumed that such misfortune could befall anyone since even the noblest warrior might be captured in battle and reduced to slavery.

(3) Since education enhanced a slave's value to an ancient slaveowner, it was encouraged and prized. Seneca laughs at the wealthy but addle-pated Calvisius Sabinus, who wanted to appear learned and "paid fabulous prices for slaves—one to know Homer by heart and another to know Hesiod; he also delegated a special slave to each of the nine lyric poets."[97] They would feed him lines to recite at banquets, which he usually botched in mid-sentence. Seneca sneeringly says that Sabinus "held to the opinion that what any member of his household knew, he himself knew also" (27.7). Skilled slaves in Roman times could have significant power over other slaves and even freedmen. Not all slaves in antiquity were haggard field hands or household drudges. Many were placed in sensitive positions and performed crucial work. To be sure, many more were assigned onerous tasks, but a free person might also be doing the same kind of work.

In modern slavery, by contrast, slave owners did not want their slaves learning too much or developing technical skills because they feared that it might undermine their control over them. "Slave illiteracy was often required by law."[98] Everything was done to keep slaves submissive by making it difficult for them to survive on their own or to be easily integrated into society if they were freed.

(4) Since race did not destine one for slavery, most ancient slaves did not think of their slavery as a permanent condition. Slaves were also permitted to keep tips and allowances, which they could save to buy their freedom. Manumission, in Rome at least, was normal; and most domestic slaves were set free at the age of thirty. Slavery and manumission were viewed as a means

---

96. J. Albert Harrill, *The Manumission of Slaves in Early Christainity* (Tubingen: J. C. B. Mohr [Paul Siebeck], 1995), 52.

97. Seneca, *Epistles* 27.5.

98. Harrill, *Manumission*, 47.

to integrate outsiders into Roman society and provide soldiers to serve in the army.[99] If their masters were Roman citizens and followed the proper ceremonies, a freedman over thirty years of age could also become a citizen.[100] The poet Horace was the son of a freedman.[101] His status shows that the offspring of a freed slave could become fully integrated into Roman society within the next generation and even be accepted in the wealthy class.

By contrast, manumission was rare in American slavery; and when Negro slaves were freed, they did not receive rights as full citizens. Many whites believed that they still had no rights at all. Consequently, the freed Negro lived in a kind of "legal limbo" between slavery and freedom. The poison of that racism still ravages American society. Over a century after emancipation, African Americans still feel slavery's invisible shackles. Even those who have become famous as celebrities, business people, scientists, and educators can face situations where they are spoken down to as though they were lowly servants. The dream of Martin Luther King Jr. "that one day on the red hills of Georgia the sons of former slaves and the sons of former slaveowners will be able to sit down together at the table of brotherhood" remains only a dream for many.

(5) In contrast with the average inhabitant of Paul's world, the average Southerner had little personal contact with slaves. The "typical Southerner was not only a small farmer but also a nonslaveholder." In the ancient world slaveholding was *not* the "exclusive domain of the very wealthy, but extended far down the social scale."[102] Even persons of modest means owned slaves, and some slaves could be given authority over other slaves who, in effect, became their own slaves (a *vicarius*).[103]

These five contrasts clearly show that the slavery Paul confronted was significantly different from what we may be familiar with from our recent past. We should not fault Paul for not speaking out in moral outrage at the injustice of slavery.

---

99. Wiedemann, "Slavery," 578–79, notes: "At Rome the freeing of slaves (Manumission) was so much more frequent that it amazed Greek observers." Wiedemann explains that Greece was a poor country, suffering from chronic overpopulation, and could not afford to integrate the large number of slaves into society. Rome, however, "needed soldiers to fight its wars; the Roman elite needed dependents to support them in the struggle for political power and status." The freed slaves helped man the army.

100. See Gaius, *Institutes* 1.17.

101. Horace, *Satires* 1.6.65–92.

102. Harrill, *Manumission*, 44, cites Kenneth M. Stampp, *The Peculiar Institution: Slavery in the Antebellum South* (New York: Vintage Books, 1956), 30.

103. Wiedemann, *Greek and Roman Slavery*, 123–24, cites an inscription in which the emperor Tiberius's finance officer, who was a slave, was accompanied on a trip with sixteen of his own slaves.

Slavery and Christianity. We find the condemnation of slave traders in 1 Timothy 1:10 along with other godless sins, but we might wish that Paul had been more forceful in challenging slavery. Several mitigating factors in his world may help us understand why he did not.

(1) Slavery was a time-honored and accepted part of the fabric of life. Wiedemann observes: "The treatment of slaves may have been more or less harsh in different periods of antiquity, manumission more or less frequent, and the tasks assigned to slaves various in nature; but it did not occur to anyone, pagan or Christian, that the institution as such should be dispensed with."[104] People living in this age could not even envision "a society where all were in theory free, much less of appreciating the worth of such a system."[105]

From the perspective of the ancients, a world without slaves was an enchanted never-never land in which tools fetch themselves and work on their own, bread bakes itself, fish catch, baste, and cook themselves, and dishes wash themselves.[106] Hardly anyone in antiquity could conceive of a world operating without slaves, in the same way that most people today cannot conceive of living without an automobile, electricity, or television, in spite of the pollution they spew into the environment or into our minds.[107] Slavery was accepted as a natural part of life. The slaves involved in the slave revolts of the past had no intention of abolishing slavery; they only wanted to set themselves up as the new masters.

Paul, like most of his contemporaries may have looked upon slavery as an unchangeable feature of this fallen world. Centuries later, Augustine accepted slavery as a punishment justly imposed for human sin.[108] The Therapeutae (Egypt) and the Essenes (Palestine) were the only two groups in antiquity who openly renounced the use of slaves.[109] Both groups were Jewish and both lived in self-contained, desert communities where they could put into practice their private idealism without being disturbed. Barclay argues, "To ask why [Paul] did not advocate the abolition of slavery in its entirety is perhaps to pose an anachronistic and inappropriate question."[110] The early Chris-

---

104. Wiedemann, "Slavery," 588.

105. William J. Richardson, "Principle and Context in the Ethics of the Epistle to Philemon," *Int* 22 (1968): 307.

106. See Athenaeus *Deipnosophistai* 6.267. Philo (*On the Special Laws* 2.123) writes: "For the course of life contains a vast number of circumstances which demand the ministrations of slaves."

107. If one wants to spark a serious argument in America, we could add guns to the list.

108. Augustine, *The City of God* 19.15.

109. According to Philo and Josephus. On the Essenes, however, see the instructions concerning slaves in CD 11.12; 12.10–11.

110. John M. G. Barclay, "Paul, Philemon and the Dilemma of Christian Slave Ownership," *NTS* 37 (1991): 177.

tians did not retreat to some desert utopia but decided to live in the real world and cope with its evils as best they could.

People in the ancient world did not debate whether slavery should exist, but how owners should treat their slaves. On this issue, Paul definitely took a humane view in his instructions about the relationship between slaves and masters. As Dodd puts it, Paul "accepts the situation in which the law and custom of the time had placed Philemon and Onesimus and asks what, in that situation, is the Christian duty of Philemon. His answer is in effect that the relation between them is to be wholly ruled by the Christian principle of love or charity."[111] Such a viewpoint apparently appealed to slaves, who joined this new religious movement in droves.

(2) Had Paul assailed the institution of slavery, such an attack would have been utterly futile, a quixotic tilting at windmills. It would have been as effective as a modern preacher railing against the evils of "the internal combustion engine."[112]

(a) Slaves had no sense of class consciousness since race, occupation, and dress did not reveal that one was a slave. Slaves did not comprise a homogeneous lower class but were "embedded in the class of their owners."[113] Their honor and economic situation depended entirely on the honor and economic situation of their masters. Consequently, a significant discrepancy could exist between a slave's social and economic status and his legal status. The urban slaves who served the members of the upper Roman orders would have felt no sense of class solidarity with the field hands toiling in agriculture or the miners digging in pits. Slaves who belonged to wealthy, influential families were more powerful and enjoyed greater privileges than many free persons, and certainly more than the landless laborers or smallholders. This incongruity explains why some individuals sold themselves into slavery for the privilege of serving the wealthy or for job security. Bartchy correctly contends that "any such call, 'Slaves of the world unite!' would have fallen on completely deaf ears."[114]

(b) Freedom did not always lead to a better life. Many in America take upward social mobility for granted and would naturally assume that freedom would be preferable since former slaves could take control of their own destiny. Slaves in the ancient world who gained their freedom did acquire a legal identity, and any children they might have in the future would be born free

111. Dodd, "Philemon," 1292.
112. Wright, *Colossians and Philemon*, 150.
113. Carolyn Osiek, "Slavery in the Second Testament World," *BTB* 22 (1992): 175. K. R. Bradley, *Slaves and Masters in the Roman Empire: A Study in Social Control* (Collection Latomus 185; Brussels: Latomus, 1984) 15, notes that "the neat cleavage" between slaves and masters did not mean that slaves formed a "rigid social class in the modern sense of that term."
114. S. Scott Bartchy, "Slavery (Greco-Roman)," *ABD*, 6:66.

and could inherit the family goods. But manumission did not always bring benefits or eliminate human misery; sometimes it increased it. Although wealthy freedmen became legendary figures, the reality was quite different. Life for freed persons was not easy. Most of those in Rome, for example, were on the dole. Epictetus imagines that a slave who gained his freedom might regret it. After the initial euphoria wore off, he realized that he had no place to eat.

> He looks for someone to flatter, for someone at whose house to dine. Next he either earns a living by prostitution, and so endures the most dreadful things, and if he gets a manger at which to eat he has fallen into a slavery much more severe than the first, or even if he grows rich, being a vulgarian he has fallen in love with a chit of a girl, and is miserable, and laments, and yearns for his slavery again. "Why, what was wrong with me? Someone else kept me in clothes, and shoes, and supplied me with food, and nursed me when I was sick; I served him in only a few matters. But now, miserable man that I am, what suffering is mine, who am a slave to several instead of one!"[115]

Slaves in good situations, on the other hand, knew a measure of security. They belonged to a household, the basic unit of production in the ancient world, and had their physical needs met. Unlike capitalist employers today, who generally take no responsibility for the welfare of their employees outside the workplace, slave owners did feed and look after their slaves who were too sick or too old to work. Some slaves, therefore, might have preferred remaining as slaves because it offered greater economic security than the impoverishment of being freedmen who, even when freed, still had to be subservient to their former masters.

(c) Since slavery fueled the basic economy, it would have created monumental social upheaval if large numbers of persons suddenly changed their status from slave to free. One might compare the mass emancipation of the slaves to millions of people being laid off today. The prospect of such economic dislocation made any call for the abolition of slavery seem foolhardy.

(3) Not only would it have been useless for Christians to press for the emancipation of slaves in the first century, it would have been politically suicidal. Such a stance would have given more reason for opponents to brand the Christian movement as a subversive group intent on destroying the underpinnings of society and fomenting revolt.[116] Unlike modern liberal

---

115. Epictetus, *Discourses* 4.1.35–37.

116. Ironically, the failure to attack slavery brings Christianity into disrepute in modern times when slavery has been abolished and is perceived as a abomination that cannot be tolerated.

---

democracies where minority interest groups can bring pressure to bear on governments without fear of serious reprisal no matter how shrill their protest, no such possibility existed in the ancient world. The social realities and political power structures made it impossible for Christians to redress any social wrongs through rebellious protests.[117]

Christians did not want to catch the unfriendly eye of civil authorities as loudmouthed troublemakers or do anything to make it harder for others to come to faith.[118] Paul's advice to the Colossians to act wisely toward outsiders (Col. 4:5) was typical of his strategy. Consequently, slaves are encouraged to be subject to masters in everything "so that in every way they will make the teaching about God our Savior attractive" (Titus 2:9–10). They are told to show masters respect "so that God's name and our teaching may not be slandered" (1 Tim. 6:1).[119]

Bousset's contention is certainly correct: "Christianity would have sunk beyond hope of recovery along with such revolutionary attempts; it might have brought on a new slave-rising and been crushed along with it. The time was not ripe for the solution of such difficult questions."[120] Lightfoot was also correct: "While the Church was still kept in subjection, moral influence and private enterprise were her only weapons."[121] The shame is that when the church was no longer politically threatened or in subjection, she did not act on the principles we find in this letter.

The quietism of the early Christians does not give us license to ignore injustice. Nor does it justify an easy alliance with an evil social and political order. In bridging the contexts, we should not ignore the question: When is the time ripe for protest? Since Christians did protest the idolatry and immorality that engulfed their culture at great cost to themselves, we should also ask: What requires our protest most and what does not? What criteria

---

117. We can see a sampling of what the reaction to such a message would have been like in Acts 16:16–24.

118. Allan Callahan, "Paul's Epistle to the Philemon: Toward an Alternative *Argumentum*," *HTR* 86 (1993): 366–67, describes how Chrysostom used the letter to Philemon to counter the antislavery wing of the church. He "stood firmly on the side of 'law and order' and was anxious to dispel the disestablishmentarian reputation of the Christianity of his day with respect to slaves."

119. Ignatius warned against giving the Gentiles any pretext to slander the congregation of God (*Trallians* 8.2).

120. Wilhelm Bousset, *Die Schriften des Neuen Testaments* (Göttingen, 1929), 2:10, cited and translated by R. P. Martin, *Colossians and Philemon*, 121.

121. Lightfoot, *Saint Paul's Epistles to the Colossians and to Philemon*, 327. Dunn, *The Epistles to the Colossians and to Philemon*, 253, contends that "pragmatic quietism was the most effective means of gaining room enough to develop the quality of personal relationships which would establish and build up microcosms (churches) of transformed communities."

do we use to decide? What means may we use to bring about the desired social change?

(4) Paul considered Christianity to be far more than a social crusade. Many revolutionary crusades have hoisted the flag of the universal brotherhood of humankind and have left only a bloody trail of bitter divisions in their wake. History should make us aware that the reformation of one social evil does not solve the deep-seated problem of human sin. Social tinkering here and there will not redeem humankind from the web of sin that besets us all—victim and victimizer. When the slaves were emancipated in the American South, for example, slavery was replaced by legalized segregation, convict chain gangs, share cropping, and Jim Crow justice. That sad history reveals that human beings and human society need total transformation.

While Paul did not overtly challenge the prevailing social structure, he also did not sanctify it as part of God's design. Instead, he fastened on how conversion fundamentally transforms personal relationships with others and with God. He laid down universal principles that, when taken seriously, ultimately topple the foundations of slavery. Johnson describes Philemon as "carefully crafted witness to an emerging Christ ethos, showing at once its power to transform symbols and attitudes, as well as its struggle to transcend social forms."[122] Preiss writes: "The Gospel penetrates systems and civilizations but is never identified with them. In particular it is more realistic than all idealism and all so-called political realism: for it attacks the heart of problems, the personal centre and personal relations."[123] It laid the groundwork for future transformation.

Another factor may have influenced Paul's approach to the slavery issue. Richardson contends that "what has been construed as indifference to social problems on Paul's part may be the reflection of the priority of mission in his thinking and the distinction he made between the spheres of action defined by the twofold nature of that mission, namely evangelism and edification."[124] Paul showed little concern with social questions beyond the boundaries of the church. For him, the church's primary mission was to confront the pagan world with the proclamation of Christ crucified and Christ regnant. All other issues were subjugated to it.

It was a different matter, however, when dealing with issues within the church. The mission there was to help Christians see the implications of the

---

122. Luke Timothy Johnson, *The Writings of the New Testament: An Interpretation* (Philadelphia: Fortress, 1986), 354.

123. Theo Preiss, "Life in Christ and Social Ethics in the Epistle to Philemon," in *Life in Christ* (Chicago: Alec R. Allenson, 1954), 33.

124. William J. Richardson, "Principle and Context in the Ethics of the Epistle to Philemon," *Int* 22 (1968): 315–16.

gospel for their personal lives and relationships. In his letter to Philemon, Paul did meddle in something that Christians had control over—the Christian household, which was the locus of Christian mission in the world.

In the Original Meaning section, we demonstrated that it was unheard of for Paul to ask a master to accept his runaway slave back as a brother in Christ and his equal before God and to suggest that instead of punishing him, he should grant him his freedom. The whole fabric of slavery was based on fear and coercion, and Paul's insistence on love and brotherhood in Philemon begins its unravelling. Paul affirms that the legal, racial, and biological categories that divide the human race belong to the old order and have no importance to God (1 Cor. 7:17–24; 12:13; Gal. 3:28; Col. 3:11).[125] In Christ there is no distinction between slave and free. All are brothers and sisters in the Lord. Both slave and master owe allegiance to a heavenly Master, and the earthly master will be accountable for how he treats his slaves. When a master is expected to treat a slave as a brother in Christ, as the representative of the apostle Paul, as an equal partner, and as a morally responsible human being who has rights, not just duties (Col. 4:1), the institution of slavery is being subverted.

In other words, while we do not find a frontal attack on slavery in the New Testament, we do find the seeds for its final eradication. Slaves can join their owners as equals at the Lord's table. How difficult it was to surmount deeply ingrained social conventions is evident from Paul's discussion about the Lord's Supper in 1 Corinthians 11:17–34. But when fellow Christians do accept one another as equal members of Christ's body, the social structures that segregate us from one another begin to crack.

A Christian slave in America recognized the incongruity of being a brother and a slave:

Am I not a man and brother?
Ought I not then to be free?
Sell me not one to another.
Take not thus my liberty.
Christ, our Savior
died for me as well as thee.[126]

---

125. Pokorný, *Colossians*, 176, points out that men who bear slave names, Tertius and Quartus, are on the same level as anyone else mentioned in the list of Paul's greetings in Romans 16:21–23. It provides evidence how the respective social orders were relativized in the Christian community.

126. Austin Steward, *Twenty-Two Years a Slave* (Rochester, N.Y.: William Alling, 1857), 21; cited by Willard M. Swartley, *Slavery, Sabbath, War, and Women* (Scottsdale, Pa./Kitchener, Ont.: Herald Press, 1983), 58.

Spiritual regeneration in individuals will set in motion social reform. If God's purpose is to produce a humanity that is the image of Jesus Christ, then those who think they are made in that new image must think twice before taking ownership of another human being. God wills us free; fallen humanity wills that others become slaves. God's purposes will prevail.

(5) Today, some consider Paul's inattention to the social inequities of slavery to be a deplorable blind spot, but it may instead be based on his unclouded vision that such things are ultimately meaningless. He was fully aware that the existing social order was deeply flawed (see Rom. 1:18–32), but he expected the present scheme of things to pass away soon (1 Cor. 7:29–31). It was, at best, only makeshift, still awaiting the transformation of God's reign. In the meantime, Christians lived their lives in Christ, who sits at the right hand of God. That assurance meant they lived in unbending devotion to their Lord, unintimidated by fearsome foes, unbeaten by their conditions in life, and unshaken in their everlasting hope.

The meaning of slavery was therefore transformed. Christians could serve the Lord in whatever situation or station they found themselves in life. This Lord accepted slave status himself in dying on the cross (see Mark 10:45; John 13:1; Phil. 2:7). Unlike today, when many believe that freedom simply means you can do as you want, Christians in Bible times understood that true freedom came when the transforming power of the Spirit enabled them to do what they ought. The New Testament also recognizes that people can be shackled by an inner bondage far worse than any external enslavement. True freedom can only be known when one is in Christ, whether that person is legally free or not.

The epitaph on the gravestone of John Jack captures this truth: "A Native of Africa, who died March 1773, aged about 60 years. Tho' born in a land of slavery he was born free." Paul proclaims that "he who was a slave when he was called by the Lord is the Lord's freedman; similarly, he who was a free man when he was called is Christ's slave" (1 Cor. 7:22). The freedom given in Christ is therefore far more valuable than even earthly freedom, although Paul encourages slaves to take advantage of any opportunity to receive it.[127] Since slavery was regarded simply as a temporary condition of the flesh that could not compare to the eternal glories with God that awaited Christians, some were motivated to sell themselves into slavery to liberate others.[128]

---

127. The Negro spirituals, composed under the harshest conditions, reveal the triumph of the human spirit infused with Christ. The novels of William Faulkner depict the ravaged spirit of the slaveholders and their heirs. The evil of slavery is manifest in the moral effects it has on society, and we are still facing those consequences.

128. Clement writes at the end of the first century: "We know that many among ourselves have given themselves into bondage that they might ransom others. Many have

Theological nuggets. The slavery issue is the most prominent feature of Philemon, but we should not ignore the theological nuggets that can be mined from this brief letter. Paul's extraordinary tact in making his request to Philemon gives us a model for using authority and leading others to make the right moral decisions. His implicit request that the master should forgive the one who wronged him also helps us examine the issues involved in forgiveness with a real life case study. Finally, Paul's delicate phrasing of Onesimus's departure from Philemon's household—"Perhaps the reason he was separated from you for a little while was that you might have him back for good" (v. 15)—allows us to examine God's providence in human affairs.

 THROUGH THE CENTURIES interpreters have drawn on Philemon primarily to convey moral lessons on Christian living. It reveals Paul's sublime spirit of humility and care for others, which we can emulate.[129] Calvin thought it was important "to note the depths of his condescension in calling one who is a slave, runaway and thief his own son."[130] We will look instead at how this brief letter applies to the facing of moral dilemmas and how Paul serves as a model for exercising leadership in the church. We will then turn to its theological implications for understanding the miracle of grace, forgiveness, and the mysterious providence of God.

Facing moral dilemmas. Philemon was in an awkward position. He must "placate Paul, keep his other slaves submissive, maintain his family estate, offer the most magnanimous example to his comrades in faith, and retain the trust of his fellow slaveowners in the neighborhood—all at once."[131] It cannot be done. Something must be sacrificed. Individual Christians and Christian groups frequently make the wrong decision because they are directed by the desires of the flesh rather than the Spirit. Injustice flourishes and becomes so deeply rooted that it seems impossible to eradicate.

Buttrick perhaps goes too far when he says that "this letter is a seed that finally split the rock of slavery."[132] Slavery continued for centuries. The moral

---

delivered themselves to slavery and provided food for others with the price they received for themselves" (1 Clem. 55:2; see *Shepherd of Hermas: Mandates* 8.10; *Similes* 1.10).

129. Marion L. Soards, "Some Neglected Theological Dimensions of Paul's Letter to Philemon," *Perspectives in Religious Studies* 17 (1990): 209–10.

130. John Calvin, *The Second Epistle of Paul the Apostle to the Corinthians and the Epistles to Timothy, Titus and Philemon*, Calvin's Commentaries (Grand Rapids: Eerdmans, 1964), 397.

131. James Tunstead Burtchaell, *Philemon's Problem: The Daily Dilemma of the Christian* (Chicago: Foundation for Adult Catechetical Teaching Aids, 1973), 31.

132. Buttrick, "Philemon: Exposition," 561.

---

dilemma of how a master reconciled owning slaves while regarding them as dear brothers or sisters apparently did not cause many Christians to lose much sleep.[133] Extant slave collars designed to impede a runaway slave from escaping again have Christian symbols on them. Since Christians objected to branding slaves on the face, Constantine decreed it should be done on the hands and legs[134]—not much of a humanitarian advance. Veyne cites the council of Elvira, which condemned Christian mistresses who "out of jealousy rage beat their servingwomen so severely that they died, provided that said death occurs within four days."[135]

Some have argued that factors other than the spiritual force of Christian principles were at work in the abolition of slavery. Slavery began to decline in the second century because it was a cost intensive means of production and inefficient. Fear and coercion were not as productive as providing incentives for achieving maximal profit updating technology.[136] When slavery disappeared from Europe after the fourteenth century, a more virulent and evil slavery, based on race, was allowed to take hold in the fifteenth and sixteenth centuries as slaves were imported from Africa. This happened when Christianity was the state religion. Philemon may contain the seed to split the rock of slavery, but Christians have not always allowed that seed to germinate and mature. Radford comments, "Christian teaching was not always true to its own principles."[137] What can we learn from this checkered history?

(1) Christians court danger when they spend so much time theologizing about moral issues that they never get around to doing justice and mercy. Radford explains that "Chrysostom and Theodore of Mopsuestia in the East and Ambrosiaster and Augustine in the West regarded slavery as a consequence of sin, a providential discipline for the control and correction of sinful men, though not an original part of the divine ideal for human life."[138] This view may have contributed to moral indifference and inertia. When a more sinister form of racially grounded slavery crept in, Radford also suggests that Christians were too caught up in the theological battles of the Reformation to notice or challenge it.[139]

---

133. Radford, *The Epistle to the Colossians and the Epistle to Philemon*, 331, notes that Jerome, Chrysostom, and Theodore of Mopsuestia defended the charm and merit of the letter but failed to see how its message had any bearing on the slavery issue. They consciously reacted against the radical wing of the church that advocated the abolition of slavery.

134. *Theodosian Code* 9.40.2.

135. Veyne, "The Roman Empire," 66.

136. Osiek, "Slavery in the Second Testament World," 178, citing T. F. Carney, *The Shape of the Past: Models and Antiquity* (Lawrence, Kan.: Coronado, 1975), 102–3; 214–15.

137. Radford, *The Epistle to the Colossians and the Epistle to Philemon*, 342.

138. Ibid.

139. Ibid., 343.

(2) The triumph of basic Christian principles is painfully snail-like in our personal lives, let alone in whole societies. Moral progress occurs by fits and starts with one step forward and what seems like two steps backward. God allows each individual to make moral decisions in his or her social context, just as Paul allowed Philemon to make his. Most of us, however, do not have an apostle writing to us individually to show us the right thing to do and to encourage us to do it. Vested interests discourage us from accepting the high cost of obedience to the truth of gospel. The pressure to do the most expedient thing is immense, and our minds work overtime in finding ways to rationalize our disobedience and salve our consciences.

Even those with genuinely held Christian principles have to struggle between what is culturally accepted and what their Christian conscience tells them is wrong. We see such a personal struggle, for example, in John Woolman (1720–1772), who wrote about his involvement with slavery with pain. He recorded in his journal, "They who know the only true God, and Jesus Christ whom he hath sent, and are thus acquainted with the merciful, benevolent Gospel Spirit, will therein perceive that the indignation of God is kindled against oppression and cruelty, and in beholding the great distress of so numerous a people will find cause for mourning."[140] His complicity in writing a bill of sale for a slave caused his anguish:

> Though the thoughts of writing an instrument of slavery for one of my fellow creatures felt uneasy, yet I remembered that I was hired by the year, that it was my master who directed me to do it, and that it was an elderly man, a member of our Society, who bought her; so through weakness I gave way and wrote it; but at the executing of it I was so afflicted in my mind, that I said before my master and the Friend that I believed slave-keeping to be a practice inconsistent with the Christian religion. This, in some degree, abated my uneasiness; yet as often as I reflected seriously upon it I thought I should have been clearer if I had desired to be excused from it, as a thing against my conscience, for such it was.[141]

Others have no moral struggle at all. A candidate for a national office declared: "People who are bitter and hateful about slavery are obviously bitter and hateful against God and his Word, because they reject what God says and embrace what mere humans say concerning slavery. This humanistic thinking is what the abolitionists embraced." Such a statement recalls the

---

140. John Woolman in *The Journal and Major Essays of John Woolman*, ed. Phillips P. Moulton (New York: Oxford Univ. Press, 1971), 66.
141. Ibid., 32–33.

bitter eighteenth-century debate between Christians who were pro-slavery and those who were abolitionist.

Christians gave slavery a biblical footing that enabled it to survive in the United States for so long. Mark Twain confessed in his autobiography:

> In my schoolboy days, I had no aversion to slavery. I was not aware that there was anything wrong with it. No one arraigned it in my hearing; the local papers said nothing against it; the local pulpit taught us that God approved it ... if the slave themselves had an aversion to slavery, they were wise and said nothing.[142]

The pro-slavery forces argued from Scripture that God sanctioned slavery. They appealed to the example of the patriarchs, the Mosaic laws on slavery (e.g., Lev. 25:44–46), and the absence of any specific protest against it by Jesus or Paul. Paul did not challenge the slavery he met in his world the way he did its idolatry and immorality. His admonition that slaves should obey their masters in all things and be content with their state unless they were lawfully set free confirmed slavery's legitimacy in their eyes.[143]

Most devout Christians today would find it morally reprehensible to own another human being and find such use of Scripture to defend the monstrous New World slavery more than a little embarrassing. They agree with Knox's contention that to assume that Paul "would have been equally tolerant of slavery in *our* world, so different from his that he could not even have imagined it, is to be ignorant almost beyond belief."[144] The Scriptures were used to buttress the slaveholders' positions, but they also fed the abolitionist movements in both North America and England, which assailed the evils of the slave trade.

The past conflict raises interesting questions. Sincere Christians drew contradictory conclusions from Scripture about slavery. Similar things happen today when different sides in a debate find scriptural warrants for their positions on current issues. Examining the sad history of slavery in the New World cautions us that we cannot resolve serious moral dilemmas by breezy appeals to individual passages from Scripture. The Pharisees also had their scriptural warrants. Swartley comments, "They took care to observe every specific command but directly opposed God's will, intention, and revelation in Jesus Christ."[145]

---

142. Samuel L. Clemens, *The Autobiography of Mark Twain* (New York: Harper & Row, 1959), 6.

143. See Larry Morrison, "The Religious Defense of American Slavery before 1830," *The Journal of Religious Thought* 37 (1980–81): 19. See also Swartley, *Slavery, Sabbath, War, and Women.*

144. John Knox, "Paul and the 'Liberals,'" *Religion in Life* 49 (1980): 419.

145. Swartley, *Slavery, Sabbath, War, and Women,* 61.

We always face the danger of straining out gnats and swallowing camels, majoring in minors while ignoring what is most crucial—justice, mercy, and faith (Matt. 23:23–24). When approaching current issues, we need to look for overarching principles drawn from the whole tenor of Scripture and must always be alert to cultural blinders that keep us from recognizing evil for what it is. We can become prisoners of our times and culture and slaves to our own self-interest, unable to recognize the blatant injustice surrounding us.[146]

The moral problem of reading the Bible selectively is captured in the correspondence between a slave owner, Sarah Loguen, and her runaway slave, Jarmain Wesley Loguen. Mrs. Loguen wrote to complain of the loss his running away caused the family.

> Maury Co., State of Tennessee
> February 20th, 1860
>
> To Jarm:
>
> ... I write you these lines to let you know the situation we are in—partly in consequence of you running away and stealing Old Rock, our fine mare. ... I am cripple, but I am still able to get about. The rest of the family are all well. ...
>
> Though we got the mare back, she was never worth much after you took her, and, as I now stand in need of some funds, I have determined to sell you. If you will send me one thousand dollars and pay for the old mare I will give up all claim I have to you. ...
>
> In consequence of your running away, we had to sell Abe and Ann and twelve acres of land; and I want you to send me the money that I may be able to redeem the land that you was the cause of our selling, and on receipt of the above named sum of money, I will send you your bill of sale. If you do not comply with my request, I will sell you to some one else. ...
>
> I understand that you are a preacher. ... I would like to know if you read your Bible? If so, can you tell me what will become of the thief if he does not repent? and, if the blind lead the blind, what will the consequence be? ... You know that we reared you as we reared our own children; that you was never abused, and shortly before you ran away, when your master asked you if you would like to be sold, you said you would not leave him to go with anybody.
>
> —Sarah Loguen
> Syracuse, N.Y., March 28th, 1860

---

146. Albert J. Raboteau, *Slave Religion: The "Invisible Institution" in the Antebellum South* (Oxford: Oxford Univ, Press, 1978), 98–99, writes that colonial slaveholders were reluctant to allow anyone to preach to their slaves lest their baptism made it necessary to free them. Six colonial legislatures passed laws by 1706 denying that baptism affected a slave's bondage to the master.

Mrs. Sarah Loguen:

... You sold my brother and sister, Abe and Ann, and twelve acres of land, you say, because I run away. Now you have the unutterable meanness to ask me to return and be your miserable chattel, or in lieu thereof send you one thousand dollars to enable you to redeem the *land*, but not to redeem my poor brother and sister! If I were to send you money it would be to get my brother and sister, and not that you should get land. You say you are *cripple*, and doubtless you say it to stir my pity, for you know I was susceptible in that direction. I do pity you. ... Wretched woman! Be it known to you that I value my freedom, to say nothing of my mother, brothers, and sisters, more than your whole body; more indeed, than my own life; more than all the lives of all the slaveholders and tyrants under heaven. ...

You say, "You know we raised you as we did our own children?" Woman, did you raise your *own children* for the market? Did you raise them for the whipping post? Did you raise them to be drove off in a coffle in chains? Where are my poor bleeding brothers and sisters? Can you tell? Who was it that sent them off into sugar and cotton fields, to be kicked, and cuffed, and whipped, and to groan and die; and where no kin can hear their groans, or attend and sympathize at their dying bed, or follow in their funeral?

... You say that I am a thief, because I took the old mare along with me. Have you got to learn that I had a better right to the old mare, as you call her, than *Manasseth Loguen* had to me? Is it a greater sin for me to steal his horse, than it was for him to rob my mother's cradle and steal me? If he and you infer that I forfeit all my rights to you, shall not I infer that you forfeit all your rights to me? Have you got to learn that human rights are mutual and reciprocal, and if you take my liberty and life, you forfeit me your own liberty and life? Before God and High Heaven, is there a law for one man which is not law for every other man?

If you or any other speculator on my body and rights, wish to know how I regard my rights, they need but come here and lay their hands on me to enslave me. ... I stand among a free people, who, I thank, God, sympathize with my rights, and the rights of mankind; and if your emissaries and vendors come here, to re-inslave me, and escape the unshrinking vigor of my own right arm, I trust my strong and brave friends, in this City and State, will be my rescuers and avengers.

Yours,

—J. W. Loguen[147]

---

147. Cited in Charles L. Blockson, *The Underground Railroad: Dramatic Firsthand Accounts of Daring Escapes to Freedom* (New York: Berkley Books, 1987), 74–75.

Sarah Loguen's letter reveals a whining selfishness that can only see herself as sinned against. She cannot recognize the sinfulness of slavery and therefore cannot recognize any complicity in this world's sinfulness for which she needs forgiveness.

In his study of three theologians under Hitler, Gerhard Kittel, Paul Althaus, and Emmanuel Hirsch, Ericksen shows how they found themselves in the orbit of Nazism supporting its ideology and even providing a theological foundation for the oppression of the Jews. They were not eccentric extremists or cranks but conscientious Christians who thought they were acting on authentic Christian principles. They saw themselves fighting off the evils that the crisis of modernity and individual freedom and pluralism wrought. Ericksen concludes:

> The world has always contained injustice: rich and poor, rich nations and poor nations. Minorities and the poor have always been put down. And the methods of the rich have often been those of the Nazis, though not usually so blatant. Nineteenth-century Britain abused India to get ahead; nineteenth-century America abused Indians to get ahead. Racism and notions of white, middle class superiority have only just begun to recede in America to give some political meaning to the phrase, "all men are created equal," with the additional change that women are sometimes acknowledged as well. But the social adjustments and the pain produced when the "haves" really give political freedom to the "have-nots" are intense.[148]

Sometimes social evils can overwhelm us. We may hear descriptions of an urgent need, the deplorable conditions, and a desperate plight and become immobilized because we suffer from compassion overload. We may also think to ourselves: How could we possibly do anything to alleviate so much suffering in so many places? Craddock writes: "Overwhelmed by the totality, the church can easily disregard as puny and ineffective the cup of water, the loaf of bread, the small chapel, the family altar, the covey of children listening to a Bible story on Sunday evening." He then gives a parable:

> It came to pass that there was a certain minister who preached to his little flock of "the world today," "the twentieth century," and "the human race." A layman complained of not being addressed by the sermons, but his complaints were turned aside with admonitions against small-mindedness and provincialism. In the course of time, the minister and the layman attended together a church conference in a distant

---

148. Robert P. Ericksen, *Theologians Under Hitler: Gerhard Kittel, Paul Althaus and Emmanuel Hirsch* (New Haven, Conn.: Yale Univ. Press, 1985), 200.

city. When the minister expressed anxiety about losing their way in the large and busy metropolis, the layman assured him there was no reason to fear. With that word, he produced from the rear seat of the car a globe of the world.[149]

Tackling the big-picture issues of the day as one small group or as one lonely individual may seem absolutely unmanageable. Paul's letter to Philemon guides us to look at the person on our very doorstep. Craddock points out that while Jesus was hanging on the cross, taking away the sins of the world, he made the effort to say, "Take my mother home."[150] Brian Dodd is surely correct in his comment about what Paul did in this letter to Philemon: "Paul did not stand against the might of Rome by opposing all slavery everywhere, but he did stand with the slave Onesimus in his hour of need."[151]

We may not be able to undo all the injustice in the world, but in our local neighborhood we can stand with those individuals who are oppressed victims who need a friend and a loving hand. God's spirit will transform the world as individuals open themselves up to its power. Willimon tells of a baptismal font at Belmont Abbey College in North Carolina, which shows just how God's Spirit can recast something evil into something good. The font had been hollowed out from a huge stone used to auction black slaves off to the highest bidder. The inscription on the font reads: "On this stone men were sold into slavery. From this stone men are now baptized into freedom."[152]

Authority and leadership. Lohse remarks that obedience "is the only appropriate response that the addressee can give to the word of the Apostle. Therefore, it is not left to his discretion whether he is willing to act out of love or not. Rather, he is obligated to obey the apostolic word."[153] I could not disagree more. I have shown in the Original Meaning section that Paul did not dictate to Philemon what he thinks needs to be done. Paul advised the Corinthians on sexuality and marriage and makes it clear that he does not try to throw a noose around people's necks by speaking *ex cathedra* (1 Cor. 7:6, 25, 35, 40). He gave them authoritative advice but is not authoritarian. The Corinthians had to decide for themselves. He had no desire to lord over others (2 Cor. 1:24) but wanted to develop his readers' own sense of moral responsibility. The same is true for Philemon. Paul wisely recognized that

149. Fred B. Craddock, "From Exegesis to Sermon: 1 Corinthians 12:4–6," *RevExp* 80 (1983): 425.

150. Ibid.

151. Brian J. Dodd, *The Problem with Paul* (Downers Grove, Ill.: InterVarsity, 1996), 109.

152. William H. Willimon, *Remember Who You Are: Baptism, a Model for Christian Life* (Nashville: The Upper Room, 1980), 61.

153. Lohse, *Colossians and Philemon*, 206.

most people do not respond well when ordered to do something by someone who seems condescending and paternalistic.

Paul does not choose to throw his apostolic weight around in this letter or win obedience by compulsion. Luther commented on Paul's statement in verses 8–9, "Therefore, although in Christ I could be bold and order you to do what you ought to do, yet I appeal to you on the basis of love," by asking, "When has the Pope ever acted so?"[154] Anne Lamott has said so well: "You don't always have to chop with the sword of truth. You can point with it, too."[155] Paul does not leave Philemon to agonize over what to do alone; he points the way for him. Nordling observes that "Paul's requests are really invitations—'encouragements'—for his original readers to offer him service out of hearts which have been freed by the gospel (cf. Rom. 6:20–23; Eph. 6:6; 1 Tim. 1:5)."[156] He takes their freedom seriously.

Again, Wall's comments are insightful: "When we continue to position ourselves to gain power over others rather than to empower them as agents of God's grace, our congregations and families will simply fail to bear witness to God in our world."[157] Paul does not dictate or employ any heavy-handed coercion or intimidation to get Philemon's grudging consent. Jewett shares how a theological student from Zimbabwe helped him he see the ethical implications of Paul's diplomacy in this letter. Had Paul ordered Onesimus's release on his authority as an apostle, he would have validated the domination system that perpetuated slavery. He writes:

> Slavery is a system of bossing people around. If Paul had bossed Philemon, the slavemaster might submit and grudgingly free Onesimus, but the principle of domination would still be intact. And slavery would spring up again inside the church, in more ways than one. Instead, Paul subverts the entire system of domination by appealing to Philemon's free decision, to act in a manner consistent with the equality and love between brothers and sisters in Christ.[158]

Paul does not employ the language of fear and guilt because that would reduce Philemon to the level of a slave.

Paul chooses the more excellent way in this letter. He expects Philemon to respond to Onesimus with love, and consequently he responds to Philemon with love. His gentle coaxing of Philemon embodies Jesus'

---

154. Cited by Joachim Gnilka, *Der Philemonbrief*, 42.

155. Anne Lamott, *Bird by Bird: Some Instructions on Writing and Life* (New York: Doubleday, 1994), 156.

156. Nordling, "Onesimus Fugitivus," 112.

157. Wall, *Colossians and Philemon*, 188.

158. Jewett, *Paul: The Apostle to America*, 68.

reproof of his feuding disciples in Luke's account of the Last Supper (Luke 22:25–27):

> Jesus said to them, "The kings of the Gentiles lord it over them; and those who exercise authority over them call themselves Benefactors. But you are not to be like that. Instead, the greatest among you should be like the youngest, and the one who rules like the one who serves. For who is greater, the one who is at the table or the one who serves? Is it not the one who is at the table? But I am among you as one who serves."

Paul's manner of dealing with Philemon on such a delicate topic is a model for Christian leadership on how to form Christians and how to influence others' behavior in the church and in the home.[159] He wants to win obedience, not force compliance that is only a superficial conformity to expectations ("eye-service," Col. 3:22). Paul trusts Philemon's Christian faith and believes that it will guide his decisions. He refuses to bulldoze his moral responsibility by dictating to him what he must do. Developing morally wise Christians is like helping a child learn to ride a bicycle. The child needs encouragement, steadying, and pointing in the right direction; but the parent must finally let go if the child will ever learn to pedal, steer, and balance alone. If Christians are ever to grow in Christ, leaders need to point them in the right directions, but they must let go and let them decide for themselves the obedience Christ requires of them.

Many churches suffer from leaders who will not let go and instead want to control everything and dominate others. They operate by force and intimidation to get others to conform to their vision and wishes. This pattern of leadership reduces open conflict but destroys fellowship. Such leaders may fool themselves into thinking they are getting others to obey God's will. In truth, this leadership style only breathes new life into the principles of domination and exploitation that govern the old aeon and worse, turn brothers and sisters in Christ into vassals and slaves. This leadership style therefore only opens the door to Satan and produces unformed and immature Christians. Their charges may do the right thing but for the wrong reasons because they are only capitulating to external pressure.[160]

(1) Wise Christian leaders will motivate their charges by creating a sense of unity: We are in this together. They will explain their vision persuasively, using symbols from our shared faith. Paul allows Philemon to work out what is demanded by love, a love he knows from what God has done for him in

---

159. E. D. Martin, *Colossians and Philemon*, 268–69.

160. Caird, *Paul's Letters from Prison*, 215, notes that people "ought not to have generosity thrust upon" them.

Jesus Christ and his fellowship in the community of faith. That means he also allows him to make the wrong choice. This possibility has been captured by Barton's imaginary recreation of Philemon's response to Paul. The slave owner could write back to Paul:

> ... Am I to understand that your wish is for Onesimus to be granted his liberty?... Brother Paul, I do not think you realize what you are asking. Forgive me for doubting your wisdom. But your expectation goes against all my natural inclinations.
>
> ... Then there is the problem of the other slaves. They would want their freedom too! What would become of us then? And I would be a laughing-stock. Who ever heard of a master without slaves? No one at the agora would deal with me any more. They would think I'd thrown it all in and become a mad Cynic!
>
> Beloved Paul, is it not important to maintain order? Is it not possible for Onesimus to be both my slave and my brother? Is it not possible for us to be one in the Spirit but master and slave in the world?[161]

But Paul trusts that love is resourceful enough to find the right way in accomplishing the good. He trusts that Philemon's maturity in Christian love will be creative enough to lead him to do the right thing.

(2) Wise Christian leaders will live out themselves what they ask others to do. Paul makes his request as one whose own devotion to Christ is manifest in his bonds. He does not ask Philemon to make a greater sacrifice than he has made himself.

(3) Wise Christian leaders will keep potentially divisive issues from becoming an "I win, you lose" situation, but instead will try to turn them into a "you win, we all win" decision. Paul does not threaten to renounce or punish Philemon if he fails to do what he wants. He frames his request so that Philemon can see how his generosity contributes to God's work and his own welfare.

The miracle of grace. The belief that the poorest and weakest sinner can become a beloved brother in the Lord forms the theological core of Paul's appeal. In many ways the letter to Philemon with its appeal, "This is your brother," is a real life counterpart to the parable of the Prodigal Son. "'But we had to celebrate and be glad, because this brother of yours was dead and is alive again; he was lost and is found'" (Luke 15:32). Lloyd A. Lewis cites the eloquent words of Samuel D. Proctor from his sermon "Finding Our Margin of Freedom":

> It does not matter where we were born, what kind of rearing we had, who our friends were, what kind of trouble we once got into, how

---

161. Stephen Barton, "Paul and Philemon: A Correspondence Continued," *Theology* 90 (1987): 99.

low we sank, or how far behind we fell. When we add it all up, we still have some options left, we still have some choices we can make.[162]

A derelict slave can become a herald for the kingdom. A shyster like Zacchaeus can be redeemed as a son of Abraham (Luke 19:9). A menacing Saul, "breathing out murderous threats against the Lord's disciples" (Acts 9:1), can become a "chosen instrument to carry my name before the Gentiles and their kings and before the people of Israel" (Acts 9:15). A privileged slaveholder can learn that Christian charity extends to all persons, including slaves.

The stories of redemption in the Bible confirm the truth of Buttrick's statement, "Every man is a bundle of infinity."[163] This applies equally to those who are classified as nonpersons or who are dismissed as the dregs of society. God's grace can transform them into something holy and profitable. From the mulch pile come beautiful flowers. We can see the grandest visions of God's love and purposes being worked out in those who are downtrodden and oppressed.

Many people in our world need to have someone convey this grace to their lives. Stephen O'Connor shares his experiences of trying to teach inner-city children how to express themselves through writing and shares a poem by Clara Ritos:

> I am a tree
> that's being picked on.
> I am a tree,
> my heart is being split in half.
> I am a tree
> that's being cut into pieces.
> People use me for firewood
> to keep them warm,
> and use me to make
> tables and chairs.
> I am a wooden floor
> that's being stepped on
> and scraped so hard
> that I can feel it
> in my heart.[164]

---

162. Lloyd A. Lewis, "An African American Appraisal of the Philemon–Paul–Onesimus Triangle," in *Stony the Road We Trod: African American Biblical Interpretation* (Minneapolis: Fortress, 1990), 232.

163. Buttrick, "Philemon: Exposition," 567.

164. Stephen O'Connor, *Will My Name Be Shouted Out? Reaching Inner City Students Through the Power of Writing* (New York: Simon and Schuster, 1996), 46.

God's grace picks up the trampled soul and hydrates desiccated spirits with a new hope. Anne Lamott comments on a famous work of Samuel Beckett, "The redemption in Beckett is so small: in the second act of *Waiting for Godot*, the barren dying twig of a tree has put out a leaf. Just one leaf."[165] Brother Lawrence, a medieval monk, saw things quite differently and said that God saw all of us as trees in winter with little to give, stripped of leaves, color, and growth, whom God loves unconditionally anyway. He turns useless, profit-less, barren trees into flowering trees planted by streams of water, whose leaves do not wither and yield its fruit in season.

A lesson in forgiveness. Paul does not specifically ask Philemon to for-give Onesimus, but he must assume that if Philemon can bring himself to accept Onesimus as a dear brother, he will have forgiven him.[166] In the Lord's Prayer, Jesus teaches us to request forgiveness of our debts *as we have forgiven others* (Matt. 6:12).

> Forgiveness is not dependent on our having forgiven others first. But persons should not expect to receive from God what they are not pre-pared to bestow on others. . . . A forgiving spirit is the outstretched hand by which we grasp God's forgiveness (5:7). When we close that hand tightly into a fist, we give nothing but also can receive nothing.[167]

C. S. Lewis has said, "We all agree that forgiveness is a beautiful idea until we have to practice it." Forgiving real-life sinners who have seriously dam-aged us is difficult. It takes work and prayer. Lewis perceptively recognized that "we need to forgive our brother seventy times seven not only for 490 offences but for one offence."[168] Forgiveness may therefore take time. Lewis wrote to a friend:

> Do you know only a few weeks ago I realised suddenly that I at last had forgiven the cruel schoolmaster who so darkened my childhood. I'd been trying to do it for years . . . this time I feel it is the real thing . . . one is safe as long as one keeps on trying.[169]

---

165. Lamott, *Bird by Bird*, 200.

166. Perhaps Paul knows that there is nothing more irritating than for someone to tell us that we need to forgive another.

167. David E. Garland, "The Lord's Prayer in the Gospel of Matthew," *RevExp* 89 (1992): 223–24.

168. C. S. Lewis, *Reflections on the Psalms* (London: Geoffrey Bles, 1958), 27.

169. Clyde S. Kilby, ed., *C. S. Lewis: Letters to an American Lady* (Grand Rapids: Eerdmans, 1967), 117. Lewis wrote to his fictitious friend Malcolm that he rose from prayer and felt that he "had really forgiven someone I had been trying to forgive for over 30 years" (C. S. Lewis, *Letters to Malcolm: Chiefly on Prayer* [New York: Harcourt, Brace and World, 1964], 106).

Our natural inclination leads us to disregard the obligation to forgive whenever it brings a high price. In Philemon's case, receiving Onesimus back as a brother and desisting from punishing him severely may very well have brought him public ridicule. He would have appeared weak—soft on slavery—and a threat to a whole system that depended on the oils of fear and swift and certain punishment to run smoothly. Such forgiveness went against the grain of everything society accepted as normal.

The growing number of slaves in the Roman empire made the ruling classes uneasy, always fearing that slaves would murder them, revolt, or run away. The typical Roman solution was the threat of serious reprisals as a deterrent. The slaveholders would regard treating a miscreant slave indulgently with a jaundiced eye. Any leniency, they feared, could only lead to a catastrophe down the road. But forgiveness is the only way to break the cycle of evil. By forgiving Onesimus, Philemon can join in God's recreating work and the reclamation of a sinner.

Some modern readers of Philemon take umbrage over any suggestion that Onesimus needed forgiveness for trying to escape oppression. Philemon was an oppressor by virtue of his owning slaves. Onesimus was the victim, not Philemon. This attitude fails to take seriously how we are all—victim and victimizer—caught in the web of sin. An evil system makes it hard for anyone to be pure, to do good, and to avoid harming others. We tend to regard ourselves as the wronged innocent one and fail to see how we have contributed to a problem. We would like to dump all the blame on one party in a dispute and consider the other party innocent.

In the context of Christian theology, both Philemon and Onesimus are sinners; and we may safely assume that Onesimus has forgiven Philemon any wrong done against him because he has decided to return to his household. The issue that Paul deals with is not who is or is not most guilty, but how to restore broken relationships. Before there can be any restoration, both must repent and forgive the other for real and perceived wrongs.

The problem is that forgiveness in our age has become too sentimental and trivialized. True forgiveness does not excuse the sin. It also does not forget that anything ever happened. The demons of remembrance may be kept at bay during our waking hours, but they often run riot just before we fall asleep or in our dreams. The sin keeps being replayed in our memory, and the anger burrows ever more deeply into our psyche. We may think we have buried the hatchet, but we have left the handle sticking far enough out of the ground that we can reach for it when the next offense occurs. How can we as Christians absorb evil without passing it on to others or allowing it to fester in our own souls? If forgiveness is to happen, we must face the sin and the anger it caused.

Paul does not tell Philemon to let bygones be bygones or parrot a meaningless cliché, "All's well that ends well." His delicacy in broaching the subject of Onesimus's restoration recognizes that the offense, whether justified or not, caused anger in Philemon and probably others.[170] Philemon understands himself to have been wronged, and Paul does not ignore that fact or sweep things under the carpet. God may have forgiven Onesimus, but Onesimus also sinned against Philemon. Paul's diplomatic letter encourages Philemon to allow his goodness to have mastery over his anger so that the relationship with Onesimus is not irrevocably destroyed.

The less malicious intent that we attribute to the person whom we think has violated us in some way, the less anger we feel toward him or her. Paul wisely seeks to relieve Onesimus of any malicious intent by attributing the whole thing to God's purposes (v. 15) and thereby defuses Philemon's anger, which may hide beneath the surface. Forgiveness, then, is "not some pious hope, but something gritty, rough-edged, an act of will, a recognition of pain, a genuine gift."[171] It "does not mean letting the other person off the hook of responsibility, but taking the hook of pain out of your mouth."[172]

Forgiveness also recognizes that any wrongdoing requires some just and commensurate punishment. Paul makes it clear in addressing slaves in Colossians that "anyone who does wrong will be repaid for his wrong" (Col. 3:25). In this letter he acknowledges that Philemon deserves some restitution (vv. 18–19). In a family, however, justice must be restorative rather than retributive. Suchocki defines forgiveness as "willing the well-being of victim(s) and violator(s) in the context of the fullest possible knowledge of the nature of the violation."[173] It frees both victim and violator from the web of sin.

Forgiveness brings healing in the relationship and healing for the victim and the victimizer. Paul frames his request so that forgiving Onesimus will comfort his heart and fill Philemon's heart even more with God's love. Jesus' parables about the servant who owed ten thousand talents (Matt. 18:21–35) and the two debtors who both are bankrupt and both are for-

---

170. Surprisingly, Paul says nothing of Onesimus's contrition (compare Pliny's appeal for the freedman of Sabinianus). His contrition may be assumed, but in the New Testament the requirement to forgive is not conditioned on their penitence (Matt. 6:14–15; 18:21–22). Nordling ("Onesimus Fugitivus," 101, n. 1) contends that Onesimus's willingness to return to his master signifies repentance.

171. Anne Borrowdale, "Right Relations: Forgiveness and Family Life," in *The Family in Theological Perspective*, ed. Stephen C. Barton (Edinburgh: T. & T. Clark, 1996), 209.

172. Ibid., citing J. Conway, *Adult Children of Legal or Emotional Divorce* (Eastbourne: Monarch, 1990).

173. Marjorie Hewitt Suchocki, *The Fall to Violence: Original Sin in Relational Theology* (New York: Continuum, 1995), 144.

given (Luke 7:36–50) would have been appropriate for the situation. The first parable about an unmerciful servant reveals that forgiveness can become far more problematic for people when it involves money. When money is involved, we may be less willing to forgive. The gospel, however, puts financial issues in proper perspective. Paul could ask Philemon, What does it profit a master to gain back a slave and forfeit his compassion in Christ and ultimately his life? In the second parable we can compare Onesimus to the large debtor who has been forgiven much by God. Can Philemon remember that he also is a bankrupt debtor who has been forgiven by God? Can he then accept God's forgiveness of Onesimus and accept him back as a brother?

The situation also has parallels with another of Jesus' parables. Philemon is like the elder brother in the parable of the Prodigal Son. Paul is like the father, who braves the chill of the night air to beg him to forgive his brother and to join the party that celebrates his restoration. "This brother of yours was dead and is alive again; he was lost and is found" (Luke 15:32). If Philemon does not yield to this request, he will show that he is not a brother, not a partner, but one who begrudges forgiving the debts of others. When wrestling with the demanding task of forgiving others, we may find that our resentment erases our memory of how much God has forgiven us.

It is so easy for us to preach how important forgiveness is for others and not apply it to ourselves. But Paul models the life and teaching of his Lord Jesus. We learn from the Corinthian correspondence that someone has hurt Paul (2 Cor. 7:12). The apostle does not seek vengeance. When his antagonist is down (2:5–11), he does not gloat over the fact that this one has finally got his comeuppance but asks everyone to join in helping him. He says, "Forgive and comfort him . . . reaffirm your love for this one . . . forgive him." Forgiveness does not mean we ignore what has happened. It means that we still relate to that person in spite of what has happened, and also in light of what has happened.

The mysterious ways of God's providence. Onesimus's unlawful flight was regarded by the propertied class in his culture as flagrant disobedience. Other dutiful slaves, perhaps fearing reprisals and annoyed by the extra work that now fell to them, would have frowned on his escape as well. Even a compassionate Christian master would have been worried and more than a little perturbed. If sin is something that brings harm to another, we may look at Onesimus as one who was sinned against but also one who sinned.

Patzia helps us to see Onesimus's disobedience from a different angle. "Onesimus' action was deliberate; but his departure did not remove him from the sovereignty of God." Patzia observes that "human failures often become God's opportunities! Here is a case in which a temporary loss was turned into an eternal gain."[174] Chrysostom long ago noted the parallels with the story of Joseph in Genesis 45:4–8; 50:15–21. Joseph understands that God's redemptive purposes were being worked out when his brothers betrayed him and their father by selling him into slavery. He tells them, "But God sent me ahead of you to preserve for you a remnant on earth and to save your lives by a great deliverance" (45:7). "You intended to harm me, but God intended it for good to accomplish what is now being done, the saving of many lives" (50:20).

In the story of Onesimus we can see the mysterious providence of God at work. We will never know how Onesimus eventually met Paul after making good his escape. We can only know from the use of the passive voice, "he was separated from you" (v. 16), that Paul believed that God's hand was in what had happened. The escapade turned out differently than any might have expected, in that Onesimus ultimately escaped into the arms of God's grace. He could not escape God's eye on him. We cannot straighten the lines of our crooked paths in life, but God can. God can take our worst intentions and turn them around for good, healing broken lives and broken relationships. In Onesimus's culture, others could only see a slave, a useless slave, and worse a runaway slave. God saw more and purposed greater things for him.

Everything turns out differently from what was foreseen by either master or slave. God was using this escape to bring Onesimus to Paul.[175] Paul sends him back to his master as a brother who, he trusts, will send him forth as a coworker in the gospel. We usually can only see the traces of God's hand in our lives in retrospect. The story behind the letter can help us see that even our darkest moments, deepest despair, and most dreadful disobedience can have some meaning in God's purposes. We are all part of some great tapestry, but usually we can only make out the individual threads.

---

174. Patzia, *Ephesians, Colossians, and Philemon*, 113.

175. The "perhaps" in verse 15 reveals the input of human freedom in this process. God's purposes are accomplished through the agency of humans. Paul could have spurned this runaway slave; instead, he "begot" him in the faith (v. 11; NIV, "who became my son"). Philemon is free to balk at Paul's request, but Paul trusts that God's purposes for both will prevail.

Scripture Index

Subject Index

The NIV Application Commentary Series

When complete, the NIV Application Commentary
will include the following volumes:

Old Testament Volumes

Genesis, John H. Walton

Exodus, Peter Enns

Leviticus/Numbers, Roy Gane

Deuteronomy, Daniel I. Block

Joshua, Robert L. Hubbard Jr.

Judges/Ruth, K. Lawson Younger

1-2 Samuel, Bill T. Arnold

1-2 Kings, Gus Konkel

1-2 Chronicles, Andrew E. Hill

Ezra/Nehemiah, Douglas J. Green

Esther, Karen H. Jobes

Job, Dennis R. Magary

Psalms Volume 1, Gerald H. Wilson

Psalms Volume 2, Jamie A. Grant

Proverbs, Paul Koptak

Ecclesiastes/Song of Songs, Iain Provan

Isaiah, John N. Oswalt

Jeremiah/Lamentations, J. Andrew Dearman

Ezekiel, Iain M. Duguid

Daniel, Tremper Longman III

Hosea/Amos/Micah, Gary V. Smith

Jonah/Nahum/Habakkuk/Zephaniah,
   James Bruckner

Joel/Obadiah/Malachi, David W. Baker

Haggai/Zechariah, Mark J. Boda

New Testament Volumes

Matthew, Michael J. Wilkins

Mark, David E. Garland

Luke, Darrell L. Bock

John, Gary M. Burge

Acts, Ajith Fernando

Romans, Douglas J. Moo

1 Corinthians, Craig Blomberg

2 Corinthians, Scott Hafemann

Galatians, Scot McKnight

Ephesians, Klyne Snodgrass

Philippians, Frank Thielman

Colossians/Philemon, David E. Garland

1-2 Thessalonians, Michael W. Holmes

1-2 Timothy/Titus, Walter L. Liefeld

Hebrews, George H. Guthrie

James, David P. Nystrom

1 Peter, Scot McKnight

2 Peter/Jude, Douglas J. Moo

Letters of John, Gary M. Burge

Revelation, Craig S. Keener

To see which titles are available,
visit our web site at www.zondervan.com